MEMOIRS OF A FORTUNATE JEW

Memoirs of a Fortunate Jew

An Italian Story

Dan Vittorio Segre

HALBAN
LONDON

Published in Great Britain by
Halban Publishers Ltd
22 Golden Square
London W1F 9JW
2005

www.halbanpublishers.com

Originally published in Great Britain by Halban Publishers, 1987
Published in paperback by Paladin, Grafton Books, 1988
Reissued in paperback by Halban Publishers, 1998

A CIP catalogue record for this book is available from the British Library.

ISBN 1870015 00 2 (cased)
ISBN 1 870015 69 X (paperback)
Original Italian edition published in 1985 under the title
Storia di un Ebreo Fortunato
Copyright © 1985 Gruppo Editoriale Fabbri, Bompiani, Sonzogno,
Etas, S.p.A

Translation copyright © 1987 by Dan Vittorio Segre

Dan Vittorio has asserted his right under the Copyright,
Design and Patents Act, 1988 to be identified
as the author of this work.

Printed in Great Britain by MPG Books Ltd.,
Bodmin, Cornwall

In the same manner in which the just are rewarded in the world to come even for their smallest merits, so are the evildoers in this world.

Babylonian Talmud, Tractate *Ta'anit*

Dispersed in diaries written daily or intermittently since 1940, the memories contained in these pages would not have been turned into a book without the encouragement of many friends.

The Rockefeller Foundation, to which I owe the generous invitation to stay at its Villa Serbelloni during the winter of 1983, will probably never know to what extent the enchanted silence of Bellagio contributed toward persuading the phantoms of my past to allow themselves to be imprisoned by the typewriter on which my wife patiently produced the many drafts of the original Italian manuscript.

As for the English translation, it would certainly not be intelligible without the compassionate help of Devorah Bar-Zemer, who worked with me on every page of the English version. I am deeply indebted to Martine Halban and Amy Pastan, who read through the manuscript with great care and suggested many improvements. If I have been able to convey to the English reader some of the original Italian flavor, I owe this to Susan Rose, who unstintingly gave me the benefit of her sense of both languages and sensitively edited many pages of the manuscript.

I

The Pistol

I WAS probably less than five years old when my father fired a shot at my head. He was cleaning his pistol, a Smith & Wesson 7.65, when it went off —nobody knew how.

My father was sitting at the same desk at which I am writing these lines, a massive oak table, well fitted for the huge ledgers in which he carefully entered, in his clear handwriting slightly slanted to the right, the daily expenses, purchases of animals and seeds, income from the sales of wine and grain, the taxes he paid, as well as the small sums he put in the neck pouch of Bizir, his massive Saint Bernard dog trained to fetch his cigars from the tobacconist. In the village everyone knew the hairy, good-tempered dog of the village mayor. If the tobacconist was not prompt enough in giving Bizir the correct packet, it was only to make him growl for the admiration of the villagers. On the oak table, now mine and still unburdened —as before—by modern gadgets such as a telephone, transistor radio, typewriter, or calculating machine, I keep my father's photograph. Bizir is standing on his hind legs, his forepaws on my father's shoulders. The picture is fading and still smells of tobacco like the desk drawers full of aging possessions: pipes, spring tape-measures, erasers, rusty compasses, penholders, a dry inkwell—things I no longer use but carefully preserve as remnants of the vanished world of my family.

On the day I was shot, in the sixth year of the Fascist revolution, I would certainly have been killed had my father held his pistol at a slightly lower angle. I had crawled into his study, placed myself in front of the huge desk without his noticing me, and suddenly stood up at the very moment when the pistol went off. The bullet grazed my head, burned—so I was told time and again—a lock of my then-blond hair, and penetrated an Empire-style armoire behind me.

This was one of those pieces of furniture with a front panel opening into a desk, which was known incorrectly in the family as a *serre-papier*. I still occasionally see this type of desk-cum-drawers in the windows of antique shops, converted into bars with places for bottles and glasses. My wife, who is convinced that furniture, like flowers, has a dignity of its own, is furious whenever she sees one of these aberrations. She regards them as a perversion of nature. I do not share this belief with her, yet I am convinced that this particular *serre-papier* possessed a personality of its own. I wonder how it would have perceived my funeral after having witnessed my death.

There would be a small, white coffin at the center of my father's library, transformed for the occasion into a funeral parlor. The rabbi would arrive from Turin with a hexagonal black ceremonial hat on his head, standing just in front of the Sisters of Saint Vincent—who nursed in the village hospital —with their wide, starched caps, rosaries in their hands, praying for the salvation of my soul. I would be carried to the cemetery in a hearse drawn by two, or perhaps even four, horses with white plumes on their heads and embroidered caparisons as in Paolo Ucello's pictures. A lot of people would be weeping around my bier. Our faithful maid, Annetta, would be there in her black uniform and white cap; Cecilia, the cook, with the special chocolates she made for my mother's Thursday tea parties; Vigiu, the coachman, with a top hat adorned by a pheasant's feather; the two collies, the huge cat, my tin soldiers, and, naturally, the entire family crying around me.

Their sorrow did not affect me. Even apart from dreams of this kind, I have always asked myself what it really means to share someone else's sorrow. The cases in which people genuinely empathize with other people's feelings are few. After all, an ingrown toenail hurts one more than the death of a thousand Chinese, and we live in a world where we share our "deep grief" or our "great joy" with distant people through cabled messages, which cost less if transmitted by a coded number. Nobody ever seems to learn from the suffering of others; rarely from his own. Only in the look of confidence and love of a dog, or of fear in a wounded animal is it possible to catch a fleeting instant of the pain of the world.

For years I have empathized with that piece of furniture wounded in my place. I do not claim that it felt pain instead of me, but I have often thought that the shot established a peculiar link between us; that that piece of oak, old and polished, possessed a strange vitality, as if it were holding a particle of my destiny. The little hole, round and clean-cut, discreet and unexpected in the folding panel, has winked at me for years. Long before I was told so by a gypsy, it convinced me that I had been born under a lucky star. Not one supposed to grant glory, wealth, and social success, but a minor star, full of a sparkling life that still gives me courage in the ever more frequent hours of doubt and sadness.

Late in the 1950s I once accompanied an Algerian sultan to Nazareth. According to his calling card he was a direct descendant of the caliph Abu Bakr, and he wanted to visit the lodge of the Clarisses convent. Here the viscount of Foucauld, touched by grace, had prepared himself for his mission of conversion of the Arabs in the Sahara, where my sultan's grandfather had murdered him. The nuns of the Order of the Père de Foucauld, who had transformed the lodge into their small convent, received my companion with the enthusiasm due to those who are clearly part of a divine design.

We sat on low, rush-seated stools, chatting quietly in the big room, clean and tidy, smelling of new whitewash, opening on two sides onto a secret, shady garden. Gusts of wind carried in the perfume of orange blossom while we kept measuring out, like the beads of a rosary, polite phrases and conspiratorial smiles, full of spent hatreds and aging vanity. We had left outside the thick convent walls the diversities of our religions, politics, and cultures. All that reached us from the outer world was the muffled sound of traffic, waves of flower scent, and the smell of burning charcoal spattered by mutton fat.

History had lost its dimension. The conversation veered almost naturally toward the idea of death. The sultan was saying that life is made up of bursts of energy constantly struggling with death. To exist was, for him, to be like a flicker of light shining for shorter or longer periods on the black inertia of matter. This descendant of Abu Bakr, to whom the French had for a moment thought of handing over control of the French Sahara, spoke, in this place of peace and faith, so remote from my village in Piedmont, in the same manner that my father spoke to me for the first and last time about his soul, two weeks before he died.

We were looking down from the top of our terraced garden into the valley, soft and green, which sloped gently down to the Tanaro River. To our left, like a caravan of brown roofs and whitish walls, the houses of San Defendente undulated above vineyards already dressed in autumnal red. The farmhouses and the courtyards stood aligned in their ancient order, still unaffected by the new, undisciplined way of life with which the farmers now had to cope. From the tops of the hills the houses overlooked the plants still growing in their appointed seasons. Here and there, however, one could already see the first signs of change. Men who only yesterday had been at the mercy of drought and hail, now crushed the land with tracked vehicles, dusted crops with small planes, and tricked the climate with plantations of imported pines and aspens. Here too, as in the Levant, one was able to perceive the deep wounds that modernity was opening in the old system of cultures. Yet at the end of the fifties, the valley still showed the face that, like that of my father, I had known since my childhood.

Scattered over the fields were bushes of cobnuts and a few lines of poplars, slim and wavering up to the sky; there were orchards that by that time had already given their crops of peaches, figs, and apricots. The land, tired by the summer toil, was lying exhausted, like a woman's body resting after the élan of love. Punctuating the deep silence, crickets chirped, thirsty birds darted from tree to tree. The hay was drying, fragrant, in the meadows. Unpicked clusters of grapes rotted on the vines amid the buzzing of wasps and in the shade of vine leaves spotted by copper spray.

From every side it seemed as though a message of farewell was rising to us. It was still hot, but my father sensed a chill overcoming his body. He calmly explained to me how the feeling of death was spreading, surprised at not feeling any fear. He had the impression, he told me, that his bones, sinews, and muscles, which still held him upright in spite of his years, were no longer his own; that his life was leaving his body like a flickering flame, deserting the cinders of his earthly life. Sooner or later, he said, these cinders would disperse into nothingness, and the flame of his soul mount, with travail, to the place from which it had come.

He was speaking slowly, to himself, about himself, head slightly bent to one side as if he wanted to catch a consensus from the rustling of the leaves in the vineyards he had planted in his youth. His eyes wandered along the rows of vines, from the houses to the dusty paths, from sky to valley, caressing the brooks, stopping at every milestone on the provincial road, following the tracks along which he had ridden, the meadows over which he had hunted hares, the poplars under which he had dismounted to drink wine with his peasants and eat slices of bread, tasting of olives and garlic.

I looked at his purplish hands, clutching the railing of the steps leading down from the garden to the bowling green. From here he had called on the youths of the village to go and fight and get killed in the war that was to have given back to Italy the towns of Trento and Trieste and brought perpetual peace to the world. His patriotism had not been the reason for his becoming the youngest mayor in Italy. The villagers had consistently voted for him because he was the largest landlord and a Jew, two things that made him more credible than others in matters of money. Villagers who had emigrated used to send him money to have mass said for their dead, trusting him more than the local priest. He had sold many tracts of land to his peasants with deferred payments and without interest. To those who suggested guarantors, he used to answer that the mouths to be fed in the buyer's family were as good as any security. At that time he was loved, admired, and respected.

It was only natural, therefore, that when he decided to volunteer in the Great War, many of the villagers followed his example, believing that it would be, as he had promised, a glorious and short war. Instead it had been just the opposite, long and painful, with few of the soldiers coming back from the front. Although there were fewer than half a dozen socialists in the village and nobody really held him personally responsible for the slaughter, the dead had been too many not to reproach him for the military interventionism he had defended with such fervor. Insulting graffiti appeared on street walls, his poplars were slashed, subversive slogans were shouted at him as he drove through the village in military uniform. They did not appreciate the garden he had planted on the castle grounds in memory of the fallen soldiers. My father felt deeply wounded; he became convinced, like many other landowners of the time, that nothing would stop the "Bolshevik hydra" except a new, strong, patriotic regime, capable of forcing draft dodgers to recognize the contribution of blood and suffering that the veterans had given the country. He could not accept emotionally the social changes that war had brought, even though intellectually he understood them. More out of anger than ideology, he enrolled himself in the Fascist party, which was gathering strength and credibility with the help of enraged war veterans like himself and with the covert support of the police and the army.

After the March on Rome, which he understood as the triumph of order over anarchy and of which he totally missed the political consequences, he threw himself with enthusiasm into the burgeoning electrical industry. He invested the income from the sale of his magnificent estate in the building of dams. In this way he ruined himself twice over: first in politics and then in the financial chaos created by the Great Depression. However, these were things of the past, memories faded by time. The more recent ones, of anti-Jewish persecution, had been mellowed by the help extended to him by those very farmers who had forced him to run away from the village at the end of the Great War. During World War II they had risked their lives to save him and his family from the Germans. In these more recent memories I had no share. Our lives had evolved in different directions. We had parted too early and for too long to share common adult experiences. If my father now allowed himself to speak to me of his innermost feelings, something he would never have done before, it was because he knew he was on the point of leaving this world forever.

Listening to him talking about his image of his soul, I had the impression of quite literally seeing a flicker of life emerging from his shabby, gray, peaked cap. It was a flickering, bluish flame of delusion and failure. I was his only triumph in life, but for the wrong reasons. The long war, from which we had both emerged unharmed, was a conflict in which a third of world Jewry had disappeared; in it he had lost his motherland, Italy, and I had found a new one, Israel. I had returned home victorious but dressed in a foreign uniform; he had survived six years of civil ignominy, two of flight into the mountains, and had witnessed the defeat of his country. Humiliated by the king, whom he had personally served, persecuted by the Fascist regime that he had helped to create, he had no other reason for pride except my contribution to that Zionist cause against which he had so tenaciously fought as an Italian nationalist.

I perceived his embarrassment toward me as soon as I saw him after five years of separation. In May 1945 I discovered that, after years of being in hiding, he was still alive and living in our old village home. I rushed in my command car to look for him, on roads still torn up by Allied bombing and Partisan operations. I felt an arrogant satisfaction in making peasant carts move out of my way, in the stupefied and frightened looks of local people seeing a British uniform for the first time.

When I got to the village I stopped under the outer archway of my home, uncertain how to behave. I was sensitive to the silent feeling of awe and curiosity in the villagers gathering in the street behind me, brought together by an event that was breaking the monotony of life in the small, rural center, forgotten by history and overlooked by war. I did not dare enter the courtyard, afraid that a sudden meeting with my father might be too much for him. At the same time I was trying hard to remember his face. I was terrified at the thought that he might recognize me first, while my expression might give away that I did not know who he was. We had not written to each other for years. The last Red Cross card I received from my family was dated 1941, before I joined the British army. I was wondering how he would react to seeing me dressed in a foreign uniform (he who had dreamt of a military career for me in Italy), discovering that without his permission I had abandoned the agricultural studies on which he had spent so much money. Behind my back people surrounded my Italian driver, bombarding him with questions and telling each other who I was. I could feel, without turning around, that they were pointing me out, could hear them mentioning my name and that of my father, exchanging comments without daring to approach me. To them I was the representative of the new authority, of those Allied forces who had won the war and whom they had not yet had a chance to meet.

From the inner courtyard of my home one of our tenants emerged. Pinin was his name. I recognized him by his thick, drooping moustache and the black scarf tied around his neck, looking exactly as he did when he used to help me mount my horse. I told him who I was. I asked him about my father. When I heard that he was in his study, in good health, and that my mother was alive and living with my sister in a nearby convent, I asked him to inform my father that I had returned. I was nervous. I had assumed a brisk tone of command that, in those circumstances, made me feel I was acting a part. With all those people clustered behind me, I stood facing the big gates that opened onto the inner courtyard. I lacked the courage to go through them, wondering if somebody would pull the iron chain of the entry bell in my honor, feeling like part of a cheap theatrical piece, of one of those serialized novels that I remembered from my father's library. Shamefacedness prevented me from crossing the threshold of a world of affections and hopes that I felt was no longer mine but that my father probably still associated with me. I had a confused premonition that a breach, deeper than that opened by time, had developed between us: between his Italian world, which had been destroyed, and my new Jewish one in which, as Joachim Murat, who Napoleon made King of Naples, once said proudly, I was my own ancestor.

My father suddenly appeared under the archway. He was panting; he must have run all the way from the library. He stopped abruptly in front of me, wondering if someone was perhaps playing a trick on him. We scrutinized each other for a moment, suspiciously, because we were both greatly changed. The man with his military beret at an angle over one ear, a blond moustache, the silk scarf of the Special Units around his neck, a pistol dangling in its canvas holster at his side, must certainly have looked to him very different from the boy, dressed in navy blue jacket and linen collar, whom he had accompanied to embark at Trieste in 1939. He, with a long white beard that had grown during his life underground, his hair thinner but still black, his leaner body barely filling a crude corduroy suit, had a patriarchal look quite new to me. Only his button-up boots were familiar.

He did not stretch out his hand or make any gesture of affection. We both stood silent and still, unable to disentangle ourselves from the images of each other that we had preserved during the long years of separation. Changed in our outward appearances, we felt both the same and different inside: linked by blood ties but separated by experiences so divergent. All this, of course, lasted only an instant, but the shock was great for us both. He spoke first, asking me which regiment I belonged to. I answered him: the Palestine Regiment. Probably he did not understand what I meant, but it was only after that answer that he stretched out his right hand and then hugged me with his left arm. By this time people behind us were talking at the tops of their voices. Someone even started clapping. We paid no attention. With our backs to them so that no one could see our emotion, side by side, we slowly crossed into the inner court and moved toward the garden, now full of weeds. My father had his arm around my shoulders. In silence we stopped at the top of the steps leading to the bowling green, untended and overgrown, to look at the valley that had been his domain and that of his parents.

The valley was unchanged except for the airfield that the German army had built near the river Tanaro. It held part of our common memories and had witnessed the sadness of our parting five years earlier. Here, we felt, we could again converse in silence, overcoming that void of disappointed experience that neither of us had been able to fulfill. For this reason, when my father suddenly chose this spot to speak to me about his soul, I knew that he was nearing his end. Convinced as he was of having failed in his task of guiding me in my life, his halting words had no other aim but to teach me how to face death, with dignity and detachment.

I, too, as I grow older, find myself thinking about death while standing at the top of the steps that lead to the bowling green, looking at the shadows drawn by the sun on the banks of the Tanaro. But I am unable to imagine my soul as a small flame flickering out of the cinders of my life. My soul looks more to me like a light reflected by an insignificant star, one of those that Saint Exupéry would have given his Little Prince to ride on: a happy and sociable star, which at least twice helped me to escape my mortal destiny, once as a child and again on a rainy evening in still-occupied Bari.

I had gone to look for a cardigan in the kit bag that the king of England had lent me, together with two sets of underwear, two winter shirts and three summer ones, two pairs of trousers, and a leather jerkin, all to make me fight better in the war. I had also been issued a jackknife, one pair of boots, a pouch with needles and thread, two gaiters, and that combination of webbing, pouches, and packs that, with the help of a flat steel helmet, made us look like ancient warriors in a modern world.

At the bottom of the kit bag I kept a big revolver taken from a captured Italian arms depot. It was heavy, cumbersome, and I had forgotten that it was loaded. I took it out of the kit bag and laid it on the corner of my bed, which I then inadvertently hit with my knee. The weapon fell onto the cement floor, butt downward. It was a fall of less than half a meter, but it was enough for the hammer to jerk and the bullet to explode.

At that moment I was crouched over the weapon. The flash blinded me for a second, and I still carry with me, intact after all these years, the memory of a deafening bang. I am surprised today at not having felt any fear, though I am not by nature particularly brave. But I cannot rid myself of the image that flashed through my mind, of myself bent forward as if I were stretching my neck on the block, looking like an illustration from the *History of Illustrious Men,* which my father kept, bound in three volumes, on the second shelf of his library.

As a child I used to spend long hours leafing through these books that, more than any others, I think, infected me with a romantic taste for the heroic. Each volume contained a collection of primitive watercolors protected by tissue paper, torn at the corners and spotted with rust. I recalled them, looking at the rust spots on the barrel of the revolver, now lying warm and vulgar, on the floor near my bed.

I do not remember how long it took before I found the strength to pick it up and unload it—three seconds, two minutes, three hours? But I know that when I looked at myself in the mirror hanging askew from two hooks on the wall over the dirt-encrusted washbasin, I saw the reflection of a pallid face, not belonging to me, with a lock of burned hair standing up over a pair of eyes that had stared, without seeing, at the void of my death.

There was deep silence in the room. On the floor below nobody in the mess seemed to have heard the noise of the explosion. If I had died they would certainly have attributed it to suicide. In a way it was true: I had that day thought of killing myself, and I felt now as though I had wriggled out of my human destiny.

I went on believing in my special lot until the day my wife, without my knowledge, decided to repair the *serre-papier* and plug up the hole made by my father's pistol. The spell is now broken. Yet from time to time I find myself believing that hidden in the shining oak there still slumbers a shred of my peculiar destiny.

2

Faith and Boredom

My MOTHER, born Jewish, is buried in a Christian cemetery. In her case destiny really seems to have played tricks with our family. True, she loved to travel, yet nobody could have imagined that after having provoked such dismay by her conversion to Christianity in reaction to my departure for Palestine, she would become the first member of our family in two thousand years to go and die—as is the custom among pious Jews—in the Holy Land.

My mother rests in the small cemetery of the nuns at Ein Kerem, the meeting place of Mary and Elizabeth. She is buried in the shadow of tall cypresses in a square of ground surrounded by high walls, which naturally invite one to raise one's eyes to the sky. Wild geraniums and lazy lizards follow the sun's rays around the stone that covers her body and that is slowly sinking into the earth. The smell of rosemary always reminds me of the black square beneath which Camus lies in a little Provençal cemetery. "The Motherland," he wrote, "is the land which covers the bones of one's ancestors." If this is true, I have, thanks to my Christian mother, planted roots in my Jewish ancestral land, though fifty years of active life have not succeeded in making me feel it is mine.

Be that as it may, nobody would have imagined such an ending for my mother who, at the beginning of the century, was not only one of the most beautiful Jewish girls in Piedmont but also one of the most sought after *partis* in Turin. In the miniature painted on the occasion of her marriage she looks like a fairy: the mass of brown hair combed up in the fashion of the time crowning the perfect oval of her face; the long neck, adorned with three rows of pearls falling over the laced bodice; the long, white, manicured hand catching them with the gentle gesture of a palm already destined to play with a rosary. There is another picture showing her in all her beauty dressed in a Japanese kimono. It was taken on the eve of World War I, in the small trellised pavilion of the garden, with Mrs. Petrella, an artist who for a fleeting moment had some fame in provincial theaters, sitting admiringly next to her. This poor woman ended her days in the village old-age home which, before being restored and modernized in the 1960s, was a hovel where inmates had to eat out of tin bowls, using their beds as tables.

In the 1950s Mrs. Petrella shared the misery and dirt of her room with two other skinny old women. When I visited her from time to time, she liked to talk about the parties that my mother gave in our country home. Today, no one could imagine the past splendor of these rooms, emptied as they have been of their furniture, smelling of mold and invaded by woodworm, which has eaten the gilded reliefs of the door frames and the wood of the old window sashes. Yet many years before I was born, the bishops of Cuneo and Alba used to converse in the hospitable atmosphere offered by the Jewish mayor of the village, with the count of Mirafiore, offspring of the morganatic marriage of Victor Emmanuel II. On other, less official occasions, when the notables of the area gathered in these salons to talk about wine, cattle, and the fight against

Phylloxera (the American pest that was ruining their vine-yards), it was my mother who set the tone of the meetings, playing the spinet and inviting some guest to exhibit his singing talents. Mrs. Petrella loved to linger over the description of this village society, which for her had been the unsuccessful springboard into the Italian fin-de-siècle society. She was easily moved when recalling for me the luxury of the white silk-lined landau in which my mother drove with her to the nearby towns of Alba or Asti. Mrs. Petrella, an expert in city fashions, advised her what clothes to buy for the forthcoming theater season, or for one of those special "family evenings," when the ladies played rummy and the gentlemen "three-seven" until they all gathered together to admire the performance of the newly acquired magic lantern.

Mrs. Petrella apparently never realized how much my mother hated the country life she was forced to live after her marriage. She did not share my father's passion for riding and hunting; she found no interest in the conversation of the local gentry, even less in political discussions. She was not even excited by such extraordinary events as the arrival in Asti of the Buffalo Bill Circus or by Colonel Cody's invitation to my father to race his horses against ours. She was bored to death in the gilded cage in which my father had imprisoned her. Childless for over ten years, she envied her more fortunate friends who could enjoy the amusements of Turin's society life, still gravitating, as it did at the time, around many members of the royal family.

The Jews of Piedmont recently had emerged from the ghetto: my great-grandfather on my father's side had grown up in that of Ivrea, on my mother's side, in that of Turin. They did not belong to the families that had distinguished themselves in the wars of the Italian Risorgimento—the nineteenth-century movement for Italian political unity—but they had fought for their emancipation and were fiercely faithful to the House of Savoy which, in 1848, had granted them civic equality. In the thirty years that followed they had forgotten most of the rites and values of their ancestral faith. My grandfathers were already unable to read Hebrew, still a language of current knowledge in the preceding generation. My maternal grandmother used to recite her daily prayers in a shortened form without understanding their meaning; for over seventy years she apparently recited in Hebrew the morning blessing in which a Jew thanks the Lord for "having made me a man."

Italian Jewry at the time suffered from the effects of emancipation for reasons common to other European Jews but also quite particular to Italy. First of all there was the question of numbers. The Italian Jewish population at the end of the last century was slightly over thirty thousand, one-tenth of the Jewish population of France and less than a fraction of the Jewry of the Austro-Hungarian Empire. Italy did not have—and to a certain extent still does not have—a capital city like Paris, London, or Vienna polarizing the intellectual, political, and economic establishment. In these metropolises, Jews had become numerous and rich enough to carry out the responsibilities of modern, communal religious institutions. In Italy, Jews had remained for centuries scattered all over the peninsula in small communities that at times were no more than a dozen families strong. From these Italian villages or country towns they had taken their new names when the state authorities required them to drop their old Jewish patronymics: Moses, son of Jacob or of David, became Alatri, Orvieto, Sermoneta, Padua, or Pavia. The "universities," as the Jewish communities were called, had developed, in the separateness of the ghettos and notwithstanding the outwardly miserable appearance of their members, strong cultural traditions in the fields of music and art unparalleled by any other European Jewish community. With the emancipation, however, they rapidly lost their members to the urban centers, former capitals of the states that the united Kingdom of Italy had meanwhile turned into provinces. In the course of these rapid social and topographical

changes, the centuries-old tissue of Italian Judaism, still strong
in the eighteenth century, had frayed, while the falling of the
ghetto walls put an end to an isolation that discriminated
against, but at the same time protected, the integrity of these
communities.

The Italian Jews at the beginning of the twentieth century
had not lost their pride in their origins. They understood that
the events that allowed them to become financially richer, and
politically equal with the rest of the population, also made
them religiously poorer. They compensated for the loss of
content in their separate collective identity by constructing
grandiose synagogues, in which liturgy and decorum tended
to imitate church pomp, while increasingly moving away
from the atmosphere of sacred life and study that had per-
meated the small, beautiful synagogues of the Italian ghettos.
In Turin this process reached a significant peak—fewer than
three thousand Jews, already forgetful of their ancestral traditions, decided to build a synagogue competing in height and
architectural originality with the Eiffel Tower. Lack of funds
finally prevented the Mole Antoneliana from becoming the
Jewish house of prayer, and this enormous and useless building
eventually became the symbol of the capital of Piedmont.

The need to compensate for long centuries of misery and
oppression, however, pushed the Italian Jews to use the new
riches acquired through the emancipation to purchase—whenever and wherever they could—lands and castles, less as an
investment than as a natural reaction to the state of inferiority
in which they had lived for so long. To buy, as my great-
grandfather did, a castle that had belonged to a branch of the
royal family, the dukes of Genoa, was a doubtful investment
but a social consecration. This desire to climb socially, shared
at that time by all the Jews of Western Europe, was probably
less resented in Italy than elsewhere. Yet it helped to link the
traditional currents of church hostility to the Jews to the new,
secular forms of anti-Semitism on both Right and Left, the

strength of which Jews seemed unable to measure and in most cases refused even to perceive. In Italy, as elsewhere, the nationalist Right regarded them as intruders, and the Left as marginal people who preferred to join the bourgeoisie than to identify with the proletariat. However, the success of the House of Savoy in uniting the peninsula, and the unlimited support that the Jews gave to this nationalist, unitarian Italian policy, allowed them to integrate into the Gentile society more quickly and more deeply than in any other country, including the United States, and to believe in the existence of unique historical conditions.

Indeed, it was not by chance that Italian Jewry was able to provide a minister of war, the first in modern Jewish history, and two prime ministers as well as contribute to the Italian wars of independence and to Garibaldi's militias thirty times more, proportionally, than the rest of the population. In the thirty most crucial years of the Risorgimento, from 1840 to 1870, the Jews in fact felt more Italian than the Italians, because, unlike most of the inhabitants of the peninsula, they had no links of loyalty to the aristocratic and Catholic regimes of the Italian states, which had traditionally kept the Jews apart from the rest of the population. By supporting the cause of the Risorgimento, guided by men like Mazzini, Cavour, Garibaldi, and Victor Emmanuel II, the Jews stood squarely behind a political movement that justified its territorial conquests and the reunion of the various Italian regions into one kingdom with an aggressive nationalist, liberal, and anticlerical ideology.

The Jews thus found themselves also defending ideas befitting not only their particular communal interests but also those of a rising political and military power—the Piedmontese, who could not rely on the unequivocal support of the Italian masses. Indeed, the Piedmontese government, especially after the military defeat suffered in the years 1848–1849 at the hands of the Hapsburgs, could not rely on wide popular sympathy.

Neapolitans, Romans, Florentines, Modenese, Venetians, tied to ancient local regional loyalties, hesitated to throw in their lot with the ambitious but—to many—foreign Savoy dynasty. The Jews, however, as a "landless tribe," were ready to serve it unconditionally and work for the creation of a new "fatherland" in which they could feel equal to others. They therefore brought to the Risorgimento an unlimited enthusiasm and faithfulness, supported by a relatively high cultural and economic level and reinforced by valuable international relations. The marriage between the dynastic Piedmontese interests and the communal ones of the Jews opened for the latter all the doors of political, cultural, and economic influence as nowhere else in Europe. Thus, for some decades, Jews like my great-grandfathers and grandfathers felt themselves to be not only the citizens but also the founding fathers of a new nation. This transitory but exhilarating situation also gave the majority of the Piedmontese Jews a psychological compensation and moral justification for the abandonment of their ancestral traditions, making them believe that they were both "true Italians" and "true Jews"—a hybrid situation and the source of that "fascination" that would later on so greatly surprise a Zionist leader like Chiam Weizmann, the future first president of the State of Israel. In the thirties he could not fathom how Jews who were so assimilated could be so free of what he called in his memoirs, the "fatuous presumptions of the so-called Frenchmen or Germans of the Mosaic persuasion."

My grandparents on my father's side had become bankers. On my mother's side they traded successfully in land and cattle. In both cases they had become affluent and—to judge by their portraits—fat bourgeois, with all the prejudices, aspirations, social conformism, moral values, and weaknesses common to a generation of "new" Italians interested in the greatness of their fatherland as much as in the success of their own affairs.

To preserve Judaism in these conditions was an unrewarding

and difficult task for them. In 1848, when a group of Jewish students in Turin on the fiftieth anniversary of Jewish emancipation in Piedmont asked Max Nordau, the then-popular French writer and ardent Zionist, to contribute an article to their paper, he answered with a message that analyzed correctly the new situation of Italian Jews:

> Up to 1848, oh Italian Jews, you were Jews in Italy; since then you have become Italians of Jewish extraction. What will you be in the future? Pure and simple Italians, without even the adjective "Jew" which reminds you of your past? People assure me that this is what will happen. They tell me that the majority of the Jews in Italy—excuse me—of the Italian Jews, have forgotten their origins, have no longer any Jewish interest, do not know or want to know the history of their race, are indifferent to the sufferings of their brothers in other countries, do not even admit the existence of a brotherhood of faith and do not desire to preserve any link with those of their blood who live under less blue and sunny skies. Is this true?

For my family, at least, this was perfectly true. I do not claim that my grandfathers were ashamed of their Jewishness—quite the opposite. But their Judaism had become something purely formal, devoid of its ancient values. Mixed marriages were considered shameful, but Jewish girls of good families, like my mother and her sister, were sent to study (little and badly) in convent schools where they would acquire a "better education." No self-respecting Jewish family of the time would have dared to eat bread during the eight days of Passover (during which Jews are required to eat only unleavened bread in memory of their liberation from slavery in ancient Egypt). Both my maternal and paternal grandmothers were proud of their beautiful Pesach (Passover) porcelain dinner services, used only for that one particular week of the year. But the thought of not having bread in the kitchen for the use of the servants, or of not consuming forbidden foods or wines would never cross their minds. When, out of respect for some elderly and "bigoted" member of the family, they observed some "unusual" details of the Mosaic tradition, they did it convinced that such rituals had no further reason to exist in modern society, although most of the assimilated families continued to exalt the value of Jewish tradition.

Nobody, for instance, had taught my mother Hebrew, or explained to her the rudiments of Jewish traditions, with the exception of some vague notions in preparation for her bat mitzvah, celebrated in the style of a Christian girl's confirmation. My father used to recite by heart, morning and evening, a small section of the Shema, the Biblical passage that forms the center of the daily liturgy. He also carried in his wallet the text of a Kaddish, a sanctification of God also recited by mourners, printed in Latin characters on a card. On the back of this card there were lines on which to record the names and dates of the "dear departed" according to both Jewish and Gregorian calendars. On these anniversaries even the least observant Jews felt it their duty to visit the synagogue. On the Sabbath preceding the Jahrzeit, that is, the anniversary of the burial, my father made sure to be called up to the podium in the synagogue, next to the rabbi, to attend the reading of the weekly portion of the Bible. At the end of the reading, of which he did not understand a word, he had the name of the departed relative announced together with the sum of money he was offering in his memory. For the rest, and in spite of his pride in being Jewish, my father was totally ignorant of Jewish culture. One could not accuse him of consciously breaking the Mosaic law, since nobody had ever taught it to him. He knew that pork and hare, which he enjoyed immensely, were forbidden foods according to some outdated Jewish ideas. He would have been sincerely surprised to learn that it was also forbidden to light a fire on the Sabbath.

Thus, almost as a reaction to this ignorance, his generation and that of my mother had invented, faute de mieux, a series of their own private "rites" to mark the Jewish holidays. God forbid that at the end of the Yom Kippur fast, which in my family only my father kept, we should not eat the *bruscadela,* a traditional Piedmontese dish consisting of slices of toasted bread soaked in strong wine. Yet the idea of stopping work or giving up a business deal or trip because of a Jewish festival would never have crossed their minds.

We children had all made our entry into *da-minyan,* a corrupted Jewish expression indicating our coming of age. Jews of thirteen years of age enter into a minyan, or group of at least ten men, without which it is not possible to recite most of the prayers in the synagogue. To prepare for this they used to send us to Talmud Torah, courses of Judaism, on Thursday afternoons, a day chosen to avoid the study of religion clashing with a tennis party or a skiing outing, which usually took place on Saturdays and Sundays. Between the solemn engagement to uphold Judaism, which the young Jew undertook on the day of his religious initiation in front of happy, proud, and usually tearful families, and the subsequent observance of Jewish precepts there was, of course, no theoretical or practical connection. It was obvious to us that "Jewish life" and "normal life" belonged already to two separate spheres. They usually overlapped in the request of Jewish parents to exempt their children from the study of Christian religion at school, a request automatically granted by the school authorities (and regarded as a privilege by one's non-Jewish schoolfellows).

My mother, therefore, like my father, grew up in a climate of obsolete Judaism and of vigorous Italian nationalism, and, as a result, she shared all the virtues and prejudices typical of a generation of Jewish bourgeois sure of themselves, affluent, and respected, and totally unconscious of the dangers that lay waiting for them in the future.

As was proper for young ladies from good and wealthy families, my mother had not followed a regular course of study. She could play the piano, embroider, had tried painting with little success, knew French and German, read fashion magazines, and took a passionate interest in books that dealt with religious questions. Her interest in such subjects was part of her inner nature. It had been developed by the nuns in the school in which my grandmother had enrolled her, convinced as the old lady was that the proximity of the *munie* (nuns) and a better knowledge of their system of life would immunize her from any "religious phobias." This turned out to be a correct forecast. My mother never turned into a bigot. Yet once she was installed on my father's estate it became natural for her to fill the long hours of boredom, while she waited for her husband to return from hunting parties or tours of inspection in the fields, by reading stories of the saints and martyrs of Christendom supplied by the local church, together with the picaresque novels about royal courts that my father had brought into his library during his bachelor days.

The emotional relationship between my parents ran on different levels throughout their lives. From the day he met her, by chance, at a university students' party, my father's love for my mother became his principal reason for living, and so it remained in spite of all the unexpected trials it underwent. "Neither of you," he used to say to my sister and me, half serious and half laughing, "is worth your mother's little fingernail." She, on the contrary, had an entirely different idea of married life—she looked on it as a duty of faithfulness, without burning love. The kindest and most thoughtful of people in her behavior, there was in my mother a core of coolness that married life was never able to warm, a coolness that inclined her to search for violent spiritual adventures, leaving the physical ones to remain part of a cluster of social and material interests that people of her class and generation believed could best serve the contractual engagements of respectful marriages.

Strangely enough, my father's and mother's families had not

previously been acquainted in spite of the fact that they had lived for a long time in the same city. One originated in Spain and had lived for generations in the ghetto of Ivrea. The other came from France and had settled in a small village near Turin. My father had to work hard to obtain permission to marry my mother. Her parents did not regard favorably the union of their daughter, "beautiful, delicate and innocent" (this was written in a song composed by a poet on the occasion of their betrothal), with a dowry of three hundred thousand golden lire, with a "good-for-nothing." This is how my father was regarded because of his inexplicable retirement at the age of twenty-four into the country after having tried in vain to persuade his mother to allow him to follow a military career instead of banking. As a compromise he had agreed to study law and for a time was even apprenticed to a famous lawyer. But the heavy sentences that a couple of his clients, petty thieves, had received at the conclusion of his impassioned defenses, had convinced him that he should withdraw from the bar and follow his un-Jewish passion for agriculture.

My maternal grandfather, who was a shrewd dealer in grain and land, suspected that this flight into the province concealed something shady. Before giving his consent to the marriage, he dressed himself in the shabby clothes proper for a cattle dealer and went to the village where my father was the mayor and the largest landowner. He took a room in the local inn and, between a glass of wine and a query about the price of cows, began to make some sly insinuations about Jews who had become heads of local administrations. He barely escaped being beaten up. Ashamed but happy, he returned to Turin convinced that my father, although indeed a queer fellow, was an honest one, capable of taking good care of public property as well as of his own, which consisted of four hundred hectares of excellent land, a rich hunting reserve, broad meadows along the Tanaro River, and a kiln for making bricks. My mother accepted her suitor without enthusiasm but also without reservations, happy to get married and in this way put an end to her parents' fears that she might elope with a non-Jew.

My father's love for her, especially after the late birth of my sister and myself, grew with the passing years. However, when the marriage was celebrated in June 1908 with great pomp in the Turin synagogue, the feelings between the two spouses differed profoundly from the type of sentiment engraved on the gold medallion struck for the occasion. Among the numerous sources of friction between the two were also my mother's refusal to be separated during her honeymoon from a little fox terrier, which my father hated, and his refusal to drop his habit of smoking smelly Tuscan cigars, which she loathed.

On a warm July day, my parents arrived at their village home, tired from their long and uneventful honeymoon trip. Vigiu drove the landau, lined with white silk and shining with black varnish outside, drawn by two lively black trotters. He wore a top hat with yellow and green pheasant feathers, a long gray coat decorated with golden frogs, and with his gloved hands barely controlled the horses, excited at the clapping of the villagers and the firecrackers. The municipal council had lit up the main street of the village with Chinese paper lanterns and with torches in the windows of the castle that my grandmother had sold to the municipality soon after her husband's death. A deputation of notables offered the newly married couple a message of good wishes embroidered on silk, in a wide oak frame decorated with their two portraits, the work of the orphanage nuns. In this message my mother was described as "a woman of sublime beauty and virtue." The village priest accompanied by the clerics, one of them a future cardinal, had organized a torch parade for the evening from the Chiabo quarter to the gate of the castle park. The carabinieri in full uniform maintained order; the municipal band played lively tunes; my father's peasants who, at that time, made up the majority of the village population, were lined up in the outer court of our home. Dressed in festive attire, their black kerchiefs around their perspiring necks, their Sunday jackets creased, they stood next to their wives and children, clapping and shouting at the tops of their voices, "Long live the mayor," "Long live Madamin," and anxiously waiting for the golden half sovereign that had been promised to every head of a family. They certainly did not think that a few years later my father would ask them to go and get themselves killed in battle. That night nobody thought of war or of the possibility that in the course of yet another bloody conflict my father and mother would be chased out of their home because they were Jewish.

My parents' total assimilation did not prevent them from being conscious of their difference from other people. Annetta, the maid who had entered my father's service before he married, also knew that there was something wrong with "the master." A minute person, deeply religious without being a bigot, she became my mother's confidant almost from the day she was promoted to the rank of personal maid. She carried out her daily work as though it were a mission, never tired, never sad. I could not understand why she had not married. In the course of the fifty-five years she remained in our service, with the exception of the brief period during which the Fascist laws against the Jews forbade her to work for us (though she continued to come secretly to help my mother), I do not remember ever having seen her in tears. On the contrary, she was always ready to laugh, even when things went wrong for her. When she was nearing her end, she kept telling my sister and me how fortunate she was to be dying in the apartment we had arranged for her in the attic of our village home. The only thing she could never understand or admit was how decent people like us could not be Christians. She consoled herself, in the course of the years, with the idea that there must exist some strange links between us and God since on certain days of the year my parents used to go to pray in Turin and on other occasions they ate food that appeared sacred to her, although quite different from the consecrated host she took every morning at communion. For this reason, and although nobody ever asked her to do so, she had taken upon herself the task of cooking the family's "religious dishes." She did not know a thing about Jewish dietary laws but it was she who, more than anybody else, took care that we should follow, at least as far as the kitchen was concerned, our strange religious obligations.

Naturally it was at Passover that Annetta felt in her element. The great spring cleaning suited her Christian principles. Although she never understood why, at Easter time, we suddenly stopped eating pasta, bread, and cakes, she took over from the cook for an entire week and sent up to the table the *quaietta d'Pitu*—salted turkey meat, and unleavened bread soaked in meat gravy with peas, instead of the usual meat, ham rolls, and roast rabbit.

On Yom Kippur it was she who, at the end of the fast—which she thought inhuman because of my mother's migraines—carried to the table the famous *bruscadela,* with which my father liked to break his twenty-five hours of total abstinence. At Purim, the Jewish carnival, which usually coincided with Lent, Annetta prepared small crisp squares for us. They bore little resemblance to the "Haman's ears" with which Jews celebrate the victory of Esther and Mordecai over the Chaldean prime minister who, in the Bible, symbolizes the prototype of the political anti-Semite; but they were equally tasty and agreeable to our Christian friends.

Annetta certainly would have liked to see us become Christians, but she would not have dared to interfere in such a delicate matter. Without knowing what it was all about, she never forgot to ask me when she tucked me into bed whether I had recited the Shema. I believe she imagined this prayer to be a pagan version of the Pater Noster and Ave Maria. I always answered "yes," and then she sat next to my bed, falling asleep before me. In the twilight I liked to listen to her breathing, looking at her miniature features drowsing in the deep arm-chair. Only once did I have a conversation with her that I could define as religious, and the initiative was certainly not hers.

I must have been six or seven years old, and we lived then in a villa in the center of the estate near Turin bought with my mother's dowry. Running away from the clutches of a French governess whom I detested, I sneaked up one quiet afternoon to the servants' quarters—absolutely forbidden to the children—and entered the room where Annetta was rest-ing. It was a large, clean, tidy room, with a big window from which one could see the Castle of Rivoli on top of the hill and get a new view of the gardens and fields of the estate. Annetta got up from her big, iron-framed bed and offered me small pieces of licorice, which she kept in a candy dish on her bedside table. I noticed a bunch of dried leaves tied up with a blue ribbon at the head of her bed and asked what they were. She explained to me that these were olive leaves blessed by the priest at Easter. She also showed me the small picture of a saint she kept next to the bowl of licorice and told me that it possessed great power. She had tested it each time she asked for help in looking for something she could not find, for instance the gloves that my mother regularly lost in the house. It was enough to hold the image in one's hand and murmur in Piedmontese, "Saint Anthony, full of virtue, help me to find what I have lost," for the sought-after object to jump out of its hiding place.

I asked her whether this picture understood only Piedmon-tese. She laughed and explained to me that saints like Saint Anthony of Padua understood all languages even if they had never studied them, as Jesus did. This last name was familiar to me since I had heard it pronounced on occasion in the family, though in muffled tones, as if it were a relative who had gone bankrupt. I thought the time had come to elucidate the matter. Annetta looked highly embarrassed. She explained to me that Jesus was the son of God; that many years ago he had been crucified by the Romans after having been denounced by a disciple called Judas; that he had died on the cross but been resurrected; and that upon him depended the salvation of every human being. "Also of those who don't know about his existence?" I asked her. She answered, "Of course." It was at that point that, blushing and sweating slightly, she took the black and silver crucifix down from the wall and gave it to me to kiss. I found this strange but not repulsive because the crucifix had a strong, sweet taste of licorice.

It was not Annetta who influenced my mother to convert. Her conversion was the result of a dramatic affair during World War I and my departure for Palestine during World War II.

My mother's sister, educated like her in a convent school, had converted to Christianity—I believe in 1908 or 1909—after a long struggle with her family. Unlike my mother, who had a docile and mystic temperament, my aunt possessed an anxious and aggressive character. She was still very young when she fell madly in love with a lawyer in Turin, a fervent Catholic and the son of a noble family. Concerning this gentleman's birth, various versions were current in the family, all of them false, due partly to envy, and to the fact that he was physically and psychologically different from his two brothers. One, a well-known doctor, lived in an odor of sanctity; the other was to reach the top of the Italian naval hierarchy. When the lawyer met my aunt, none of his family had yet become famous. This, of course, made it even more difficult for my maternal grandparents to agree to the romance of their daughter. Their opposition only made her passion fiercer. In the bourgeois romantic atmosphere prevailing at the time, it was only natural that she threatened to commit suicide or run away from home with her lover. This second alternative would have been even more dishonorable than self-inflicted death, so after my grandfather died, consent was grudgingly given. My aunt converted and married, and the entry of this Christian uncle into the family made relationships within the "clan" even more complicated than before.

This uncle whom I acquired by marriage was a tall man, thin as a rake, a frequent sufferer from rheumatic pains, austere and authoritarian as befitted his profession, and with little sympathy for Jews. He was certainly not an anti-Semite. He had broken openly with the Fascist party—which he had supported in the beginning—after Matteotti's assassination, a gesture that showed his political farsightedness and his moral stamina. But to him, the utilitarian and bourgeois conformism that my family had developed toward the Fascist regime made "certain types of Jews," as he used to say, unbearable to him. I knew him too little and I was too unaware of our family intrigues to discuss the judgment I often heard people passing on him. His long, drawn face, the offensive tone he often used to underline his ideas, his fits of temper, about which I often heard but never witnessed, made him unlikable.

In fact he scared me. An unpleasant remark he made about the Jews the day I went to say good-bye to him before leaving for Palestine gave me, quite unjustly, an excuse to break with him. After the war he let me know that he wanted to see me and clear up the misunderstandings that were keeping us apart. I refused to meet him. I was certainly wrong; as one of the first Piedmontese intellectuals to join the Fascist party and one of the first to give back his party card—something that for a man in his position was neither easy nor convenient—he could have enlightened me on many political and family matters for which I cannot find answers in the family archives. But another fact, which I learned only after my return from Palestine, had in the meantime helped to raise a barrier between us: that uncle had played an important role in the life of my mother.

At the outbreak of World War I my father found himself exempt from military service because he was a mayor as well as the firstborn son of a widowed mother. His filial duties had prevented him from entering the military academy as he had wanted. In 1916, a year after Italy's entry into the war, it became impossible for a fervent nationalist like him, who had preached participation in the war, to stay at home. He felt ashamed each time he had to take news of deaths to the houses of his villagers, transmitted to him ever more frequently by the military authorities. The event that finally drove him to join up as a volunteer, however, was the death of his favorite horse.

The army had requisitioned three of his horses at the outbreak of the war. He had seen them leave the stable for the front line, one after the other, docile, clean, full of energy: the gray, his hunting mare, and Bayard and Harlequin, who were the matched pair for his landau. Only Blackie, a wonderful six-year-old gelding, born and reared in his stables, was left behind. My father succeeded in having him classified as a workhorse, although he had never pulled a cart or a plow in his life. I never understood why the army, which was already stuck in the trenches, needed so many riding horses. In any event, my father's first three horses were sent immediately to the front line, and soon came the military postcards announcing their deaths. Each time the unknown hand of some possibly romantic or melancholy officer had written to my father expressions of condolence more suited to the death of a man than that of an animal. But in that first year of war the peasants who filled the trenches counted little. Italy, as much as other European countries fattened by forty years of peace, seemed to need—as Churchill said—a good bloodletting.

At the beginning of 1916 they came to take Blackie. Before he left my father photographed him. This picture, enlarged to life size, was framed and hung in Blackie's stall in the now empty stables. Later the photograph was moved to the attic. Yellowed by time, it still shows, under the glass, a military postcard signed by a certain Colonel Depaoli of a cavalry regiment and dated April 12. It reads: "Most illustrious lawyer:

I am sorry to have to announce to you that Blackie has died a hero's death. He was hit by a grenade which also killed seven men and a sergeant-major. He was a courageous and faithful animal. He gave the best of himself to the Fatherland. Please accept the expression of my most sincere sympathy." Three weeks later my father enlisted, unrequested, at the nearest recruiting depot.

He was short in stature and for this reason he was registered in the infantry. After a few weeks as a private, they discovered that he had a university degree and sent him on an officers' training course and from there straight to the front. For him, as for so many other members of the Italian bourgeoisie who had been in favor of Italy's entry into a war supposed to be short and heroic, the discovery that it had turned into a senseless and endless slaughter was a terrible shock. He bore life in the trenches in silence, like so many others, convinced that he was fulfilling a moral and historical duty.

I do not have any of his letters from this period: he destroyed them all when he returned from the front. I doubt if he ever kept a diary as some of his cousins did. I am grateful to him for his modesty, because when I read the correspondence of other members of my family that found its way into the nationalist press of the time, I feel a deep embarrassment at the cloying banalities, the forced romanticism, and the spiritual emptiness concealed behind the literary efforts of people whom I respected and whose hospitality I had often enjoyed. Already many years before the Fascist racial laws, this type of war writing and memoirs showed up the empty public morality of a generation of Jews who had lost both progressive social conviction and genuine religious and cultural belief. The great flare-ups of patriotic sentiment that had driven Italian Jewry wholeheartedly to support the Risorgimento, and made them believe that nationalism represented the heroic epilogue of centuries of discrimination, had died down with the political achievement of Italian unity. Only in the schoolbooks had the new Italy remained the epic and pure country of Mazzini, Garibaldi, and Cavour; in practice it was a new, disorganized state, open to speculation and scandals. The Jews may have appeared less opportunistic than others, thanks to a certain reticence to exposing their financial success, due to their status as late arrivals. At least in our family, in spite of the break with our traditions, people still followed a style of life that united Risorgimento ideals with remnants of Jewish austerity.

During the war, however, I am convinced that for most of them Jewish sentiment often prevailed over other feelings. In my father's case this was certainly so. Facing death in the trenches, he tried desperately to reestablish contact with his Jewish origins. Among the books in his library I found one, torn and stained with sweat and mud, full of annotations, that clearly shows it was carried close to his skin for long periods of time. It was one of those books that the Italian rabbis of the time presumably thought could save Judaism through its linguistic tricks. Their idea was to revitalize the ancient Hebrew language through literal translations into Italian. In this particular book every word of the prayers written in Hebrew characters was divided from the following one by a stroke, and below each word, also between strokes, was the corresponding Italian meaning. How it was possible to pray with such a text is beyond my comprehension: Hebrew is written from right to left, Italian from left to right. The translated words follow each other not only imprisoned between bars but also in the wrong order. They looked like a line of ants with their front legs touching their neighbors and produced a visual and verbal discrepancy that made these texts look as though they had been composed for retarded stutterers.

Yet every page of the book had been annotated, underlined by my father as no other book in his possession. I often imagine him, sitting on a rock in a wet, muddy trench waiting for an assault, or checking his sentries, searching for courage and hope in the magic produced by this confusion of Latin and Hebrew characters. These printed words had lost their original meaning for him, and even if they had still retained something, the translation would have destroyed the rhythm they might once have possessed. But to my father, in those circumstances, they must have transformed themselves into mysterious links with an ancient and faraway world about which he was totally ignorant. Faced by a European civilization in the process of committing suicide in the mad war he had preached, that of his ancestors probably appeared to him as more solid and credible. One thing is certain: on Yom Kippur in 1916 my father rejected all attempts by his fellow officers to make him eat or drink before leading his platoon into one of the many deadly and useless assaults. He described that terrible day to me many times. Thirty men went out; six came back. His luck was rewarded by a brief spell of leave. He rushed back to his country home to find my mother had decided to become a Catholic.

Only after I returned from Palestine in 1945 did my father tell me the full story of this first attempt at conversion, about which I had previously acquired only fragmentary information.

My father, still amazed at being alive, had gone to the town nearest to the front to be deloused and had sent my mother a long, excited telegram to announce his forthcoming arrival. Therefore, he was quite surprised not to find her at the railway station; his blacksmith, too old to be mobilized, was waiting for him with a calèche. This blacksmith—Carlin was his name—born and reared on one of our farms, considered himself, and was considered, a member of the family. To my father, who questioned him anxiously about my mother's health, he was unable to give a satisfactory answer. He kept saying that Madamin had looked a bit agitated during the past few months; that she had been seen walking a lot in Annetta's company; she had spent long hours in church praying for his safety. The village clerk had shown him a newspaper that described the heroism of, and the terrible losses sustained by, my father's regiment. It must indeed have been a horrible day. It was certainly thanks to Madamin's prayers that he had come out alive. She was doing a wonderful job helping refugees and giving out a lot of money to the village poor, while spending most of her evenings sewing with the orphanage nuns. My father knew of my mother's religious bent but never expected that instead of welcoming him with the warmth due to a returning soldier, she herself, tense and excited, would announce to him her decision to become a Christian. He felt the most atrocious pain of his life.

He did not try to argue with this woman he loved. Wounded both in his masculine and his Jewish pride, he shut himself in his library for a day and a night, refusing, to Annetta's consternation, to eat in the dining room or to receive the friends and farmers who came to greet him. When he ordered the old gardener to hurry up and summon the village priest, the rumor ran through the village that something serious was taking place in our home.

The priest, a friend of the family with whom my father had spent many evenings playing chess and emptying bottles of wine, was the only person who had not yet come to welcome him back. My father trusted him fully and quickly understood that he was waiting to be called. Questioned as to what had happened in my father's absence, the priest gave him all the necessary information in detail.

With my father far away, my mother was even more bored than usual by country life. The assistance she gave to the war refugees, the knitting of vests, balaclava helmets, and scarves for the soldiers who were freezing in the trenches, was not enough to fill up the days of a woman who aspired to be involved in something different, more beautiful, greater. In the village, the war, with its unending slaughter, brought to every family with a relative in the front lines, a feeling of anguish, of terror, but also of anger and revolt against those who preached the war (and who now were more despicable than the workers who stayed home). The Jews, moreover, did not have special interests to defend in this conflict, as they did in the wars of the Risorgimento. They wanted to protect their newly acquired positions but no longer felt part of the country's elite. On the national scene there was no longer a Nathan, mayor of Rome, to shield Mazzini in his home, nor an Artom to work as a private secretary with the count of Cavour to unify Italy, nor an Ottolenghi, who, after serving as an officer with Garibaldi's troops, had been rewarded with a title and the war portfolio.

The Jewish community, from which my mother felt estranged in any case, had little to offer its members in those days. The synagogue imitated the church wherever possible, introducing, for instance, the organ on the Sabbath and High Holy Days, and dressing its rabbis in ludicrous black gowns and hexagonal hats. The patriotic rhetoric that these rabbis spouted from the pulpit sounded less convincing than the patriotic sermons of the priests in their churches. It was more difficult for a Jew than for a Christian to think of a Jewish soldier in the enemy camp as an enemy. The church, with its symbols of human and divine sacrifice, offered messages of faith and hope befitting the mentality of Christian soldiers. The synagogue, however, had nothing similar to offer its own faithful. The rabbis prayed for the return of Zion while Jews were asked to die for the recovery of lost Italian provinces; they exalted the Exodus from Egypt while millions of people knew that they would never leave the trenches alive. The war eroded, for everybody, moral values, the links between the classes, and the reciprocal feelings of respect and authority between them. My father, who had voluntarily chosen to share the horrors of that war, clutched at the meager advantages offered by the army: the authority of a military uniform that at last he could wear; the solidarity of the fighting men; the respect he aroused in others by his fatalistic approach to death;

his belief in the just cause of Italian arms; the simplicity of the choices facing him—recover Treno, Trieste for Italy—or death.

My mother, however, was seeing her *belle epoque* world crumble in an atmosphere of growing vulgarity and social promiscuity, in the dissolution of that aristocratic ambience—in fact already well and truly dead—that the Jewish middle class aspired to join like the rest of the country's petty bourgeoisie.

The war, viewed from the leisure of a quiet country life, increased her desire, indeed her need—more out of boredom than out of a sense of adventure—to go beyond good and evil. She felt herself swept away by events greater than herself, without support within the family, guidance in her religion, or advice from her friends. Desperately searching for values to hold on to, for occasions to feel different, she found in her brother-in-law someone ready to listen to her doubts and offer dispassionate counsel. Free—I have never known why—from military service, or perhaps serving locally, he used to visit her frequently, bring her religious books, and put her in contact with a friar gifted with eloquence and a desire to conquer for the Christian faith a Jewish soul so naturally prone to religious enthusiasm. This friar quite possibly thought he was acting in the same spirit as Italian soldiers conquering Austro-Hungarian positions in the front line. He had understood that my mother, separated from a husband who had preferred war to the boredom of country life, rich, without children, and searching for her identity, needed to do something exceptional, to make a gesture that might correspond with the general atmosphere of heroism created by the war. The church attracted her with its liturgy full of music, its paintings, its literature soaked in sacrifice and passion. It offered her an opportunity to realize herself, within a strong, confident hierarchy, capable of understanding, comforting, and bestowing social approval.

The village priest talked at length to my father. He did not conceal the failure of his weak efforts to postpone, in time if not in spirit, a decision that he thought improper for my mother to make as long as my father was away from home. But what could he, a poor village priest, do against so many persuasive and influential people? There were also limits that his cassock imposed on him in such circumstances. To save a soul, to bring a lost lamb into the church, was a duty he could not hinder even if he felt, out of friendship for my father, unable to participate actively in such a mission. He had spent many unhappy hours, he told my father, torn between his religious duties and his human obligations. In the end he had decided to withdraw from the whole affair. His conscience, naturally, was not at ease. But who on earth could sleep peacefully with what was happening in the world these days? His eyes shone with unshed tears as he finished speaking. He blew his nose several times into his big, red, snuff-spotted handkerchief, shook hands with my father, and returned to his parish after exchanging a few words with Annetta, who was anxiously waiting to report back to my mother anything she could learn about the meeting.

My father understood that in such circumstances there was little to be done on the spot. He could not hope to persuade my mother to return to an ancient faith about which he himself knew so little. He could not expect, by his brief presence, to neutralize the effect of months of persuasion by so many missionaries. Without greeting my mother, he took the first train to the city of Cuneo and asked to speak with the bishop. They were not friends, but they knew each other well enough for him not to be kept waiting. In any event, his bearing was so stern that nobody dared to hold him up. In a few short, well-chosen sentences he explained his problem to the bishop. He told him that he was due to return to the front lines and therefore could not care less how he would die. He knew that the friar who had got into the habit of visiting his wife belonged to the bishop's diocese. If he did not receive on the spot a promise that no priest would be authorized to baptize her before the end of the war or prior to his death, if the bishop did not give him a formal guarantee that neither the friar in question nor any other priest would enter his house in his absence, he would look for the friar and put an end to his life. Then he would decide what to do: commit suicide, stand trial, or go back to the front lines and get killed. He had already informed his lawyer, in writing, of his intentions and prepared a communiqué for the press. Should the bishop refuse his request, he would see to it that people would be informed how the Church was stealing the souls of the wives of Jews who were away from their homes fighting for their country. He gave the bishop five minutes to decide.

Standing upright, with a theatrical gesture he took his watch out of his pocket. It was a gold Longines, with the monogram and the profile of King Victor Emmanuel II engraved inside the cover. He had inherited it from his uncle, to whom the king had presented it in return for delicate services performed for the "beautiful Rosie," the morganatic wife of the king, when she was still the mistress of the monarch. The watch, my father told me, showed ten past eleven in the morning. With his eyes fixed on the hands, he stood there waiting for the answer of Holy Mother Church.

I do not know what impressed the bishop most: the compressed fury of a man known to be one of the influential notables of the province, or the threat of a scandal. He asked my father to sit down. He ordered a very strong coffee. He offered him a Tuscan cigar from a box well-concealed in his table drawer. He tried to calm him down in every possible way. Then he promised "to do his best" and in my father's presence ordered the friar to be summoned to his office. My father left the episcopal palace not entirely reassured but convinced that he had done his utmost. The idea of returning to the front lines now seemed to him almost pleasant. Death would free him from a painful situation, just as the conflict with his wife was freeing him from the fear of going back to the trenches.

During the whole of his leave, he did not speak of religion to my mother and tried to enjoy as much as he could the warrior's rest. The detached behavior of a man who was ostensibly preparing himself to die probably made my mother hesitate to make the final decision. Before he left for the front, he learned from the village nuns that the friar no longer had the right to come to the village. Thus the conversion was postponed by twenty years to the day when, following the Fascist anti-Jewish laws and my departure for Palestine, my mother was again shaken by a violent religious crisis.

In the meantime, however, another factor helped to consolidate the religious truce between my parents—my father was in danger of being shot for high treason. Back at his regimental headquarters, he found an urgent call from the General Staff Office; they needed, he was told, a cipher officer in the personal secretariat of the king. The position was being offered to him on condition that he knew how to type. For an entire afternoon and throughout the night, my father worked unceasingly on one of the strange, new office machines. The following day he successfully passed the examination. Thus, he moved from the mud of the trenches straight to the luxury of a Venetian villa, in direct contact with the king and the top commanders of the Italian and Allied armies. This period of rubbing shoulders with the "top brass" he had so much longed to join probably influenced his opting for Fascism later. It also produced a valuable collection of photographs of the great personages of that time, which I have inherited and like to admire whenever I can, always asking myself how so many important and apparently honest and intelligent people could have allowed such a slaughter to continue unchecked for five years.

For my father the transfer also meant taking my mother away from the estate in Piedmont and bringing her to Udine, the nearest big town to the front lines. He obtained all the necessary permits for her arrival and chose appropriate accommodations for her. Then, just before her arrival, on a January night in 1917, he had to decode a personal message from Czar Nicholas to King Victor Emmanuel, in which the Russian emperor announced an offensive against the Germans. There was nothing strategically or tactically decisive in this action. The operation ended with a slight advance in the Riga area, during which the Russian troops, exhausted and already undermined by revolutionary propaganda, conquered a few German positions in the marshy area of Tircul. But for the Allies, pressed as they were by the armies of the Central Powers, this was excellent news. My father decoded the message and then made four copies, as was his procedure for top-secret documents: one for the king, one for the chief of staff, one for a certain General Porro, whose position at that time I do not know, and the fourth one for the file to which he alone had access.

I have heard the story so many times that I remember every detail by heart. It was January 4. There was quite a crowd of officers at the café in the Piazza dei Mercanti in Udine. A war correspondent approached a Russian liaison officer, slapped him on the back and said at the top of his voice: "At last you are moving!" People immediately crowded around the journalist, who retreated behind a mysterious smile, while the Russian ran to his office to report the matter. In the evening, while my father was busy at his decoding work, two officers came to his office, declared him under arrest, and took him straight to the commander in chief, General Cadorna, for interrogation. To whom, he was asked, did you reveal the contents of the coded telegram? My father did not know what they were talking about, but in such circumstances hypotheses were of little use. Since only four people could have known the contents of the telegram, and nobody could suspect either the king or the two generals, it was natural that suspicion should fall squarely on the fourth, the junior officer who knew the contents of the message.

By chance, a military police officer, in civilian dress, was present in the café when the war correspondent made his remark. He interrogated him and learned that he had entered the office of General Porro when nobody was there. He had cast an eye on the dispatches lying on the table, read the czar's telegram and been unable to stop himself from showing off.

However, it took more than two weeks for the matter to be clarified during which time my father was kept under house arrest. A court-martial was set up, and the danger of being sentenced to death became very real. Equally serious was the fact that a rumor began to spread that a Jewish officer had committed a serious crime. Jews who heard the rumor—and the many members of my family who were in uniform immediately became aware of it—thought a new Dreyfus case was being prepared. My father's brother, who already held an important position at GHQ, came to see him accompanied by one of Italy's leading lawyers.

Meanwhile, my mother had arrived in town, unaware of the events and totally confused by what seemed to be a major family, and perhaps national, tragedy. She knew my father too well to doubt his innocence. It was natural for her to come to his defense, to offer him her moral support, while finding in this affair an exciting diversion from her religious problems. For a few days the situation was serious. My mother, connecting her husband's troubles, through who knows what sort of logic, with her attempted conversion, already felt herself responsible for what was happening to him.

Then suddenly the charge against my father was dropped, official apologies were offered, and he regained the trust of the king. This happy ending smelled too much like a miracle not to be regarded by both my parents as a sign from heaven. And thus it was in Udine, a sleepy provincial town where many years later I would celebrate my bar mitzvah, that my mother promised my father to abandon the idea of changing her religion. It was a promise she kept strictly for more than twenty years and to which I owe the fact that I was born and raised a Jew. However, when the Fascist anti-Jewish laws were published and the world crumbled around my parents, my mother found herself once again isolated and unprepared to face events greater than herself.

My departure for Palestine, a country she could not even locate on the map, catalyzed her religious crisis. This time my father no longer had the courage nor the authority to dissuade her. His world, too, was shattered, the world of a Jew who had been a faithful servant of the House of Savoy, a Fascist and a confirmed Italian nationalist. He himself felt little comfort in the few Jewish rites he still observed, nor was he able to explain to himself the sudden social thunderstorm that was hitting him together with the rest of European Jewry. The only thing he could count on was the affection of the woman he loved. If the Christian faith—he explained to me—could comfort her in the midst of such a disaster, he had neither the right nor the desire to oppose her decision.

One day, when he was particularly open with me about these very personal matters, he told me what he did on the day my mother, on her confessor's advice, made a public act of repudiation of Judaism. The whole family (including those members who had already converted in secret) took this formal public statement very badly and denounced it as an act of treason, aggravated by the unnecessary publicity. But my father preferred to send to the convent, where she had retreated to prepare herself for her baptism, a bunch of red roses, like the ones he used to offer her on the occasion of their wedding anniversary. Then he went into the fields to prune his vines.

My mother saved two of these roses. She asked me to put one on my father's coffin, which she felt she could not follow to the Jewish cemetery in Turin; she took the other with her to Israel, where she went every winter after my father's death instead of going alone to the Riviera.

In Jerusalem, where everything was new and strange to her,

she seemed at last to find some peace of mind. On Sundays she used to go to mass, with great discretion, in a monastery where most of the monks were, like herself, converts from Judaism. With their help, she started learning Hebrew. One evening I surprised her teaching my son the same prayers that I had heard my father recite near my bed when I was a child. She spent long hours walking in the garden of the Convent of the Sisters of Zion at Ein Kerem, a convent built at the end of the last century by a rich French Jewish banker who converted to Christianity. In this place of peace and faith, she used to tell me, the little Judaism she had learned as a child revealed itself to her as the roots of the Christian gospel, while the catechism that the priests had taught her appeared to be dressed in Jewish robes.

Sometimes, in the afternoons when she looked at the shadows of the olive trees lengthening on the Judean Hills and the square stones of the convent turning first red then purple under the rays of the setting sun, she felt herself overtaken by a sweet languor. It seemed to her that time was melting her doubts, that the ancient landscape made her pains and anxieties minuscule in the face of the mystery that here, more than anywhere else, weighed on the conscience of the living and on the oblivion of the dead.

When she suddenly fell ill, she asked for and was given permission to be buried in the cemetery of the convent. The gravestone only bears her name, the dates of her birth and death, and a cross. Every year it sinks a little deeper into the earth, as if the body it covers is asking for a closer embrace. One day it will disappear, I imagine, sucked in by the soil perfumed by the winter rains, concealed like the other tombs by the broom and the wild gladioli that blossom in spring and disappear at the first sign of summer—the scratch left by a life on the face of eternity.

3

My Jewish-Fascist
Childhood

I WAS born at the end of 1922,
a month after the March on Rome, and I lived for sixteen years
in Fascist Italy. Those years of Italian life were for me an
existence so regular, normal and carefree, so devoid of events,
that I would find it very difficult to say what was special about
Fascism.

Those who have experienced situations whose daily normality blurs the perception of their extraordinariness may perhaps
feel more keenly to the contrary. I never entered into the
Mussolini regime—I was born into it. As a totally assimilated
Jew and as an Italian raised under a political regime of which
my family and all my friends approved without any reservation, I, too, saw Fascism as the only natural form of existence.
I was not aware of its particularism, because I had no way of
comparing it with other political systems. It may sound incred-
ible, but the first time I heard socialism mentioned as a political
reality, not as a historical fact, was in 1939, in a kibbutz in
Palestine. As for democracy, I knew it was plutocratic and

decadent, and I did not understand (though the thing did not interest me in the least) how it could continue to exist.

This childhood experience of total adaptation to the environment allows me today to understand better situations that appear to be inconceivable to others: the ability, for instance, of the Israelis to lead a normal life, day after day, in the midst of an unending state of war; the ability of the citizen-soldier to bear and often enjoy military service provided that it lasts long enough to assume a regular rhythm; the ability of men and women to love, work, buy, and sell in a city like Beirut, ravaged by civil war.

The Fascist youth organizations to which I belonged from my earliest years—the Balilla and the Avanguardisti—were part and parcel of the school system. I respected them in the same way I respected my teachers at the Royal Gymnasium, but they did not interfere with my life. They wanted me for the end-of-year gymnastics exhibition, not for my ideas. In any case, my mother's "justification," written in her beautiful handwriting on handmade Fabriano paper with her name gracefully engraved on the top left-hand corner, was sufficient to free me at any time without question to go to the dentist, play tennis, or attend a Hebrew lesson. I do not remember, either in school or outside, one single occasion when I felt uneasy because I was a Jew. I was convinced that being Jewish was a treat no different from Cirio brand marmalade, the more so because I was the constant object of jealousy among my school friends for being allowed "for religious reasons" to be absent from the boring lessons of the Gymnasium priest.

The Judaism practiced in my home did not entail any special obligations. Except for the fact that I had to go on Thursday afternoons to the lesson at the Talmud Torah to prepare for my bar mitzvah, to be a Jew was not, in my case, any more inconvenient than being a Catholic or a Protestant. The Sabbath was like any other day: school in the morning and horseback-riding or fencing in the afternoon. There was no special food to be eaten or avoided at home or outside. As a Jew I was exempt from going to mass on Sunday mornings and free from the obligation to observe the forty days of Lent, but my mother took great care always to have fish on Fridays "out of respect for the servants." The Jewish High Holy Days of Rosh Hashanah and Yom Kippur usually fell at the end of the summer vacation. I spent them in the mountains playing cowboys and Indians. My father, secluded for the day in his library, used to read his big prayer book, translated into Italian; he used to call us into his room on the afternoon of Yom Kippur to read us the story of Jonah, and that was all.

At Passover, we ate matzoh, but naturally the servants always had their bread. I never attended a Passover seder until I arrived in Palestine. Of the other main Jewish holidays, Shavuot and Succot, I knew nothing at all. I was, however, well aware of a feast called Purim, the Jewish carnival, because my maternal grandmother used to bring us a round cake covered with glazed fruit, called *brasadel* in the Piedmontese Jewish jargon, which my mother tried in vain to imitate after my grandmother's death.

Hanukkah, the Festival of Lights, fell too near Christmas for me to be able to distinguish clearly between them. We used to celebrate both in the mountains. I attended midnight mass with my father and with my Christian cousins, all very excited by the long ride in the snow in the horse-drawn sleigh, skimming through the darkness to the accompaniment of the galloping horses' bells. We were aware (especially my cousins, who knew at the time that my uncle expected to be made a baron or a count) of our duty to receive with grace and reserve the greetings of the workers from the family estate. After singing the carols from the benches behind us, the workers formed a pathway down the aisle of the church for our passage; never did it cross my mind that the fact that they were Christians and I was a Jew might be considered peculiar. It was as natural as the pine trees around the church, the little cemetery and its crosses, the river bubbling by among the patches of snow, the old sawmill, the mountains, the wind, and the old cook who waited for us at home with mulled wine and biscuits.

Since I had no contact with the world outside Italy; since I read only school textbooks, adventure stories and, from time to time, the local newspapers to look up the titles of films or the sports programs; since I lived first in the gilded cage of my mother's estate in Piedmont and then in the cotton-wool climate of a Venetian provincial town in which my family occupied a certain position; since I had no political or social reasons to become interested in events or ideas beyond those of my daily routine, so full of small duties, of cycling and riding competitions, of social satisfactions, I lived in the belly of the monster, totally unaware of its existence.

The first sixteen years of my life were divided into periods of equal length—from 1922 to 1930 on my mother's estate near Turin, and from 1931 to 1938 at Udine, a small provincial town in the Friuli region. It was the nearest place with a high school to my uncle's fiefdom in the mountains along the Austrian and Yugoslav border, where my father worked after losing most of his fortune in the 1929 stock market crash.

After the publication of the laws against the Jews in July 1938, we returned to the Piedmont region and I went to live in my grandmother's house in Turin, one of the few cities in Italy where the Jewish community was able to organize secondary schools for students who had been thrown out of the public schools. Here I discovered for the first time a world different from mine; here took place the first brutal meeting with the particularism of my Jewish condition, my first contacts with a literature, a history containing ideas totally different from those with which I had grown up. In Turin I also met many people whose names have since been inscribed in the history of the Italian resistance movement and of the Jewish tragedy: Leon Ginsburg, the Russian-born writer; and Emanuele Artom, the mathematical genius who was later tortured to death by the Fascists; Franco Antonicelli, a future senator and leader of the anti-Fascist Piedmontese resistance; Primo Levi, the chemist whose account of life in concentration camps would become a classic of the literature on the Holocaust. However, I did not establish strong relations with any of them, since I left almost immediately for Palestine in order to escape from the new, and to me totally incomprehensible, situation in which I suddenly found myself trapped.

I felt, indeed, like a fish out of water. I had never been a Zionist, and I could hardly have become one since my father strongly opposed the Jewish national movement, which to his mind undermined the patriotism of the Italian Jews. I knew that there existed strange boxes, blue and white in color, in which my new schoolmates put coins on Jewish holidays. But my father refused to have such an object in his house, even after the publication of the anti-Jewish laws. I was also completely ignorant of Judaism, if one excepts the few notions I had learned at the Talmud Torah classes while preparing for my bar mitzvah. If, nevertheless, I was to be one of the first Italian Jews to leave for Palestine after the publication of the Racial Laws (after having tried without success and without the knowledge of my parents to join the foreign legion in France), this was only due to the attraction of romantic adventurism and to the hope of being able to imitate, in a country that did not yet have a political identity of its own, some of the deeds of Garibaldi. Unnoticed by everyone, I even tried to teach myself to make candles as Garibaldi had done in Latin America to make a living before joining the Italian legion, fighting for the liberation of Uruguay. Feeling deeply offended by the behavior of the Fascist party and the king toward me and my family, I broke my ties with the Italian nation in a series of secret, nighttime ceremonies, during the course of which I buried, under the great cedar of Lebanon in

my mother's garden, my black Fascist dagger, a wooden toma-
hawk, and my collection of tin soldiers—the symbols of my
now-shattered hopes of joining the Royal Military College.

To the psychological shock caused by these sudden changes
(which were continued in Palestine with my passing—in less
than two years—from a kibbutz to an agricultural school, and
from that school to the British army), I attribute in part the
tenacity with which the uniformity of my life under Fascism
—the only normal existence I ever knew—has stuck in my
memory. It is as if my subconscious has refused to abandon the
illusion of the quiet, happy years of my youth and blocked all
attempts to look more deeply at those early periods of my life
that must, in some way, have recorded the events that shook
my family and the country of my birth during this time—for
instance, the stock exchange crash of 1929.

Of this event, which ruined my father, causing us to leave
Piedmont for Udine, and forcing him to work for the first
time in his life so that we became, in the eyes of our ramified
and still very wealthy relations, the poorest and therefore the
most stupid branch of the clan, I do not remember a thing. I
recall only some mnemonic flashes from the time just before
our move, completely detached from the events that were
shaking our family existence; for instance, a night drive on the
not-yet-asphalted road leading from my mother's estate, in my
father's 509 Fiat limousine, sitting next to the uniformed chauffeur, who allowed me from time to time to put my hands on
the wheel. I was full of excitement at the sight of the speedom-
eter needle jerking around the fifty-mile-an-hour mark, and I
kept turning around toward my parents to make them conscious of this extraordinary adventure. I could see them
through the movable glass partition that separated their seats
from that of the driver, totally indifferent to my enthusiasm.
They were talking to each other with agitated gestures that
seemed to mime the anguished movements of the two red roses
stuck in the silver vase next to the door. My mother, wearing

a big silver fox fur around her shoulders, crushed in her hand a handkerchief embroidered with her monogram and frequently touched her lips with smelling salts. It was the day my father, having lost all his money, understood for the first time that he was completely ruined. We were saved by a loan from his cousin's bank and by the job, offered by his brother, of running a chain factory somewhere in the Venetian mountains. To him this was the end of his world, of his material security, which for the last two generations had seemed indestructible; for me it was only a high-speed drive in my first—and last—private limousine.

Another clear memory of that time is linked to a rat. My sister and I were children prone to illness. She had had a mastoid operation; I used to progress from sore throats to bronchitis, which my parents tried to prevent by forcing me to drink great quantities of castor oil and by stuffing my nostrils at night with cotton swabs soaked in some strange and evil-smelling liquid. If to all this one adds my tendency to wound myself in the strangest ways (I once poured boiling water on my arms; another time I cut my scalp open with an ax, which I was using upside down to knock in the pegs of my Indian tepee), it will be clear why, as long as we remained in Piedmont, my parents preferred to have me taught privately rather than to send me to the public school. This resulted in my not studying anything seriously, not knowing boys my own age, and in living in the golden cage of a big country house among teachers, servants, and gardeners who, in the main, looked after their own affairs.

My mother's estate was surrounded by a long wall that cut me off from the mysterious world of the village. There was nothing much to see from three sides of the wall since it overlooked open fields, and agricultural life was far more interesting at home than outside. The farmers never objected to my joining them in their haymaking; whenever I asked they put me astride one of their big workhorses or allowed me to hold the reins of the two-wheeled Piedmontese carts, which looked to me like Roman chariots. Sometimes they even allowed me to steer the plow or shell the maize, or to collect frogs and snails from the ponds, which both they and my father liked to eat. From them I learned much more than from my teachers, and to them I owe the ease with which I was able to adapt to work in the fields when I reached Palestine.

The fourth side of the wall extended for hundreds of yards along the main road of the village, into which I was not allowed to go unaccompanied. I was only permitted to stand near the great iron gate at the end of the acacia-lined drive, to peer like a monkey through the bars into the world of free men.

The Via Maestra was narrow and full of life with two stone ruts down the center for cartwheels. To the left of the gate were some artisans' workshops, one of which belonged to my mother's cobbler, whose son eventually bought her estate. In these workshops wonderful things happened: from rusty pieces of iron there came forth delicate iron tracery; from masses of cane, all sorts of beautiful baskets; from big tree trunks, window frames, tables, and doors and—most important of all—my wooden shields and swords.

To the right of the gate one could see the beginning of a small winding lane, leading—so I was told in great secrecy by Cecilia, the kitchen maid—to a restaurant where one could rent rooms by the hour, which always seemed to me to be an excellent business. At the corner of the lane, soldiers of the local garrison used to wait in the evening for their girls, and women exchanged gossip during the day. The Via Maestra was crowded with carts, either filled with hay and corn, or empty with a farmer asleep inside next to a flask of wine, at the mercy of his horses' loyalty and sense of direction.

However, the most important things in that street for me were the parades organized by the local branch of the Fascist party and the processions of the local parish. They competed between themselves with their uniforms, their flags, their songs, their music, and the very impressive gestures that the participants made while walking—either raising their hands in the Roman salute or waving them in Christian blessing. My preference had been for the Fascists since the day my father, giving in to my insistence, put me between two of his militiamen in black shirts and armed with carbines and daggers, to march in front of the flag. I felt exalted and terribly important. Only many years later, when I saw for the first time a British regiment marching along with a goat as its mascot, did I realize that I had filled the role of the goat in my first Fascist march.

The Catholic processions were quite different. I was never given permission to join them and to swing the censers like the little village boys whom I so much envied. They succeeded, while marching and singing in unison, in raising white clouds of perfumed smoke, something I never could manage when I tried to send Indian smoke signals to my sister across the garden. The blue and gold garments of the priests, the crosses, the white, embroidered smocks of the choirboys, the white headscarves of the women of the Daughters of Mary, impressed me more than the black shirts of the Fascists. Yet an event once took place that created between me and the church procession that psychological barrier that still keeps me away from any form of collective liturgy.

It was a hot summer afternoon; the church bells had been ringing for hours; the Via Maestra was packed with people. The carabinieri wore their gala uniforms with blue and red feathers on their bicorne hats. The bishop was there, surrounded by priests, walking behind the statue of the Madonna with a golden crown on her head and a blue silk scarf draped around her wooden shoulders, carried by eight farmers dressed in their Sunday best. There were the boys from the elementary school, the Daughters of Mary, the canons and the clerks, and the association of ex-soldiers with their banners full of medals. There was the old soldier from Garibaldi's army with his red shirt, an antiquated military cap on his head, hobbling along with a walking stick. The smell of incense mingled with that of the hay still in the fields. The municipal band led the march, followed by my father, who had just been appointed mayor, wearing his tricolor sash of office and a black jacket, which had miniatures of his military medals pinned on the lapel.

Our farmers sat on top of the wall with their legs dangling near the heads of the passing crowd. My mother's maid and my French governess stood side by side near the iron gate. They gave me a special place at their feet; I sat on a little stool from which I could look down at the procession without getting tired. My sister, however, stood a few yards away under the last acacia tree of the avenue, next to the canal that crossed our property. Just before the bishop and his entourage passed in front of the gate, my sister let out a scream of terror at the top of her voice. Half a century later I still remember the scene: she stood petrified, pressing her little leg with both hands and screaming, "he's bitten me!" Her shrieks were soon echoed by the screams of the French governess, who was terrified of being thought responsible for whatever had happened.

The strange thing that was the cause of all this commotion stood motionless, like part of one of those still-life scenes that my mother used to organize in her sitting room among her guests when she felt that gossip and sweets were no longer able to keep people from yawning. It was a rat—to my eyes it looked monstrous—an aggressive sewer rat, not a field mouse, since it had the courage not to run away amid all the uproar. After having bitten my sister, it stood there looking at her and at the French governess with two small, red eyes and with tiny, bared, pointed teeth, which looked to me like elephant's tusks. The first to react was Gusto, the son of a tenant, who, swearing loudly, and with a hoe in his hand, threw himself at the rat but was not fast enough to hit him. The rat disappeared into the hay; my sister continued to scream and the French governess to cry. My father, who had recognized my sister's voice, rushed from the procession in the street and started asking worried questions from his side of the gate. The bishop, however, remained unperturbed and continued his march, only irritated by the fact that the people following him had stopped intoning and were asking each other what was happening in the farm of the Jews. I sat on my stool, in a way enjoying the whole scene through the legs of the people around me and outside the wall, but growing worried by the screams of my sister, which were mingling with the litany of the priests.

From that day I developed a great fear of rats, and the physical impression that life is a procession of mortals who pass by your anguish without feeling your existence.

During the eight years that followed our move from Piedmont to the Friuli region, my life went on, divided between school and holidays. Of the first class I attended in a public school in Udine I remember only the shining smile of my teacher, with whom I fell madly in love, only to learn later from my mother that she had false teeth. I was still not well enough to share in all the games of my new schoolfellows, and I spent most of the first year in our new residence in bed with fever. It was only in 1931, when we moved into a new apartment thanks to the growing income from my father's work, that I started living a normal life.

We lived in a large apartment, which my mother continued to describe in her letters to her relatives as "two rooms." Annetta, previously my mother's personal maid, was now the housemaid, and Cecilia remained as cook. We did not own a car, but for long trips we used the factory limousine. Usually my mother was "at home" on Thursdays, and on that day I was authorized to invite my friends to come in the late afternoon to finish up whatever cakes or sweets her friends had left for us.

My father lived apart from us in a mountain village, where he ran one of his brother's factories. We saw him only on

Saturday evenings when he came to town on the six o'clock train, only to go back to the factory early on Monday mornings, traveling second class, thanks to the special rate he enjoyed as an officer in the Fascist party. In the afternoon he used to take me to the cinema, sometimes even to see two films, one after the other. On Sunday mornings my father woke up at eight o'clock, and by nine was ready in his shining uniform of commander of the Fascist militia. He used to take out of a red cardboard box the black Fascist fez with its silk fringe falling to one side. He buckled the golden belt with his silver dagger dangling from it around his waist, and put on his gleaming boots with spurs, which Annetta had been polishing for hours, and which I had the privilege of carrying into his bedroom. In the cold weather he wrapped himself in a splendid gray-green cape that fell to his heels and left the house surrounded by an aura of authority and mystery, which many years later I suddenly recognized in the portrait of the *Fascist in Uniform* by Ligabue.

My mother, after much hesitation and pressure, finally agreed to become a patroness of the local Fascist party Women's Section. She hated wearing a uniform, even though her broad-brimmed black hat was always the most elegant among all the local ladies. At noon on Sunday she took the tram to join my father in the Piazza dei Mercanti for an aperitif. I, together with my school friends, had gone my way, dressed in the uniform first of the Balilla, afterward of the Avanguardisti, to the Sunday morning Fascist Youth meeting. These were horribly boring; they started and ended with a nominal roll call to check whether any of us had been able to disappear while the youth commander read the order of the day, gave the order to salute Il Duce, and made us march up and down in the courtyard of the school, which served as HQ for our youth organization's unit. I, too, wore my fez and carried a dagger, but both were infinitely less impressive than those of my father. I dreamed of becoming a section leader so that I could change my fez for an officer's cap and my gray soldier's uniform for the tight blue dinner jacket of the section leaders, which closely resembled the elegant dress of the Royal Naval cadets who courted my sister. It was the first of my unsuccessful attempts to rise in a military hierarchy.

Starting from the fourth year at the Gymnasium, we were forced to study Fascist culture and military history. Nobody took these lessons seriously since we all knew that our school fates would really be decided by the written examinations in Italian, Latin, and Greek, for which I took private lessons for years in preparation. My teachers were unanimous in thinking that I was "without a solid basis," and I am afraid that I have remained so to this day as far as academic culture is concerned. This intensive study did not prevent me from bicycling every day, fencing twice a week, going to Talmud Torah lessons on Thursday afternoons, skiing on winter Sundays, or from actively getting ready, psychologically and materially, for the school holidays.

The more I think of that period, such a happy one for me, the more I realize that I escaped the impact of the dramatic events already shaking the world and menacing the safety and unity of our family. The war in Abyssinia appeared to me to be a normal event, considering the fact that Italy controlled so little green space on the map compared with the red and blue patches of the British and French colonies. The war in Spain was too far away and too complicated to impress me. I did not meet any soldiers who had been involved in either war, nor school friends who had lost relatives in them. This was because most of the fighting troops were recruited from the unemployed, with whom I did not mix, or from the south, which for us northerners was beyond the pale. Indeed, when my father had to go to Rome to mount guard at the royal family tombs in the Pantheon, he used to announce his trip to my mother by saying, "I have to go south of the Po" (river), and would then send her a postcard from his military camp bearing the words "Kisses from the colonies."

In any case, I was convinced that Italy would always win any war, since the newspapers and our teachers spoke only of military successes, while the cavalry and air force officers I knew or who visited our house were young and eager to distinguish themselves in battle. Photographs of war horrors were not admitted into our home, and I was not troubled by the fact that I could not explain to Annetta why the Spanish Republican troops, which were obviously also Christian troops, took particular pleasure in killing nuns and priests. I was far more interested in collecting stamps from Abyssinia and Spain and learning about the Spanish Riding School in Vienna than in the political and military events that were preparing our ruin.

In 1935 there was a moment of agitation in our family when the police searched the house of my father's sister in Turin because of certain unclear relationships that my uncle, a well-known anti-Fascist (which meant that he had never registered with the Fascist party) had with political émigrés. Nobody was arrested. My father and his brother intervened "in the highest spheres," and things returned to normal. The only political incident I witnessed during the five years I spent at the high school in Udine was the beating up of a small boy in my class because his mother was Belgian, and Belgium had voted for sanctions against Italy. But, as in the films I used to see on Sunday afternoons with my father, justice quickly triumphed. As soon as the headmaster learned about the incident, he collected the whole school in the auditorium, brought the victim up to the podium and revealed to us that his father was an officer fighting in Abyssinia. With a rhetoric that moved most of us to tears, he promised to expel from the school and "denounce to the competent authorities" anyone who dared to bother the boy, whose only sin was to have a foreign mother.

It never occurred to me that if it were possible to beat up someone because his mother had a different nationality, it might also be possible to beat up somebody who belonged to a different religion or race.

To this very day I ask myself whence came my unshakable, irresponsible sense of security and my blessed ignorance, despite my being aware of the fact that I was a bit different from the rest of my schoolfellows. I did not attend the catechism class; my mother used to accompany me on Thursday afternoons to the Talmud Torah in the little synagogue, which was a transformed granary near the railway station. The rabbi who taught us, and who was to become a famous scholar in America and in Israel, was a Hungarian Jew, big, poor, and overburdened by a large family. Like the cantor, who was invited by our community for the High Holy Days, he wore a big beard and a stained black robe.

I knew that the rabbi and the cantor, despite their being Jews like us, were quite different. They were totally strange in appearance; they had to solve continuous problems concerning food and timetables, which I did not have; they were similar to those strange, bearded beings who from time to time used to ring the bell of our apartment and then stand immobile and silent in the doorway. Annetta, who usually opened the door in her white lace cap and frilly apron over her blue-and-white-striped uniform, used to leave the door ajar but with the chain on, to make quite sure that they could not get in. Then she would rush to my mother and tell her, in Piedmontese dialect: "Madame, there is one of those, there." My mother was always quick to understand her. Surprisingly for me, even if she were entertaining guests, she used to get up, go to her bedroom and open the cash box, taking out a small black silk bag that she had inherited from her mother and in which she collected large silver twenty-lire coins, with the head of Mussolini on one side and the inscription "It is better to live one day as a lion than one hundred years as a sheep" on the other. She would take one of these coins and go in person, to the ever-renewed astonishment of Annetta, who followed her closely for protection, unlock the door and put the coin into the hand of the strange being, who would receive it with an outstretched hand covered by a not-always-clean handkerchief. "They are dirty," Annetta used to comment. "Yes," replied my mother, "but they are very well educated, since knowing that, they cover their hand with a handkerchief." It never crossed her mind, even after she went to Israel in her last years of life, that orthodox Jews behaved in that way, convinced as they were that the women in a family like ours must surely have been impure.

Certainly some faint echo of anti-Semitism reached my ears, but it was the echo of the Dreyfus case, which was explained to me occasionally by my father, without of course any mention of the effect it had had on Theodor Herzl. They were far-off events, which some members of my family living in Paris still remembered, but which to me sounded like the deeds of Genghis Khan or Attila, reinforcing, through their unreality, my sense of security. At the Fascist party HQ in Udine, where my father had many contacts, everybody was openly opposed to the persecution of the Jews that had begun to take place in Germany, not because the victims were Jews but because the persecutors were Germans, hated by the local Italians. My father's brother, who continued to rise rapidly on the ladder of economic success, used to write to us, or tell us when we met him in the summer in his mountain resort, about his meetings with Mussolini. These meetings, always extremely friendly, never ended, said my uncle, without some allusion by Il Duce to the difference existing between the Italian Jews and those of the rest of the world. We were secure because we were different, and we could be different because we were, so far, secure.

In the military circles in which I roamed, either because my friends at school were the sons of officers or because around

Udine there were many military bases where I could ride at will, it was almost a ritual to show loyalty to the king and a detachment from Fascism, together with open hostility to the Germans. On such occasions I felt part of a quasi-secret society, since in the presence of my mother or father somebody always found a pretext to speak in favor of the Jews and against the Germans. The fact that in those years the colonel of the most prestigious cavalry regiment in town was a Jew, was enough to cut short on anyone's lips—in our presence at least—any criticism he may have had of the Jews. On Yom Kippur in 1937, when the cantor started singing the Kol Nidre prayer for the third time, three bareheaded youths entered our little synagogue with the obvious intention of disturbing the service. There was a moment of tension, even though the cantor continued singing the prayer. My father looked around him, and when he saw that nobody reacted, he left the bench on which I was sitting and with his tallith wrapped around his shoulders went straight to the intruders. Without a word, very slowly, he withdrew his wallet from his inner pocket and pulled out a document showing his position in the Fascist party. The three youngsters jerked to attention and left the synagogue. It was a small incident—one I still remember with great clarity. It confirmed, more than anything else, my feeling of total security, which was reinforced as in every previous year, by the life I lived during my summer vacation.

There were three different types of holidays, all of which were religiously kept by my mother, convinced as she was that the first two were indispensable for my health and the third for my father's psychology: a seaside holiday between June and July, a mountain holiday from July to September, and then a week or ten days back in Piedmont for the grape harvest.

The seaside holiday was the most boring period as far as I was concerned. I disliked swimming, I hated sailing, I burned easily in the sun, and I objected to playing chaperone to my sister, or as we say in Italian, "carrying the candle" for her innumerable admirers. In 1935 and 1936 the seaside holiday was replaced by two cruises in North and Latin America on board the big luxury liners *Saturnia* and *Conte Grande,* respectively, which transported, over and above many important people and rich tourists, a selected group of *marinaretti* (the maritime Fascist youth movement) belonging to families who were considered most loyal to the Fascist regime. Their task was to march in the streets of New York and Buenos Aires and promote the collection of iron and gold from the Italian communities of those cities in support of the Abyssinian campaign and as a gesture of defiance against the League of Nations' economic sanctions. I had no difficulty in being accepted for these cruises, and I was quite surprised to find that the percentage of Jewish *marinaretti* was much higher than the percentage of Jews in the Italian population as a whole.

It was during one of these trips that I delivered my first public speech, commenting on a speech by Mussolini that had been relayed to us over the ship's radio during the afternoon session of Fascist indoctrination, in which I did not usually participate because of seasickness. My speech was not a great success, partly because I spoke about the historical role of Il Duce while our commander, a teacher of calisthenics from Sardinia named Porcu (swine), was mainly interested in speaking to us about venereal disease and masturbation, which in his view were the main enemies of Fascist youth.

When we reached New York we found a very large deployment of foot and mounted police waiting for us, trying to keep away from our ship—moored to a quay near Grant's Tomb—a crowd of people shouting anti-Fascist slogans at the tops of their voices. It was a great surprise to me to discover that there were people who did not share the Fascist ideal and even more to hear for the first time some important Italian people on deck speaking openly about the connection between plutocratic communism and the Jewish International. But I quickly forgot the scene and the remarks because we were soon inundated by a much larger crowd of enthusiastic Italian-Americans who for the next three days did nothing but carry us from one feast to another, showering us with gifts and ripping from our uniforms whatever they could—stripes, medals, and so on—for souvenirs. The same thing happened in Buenos Aires. Here the highlight of the trip was a concert given by the famous Italian tenor, Tito Schipa, at the Teatro Colon. When we entered the auditorium in our bright blue navy uniforms, the people seemed to go mad with enthusiasm. I returned to Italy convinced that a military career was the one most suitable for me, although deeply upset by the fact that my stomach had proved that it would be unwise for me to enroll at the Naval Academy.

At the seaside resort of Grado, where we used to spend the first part of our summer holidays, I met the first Jewish refugees from Germany. I remember well a family by the name of Furst consisting of a distinguished elderly man, his wife, and their two daughters. They must have been quite rich and were staying at the seaside in Italy as tourists waiting for permission to go to Palestine. They used to tell my mother what was happening in Germany to the Jews, but never mentioned what they had personally suffered or lost. They listened, with interest but little belief, to what we used to tell them about the difference between Italy and Germany and the fate of the Jews in those two countries. They had not read the book by Ludwig on his meetings with Mussolini, so my father went to look for it in a library; before giving it to them he read to me some of the passages in which the German writer related what Il Duce had said to him about anti-Semitism and in favor of the Jews. The Furst family left Grado together with us, and a few years later I looked for them in Palestine without success.

In the mountains, within the large estate belonging to the factory that my father ran on behalf of his brother, the unreality of my existence and my thoughtlessness were even greater than at the seaside. My uncle's factory was the main industrial establishment in the area; he owned a whole valley with several mountains, two small lakes that produced electric power for the nearby town of Tarvis, large patches of woodland, and an entire village, the houses of which he rented to his workpeople. It was, and to a certain extent still remains under my cousin's paternalistic rule, a kind of fiefdom, and at that time I was the son of the "overlord's" brother. It is difficult to describe to anyone who has not lived in such places and during those years what it meant to belong to a family that owned the land, the houses, the roads, the woods of an entire area; provided work for three hundred families and looked after their welfare through an old-fashioned system of charity for the needy; supported the small parish; was responsible for the local sports activities; and what it was like to live in a country where trade unions were illegal, strikes were punishable by imprisonment, and work was still scarce.

In the case of my family, there were also political ingredients that made our position stronger. The valley owned by the factory was a tongue of land squeezed in between the Yugoslav and Austrian frontiers. It had been allotted to the Italians after World War I by someone who apparently paid little attention to Wilson's principle of national self-determination, since the whole of the local population was Austrian and objected strongly to being under foreign, Italian, rule. In fact, when they were given the choice, under the 1939 agreement between Mussolini and Hitler, ninety percent of the local inhabitants opted for the Third Reich and went off happily to get themselves killed at Stalingrad or by Allied bombs during World War II. I imagine that their feelings toward the Jews were not very different from those of the Nazis across the frontier, but my uncle was their source of livelihood and my father, apart from being the manager of the factory, was the highest Fascist official in the area and was also responsible for the antiaircraft defenses of the whole border region. In other words, we were the object of their natural respect for the established authorities and of their fear aroused by the representative of the conquering power. The fact that we were also Jewish only made these circumstances more sinister in their eyes.

Of all this I was completely unaware at the time, despite the fact that the former Austrian burgomaster of the village, a nice, tall, old Carinthian nobleman, had from time to time tried to explain the situation to me. He lived next to the post office in a brick and wood mansion in which he painted and collected matchboxes, tram and railway tickets, dried flowers, and stamps. My passion for stamps had given me the courage to cross his threshold, which my father did not particularly like since he was convinced that at heart the old gentleman was still an enemy of Italy. In fact, he kept in his studio a very large portrait of a man he called his "uncle" but which was none other than Emperor Franz Josef of Austria. The burgomaster had painted elegant evening attire, complete with white tie and tails, over the kaiser's military uniform. When I stood in front of the portrait and gazed at it with admiration, my host would wink at me, his bushy white eyebrows beetling over the gleam in his eyes. It was a kind of silent secret ceremony we both enjoyed, after which he would take me into the sitting room where his maid had already prepared for me long slices of black bread spread with butter and honey. While I was eating he used to show me his war and peacetime decorations and tell me about his trips to Russia and England.

My father, as I said, did not like my visiting him, but my mother defended me, saying that the old gentleman was a polite and inoffensive person, that he had been living alone for many years with his housekeeper and certainly took pleasure in the visit of a person of my age. Better him, she would say, than some of the youngsters with whom I went fishing and who probably talked to me about unspeakably dirty subjects. She was right: the old burgomaster never spoke about sex or politics, nor did he ever mention my race or religion. He liked to recall the better service that the Austrian administration had provided in his time for the local population, and I listened to him as if he were speaking about an imaginary, lost continent.

During the months I spent in the mountains, my already carefree city existence transformed itself into a continuous fulfillment of childish dreams. I fished for trout; I accompanied the gamekeeper on his long walks to check the game birds; I was free to disappear from home for hours at a time, picking mushrooms and blackberries. My father's house stood in the middle of a large garden fenced with wooden stakes, which to us children served as a forest in the Old West. It was bordered on one side by a stream with one small island in the middle that had three tall pine trees. Here my sister and I built a permanent Indian camp, complete with tents, Sioux costumes, bows and arrows, and shields. It was linked to the mainland by a small drawbridge and connected to the house by an overhead cable capable of carrying a basket. We used this to send instructions to the cook, who promptly returned the basket full of provisions.

There were no service problems in the house since, in addition to the two maids my mother brought with her from town, there were those who attended my father throughout the year. The villa was always full of guests, especially during the summer military maneuvers. My uncle, in his rather imposing mansion on top of the hill, received officers from the rank of colonel and upward; my father, partly because of his lower social rank and partly because of my sister, was responsible for entertaining those from colonel downward.

The factory had a lot of cart horses that I could ride whenever I wanted. In the winter we harnessed them in pairs to the sleighs and spent hours galloping along the empty, snow-covered roads. It was a world of dreams, unreal and feudal, which I recognized many years later in some of the scenes from the film Dr. Zhivago. For me, however, it was absolutely normal and I accepted it without scruples or doubts because I knew no other. Into this world, unpleasant echoes from the outside could not penetrate, and if occasionally politics came up, they were always dealt with in a patriotic, Fascist, and triumphalist key.

The last week of the summer holidays was spent in Piedmont on my father's farm. It was a very small farm, the remnant of the huge estate lost in the wake of the 1929 stock market crash. But the house was—and still is—a large, eighteenth-century building, which my father rented out except for his library and a few rooms where he stayed during the period of the grape harvest. He was always very busy and happy in this village where he had spent the best years of his life. Apart from rents to be collected, there were always problems with the sewage, the roofs, and the garden, as well as an unending stream of farmers who came to ask his advice, mainly on legal and family matters. He was no longer the landlord, but the royal castle around which the village was built had belonged to his grandfather and his great-grandfather before him, and there were still many people who remembered when he had been the mayor. Quite a few of them had been his tenants; most had been his soldiers during the First World War. He knew every family, and people came bearing bottles of wine and baskets of fruit to ask him to read a contract prepared by a lawyer they did not trust, or for advice about their unending litigations. He received them, sometimes late at night, in his library, under a large reproduction of Rembrandt's *Rabbi*. I sometimes listened to their conversations, always carried on in Piedmontese dialect, but I spent most of my time in the attics among old trunks full of surprises. They contained monkey skins and gas masks from the Great War; medals and embroideries; ebony animals and tin soldiers. There were also strange objects, such as portable toilets in the form of imposing armchairs, stuffed birds, alcohol distilling apparatuses, and chalk reproductions of the Parthenon friezes. Most interesting of all were the family archives, full of old documents and photographs, especially from the First World War. In the photographs all the male members of the family appeared in uniform, and there were also pictures of King Victor Emmanuel, the Prince of Wales, General Kitchener, Clemenceau, the Duke of Aosta and his wife—all people with whom my father had rubbed shoulders in the service of the king during his years of military service.

In this village and in this old house I felt strangely changed —not into a Jew but into a Piedmontese, which was quite different from being an Italian or a young Fascist. To be a Piedmontese meant, for me, to belong to Italian national prehistory, to be a member of the people (in my imagination they seemed almost like a clan) that had made Italy. In that great mythical enterprise called Risorgimento, many Jews, my father among them, felt like the Pilgrim Fathers: they were, in a sense, their own ancestors. Italy, for the Piedmontese, was not a fatherland or a motherland: it was a geographical, emotional, political expression; an ideal that the Jews of Piedmont had helped realize and to which they had contributed more than any other group on the peninsula. In a way, they were the only true Italians, since they were born—as citizens—at the beginning of the Italian struggle for national unity. They could feel more Italian than the Italians because they were neither Venetian nor Florentine, not Roman or Neapolitan. They had no roots in any national identity that preceded the Italian one. Over and above this, we were also Piedmontese, part and parcel of the state that had united Italy under the House of Savoy. And to this house we Jews belonged more than anyone else. Before we had been emancipated and left the ghetto in 1848 (but who remembered those days anyway?), we were the king's servants, a strange kind of inverted aristocracy, lower than the local nobility in status, but higher than most of the king's subjects in wealth, culture, and influence. After the emancipation, we became the standard bearers of the Risorgimento, the most ardent partisans of a political Italian unity which, by destroying the power of the many minor Catholic princes and kings of the peninsula, had created a great secular state in which everyone was equal, and some—like our family —more equal than others.

I did not know much about being Jewish, but I knew that to be a Piedmontese Jew meant belonging to that special "sect" that had given Cavour his place in the Piedmontese parliament and had financed his wars through Jewish banks; it meant belonging to the people who had sheltered Mazzini, who had given the highest percentage of volunteers to Garibaldi, and who had fought for their king in every war of independence. It was natural that we should have a privileged position under the present regime. It was a position justified by our being an integral part of that village where my great-grandfather had bought the castle from the king's brother. My grandfather had lived in it until his death; my father had turned it into the village hall, the village school, and the seat of the local tribunal, and I still played in its gardens with a feeling of natural possession.

In the twenties, before we left for Friuli, I spent many hours during the cold winters in the cow shed of Annetta's nephews, sitting in the straw and listening to the stories of the villagers who had fought and died to make the king master of Italy. They all felt they had been robbed by the ungrateful Italians, those people living south of the River Po, to whom the Piedmontese had brought unity and freedom. And still they were proud to have been the driving force of Italian political renaissance. They never spoke Italian, and I had difficulty in following their singing, French-like dialect. But it was good to be with them, playing lotto for peas, shelling maize cobs, breathing in the warm, pungent smell of cow manure, and singing the nostalgic songs of the Alpine troops to which most of them belonged. On the kitchen walls, at the side of the great fireplace, were stained pictures of the king, Cavour, and Garibaldi, never of Mussolini.

Two of Annetta's nephews, who were sergeants in an aristo-cratic regiment of mounted artillery and therefore more royal-ist than the others, carefully avoided mentioning his name. When they spoke of him they would simply say "that one," and everyone understood. I, of course, did not, and in any case was not interested: what I wanted to hear were stories about the "lady" whom Garibaldi visited when spending a night or two in the village; about the pipe and walking stick that he had left in the local doctor's house; about King Victor Emmanuel II and Rosina, the beautiful girl whom he had married morganatically and whom Annetta's sister had known before she was made the Countess of Villanova.

My father and mother, always so particular about the people I mixed with, had no reservations concerning these farmers. My parents knew them all because they had provided the family with servants for three generations. They were part of "our people," and went to bed in winter like my parents with a warming pan between the sheets and had the same sticky flypaper dangling from their kitchen ceilings as we did. I knew that we were different, socially and religiously, in our dress and in our language, but I still felt that we were the same because we were all Piedmontese.

I do not know how many people in the village still feel that way today. Probably none. I doubt if they even know why the main road, Via Roma, is still called "Cornarea" by the old people. This strange name derives from the behavior of the gentlemen of the royal court who, staying in the village during the king's summer vacation, spent most of their time ogling the village maidens, making their fiancés or husbands grow "noble horns"—corna reali—on their heads. The mixture of aristocratic and popular blood presumably contributed to the fact that this small village of no more than seven hundred souls produced for over a century a considerable number of famous people, who brought honor to the village through their weapons, their robes, or their altars.

But already under the Fascists this compact agrarian society and its houses had gradually fallen into ruin and its institutions removed elsewhere. In earlier times the farmers' fear that a spark from a passing locomotive might start a fire in the corn caused them to write a petition to the king asking that the route of the railway be changed in order to protect them from the deeds of this new mechanical devil. The result now was that the village was not on the railway map; it remained cut off from the major road network and lost the battle to draw the new motorway nearer to itself. The local court was transferred to the nearby town. The church primary school has been replaced by a state secondary school that will probably close down in a few years' time for lack of pupils. The orphanage has already done so for lack of orphans. The great Seminary of Salesian Friars has been empty for many years, and so far no one has taken up the proposition to transform it into a hotel or dance hall, as some villagers have suggested. Only the old hospital, which has been transformed into a home for the elderly, is flourishing. The number of old people grows at the same rate as the number of vineyards left untilled by the young people who move into industry. Old men and their sons have certainly become richer through state pensions and industrial salaries—yet they look sadder because of their inability to keep the family together. The priests no longer follow the funerals singing litanies in Latin. The liturgy has lost its mysterious attraction because of the use of the Italian language, which the priest, walking before the coffin, broadcasts loudly into the air through a battery-operated megaphone hidden away under his robes with the microphone dangling like a cross from his neck. The church bells do not ring as often as they used to when I was a boy: nobody knows any longer, as they did in the twenties, when a dying man enters into agony, when the priest gives the last rites, nor the precise moment in which the soul of so-and-so, better known to everyone by his nickname, has started on its journey toward the Creator. The bells ring today during the funerals, clear and precise, carrying an impersonal message, controlled by the electrical mechanism of the bell tower, through the fields where tractors have replaced the big white oxen and the vines are dusted regularly by helicopters.

During the week of the grape harvest, when I accompanied my father to renew the yearly leases of the tenants, and my grandmother to do her "cure of the grapes," I used to go to the parish hall to look at the films that the priest showed twice a week. The films were only those approved by the bishop's office but they were preceded by documentaries made to exalt the deeds of Mussolini and the glories of the revolutionary Fascist party. Nothing could have been more boring than this politicized news, and we waited impatiently for it to end and the main film to start. However, from time to time these propaganda efforts also contained pictures of fashion shows or of seashore tourism through which the regime wanted to stress the normality of life in Italy. These pictures were unacceptable to the parish priest. He used to keep a stool between the two lanes of seats and would ask one of the young clerics to be ready to stand up on it whenever he told him and block the beam from the projector with a big handkerchief, usually the huge red one used after taking snuff. From the darkened hall rose shouts of protest, stamping of feet, curses, and allusions that were certainly more sinful than the innocent view of women he had censored. The priest was not moved by these protests: he was a man of few but clear principles, which he once summarized from the pulpit in a pithy axiom. Speaking of the demons that had invaded the village society after the Second World War, he denounced the use of motor scooters, shouting to his impecunious audience: "Mothers and fathers, remember that when your sons and daughters leave their homes on Lambrettas as a twosome, they usually return home as a threesome"—a historic maxim possibly, but of doubtful accuracy, considering that the population of the village was already clearly on the decrease.

The *maresciallo* of the carabinieri, too, had a way of his own of maintaining peace and order while being kept informed of everything that took place in the village. Until late in the 1950s there was neither terrorism nor abductions in Italy; open, vulgar violence was the monopoly of the Mafia in the south and the Fascists (as long as they were in power) in the rest of the country. But cow stealing was common, poplars and vines were often cut down in the course of vendettas, and corn sometimes set alight the day before harvest.

The head of the local security forces learned about all these deeds while playing cards in the local inn or when fishing on the river. It was a known and accepted custom for anyone wanting to tell him something confidential to do so while fishing by his side. As for the remaining security tasks, it was his wife who ran the show. The carabinieri went on daily patrol with their old, 91-type carbines slung across their backs, the black celluloid hat strap under their sweating chins. The *maresciallo*'s wife, however, sat at her window, or on sunny days on the balcony of her top-floor apartment, in the big house that served as the carabinieri headquarters and the permanently empty jail. I remember her knitting, or cleaning vegetables, apparently oblivious to the world around her. In fact, from her vantage point she could dominate almost the entire territory of the village. She knew better than her husband the routes the patrols had to follow and did not forget them for a moment. When she saw the two carabinieri on duty disappear for too long behind a house or a clump of trees, she blew on a big whistle she kept hanging around her neck, and the offenders against public order hastily reappeared upon the landscape.

Life in the village was certainly not as idyllic as it may have looked to an outsider. I knew of the many court cases in which almost every family was engaged, of the illicit affairs and the complex family feuds that dragged on for years around a patch of land, an inch of guttering, or an artesian well. Once I was told about a murder that had remained unsolved for years. Since it was a family affair, Annetta explained to me, even the carabinieri had no real business to intervene.

Today such a case would be unthinkable. And yet it was to this secrecy, to this sense of family and village honor, that members of my family owed their lives after the September 1943 armistice between Italy and the Allies when German forces occupied the area. Three years earlier, at the outbreak of war and after my departure for Palestine, my parents had left my mother's estate near Turin and had gone to live in the village where my father had been the mayor for so long, believing that it would be safer for them and that life would be less expensive. My grandmother went with them, and they took up their residence in one part of the big house, the remainder of which was leased to nuns as their summer residence. From the little land my father still owned in the village he was able to derive a large part of the food needed by the family. There were enough trees in the garden to provide firewood, and although in the valley below a big new airfield had been constructed, my parents felt secure in their old family home where everybody knew and respected them, and over which the Allied bombers flew on their way to bomb Turin, Genoa, and Milan.

War events and the tragic fate of the Jews did not touch them until one day in October 1943 when the *maresciallo* of the carabinieri came ceremoniously to tell my father, who was sitting as usual in his library, that he would be coming in the afternoon to arrest him, together with my mother and sister. He did not mention my grandmother since she was not in the local population register.

In less than three hours, my mother and sister, dressed as nuns, left for the nearby convent. My father went to the mayor's office, received false documents on the spot, and transformed himself into a peddler. He had foreseen the possibility of being arrested, and as an old soldier, was convinced that the best way of avoiding capture would be to adopt a profession that would oblige him to be constantly on the move. His disguise had been prepared long since and was hanging in his wardrobe. He put on heavy boots, filled a large, wooden, folding case with shoelaces, razor blades, toothpaste, small pieces of soap, and so on, and went out into the fields, spending the following eighteen months walking from one farm to another. He was arrested three times but was released after the mayor of his village confirmed in writing to the Fascist police that he was a well-known peddler, psychologically disturbed but quite harmless.

No solution could be found for my grandmother. She was already well into her seventies, completely sclerotic, and had to stay in the village. She was not even aware that a new world war had broken out. When she went out, accompanied by her old maid, Madeleine, to take the air in the gardens of the castle that had been hers many years before, she used to acknowledge ceremoniously the salutes of the German and Italian officers whom she encountered on her way, convinced that she was still living in the First World War.

This grotesque situation, which lasted until the end of the war, combined a deep sense of human solidarity with an equally deep hate for the Germans and the Fascist Republicans. It also gave an idea of the links existing between my family and the seven hundred or so villagers and of their ability to keep a collective secret that could have cost many of them their own lives. It was a situation in which, because of the war, but not only because of it, all social relationships and economic barriers were removed and replaced by a visceral, almost animal solidarity that I do not think existed, as far as the Jews are concerned, anywhere else in the Western world.

Such was the world in which I grew up, and it was difficult for me, even after the publication of the anti-Jewish laws in 1938, to feel marginal toward the Italian society. Through my relations with my new friends at the Jewish school in Turin

I was, indeed, beginning to detach myself from my Fascist background and become aware of the harsh fate of the Jews. Yet I could not emotionally break with the human realities of my father's village or my memories of my happy life in the Friuli. It was from this small, real, but at the same time imaginary, world that I left in 1939 for Palestine, a far off and completely unknown land. What made my father decide to give his consent to my departure was an event that took place in our family—dramatic but totally consistent with the type of life I had lived up to that time.

Even before the publication of the Race Manifesto in July 1938, the Fascist press had surreptitiously tested the reactions of the Italian public to an open campaign against the Jews. At the beginning of 1937, a book by Paolo Orano, *The Jews in Italy,* analyzed the Jewish problem on the basis of all sorts of contorted political and ideological arguments. It pointed out the difference between patriotic and unpatriotic Judaism, between Italian and Jewish nationalism, and it launched vitriolic attacks on Zionism, a movement that Mussolini in fact had supported not long before as being very good for Italian penetration into the Middle East. All this threw the majority of Italian Jews and the leading members of the central organization of Jewish communities of Italy (the highest administrative institution of Italian Jewry) into confusion and divided them. Naturally nobody spoke of all these things in my home, nor of the fact that at that time some members of my family were engaged in this communal and ideological struggle. The most active was my cousin, Ettore Ovazza, the only one of my close relatives to be killed, in a horrible way, with his wife and two children, by the Fascist Republicans at the end of the war.

Ettore Ovazza had always had literary ambitions. During the First World War, in which he had served as an officer with his father and two brothers and received great distinction, he had written and published diaries that today are astonishing in their emphatic banality.

After the war, my cousin, like my father, had naturally gone over to Fascism and founded a Jewish periodical called *Our Flag,* in which he expressed what he and many other Italian Jewish Fascists thought should be the political stand of the Italian Israelites: faithfulness to the ideals of the Italian Risorgimento and Italian unity; devotion to the monarchy; opposition to Zionism as far as the movement concerned Italian Jews, but not insofar as it offered a refuge against anti-Semitism; apologetic stressing of the Jewish contribution to the Italian cause and to Fascism; and criticism of the German racial laws but also of Western democracy and of liberalism, with which Italian Jews should not—in the opinion of the journal— meddle. It was a hybrid position, which became indefensible and unbearable with the development of the anti-Jewish politics of Mussolini. Yet at the end of 1938, when Italian Jews could no longer send their children to school and Italians could no longer use textbooks written by Jews; when civil marriage between Jews and non-Jews was forbidden (the Fascist regime could not interfere in religious marriages because of its agreement with the Vatican); when Jewish parents were legally losing their rights over children who wanted to denounce them to the authorities; and when Jews could not serve any longer in the army, there were still Jews who deluded themselves into thinking they would be able to ingratiate themselves with the regime through a public demonstration of devotion to Fascism and by detaching themselves from those Jews who were considered enemies of the regime.

My cousin was one of these deluded people. The Fascist press had been attacking, with ever-growing violence, the Jewish community's main organ, *Israel,* which defended with courage and dignity the position of Italian Jews, and in particular their right to be Zionists. My cousin thought that a "punitive action" against that periodical by Fascist Jews would demonstrate their patriotism to the government, and at the same time, be agreeable to the party.

On a cold, gray, autumn day, Ettore Ovazza arrived at my parents' home on my mother's farm near Turin, accompanied by two or three people I did not know. They had warned my father of their coming, whether by telephone or letter I do not remember, and he, contrary to his habit, had asked me to be present at the meeting. We received them in the dining room, with my mother in a state of nerves serving tea and small cakes, apologizing all the time for not having a maid (because of the "Laws"). After a while, with her eyes full of tears and fear, she left the room.

As soon as she had gone, my cousin explained his plan in great detail. The anti-Semites, he said, accused the Jews of being allied with the democracies. The number of anti-Fascist elements among the Israelites was unfortunately very high. The Fascist regime, because of its new politics, underlined this negative disproportion rather than the much larger and more positive one of the Jewish contribution to Fascism and to the Italian national cause. However, he said, in spite of the Racial Laws, Mussolini had not permitted the criteria of the Nuremberg Laws to be applied to the Italian Jews. Devoted and reliable friends who had direct access to Il Duce had told my cousin that Mussolini was irritated and sad at having to follow Hitler along the path of anti-Semitism. He had to do it for higher political reasons, but it was against his better nature and the very tradition of Italian Fascism. As proof of this, my cousin pointed out that the Fascist press had stressed that the battle for the defense of the Italian race was more political and ideological than biological and racial. The Nuremberg Laws found not an imitation but a limitation in the new anti-Jewish regulations. As former members of the Fascist party, and thanks to their military service, all our families had been "differentiated," that is, partially exempted from the new racial laws. But even for the common Jews life was better and more secure in Italy than in many other European countries. Even the new regulations facilitating conversion to Catholicism were a way in which the party showed the difference between Italian and German conceptions of anti-Semitism. In sum, said my cousin, it was clear that Mussolini was acting against the Jews with great personal reluctance.

However, the anti-Fascist Jews as well as the Zionists played into the hands of their enemies in the Fascist hierarchy as well as in the Catholic hierarchy by offering a reason to attack them, and through them the whole of Italian Jewry. One had to be honest and recognize that the Jews of Italy had made themselves too prominent; every issue of the *Review of the Race* (the new, anti-Semitic publication founded after the enactment of the racial legislation) underlined the numerical disproportion existing between Jews and non-Jews in the most important fields of life in the country. Just to mention the army and the navy, one could list scores of Jewish generals and admirals as against only thirty-six private soldiers. How right —said my cousin—were our forefathers who preached to their sons not to show off, not to boast of their new privileged status outside the ghetto. However, since it was no longer possible to go back in history, it was necessary to make a clear distinction between those Jews who had always been faithful to the Fascist regime and wanted to remain so and all the rest.

His proposal was as follows: in Florence the Jewish publication, *Israel*, which should be devoting its attention only to cultural and religious matters, had instead transformed itself into a mouthpiece for political ideas that Fascism could not tolerate. It claimed that greater Jewish solidarity and consciousness were necessary to compensate for the loss of that Italian identity being forcibly torn from the Jews. This thesis went against the interests of Italian Jews. To ask to be different in such a way and at such a moment meant detaching oneself from the national body, confirming the accusations of the anti-Semites who wanted to see Italian Jews as a foreign body. It was therefore important to show on which side the Fascist Jews, the patriots, stood. A punitive action, a minor pogrom, against the print shop and editorial offices of *Israel*, which in any case would sooner or later be attacked by the Fascists, could be an act more useful to the Jews of Italy than a thousand written polemics. The operation would also remind Mussolini of the heroic days prior to the March on Rome, during which the Jews had so ardently supported him. Such an action should be carried out by people of unstained Fascist faith and of recognized national stature. My father was one of these. By joining the punitive action, he would add luster to the initiative.

To me, so indifferent to political questions and so ignorant of what was happening around me, such talk was deeply disturbing. On the one hand, I was tempted to join in an action, during this period when I felt myself harassed without the ability to react. On the other hand, it seemed to me monstrous that at a moment when the Jews were trying to find new cohesion and had proved the strength of their communal ties by creating, in less than four months, an exemplary, independent, educational system; when everyone was looking for contact with the world outside Italy; and above all, at a time when the Fascist regime and the monarchy had betrayed the constitution, anyone could think of cooperating with our persecutors in such an explicit and unashamed manner. However, I felt it was a problem too serious for me to give an opinion before my father had replied. I looked at him and felt how difficult it was for him to take a stand because of his past, but also because he had no links with people outside the Italian national establishment—unlike me, who was now in touch with Judaism and had become mildly anti-Fascist through my school contacts.

My father took a long time to reply. He balanced his pipe in his hand, filled it with great care, and lit it as though nothing was of greater importance for him at that moment than the correct behavior of a smoker. I could see that these mechanical gestures helped him to formulate his thoughts. The others, too, kept quiet, and in the silence the tension grew. When my father began to speak there was no trace of emotion in his voice. He explained that it would be strange for a man like himself, so detached from politics, suddenly to join in an action of such gravity. Those who attached importance to his past links with the Fascist party or with the royal house were completely mistaken. He was by now no more than a poor Jew who would probably not be allowed in the future even to remain a poor farmer. But even if he had not been the unimportant person that in fact he now was, he would have refused to join them in their scheme. It was true that as Italians we had lost our sacrosanct rights inscribed in the constitution, but as Jews nobody could take away our sense of dignity and honor. To attack coreligionists in such hard times as those we were going through in order to ingratiate ourselves with a regime that had betrayed us was to act as slaves, not as free men.

He had spoken in a low voice, almost as though he was asking forgiveness for what he was saying. A long silence followed. My cousin broke it by saying: "As you like; if you change your mind, let me know." Afterward he inquired about my studies, about the farm, and about my mother's and sister's health. Before they left, my father offered them some magnificent pears. They took them, congratulating him on his life as Cincinnatus. A few weeks later they burned the offices and the printing press of *Israel*.

When my father heard about it, he called me into his study and told me that he agreed to my leaving Italy. It was not important where I went, but for a young Jew there was no longer any future or hope in Italy. When I told him that I had been informed that one could obtain a visa for Palestine against a deposit in an English bank of a thousand pounds sterling, my father, who knew very well the risk entailed in illegally exporting Italian currency, went straight to the chief of the Fascist police in Turin and asked him what he preferred: that the money be transferred legally abroad or that he (my father) should become a criminal. The party chief helped him to transfer the money, an act subject to the death penalty at that time. The fact that I emigrated to Palestine with the assistance of the Fascist regime still seems to me farcical, but also a proof of the unreal situation in which a Jew in Italy could still live.

In May 1939 Mussolini ordered large-scale military maneuvers along the French frontier. The mayor of our village called my father and told him that Il Duce would probably be passing through the Via Maestra and that it was necessary to whitewash that section of the wall on my mother's estate bordering the road. Because of its length and its even surface the wall was the most suitable place to be decorated with quotations from Mussolini's speeches. The mayor knew that my father was a Jew, but being aware of his Fascist past and his culture, decided to leave him free to select the most appropriate passages. My father chose the Mussolinian phrase "Many enemies, much glory." The mayor decided that it would be best to leave the wall bare and in the end, Mussolini, quite oblivious to all this, chose another route.

4

The Tombstone

I INHERITED from my father a burial plot in the Jewish cemetery in Turin and a farmhouse in a small village near the town of Alba. Over the years the value of the plot has increased, while the value of the house has gone steadily down. I have received many offers for both, but I have never been able to bring myself to sell them, even though the money would undoubtedly be useful.

It is strange to see how in the Jewish cemetery of Turin a community of dead Jews has within one century replaced a community of living ones. Above the ground, the Jews have spread themselves at an increasing rate, over countries, cultures, and religions different from their ancestral ones. Under the ground, their number increases year by year in an enclosure that can no longer grow in size. Because of this, the prices of cemetery plots are continually on the rise, independent of the changing prices of real estate and oil, for which nobody in the graveyard has any further need.

The Jewish cemetery in Turin is located next to the Christian one and is divided into two square compounds, the old and the new. In the former, many tombstones have sunk into the ground, the names are no longer legible, and the chapels perpetuate the withered glory of unknown families, once rich and powerful. Here are the tombstones of Jewish barons, consuls, bankers, army officers; people who, if one is to believe the inscriptions, all lived exemplary lives devoted to their families; people who drove out with a horse and carriage before switching to automobiles. Only the inscriptions and obituaries in old newspapers remain to prove that they really lived. Jews do not have the habit of remembering the dear departed with the oval photographs protected by convex glass so common in Italian Christian cemeteries. Our taboo on graven images is still strong enough to prevent this. But even without pictures, a date—1840, 1861, 1914—is enough to start the visitor pondering over the lives of these people, whose names indicate ancient and faraway origins: France and Corfu, Spain and Mantua.

Among the books I cherish most in my library is an "official and definitive" register of the Piedmontese noblemen compiled during the reign of King Umberto I, in 1886. The hundreds of names of dukes, marquises, counts, and barons include half a dozen Jewish aristocrats, all of recent creation, whose origin is given as "Palestine." Some of them are buried in the old Jewish compound of Turin. None of them seems to have been capable of transferring the title to succeeding Jewish generations for more than a century, whereas as simple Jews, their families had survived for over a thousand years. The glory achieved in the modern world outside the walls of the ghetto seems to have quenched forever their tribal Jewish vitality. The tombstones of these famous, affluent Jews left without successors have always seemed to me to mark a second death to be added to the physical one: a memento of the major contribution that the "dear departed" made to their "inconsolable survivors" has boiled down to the fact of removing themselves from the social competition. Thus, in the old cemetery, most of the tombs stand without a future: the descendants have been dispersed in the turmoil of life, usually beyond the wall that separates the world of the Jewish dead from that of dead or living Christians. The new compound, however, shows clear signs of life: graves are well tended, flowers are changed frequently in the vases, and one may even meet a relative coming to visit his dead "out of season."

I often visit this cemetery, but not exclusively for religious reasons. We Jews do not have a cult of the dead because, as the psalmist says, "The dead praise not the Lord." Before we are buried, we are laid on a marble slab and treated with alternate splashes of hot and cold water to make sure that we are not simply unconscious. Then, wrapped in a sheet, and for men, also covered by a prayer shawl from which the four knotted corner fringes, supposedly meant to remind us while alive of our duties toward God, have been removed, we are put into the earth. I have a marchioness cousin who does not believe me when I tell her that some of today's common habits are derived from old tribal customs: for instance, that of tying a knot in the corner of one's handkerchief so that one is reminded of something.

Naturally customs change with time and place. In Israel the last journey is made on a stretcher, carried by friends who take turns in this pious service. Other functions are carried out by the burial society (Hevra Kadisha), whose members thereby acquire merit for the world to come and financial gratification as long as they live in this world.

In Italy, where coffins are used, Jews travel like others, on a bier from which the crosses and other Christian symbols have been removed. It is a quick, functional method of transportation. These funerals have not yet reached the levels of death mystification practiced in the United States but considerably reduce the time devoted to burials, which once played such an important role in the society of the living. In our age, in any case, nobody dies any more; we disappear from the world through accidents that should never have happened in the first place. I remember the indignation of the surgeon who had operated on my mother when he saw her suddenly die. "I don't understand it," he said to me in perfectly good faith, "there was no reason for her to die."

In modern funerals I always feel the absence of an impressive bier, drawn by at least two black-draped horses with a band in front and some flags behind. These were the performances that I admired most in Italian villages when I was a child. If the departed was an important person, he was preceded by musicians, wreaths, praying members of religious confraternities, priests, and clerics. He was followed by crying relatives and a lot of people dressed in their Sunday best. "It was worth dying," my father used to say on these occasions. With Jews and Moslems, this pomp never existed. The body is not put in a coffin; the people crowd around the stretcher with a familiarity that does not diminish the horror of the sudden disappearance of the body, dumped into a freshly dug grave. *Memento mori* is the brutal message of these Semitic burials. I have often asked myself whether these differences in funerary styles have not given assimilated Jews an additional reason for changing their religion.

My family mausoleum in the new Jewish compound in Turin follows the local custom: it consists of a big, underground, waterproof vault, with thirty-two places neatly stacked one above the other around the walls. The upper part of the tomb was constructed by a famous architect in an elegant, modern style, and thick rosebushes climb up the decorative stone columns at the corners. It gives me a strange feeling, not devoid of pleasure, to sit on the large marble tombstone and look at my own name, the same as that of my grandfather, sculpted in iron letters, which has been waiting for me for over a century. Sometimes I trace with my finger the patina of these letters that confirm the earthly passage of an ancestor I never knew. The gesture reminds me of the pride that swept over me the first time I fingered the embossed title,

"Embassy Counsellor," on my newly printed visiting cards. My grandfather, a banker whose father still lived in the ghetto of Ivrea, might have dreamt of a diplomat grandson, but never of one serving a Jewish state. I know now that even the wildest fantasies can become reality, and yet, standing in front of my own name in my family tomb, I know with equal certitude that all realities turn sooner or later into dreams of the past.

Considering my parents' propensity for dissipating their considerable fortune on unsuccessful financial operations, our family plot testifies that at least on this occasion my father invested his money well. True, when he decided to build all these niches for his parents, sons, and grandsons, he was still convinced that he bore the responsibility for a large family, which has meanwhile melted away. Between conversions, dispersions, and mixed marriages, the mausoleum in the year 2000 will not host more than a dozen permanent residents—antecedents and collaterals included. As a result, I find myself the owner of a "residence," the value of which increases from year to year thanks to the requests I receive from strangers.

So far I have not sold to anyone, not even to an octogenarian lady who asked me to sell her a niche, convinced as she was that in my family tomb she would find better bridge partners than in her own. "It has been so difficult spending a whole lifetime with boring people that the idea of being bored throughout eternity terrifies me," she told me the last time we discussed the matter.

After having visited many countries in which the existence of the living is supposed to depend on the dead, I begin to believe that my friend was right. The break between this world and the next that marks the Judeo–Christian tradition is not a universal belief. In the country of the Hova, on the highlands of Madagascar, for instance, the richer and more important the departed, the more often his family feels compelled to take his body out of the tomb, to dress him in beautiful robes, and seat him at the center of a festive family gathering. Even if the French colonial legislation put an end to the custom of transporting—especially in the hot season—a dead grandmother on the roof of a bus, or a departed uncle on the handlebars of a bicycle, no respectable person in that country would dare to begin a speech without asking permission of the dead and apologizing in advance for any foolish things he might say.

We, on the contrary, have the habit of attributing to the dead, especially to famous people we have not known and whose ideas we have not understood, the strangest statements. It is a discourteous custom, particularly common among politicians and academics. They should learn from the wisdom of the Malagasy who, as soon as they had obtained their independence from the French, asked that the legal address of the living should be identical with the domicile of the dead. This would make the departed one still share with the living in the vicissitudes of life.

One does not have to go as far as the Indian Ocean, as I did, to find eloquent examples of familiarity between the living and the dead. It has always existed in my village in Piedmont. The most expensive graves in the cemetery are those that enjoy a good view of the surrounding vineyards, renowned for their excellent wine. This fine quality is thought to be due to the fact that once upon a time the land around the cemetery belonged to a doctor who, according to the villagers, contributed greatly to helping the living reach the world of eternal rest. Or take the case of the cardinal, a famous son of the village, who insisted, by virtue of his ecclesiastical rights, on being buried in the parish church and not in his local family chapel. To those who asked him with surprise why a humble man of great wisdom like himself should avail himself of an archaic medieval privilege, this prince of the church answered with perfect candor that throughout his life he had suffered too much from rheumatism to give up the right of resting in the warm, dry atmosphere of the church.

Luigi, my uncle's cook, would have understood the cardinal perfectly. Luigi was a much-traveled southern Italian who never felt perfectly comfortable with the alphabet. Unable to fill in the census form by himself, he once asked me to put his profession down as "sculptor in butter." He had a perfect right to this qualification, having spent a large portion of his life working in the kitchens of Balkan princes. In that volatile part of the world, which he observed from the depths of his pots and pans, he had reached some firm and wise conclusions concerning the powerful of this world who, on the upper floors of their palaces, disposed of the destinies of common human beings. He understood that food, like dress or hairstyle, is a form of language, without knowing how close his culinary-political experience came to Lévi-Strauss' ideas about the "raw" and the "cooked." Luigi had learned that the blows cooks and scullions could exchange over different types of borscht, or the fights over a description of coffee as Turkish or Greek, paralleled the discussions on principles, rights, and religions that the princes conducted in the conference rooms. He once told me how Romanian chefs at a certain diplomatic meeting had refused to cook chickens in Bulgarian pots, and the Serbian dishwashers had insisted that the Macedonians should clean the plates. Eventually the political agreement worked out on the upper floors drifted down into the kitchen on the basis of a compromise on the sauces and in the form of a large iced cake upon which each national flag was precisely reproduced in candied fruit. Luigi, who felt both neutral and superior to these squabbles, crowned the sweet political monument with a big sugar star, which nobody had the courage to eat, remembering the tragic consequences that another silver star—of the Bethlehem manger—had had on Balkan politics. They all read into the innocent, "sweet" message of Luigi (who, as a good Italian Catholic, had simply thought it proper to crown the diplomatic agreement with the star of Bethlehem) a deep, political meaning. After all, it was the stealing of a silver star from the manger in the Church of the Nativity that indirectly caused the Crimean War.

However, Luigi never accepted my historical interpretation: he was, in a way, an incurable romantic. That did not stop him from vigorously defending his privilege to receive tips from any guest who came to dinner, me included, while at the same time resenting the fact that I did not ask him for a loan when he saw that I was short of money. "I have given plenty of money to Michael," (the prince who twice sat on and then lost the Romanian throne) he used to say to me, "and he certainly needed it less than you," which was true. Only once, soon after the end of World War II, when I found myself in dire need of money to buy a wedding present for my sister, did I ask him if it was possible, with great discretion, to find somebody to buy the collection of guns that I had built up during the war years. "Of course," he said, "there is Prince so-and-so, from whom you 'English' have confiscated all weapons and who wants to rebuild his collection." I gave him two German Mauser machinenpistolen, a long-barrelled gun for precision shooting, and a P38. Luigi put them into his shopping bag and two days later brought me a roll of Italian bank notes. That was the only private arms sale I have ever engaged in in my life, and I still ask myself today whether it was an appropriate way to go about buying a wedding present.

Luigi entered my family when Mussolini asked my uncle to implement the policy of economic self-sufficiency by creating in Sardinia an imaginary Ruhr, called Carbonia. Unlike my father, who had studied agronomy and law, my uncle had no formal academic education. He had taken a course of commercial studies; had gone to Germany to learn the language; and had been involved in the early stages of the creation of the Fiat motor company, which he left when the future Senator Agnelli told him in good Piedmontese dialect that there was "no place for two cockerels in the same chicken run." He had already reached an important position in an

Italian bank when World War I broke out. Called up as an officer in the Engineering Corps, he rapidly scaled the military ladder; won a number of French, British, and Italian decorations; and got involved in drafting the economic part of the Peace Treaty with Austria and, later, in a great scandal linked with iron mines. All this helped to launch him on the road to economic success, and within a few years he was in control of an industrial empire with its head office in Trieste. For a long time he remained the most sought-after bachelor in that town. In my capacity as his only male heir, he immortalized me in a marble bust at the age of six. Later on he got to know a divorced Austrian Christian lady, whom he decided to marry at the age of fifty, and with the birth of his two children I lost my special status although I retained his special affection.

From the kitchen Luigi had followed my uncle's fortunes, producing an ever-increasing number of dishes for his political and financial banquets. From his stove he also observed with sadness but without surprise his master's fall on the eve of Mussolini's anti-Jewish laws. Neither my uncle's national and Fascist merits nor his late baptism succeeded in preventing the confiscation in 1938 of all the factories he had set up. For Luigi, who had seen the downfall of thrones, the loss of ten or twenty thousand workers a month was a natural part of the game played by all the great ones he had fed. My uncle's misfortunes only increased his devotion. "When everybody abandoned him," he told me once, in reply to my question why, despite the racial laws, he had continued to keep in contact with my uncle, "somebody had to cook for him."

When the Germans took over Italy in 1943, my uncle took refuge in Vatican City, from which he emerged when the Allied troops arrived in Rome, only to embark on a long period of agonizing illness. He died just before the end of the war and his family, waiting for the liberation of northern Italy to give him an appropriate resting place, buried him temporarily in Luigi's tomb at the Verano cemetery in Rome.

Some time before the transfer of the body to a permanent family grave, Luigi asked me to accompany him to take leave of his dead master. We fixed an appointment at the Piazza dell'Esedra, in a café under the pillared portico where he used to play cards with the servants of other Roman families. I was still wearing a British uniform, which made no impression on those butlers and cooks, experts as they were in liveries and accustomed to handing hats, gloves, and batons to generals. One of them asked me why I wore on my left sleeve a badge similar to the one the Germans had imposed on the Jews as a mark of shame. I explained to him where my regiment came from; how it was made up of Jewish volunteers from Palestine; and why we had chosen that badge, blue and white with a yellow star in the center, in honor of a certain gentleman called Herzl, a Viennese journalist who, half a century earlier, had had the queer idea of creating a state for the Jews and had designed a flag for them with the Star of David on it. That Mr. Herzl, I said, would be astonished to see how the Germans, whom he had asked for help in realizing his dream when the kaiser visited Jerusalem, had turned into the worst enemies of the Jews.

Luigi listened in silence. "Maybe you won't believe me," he finally said, "but I saw that Mr. Herzl in person when he went to speak with the emperor in Jerusalem." In his unconnected way, full of confused imagery, chewing his cigar stub, spitting from time to time on the marble pavement of the portico at his feet and carefully squashing the phlegm with his shoe, he told us how in 1898, at the age of less than twenty, he had been working as a dishwasher in the service of a German prince who accompanied Kaiser Wilhelm II on his historic visit to the Holy Land. In Jerusalem, Luigi, like all the other servants, was ordered to arrive on horseback so as to increase the number and impressiveness of the imperial escort during the kaiser's entry into the walled city of Zion. The sultan had ordered a breach to be opened in the ancient walls, near the Jaffa Gate, for the entry of the imperial guest, who refused to dismount in order to clear the gateway or lower his head decorated with an egret's feather—a dubious historical curiosity that Jerusalem guides still tell to tourists.

The trouble with Luigi was that he was no horseman. To avoid possible mishaps he was put astride a donkey that apart from being big and placid was also white. On this mount Luigi entered the City of David amid a cheering crowd, some of whom were shouting "the Messiah, the Messiah" and laughingly pointing at him. "I answered them by waving both my hands," concluded Luigi.

In the tram rumbling noisily along toward the Verano cemetery, I reflected on the little stories that form the texture of history. Luigi, dishwasher of an emperor who had thought himself the greatest ruler of his time, was now sitting next to me, an Italian Jew in British uniform. I was involved at that moment in some minor plots against the British in Palestine, a semicolonial regime that had first supported and later opposed the same Zionist dream that Herzl wanted to entrust to the Germans—those same Germans who, a few decades later, were to try and solve the "Jewish Question" in the gas chambers. Together Luigi and I were on our way to pay our last respects to the mortal remains of my uncle, who had tumbled from his exalted political and financial position because of a Jewish origin that no conversion to Christianity could erase. Ironically enough, he was now lying in the grave of his cook, who had survived him and the kaiser and the many great ones of the world for whom he had plucked chickens and concocted sauces.

Luigi was carrying with him a small package wrapped in newspaper. He held it in both hands as though it were a handwarmer. This made him look even more ridiculous, huddled in spite of the warm weather, in a thick black overcoat with velvet lapels, his homburg on his head, and with a small gray moustache that made him look like Charlie Chaplin in *The Great Dictator*.

When we reached the grave, he put the package down on the marble slab, which already bore his name and date of birth and awaited the date of his death. With controlled gestures he took out of his pocket a curved, silver-handled brush, like the one my mother used to keep on the lace-bordered table in her huge bathroom. The brush reminded me of the silver-framed mirror, held by two finely wrought screws, which I was forbidden to touch while my mother's hair was being dressed, because the slightest oscillation of the mirror immediately made her feel seasick. I used to stand motionless at her side, rapt by the sight of her beautiful face: it had nothing in common with the cancer-worn visage whose eyes I closed on a warm spring morning in a Jerusalem hospital.

The childhood image that always returns to my memory is of my mother, dressed in an evening gown, long and décolleté, with a silk rose (which I still keep in a sandalwood box) pinned to her breast with a sapphire brooch. That was one of the few occasions when my father was persuaded to wear tails and accompany her to a gala performance at the Regio Theater in Turin. At that time, a few years before my father went bankrupt, our coachman, now chauffeur, Vigiu, allowed me to sit on his knee and hold the steering wheel while waiting in the driveway for my parents. Of that 509 Fiat Berline, all that now remains is a mahogany box in which my mother used to keep a small brush with which she removed the dandruff from my father's collar before they left the car. Now Luigi was doing the same thing with the leaves that had fallen on the marble slab of the tomb from the nearby trees and with some grains of dust that only a trained eye like his could have discerned.

I felt a strong need to pray, but I could not decide in what language and according to what religion I should do so. I could not recite the Kaddish, the Jewish prayer for the dead, because I lacked the requisite quorum of ten Jewish males, which in any case could not have assembled in a Christian cemetery in honor of a converted Jew. I was unable to recall in Hebrew the words of the Pater Noster, that old Jewish prayer taken over by the Church, and felt uneasy, as a Jew, about pronouncing them in Latin. Finally, I decided that it would be best to leave religion alone and pay tribute to my uncle by keeping his image alive in my mind, remembering how he was always kind and jovial with me, while being so feared and envied by the rest of the family for his political and industrial power.

I had few memories of him to rely on. When we children were admitted to his presence, we were supposed to salute him politely and then disappear as quickly as possible so as not to steal one instant of his precious time from the adults. On these occasions, when I always thought that the grownups were unjustly robbing the children of their rightful proximity to the great man of the family, I observed with disdain the way in which they behaved toward him. If they followed him about while he was pottering among the flowers of his mountain garden, their real lack of interest in the art of gardening was more than obvious. If they played bowls with him, they could barely wait for the end of the game, which they often deliberately lost to please him, to get his undivided attention. If they admired, with exclamations of surprise, the latest addition to his collection of snuffboxes (one of the most beautiful in Europe, or so I was told), they could not conceal the envy in their voices. The hope of discovering a minor imperfection in the snuffbox was similar to the hope of finding reasons to criticize my uncle's social success. He liked to boast about his meetings with Mussolini, to describe in great detail a dinner in Vienna or a lunch in Paris at which he signed a new agreement, started a successful enterprise, or established powerful new friendships. From these conversations, which usually turned into monologues addressed by my uncle to the admiring family circle, there emerged a kind of gossip filter, made up of sentences such as "my brother says . . . ," "my brother-in-law believes . . . ," "the commander denies . . . ," with which not only my relatives but also the drivers, maids, and gardeners built up their own reputations among their poorer relations, perpetually in search of recommendations and jobs.

The first time I had my uncle entirely to myself was one afternoon in early September 1939 in Trieste. I was due to embark the same evening for Palestine on one of his ships, by now already confiscated in accordance with the racial laws. My father had accompanied me to my uncle's house but had gone back immediately to Turin by train, with the excuse that the midday express was quicker and more comfortable and that he did not want to leave my mother alone. The truth was that he no longer had the courage or the physical strength to wait and see the ship sail, with the possibility of never seeing me again.

We had left Turin the previous evening, riding second class by virtue of the last reduced price ticket to which my father was entitled as a reserve officer, but without any hope of renewal because of the new anti-Jewish legislation. The loss of this small privilege seemed to pain him beyond reason, since he traveled very little. We had spent the night in a half-empty compartment, not speaking about the problems that weighed so heavily on our hearts so as not to reveal our race to the other passengers, or the fact that I was going abroad. With a stern and suspicious look on his face, the Fascist train police officer who accompanied the conductor jumped to attention and raised his arm in the "Roman" salute when he saw my father's Fascist identity card, unaware that he was standing in front of a second-class citizen to whom no respect was due. My father returned his salute with a sadness that the other people in the compartment interpreted as the feigned modesty of a powerful member of the regime. A grotesque aura of respect thus accompanied our agitated slumbers during the rest of the journey until dawn, when we changed trains at Mestre, after crossing and recrossing the bridge linking the continent with Venice.

I remembered then the emotion and pride with which, in my third year at the Royal Gymnasium, I had recited in front of my class Fusinato's poem on the siege of Venice in 1848, when the city rebelled against the Austrians. I was praised for the "heart" I had put into my recitation, which was due to my father's explanation that the president of the embattled Venetian republic at the time was of Jewish origin. "Plague is rife/ bread is lacking/ on the bridge floats the white flag," said the poem. Now it was my father's turn, I felt, through my flight to Palestine, to raise the white flag over his broken Fascist ideals, over his pride as an Italian nationalist, over the ruin of all his family hopes. I had nothing to tell him, and he had nothing to tell me, as if we had both exhausted all topics of conversation.

I was grateful to him for not accompanying me to the ship, for cutting short the adieus, and for leaving me alone with his famous brother. My uncle treated me as his peer: he made me sit facing him at the long marble table around which so many great people had once dined. Now we were together, or rather he was alone with me, with a maid not yet taken away by the new anti-Jewish legislation serving us in silent precision as in the time of his greatness. Noiselessly, she kept changing fine procelain plates in front of me, with gloved hands, quick to disappear with a slight rustle of the starched white apron she wore over her black silk uniform.

My uncle made no comments on the political situation created by the war that had just broken out. He asked me about the agricultural school in which I had enrolled without ever pronouncing the word "Palestine." I answered him with the nonchalance of a spoiled youth on the point of entering a finishing school in England or Switzerland. From the window I could see the terraced garden full of flowers, with the replica of Rodin's *The Kiss* and the jet of water in the center of the pond where red, gold, and silver fish continued their lives undisturbed. Nothing had changed on my uncle's estate except for the feeling that both of us had been torn from the reality surrounding us, that we were strange travelers in a space ship of Jules Verne's imagining, in which the refined life of the past continued under the new, unreal dimensions of the present. For my uncle this may have been a surrealistic experience; for me it was a moment of total triumph, which I owed to the new Fascist anti-Semitism and which nobody could disturb. On the eve of my departure for a foreign land I had become, thanks to the racial laws, equal to the richest and most powerful man I had ever known in my life. The fact that this was due to his social and political collapse did not disturb me in the least. This was the first of many occasions when I realized that one person's good fortune is always linked to another person's troubles.

After lunch that afternoon my uncle took me to the home of Lionel Stock, founder of the famous distillery firm and a dedicated Zionist, to ask him for letters of introduction to some of his friends in Palestine. These letters did not help me in the least in a country flooded by immigrants looking for jobs, but I recall with deep emotion the meeting of those two powerful Jewish industrialists who had not, I believe, met for years.

Lionel Stock was dressed in a dark suit with a gold chain dangling from his waistcoat pocket. My uncle wore an elegant light gray suit, which was the only spot of color in the sober office we entered after passing through the factory courtyard. The two men represented different worlds in the social and ethnic mosaic of Jewish Trieste before the war: my uncle had come from Piedmont following the victory of the Italian army; Stock had stayed put after the collapse of the Austro-Hungarian Empire. One was the epitome of economic success in authoritarian Italy; the other the symbol of economic development in traditional Mittel Europa. One was baptized and a Fascist, the other a confirmed Jew and Zionist. The only thing they had in common was their Jewish origin and their interest in me. Conscious of my position, I sat silent between them like a laboratory animal, the focus not of an experiment but of a confrontation of ideas.

Lionel Stock was saying that no Jew could escape his destiny. My uncle answered that the storm would eventually blow over and that it was necessary to trust Mussolini, who had always been friendly to Jews on condition that they kept themselves out of the public eye. Stock said that we had no hope unless we stood as united as possible, that we could no longer rely on anyone, that we had to exploit the little freedom that was still left to the Jews in Italy to get away and to help as many coreligionists as possible to escape from the Germans. My uncle answered him that the Jews, as a separate group, were the agents of their own ruin. In order to reverse an illogical, tragic, unjustified destiny, he had married a Christian woman and had his children grow up in the religion of the majority, different from the faith into which he was born. Stock replied that this was perhaps a choice open to the individual, but not to the Jewish masses, and that my uncle's recent losses underlined the fact that even a powerful individual Jew who had been baptized could not escape his Jewish destiny. Since Hitler's decision to check the religion of the grandparents, we had reached a situation in which the lineage of Jews was examined as carefully as that of the nobility used to be. In the absurdity of the racial persecution it was necessary to accept the responsibility carried by this new type of negative Jewish aristocracy. I was wise to leave Italy because the future of the Jews was outside Europe, in America, and even more in Palestine, where a day would come when nobody would be able to contest their right to lead a normal existence like any other people.

My uncle insisted that the Zionist movement, even if theoretically rational, was politically illusory. It did not take into consideration the realities of the contemporary political world. England and France were two countries in full decadence. They were unable to stop the march of powerful nations like Germany and Italy, which were in the process of rapid demographic and military expansion. Possibly the destiny of the Jews in Palestine might have been different if Italy had been given the mandate over that part of the Ottoman Empire. Now, allied with the Arab world, Italy had less interest in Zionism than England, which had already betrayed the Jews of Palestine in order to capture the sympathy of the Arabs. He was convinced that I was not saving my skin but marching straight into a trap. He could not understand how my father could have failed to try to dissuade me, but we were living in times in which nobody, and more particularly the Jews, understood what was happening. Of one thing he was convinced: out of this war a new order would arise; woe to those who stood against it; they would be destroyed.

Stock knew that he could not sway my uncle. He listened without interrupting, sighing and shaking his head in sorrow. When we parted he said to me, with a note of hope in his voice, that he hoped to see me again in less troubled times so that I could bear witness to which of the two, he or my uncle, would be vindicated by the future.

It is remarkable with what clarity my uncle remembered this, for him, unpleasant conversation many years later. He was lying on a large bed in his apartment in Via Bruxelles, opposite the villa of Marshal Badoglio, in an area that was then one of the most elegant and quiet in Rome. The room was filled with the smell of death, a death my uncle had always dreaded and now accepted with surprising resignation—only from time to time he cried without apparent reason. The anxiety of recent years, his flight into the Vatican, his separation from his wife and children, all had shaken his physique more than his economic ruin out of which, however, he had saved a considerable sum that now served to pay the fees of the most famous Italian doctors. My aunt thought she could increase the efficacy of the medical care by winding around my uncle's neck a pair of white woolen socks that the family's confessor had obtained from Sister Pasqualina, Pope Pacelli's maid. It was said that the socks had been worn by the Pope himself and might, therefore, bring about the miracle in which the doctors did not believe. In my eyes, however, they made him look pathetic.

My uncle was happy to see me again. He wanted to ask me to leave the British army, with which I had come to Rome at the beginning of 1945, as soon as possible. I do not know whether he was fully conscious or under the effect of drugs, as he described to me in a gasping voice the immense new possibilities, political and economic, that would open up in Italy once it was free of the Fascist regime. From time to time he spoke about India, which he wanted to visit as soon as the war was over; about the forests he had lost in Poland; about past conversations with Italian politicians and international bankers; about the fleet of fishing trawlers that he wanted to establish as soon as the war ended; and of the importance of always having polished shoes because—he kept repeating—the shoes betrayed the man.

Once he described to me the frontiers of the financial empire he had created. They extended from mines in Lorraine to forests in Danzig, from food industries in Trieste to a hydroelectric plant on the Austrian border. The loss of all these riches seemed to have wounded him less than the rejection by the duchess of Aosta of a gift he had sent to the Castle of Miramar on the birthday of one of the duchess's children. The box, wrapped in shiny paper, had been returned with an icy letter of thanks. Even now, after the duke had died a hero's death in Africa, my uncle still suffered from having been considered, even at the peak of his power, a parvenu, a newly rich Jew who had no place at court. None of the many personalities he had known in Europe between the two wars—Paderewski and Balfour, Rathenau and Marconi, Balbo and Dolfuss—could compensate him for that snub, which he had been unable to erase since he had narrowly missed the opportunity of being made a count by Mussolini.

While Luigi cleaned the tombstone, I remembered the sudden visit that my uncle had paid to my mother in the winter of 1938. I had never seen him so happy, and his slightly mischievous smile seemed never to leave his lips. He gave me a big fifty-lire note, although he had sent me one shortly before, for my birthday. He asked my sister what she wanted for her birthday, in April, and then he retired to another room with my mother, surrounded by an atmosphere of great secrecy. When he left in the long, shining Lancia with his monogram on the doors, the chauffeur dressed in livery, he left behind him an aura of faint after-shave and strong mystery, which my mother immediately broke by telephoning my father while I listened at the keyhole.

He—Mussolini—had let my uncle know that he was prepared to support a proposal to the king to make my uncle a count or a royal senator. It was clear, my mother said over the telephone, that in the first place one should think of an appropriate coat of arms. It could not be anything connected with the "45" (a number used in the family in front of the servants to indicate that somebody or something was Jewish; the servants knowing no more than we that the Hebrew letters of the word *adam*, meaning "man" or "Jew," corresponded to the figure 45), but it would be nice if the coat of arms were in some way connected with our family. (This was not easy since it was only in 1849 that my forefathers left the ghetto of Ivrea where they used to sell rags, with special permission to remain outside the ghetto walls every Tuesday.) In any case, my mother went on, my uncle wanted my father, who was an expert in heraldry, to give some thought to the matter. It was a real shame, she continued, that the village in Piedmont where my grandfather had owned the castle and where we still had some property, was a fiefdom of the duke of Genoa. It would have been nice if the coat of arms could have been that of the village, with its cross and sheaf of corn, which was printed on the labels of the wine bottles my father prepared specially for my uncle every year. My father laughed at the whole idea. He was right, because before six months had elapsed, the new alliance between Mussolini and Hitler had destroyed forever the heraldic hopes of his brother.

With my heart agitated by these memories and my head empty of ideas, I now stood in front of the grave, following with my eyes Luigi's arthritic fingers struggling with the knots tied around his parcel. Eventually there emerged from the newspaper a small, round jar that might once have contained jam. Inside was a yellow liquid. Luigi, with a hieratic gesture full of respect, unscrewed the lid and slowly poured the contents onto the marble slab. A strong and pleasing smell of rum reached my nostrils as a puddle of liquid fizzed over the stone. With his cigar stub dangling from his mouth, Luigi murmured loudly enough for me to hear: "Commander, this zabaglione is made exactly as you liked it." With the back of his left hand, in which he held the lid of the jar, he wiped away a tear, turning his back to me in shame.

A slight breeze caressed the cypresses: I found myself thinking that they had nothing in common with those celebrated by Respighi. These were clumsy trees, powdered with dust, swaying above the yellowing grass at their feet. Indifferent to death and pain, they looked as though they were sucking up life from the graves, witnesses of everything and nothing, in a garden dedicated to nothingness and inhabited by everyone.

Silently we left the Verano, Luigi wrapped up in his black winter coat and I huddled in my badly ironed British battle-dress. The "Red Circular" tram was just coming. Without speaking we shook hands. Anyone witnessing the scene might have thought we were two mafiosi who had just completed a deal.

5

A Fascist Cadet
in Zion

AFTER so many years I still laugh at the thought of my arrival in Tel Aviv. I was traveling on a small ship carrying a mixed cargo and about thirty passengers. I was sixteen and had a "capitalist" immigration visa, the type of visa that the British issued to immigrants with at least one thousand pounds sterling, which, in my case, my father had deposited in an English bank through the good offices of the Fascist party. I was alone in one of the six or eight first-class cabins. Traveling with me were some priests and a few Palestinian Jews making their precipitous return because of the outbreak of war. I was the only immigrant on board. The British mandatory authorities had by that time practically closed the door to Jews from Europe. With the publication of a white paper limiting Jewish immigration they had put an end to Zionist hopes of having a Jewish state in Palestine, since the percentage of the Jewish population had been fixed at one-third of the Arab inhabitants of the Holy Land.

My situation was thus particularly hybrid. I was a "deluxe" immigrant, due to join a kibbutz; I was the nephew of the owner of the ship on which I was sailing, but the ship had just been confiscated by the Italian government because he was a baptized Jew; I was under the personal care of the ship's captain at whose table I took my meals, and at the same time abandoned in every sense into the hands of an unknown fate. Nobody, and first and foremost myself, knew exactly who I was. Among the passengers, a beautiful lady seemed particularly startled by my presence. Wife of the owner of the then-largest textile factory in Palestine, she too was traveling first class, and we quickly became friends.

She could have been about thirty-five years old and told me she had a son not much younger than I. She did not mingle with the other passengers and spent long hours looking at the sea as if oppressed by nightmares. We used to take our afternoon tea together in long, quiet sessions—I too busy with myself to ask her about her troubles, she too plunged into her own thoughts. She must have left most of her family behind in Europe and perhaps had tried in vain to persuade them to follow her to Palestine. A tall, blond, sad woman, she listened to me with a strange look in her eyes, a look of curiosity and compassion. With considerable tact she kept warning me of the illusions I was weaving about the country awaiting me. I would not find anything remotely like Italy, she said, either in the landscape or in the people. It was not the physical toil that I should be afraid of but the cruelty of human relations. In Palestine the differences among people were greater than in other places because of the large number of immigrants. I would probably find myself lonely and misunderstood by other youngsters because of the type of world I was coming from. I would be caught up in a network of abrasive relationships among uprooted people who, because they were uprooted, were now busily engaged in building a world in which to forget their past. I should not expect compassion, pity, or kindness, though I would be able to rely on human solidarity. But it was a type of solidarity that shied away from privacy and individualism. Necessity and ideology privileged the group rather than the individual. For this reason it would be wise of me to find and adhere to a group as quickly as possible. I would suffer less than if I remained aloof. The price to be paid for acceptance would certainly consist of the loss of many of my dreams, not to speak of the tastes and habits I had brought with me from home, but nevertheless I should conform. The only other piece of advice she could give me was to try and develop thick callouses on my soul like those that would very soon harden the palms of my hands. Palestine, she kept telling me, is a land where caresses are made with sandpaper.

Naturally I was not convinced. Stretched out on my deck chair in the morning and the late afternoon, I enjoyed the infinite, changing blue of a bright, glassy sea—an atmosphere of well-being that made it impossible to imagine a future of pain and humiliation. The unreality that had always surrounded me was still there, even if different from before. World War II had broken out, but I was making my first cruise as a private person, free from uniforms, obligations, or discipline. I was a Jew, branded by racial laws, but served in style by Aryan waiters, protected by a captain who was perhaps wondering whether my uncle might not someday again be his boss. I was a refugee, an immigrant, a being in flight from a Europe that was tumbling into hell, but this did not prevent me from feeling free, fortunate, and happy at being able to run away from the war fronts, from college discipline, and from the oppression of Jewish life in Turin. I was full of hopes, without responsibilities, enjoying every minute of my life on board, which kept me busy from morning to night. I slept, I ate, I chatted; I read novels from the ship's library; I roamed freely around the ship, from the captain's bridge to the engine room; I talked to the boatswain, who demonstrated the knots he could make with a piece of string; I discussed the radio bulletins announcing German victories, and I was not— as I had dreaded—seasick!

During the crossing which, even near Crete, where the sea is often rough, was consistently sunny and calm, an abandon-ship exercise was carried out. The first officer called the passengers onto the top deck, checked the correct fastening of our life belts, explained the meaning of the siren blasts in case of danger, and took care to assure us that such danger was highly unlikely. Italy, he said, would remain neutral, thanks to the wisdom of Il Duce. Nobody would dare to provoke her in *mare nostrum*. Just the same, we should not allow ourselves to sink into a comfortable fatalism; not for nothing was England known as *perfide Albion*. Should we find ourselves in danger, we should face it with Italian, Aryan, and Fascist courage. The poor man, destined perhaps to die soon in some naval operation, must have learned his speech by heart. Facing a public composed mainly of Jews, his words sounded like a Marx Brothers' gag.

It was early in the morning when we anchored off Tel Aviv. To the right, clustered on the promontory of Jaffa, was a conglomeration of small houses, the bell tower of a church, and a large, castle-like building. Facing me, rising from an expanse of sand, were lines of flat roofs, colorless cement cubes with a splash of green here and there. A number of barges swayed on the water. The entire harbor consisted of a small jetty from which they shuttled back and forth to the few cargo ships waiting beyond the shallow water. An Italian priest, with whom I had gotten friendly during the trip and with whom I had discussed, for the first time in my life, the dogmas of Judaism and Christianity, explained to me that the only real harbor in the country was further north, at Haifa. The Jews had built the jetty in Tel Aviv and were handling their own cargoes because the Arabs of Jaffa had refused to unload the ships for them. "Jews and Arabs always quarrel," he said, "and they will go on quarreling for a long time to come if somebody does not put an end to the attempts of the Zionists to have a state of their own in Palestine." The war that had just started would certainly clip the Zionists' wings: the Jews were already not allowed by the British to immigrate into Palestine or to buy land from the Arabs. But after reducing them to a perpetual minority, the British government would use them to fight the Arabs, divide the country, and thus have a reason to remain *ad aeternitatem* in Palestine. In any case, he added, everyone was fighting everyone else in the Holy Land, which was supposed to be the Land of Peace. At the Church of the Holy Sepulcher the Christians quarreled among themselves no less than the Jews with the Moslems. If I visited Jerusalem one day he would be happy to take me to see it for myself. He wished me good luck and disembarked with the other passengers, including my beautiful lady companion, leaving me alone on board in the hands of the immigration authorities. They gave me permission to go ashore in less than half an hour.

As soon as the little row boat had taken me into the port, which consisted of a large shed for goods and a few hovels used as offices, a short, ugly, slant-eyed nurse got hold of me with the brisk authority derived from her white uniform and starched cap embroidered with a red Star of David. She took my temperature, measured my pulse, vaccinated me without a word of explanation, asked a lot of questions about my health and that of my family, and almost choked when I, in turn, asked her who the bearded gentleman was looking at me with sad eyes from the wall. "Theodor Herzl," she growled, "the founder, the prophet of Zionism." After which, stupefied and disgusted, she let me go.

Nobody, naturally, was waiting for me outside the port, and I wondered how to approach the passersby to get some advice. I did not speak a word of Hebrew, they would certainly not understand Italian, and I was ashamed to show how little French and English I knew. I was wearing a navy blue jacket, gray flannel trousers, a shirt with cufflinks and the detachable linen collar that dandies at that time sported in Italy, and a beautiful silk tie. To the people I saw outside the tiny port, open-shirted, perspiring, and scruffy, the men in sandals and shorts, the women in sandals and khaki bloomers hitched up to the tops of their thighs with elastic, I must have looked like the ringmaster of a circus. Next to me stood a big, leather-bound cabin trunk and a canvas bag. The trunk, a bar mitzvah gift from my cousins, was silk-lined and bore my initials; the canvas bag contained a collapsible camp bed and a small tent. These two objects were recommended items for immigrants, listed in the documents I had collected at the Palestine office in Milan. Among other useless pieces of advice, it suggested that one equip oneself with a Boy Scout hat. To find this headgear, my father and I had scoured half of Turin. Finally we came to the Borsalino shop in the station square, where we thought we had seen something like the hat in question in the window.

The shop assistant, after listening to our explanation of why we needed such a hat, told me that he still had some Boy Scout hats in stock. They had not been in demand for a long time, since the Boy Scout movement had been outlawed by the Fascist regime. He brought me a couple to try on—they were made of rich brown felt and shaped like those of the Canadian Mounties. The assistant assured me, in front of the mirror, that it fitted me beautifully. He said he was happy that I would be wearing it in a country where people could have uniforms without being trained for war. An immediate feeling of understanding and conspiracy was established between us. Hat in hand, we left without any further conversation, but I am convinced to this day that if I had stayed in Italy that shop would have become a friendly refuge for me, with the hat serving as a password for anti-Fascist action.

As soon as I landed in Tel Aviv I understood that it was safer for me to make the hat disappear. It was heavy and totally unsuited to the climate of the country. Worse, it made me look even more ridiculous than my jacket and tie in a world where women covered their heads with faded scarves of coarse blue cotton and men wore peaked caps of a Russian-Polish type. This latter fashion quickly disappeared in Israel, but at the time it symbolized adherence to Marxist principles, just as it does today, in a curious geographical development, on the heads of Chinese militants.

However, this was not the subject of my reflections when I went out under the blinding sun and stood alone, already without my jacket but still wearing a tie and a linen collar, next to my cabin trunk and canvas sack. I found myself suddenly faced with the emptiness of my future. For the first time, after months of excitement, enthusiasm, fantasies, and romantic projects, I was smitten by a feeling of utter hopelessness. In trying to analyze the cause after so many years, I probably tend to confuse the experience of that time with my present-day recollections. Yet that first fit of anguish left an indelible scar.

Leaning on my cabin trunk, which stood upright on the sand like a memorial column to my past, I did not understand the meaning of the new life facing me. But from the very first moment, I perceived the dessicated vitality of the place—the power of the people who, from ideological choice rather than from necessity, wanted to appear poorer and rougher than my father's peasants. They exuded an insolent misery; they displayed a life-style that signaled to me unequivocally I had fallen into a world of frenetic action, without reserves or counterweights, with no hiding places for the soul. It was a world devoted to deeds and burned by activism as the flat-roofed, peeling houses were burned by the sun. In the sudden, infinite emptiness of my situation, these houses seemed to eye me from across the street, graceless and only less frightening than the wooden barracks along the seashore, whose walls bore tatters of tar paper, which flapped grotesquely in the wind.

These shacks, perched on the dunes like witches' dens, looked down on the camel trains filing past along the shore. Laden with crates of sand, they made their way to invisible construction sites, their rhythmic pacing marked by the tin-

kling of the bells around their necks. From the lopsided veran-
das of some of the shacks, wash flapping in the breeze saluted
these indolent animals, pressing upon me the naked, miserable
reality of my new motherland, so different from that of my
dreams. I was unable at that time to perceive beyond the
poverty of the landscape the hidden meaning of the Zionist
adventure and the miraculous connection between the moribund Judaism of Europe and the acrid pride of a Jewish
nationalism in Palestine striving to create a new type of Jew.

In a confused way I felt that Tel Aviv had no personality
of its own, like some of the new towns Mussolini was creating
in the drained marshes around Rome. This burgeoning town,
in which a writer one day would say that people laughed in
Hebrew during the day and cried in many languages at night,
reproduced in microcosm the whole history of the human race.
It was a history of which I was totally ignorant and which now
paraded before my eyes in a living collection of tattered styles,
languages, costumes, and habits. It was a history that jumbled
together in a disorderly, unharmonic, unblended whole, the
passions, needs, and hopes brought here by fanatical idealists
and reluctant immigrants from the four corners of the earth.
In those short-long instants of my standing outside the gates
of Tel Aviv port, I experienced the first brutal contact with
infinite emptiness. But I also unconsciously perceived that
diabolical mirage that calls men to supplant thought with
action and to choke doubts with meaningful gestures: action
for action's sake.

A taxi driver, sitting in a dust-covered Ford, shook me out
of this nightmare. He was probably used to meeting stunned
immigrants like me. For a couple of shillings he offered to take
me to the bus station, the focal point where everyone seemed
to converge before dispersing into a new world that was, for
many, still without poles of attraction.

During that short trip I must obviously have absorbed
through my eyes and my pores the novelty of this ungrateful

landscape. Yet of those first visions of Tel Aviv I have almost no recollections. The shock must have been too strong for them to be recorded in my mind: this has not remained the only memory block I have experienced in my life. Anyway, on that particular morning my brain started functioning again only on my arrival at the bus station, if one can so describe the chaos of public transport that greeted me.

The vehicles of the Jewish bus cooperative—the main transport system then, as today, because the state only operates a couple of short railway lines—were parked untidily along narrow, unpaved streets branching off the main road named after Theodor Herzl. These squat, dusty brown buses had rows of hard wooden seats inside and dirty windows with wire netting on the outside to protect against the stones and sometimes the bombs that the Arabs had gotten into the habit of throwing. The streets were crowded with people dressed in every possible variety of Western and Eastern costumes and with carts pulled by donkeys or horses. I was struck by the fact that most of the latter had ulcerated skins and were not castrated. The fact that a badly cared for stallion could be harnessed to a cart seemed to me symbolic of a society in which human and animal energy kept pulsing in scarred bodies. But soon my eyes became mesmerized by an unexpected spectacle of popular magic: on one street corner a bearded man with a kind of turban around his head was making hieratic gestures while slaughtering chickens with a long knife. The sand soaked up the drizzle of blood under the attentive eyes of women carrying shopping bags.

Not far from there another man shuffled along in a pair of baggy, black Turkish trousers that fell onto his old, down-at-the-heel slippers. He carried on his back an enormous brass jar with an elongated, griffin-like beak high over his shoulder. A metal beaker dangled from three fingers of one hand; from the other was suspended by its handle a flat metal "basket" holding some dirty glasses. With the thumb and forefinger of the first hand, he drummed up customers by clacking metal castanets. "Tamarindi, tamarindi," he shouted, making his way slowly through the crowd. From time to time someone would hold out to him a coin with a hole in the middle. The tamarindi seller would then bend forward in a measured bow, allowing with the inclination of his back a yellow liquid to spurt out of the beak of the jar from above his shoulder. He caught the beverage in midair in one of the glasses that he had previously rinsed in water from the beaker. The customer drank and returned the glass to the tamarindi seller, who moistened it again with a little water, erasing with his thumb any trace left by the customer's lips. Then he moved off again to the sound of his castanets. He was an Arab, his head covered with a gray-white scarf. When he poured out the tamarindi for a Jew, standing in front of him in a peaked cap, his sunburned, hairy legs sprouting out of his faded shorts, they looked like two bizarre animals exchanging silent messages through the colored bottom of the glass.

I was also feeling thirsty, and since my cab driver had refused a tip, I invited him to have a drink. He took me to a restaurant called Istanbul where, sitting at a shaky, oilcloth-covered table, I received from this good man my first lesson in the comparative history, geography, and psychology of the country in which I was to become a citizen.

The driver wore a khaki shirt and shorts and, like the bus drivers who went to-and-fro in the restaurant, he sported knee-length socks and brown shoes. Unlike some of the others, he did not have a Mauser automatic pistol dangling from a holster strapped across his chest, nor did he wear, strapped to his belt, a strange gadget to dispense change. This odd apparatus consisted of three metal cylinders of different diameters, each with a spring pushing up a round plate the size of a particular coin. The drivers, who also sold tickets, slid the coins they received into these cylinders or took them out by a pressure of the thumb to give change. My father had a similar instrument, smaller and box-shaped, in his study. Inside were two cavities, each with a spring in the bottom, in which he used to keep golden sovereigns and half sovereigns. He took this box with him when he went to Monte Carlo to play and once described its use to me as though it were already an archaeological relic. Under the thumbs of the bus drivers, without dandified refinements, I now watched silver shillings and perforated tin piasters sliding in and out from these gadgets.

They bore the word "Palestine" in English, Arabic, and Hebrew. After the Hebrew word was a bracket enclosing two letters of the cuneiform alphabet, which the Jews had brought back from their exile in Babylon: an *aleph* and a *yod,* the initials of the words "Eretz Yisrael" (Land of Israel). My taxi driver held one of these coins under my nose and explained its political significance. The Arabs, he said, had refused to allow the Jews to have the words "Land of Israel" fully inscribed on the coins. The Jews, for their part, objected to their ancestral land being called only by the Arab name "Falastin" (that is, the land of the Philistines) which, quite apart from contemporary political considerations, was, in my driver's opinion, an anachronism, since the Philistines had been massacred by Samson a long time ago. The British, however, Solomonically added the brackets with the *aleph* and the *yod* after the Hebrew "Palestine." It could be pronounced "Ai!" and this cry of trodden-on corns was, according to my impromptu teacher, a perfect description of the situation now facing the Jews.

The driver was born in Russia and had emigrated to Palestine with his parents after the revolution. He spoke Italian and a few words of Ladino—the Jewish-Spanish speech—which he had picked up on his summer trips between Salonica and Venice. He had been shuttling back and forth on that route, engaged in a very special trade—pro forma marriages with Jewish girls who had been refused immigration certificates by the British. By marrying him, a Palestinian citizen, a girl could enter the country by right and then, through a quick divorce procedure, proceed to join her real fiancé, if she had one, or look for a husband locally. The British had eventually caught on and forbidden this type of arrangement, and he had thus lost the opportunity of making free summer trips to Europe, where because of Hitler and the war, people were now, he said, in deep trouble. Fortunately it would not last long; he knew France well, and the French army was the strongest in the world. The Nazis would be beaten after breaking their heads against the Maginot line. Meanwhile life for the Jews in Poland was turning sour, he went on; one heard terrible stories about their fate. Yet they had asked for it; they could have come to Palestine during the years when immigration was free, but they had chosen to stay among their enemies.

My man was particularly hard on the religious Jews who believed that Zionism was the work of the devil. Now they were tasting hell, he said, and could see for themselves what it meant to pray three times a day for the return of the Jews to Zion and yet stay put in their quarters in Lodz and Warsaw. They could at least have emigrated en masse to America! Instead they had waited till the Germans arrived. Like the Jews of Western Europe they felt secure because the goyim (Gentiles) had passed laws giving them legal equality. "Pieces of paper," grumbled the driver, sipping his lemonade. "Pieces of paper which all the governments will eventually tear to pieces as has already happened in Germany and Italy." The Jews of Europe now found themselves trapped with their money and their houses full of possessions that they could not get rid of. Instead, had they had a bit more *sechel* (common sense), they might have been able, with a bit of that money, to buy villas and orange groves and build factories and theaters in Eretz Yisrael, helping Zionism while saving their skins. But that's what Jews are like, he sighed hopelessly; I would find that out for myself very soon. Jews, he explained, were clever but not wise. A clever man is the one who finds ways out of an unpleasant situation into which a wise man would never have got himself. I should try to be wise, not clever, he advised me, because just by looking at me he felt that I would never have any success among the clever.

Anyway, now that I was safe I could start a new life. But to succeed in it I should turn my back firmly on the past. There was no way back for the Jews: the war would sever the physical links that still existed with Europe, and Zionism should cut the cultural and spiritual links with it and put an end to the mentality of the Diaspora. From this war the old continent and old Judaism would emerge in shambles. The Zionists, like Cortés' Spaniards in Mexico, could only go forward, in spite of the opposition of the British and the hostility of the Arabs. They should transform themselves from refugees into conquistadores. Jabotinsky (the nationalist right-wing leader) and his Revisionist party were right—one could not build a state, as the socialists were trying to do, just by adding one cow to another cow, one dunam of land to another (bought at a "golden" price from the Arabs). Only strength would permit the Jews to live in security in Eretz Yisrael. The Jewish Agency (the Zionist administration in Palestine) and the world Zionist movement were wrong in believing that it was possible to pacify the Arabs by practicing *havlagah,* the policy of self-control that authorized only to reply to attacks but never to initiate them. On the contrary, it was necessary to be the first to attack, to show one's teeth, to frighten. The Jews of Eretz Yisrael must convince their enemies that they were no longer the Jews of the ghetto; they were the new oriental barbarians, the new Hyksos. Mohammed, with four hundred riders, had destroyed the Byzantine Empire; four thousand Jews could shake the British Empire.

There was something fascinating in his words. In my imagination I saw bands of Zionist Arditi, the Italian storm troopers whose exploits in the Great War had so often been taught us at school, dressed in shining armor, galloping with flying banners to the conquest of London. But as soon as I returned to my senses, my eyes fell on the flies sipping the drops of lemonade bubbling on the table. No war cries came from the street but only the clucking of chickens and the braying of donkeys. Unknown people, looking most unwarlike, chattered around me in incomprehensible idioms. The landscape was that of a small, dusty, provincial town, of the dirty corner of a market from which the smells of cooked food and rotten vegetables rose into the air, displacing all fantasies of glorious conquest. What I saw was a perspiring and agitated humanity, not a phalanx of martial warriors. The crude white light leveled all objects into an unending succession of black and white shapes. Nothing could be further from a battleground than this inordinate ambience, in which all living things searched for cover in the miserly shade of noon.

I looked at my jacket, creased by the chair back. I had already undone my collar and tie and turned up the sleeves of my shirt, which sweat had glued to my spine. I felt undressed, dirty, defenseless, immersed in the still air of surroundings made up of sand, noise, shoving, and shadows.

My driver had to go. He helped me carry my luggage to the edge of the dirt road from which the bus to my kibbutz was supposed to depart. He assured me that I could leave everything unguarded; no one stole in the only totally Jewish city in the world. He shook my hand, wished me luck, and left in his dusty Ford, unaware of the help he had given me and for which I would never have the opportunity to thank him.

The trip to Kibbutz Givat Brenner was uneventful. I expected stones or bombs to be thrown at us and for our driver to fight off enemy attacks with his pistol, as in a Western, but nothing happened. We drove through areas of Jewish settlement, alternating with Arab villages and large tracts of empty sand. On the road we passed small groups of Arab peasants astride their little donkeys, followed by women carrying bundles of greens or firewood on their heads. The landscape was exotic but poor and the dimensions of everything were miserable.

As we left the outskirts of Jaffa, we passed in front of the bell tower of a Russian Orthodox church, standing almost opposite the minaret of a mosque. Around both buildings I could see low, flatroofed, crumbling mud houses and crowds of barefooted children. Their faces were covered with flies, their clothes consisted only of dirty nightgowns falling to their feet. There were scattered palm trees, some vineyards, and many orange groves, whose brilliant green contrasted vividly with the sandy, dusty monotony of the surroundings. Squatting women baked bread in ovens of stone and dried mud. Here and there, in the courtyards or on the flat roofs, apricots, tomatoes, and bunches of peppers were drying in the sun. In front of these hovels and under thatched roofs, groups of Arabs eyed us, sucking at their water pipes. By the doors stood water jars and bundles of sugarcane. From time to time a slow-moving, skin-ulcerated camel slowed the bus down. Chickens darted out from all sides amid the howling of skinny dogs. It was an ugly and impoverished world, from which one had to lift one's eyes to the sky, limpid and blue, to recover hope.

Next to me sat a fat, perspiring woman with a basketful of vegetables on her lap. Encouraged by the other passengers, she questioned me about my origins, my age, the family I had left behind in Italy, the people awaiting me in the kibbutz, my father's business, how much he had earned, why I had not gone to America, what I thought about Tel Aviv, why I had chosen to go to the agricultural school at Mikveh Yisrael instead of the one at Kfar Tabor, which was much better and which was where her uncle had studied. She gave me a mass of unasked for advice; inquired about my political views and offered her own in exchange; discussed my case with a man sitting in front of us; made sure three times that the driver knew where I was going; and finally got off at Rehovot, today a great science center but at that time just a spot of green and a cluster of white houses between two stretches of sand.

After a while we entered the kibbutz grounds through two revolving, rusty iron gates standing wide open over a shallow concrete ditch full of whitish water. The bus moved slowly into the water to disinfect its tires against "foot and mouth" disease, which, unchecked among the Arab herds, also caused considerable mortality in the Jewish cattle. A road of beaten earth wound through a thick orange grove leading to a bare, stony hill covered with buildings.

On the way we encountered first, on the right-hand side, workshops full of machinery under repair, welding equipment, and men dressed in grease-stained blue overalls. Next came the chicken runs and the stables; higher up, laid out in semicircles, stood three types of dwellings: there were two-story, rectangular blocks with an outside staircase in the center and two balconies, one above the other, providing access to a row of four rooms each. The balconies sported broom handles, flowers in petrol tins, and wooden crates used as cupboards. Lower down the hill, in no clear order, were many wooden huts, also divided into four rooms, with an open veranda serving as a storage space for brooms and buckets, makeshift cupboards for work clothing, and gaping shoes covered with mud. Here and there one could see large crates transformed into "private houses." Some were painted outside; one had a curtained window and looked like a doll's house; another was surrounded by a small path lined with white-painted stones and rows of flowers. Finally, there were a lot of bell tents, supported by central poles, with their flaps rolled up to allow air to circulate, revealing iron bedsteads and untidy blankets and sheets hanging to the ground.

It took me some time before I realized that this distribution of dwellings indicated a precise social hierarchy. The older kibbutz members, who were usually married, occupied rooms in the two-story cement blocks. The unmarried young people and the new immigrants lived in groups of four or six to a tent, men and women separately. Some married newcomers occupied the crates in which they brought their own or their friend's furniture to Palestine, while less senior kibbutz members lived in the huts, two to a room if they were married, four if they were single. Near the top of the hill, a spot of green on one side surrounded the children's house. Separated from their parents, they enjoyed conditions of order and comfort far superior to those of their elders.

At the very top of the hill rose the water tower, under which were situated the post office, the auxiliary police guardroom, the infirmary, the administration office, and, at some distance, large huts used as a dining room, kitchen, and clothing store.

I had brought with me from Italy a small tent, quite welcome to the kibbutz administration since the bachelor quarters were overcrowded. They allotted me a small piece of ground between the infirmary and the showers and in this way, without knowing it, I excluded myself from the social hierarchy of the kibbutz habitat.

I learned my first lesson in collective life from the latrines and the showers. The latrines were easily identifiable in daytime by their kennel-like, elongated form and their wooden doors banging in the wind. By night they indicated their position by the smell of sewage mixed with the stronger and more acrid one of Lysol. Within these constructions, partitioned inside by jute curtains, crude wooden seats standing on the slatted floor permitted the free fall of metabolic products into the trench below. In a land where water and manure were in short supply, it was a logical and economical system. Next to the seats were containers for used paper. These primitive, smelly latrines, together with the showers, fulfilled a social-cultural function no less useful than their hygienic one. Since toilet paper was a luxury the kibbutz could not afford, every-body used old newspapers. The latrines thus turned into ex-temporary reading rooms with the help of crunched up pieces of publications reporting local and foreign events, some of them well in the past.

I soon learned to accumulate stocks of printed papers in French and English. Since I did not yet know Hebrew and could not find reading material in Italian, these scraps of old news added a dimension of intellectual relaxation to my bodily one and represented moments of comfort in the crudity of the situation. In these latrines I could offer my body, untrained for physical labor, moments of delightful relaxation for my aching muscles, while the bits of news I read without fear of being disturbed transformed themselves into a multiplicity of links with the external world. Through the jute partitions one could naturally perceive signs of the existence of other human beings nearby. But once one had latched the door on the inside one could feel absolute master of one's own space. Furthermore, because collectivism dominated almost all other aspects of life in the kibbutz, nobody in the latrines tried to violate the exclusive privacy of his neighbor by talking. If two people were walking together to this place of reflection engaged in a hot philosophical or political debate, they cut short their conversation as soon as they reached the latrine doors, as though every link between them had been suddenly severed. Compelled by bodily needs, secluded in wooden and jute cubicles, each one would find himself temporarily free from the communality that continuously shrouded him elsewhere in the kibbutz. In this thinking place, as happened to Luther, great ideas and hopes may have germinated. Here, in any case, sitting above the disinfected excrement, people felt free to sigh more deeply than in the silence of their nights. Here, having ab-stracted themselves for a while from group life, individuals could bare their bodies and souls without shame. Today no trace of these latrines remains, but I do not think it is possible to describe the atmosphere of those days without taking into account the role they played in the collective society of the time.

On the kibbutz showers much has been written. As far as I know, however, no one has stressed their social role as opposed to that of the latrines. The two institutions, located one in front of the other, one long and low, the other squat and high, acted as two poles of the same communal dynamo, energizing the entire community through a kind of point and counterpoint of promiscuity and privacy, of biological individualism and ideological collectivism.

One entered the showers after having abandoned one's dirty, sweaty working clothes in a wooden box on the veranda. With a towel draped around the hips, feet pushed into wooden clogs (I thought they were a Zionist invention until the day I found a pair in a bathroom in Berlin), one then teetered along toward the purifying water, carrying the soapbox, toothbrush, and the dental powder supplied by the kibbutz in one hand and, if one could afford it, a second towel slung over arm or shoulder.

The kibbutz showers were the daily scene of an important social rite, as much as a center of hygiene. Between five and six in the evening the entire population of the kibbutz changed through this rite from one of workers to one of intellectuals. This transformation reminded me of Machiavelli's letter to Francesco Vettori, which we had to learn by heart at school: "As the evening comes . . . on the threshold of my house I divest myself of my daytime wear, full of mud and dirt, and don royal, ceremonial robes." Here a similar but reverse ceremonial process was taking place: we shed our working clothes, "full of mud and dirt," and stood in Adamic dress under the steaming water, the women on one side of the wooden partition, the men on the other. The ambience was certainly not ideal for nurturing what Machiavelli called "that food which is only mine," namely one's philosophical and political writings. Yet it helped to strengthen the psychological tissue of an egalitarian society, which aspired to create a new man in an old land.

Naked as worms, but socialized, looking forward to an evening and a night free from the biblical curse of manual toil, we appreciated the shower as a powerful means of reinforcing the links of our proletarian brotherhood. Refreshed by water that everyone knew was precious, often warmed by ideological discussion, we lingered on the humid, slippery benches to talk politics while washing our feet; we exchanged quips and darting comments through the steam that blurred the contours of our bodies; and we dried away the dribbles of water on our skin, together with the tears that sometimes overflowed unseen from the depths of our hearts.

In this daily rite the hedonistic pleasure of ancient Greeks and Romans mingled with a modern desire to overcome our Freudian complexes. In the process there was also an attempt to align the different components of the elitist and egalitarian society of the kibbutz: the strong with the weak, the introvert with the extrovert, the ambitious with the humble. There was an implicit offer of familiarity that ceased at the threshold of the showers as one left, but that made it possible, inside them, to initiate difficult conversations, admit doubts, overcome timidity, feel defenseless without shame. From the showers one emerged clean in body and renewed in spirit, feeling the impalpable flux of ideas and hopes that later, in the dining room and the "House of Culture" (the room where books and current newspapers were available), turned into endless intellectual debates, ideological quarrels, military planning, and political conspiracies. It was in that complex, watery atmosphere that I sensed the possibility of becoming freer by giving up a part of my own freedom.

Looking today at photographs of forty or fifty years ago, which every kibbutz keeps in its archives, one wonders how these collective villages were able to undergo such radical changes in such a short time. Families today live in small apartments with one or two rooms for the children, well-furnished, often air-conditioned, with private showers and kitchenettes, full of more or less useful objects and gadgets produced locally or imported. The communal dining halls are often more elegant than those of a first-class hotel. The kitchens, totally automated and deodorized, equipped with the most modern labor-saving devices, are still visible from the dining room. But bars, little taverns, reading and music rooms, game clubs, and swimming pools shaded by trees and beautified by flowers are today an integral part of the normal standard of life of a collective village.

Nobody goes anymore to a common shower or latrine. Along the cement paths winding coquettishly through the mown grass, far from the workshops area and the smell of chicken runs and cow sheds, people walk or ride bicycles with the elegance and ease of an elite that has fully accepted its new status as a rich and secure class. Whether the kibbutz members are happier today than in the past I cannot say. Happiness is a state of the soul, not a function of the environment. Something has certainly been lost with the disappearance not of a certain austerity but of the tension created by the daily contrast between collective labor and individual freedom, conformism and rebellion. Machiavelli would not have been able or willing to live in a kibbutz, but he would have had no difficulty in understanding the political role of these free communities nor in identifying them as the most original, populist aristocracy of the modern world—an aristocracy without princes, still solid and active today in spite of incipient signs of corruption, social hardening, and ideological sclerosis. When I knew it, almost half a century ago, the kibbutz was still an enthusiastic experiment threatened by external dangers but consolidated inside by the austerity and moral standards of its members.

The physical and economic hardship of those days—work was barely sufficient to cover the subsistence needs of a community constantly increased by the arrival of new immigrants —was a spur to the vitality of the kibbutz. One of the strangest and liveliest discussions at which I happened to be present, for instance, was on the moral, philosophical, economic, and biological right of the community to fix the number of children a couple could have. This right was never conceded by the "comrades" to the general assembly, but the debate showed both the difficult, material conditions at the time and the honesty and intellectual rigor with which they were faced.

It seems to me that, denuded of its ideological elements and extemporary necessities, the principal strength of the kibbutz in that difficult period (and probably still today) was its capacity to bring together, behind an image of equality, people of profoundly varied capacities and cultures. The strongest personalities could lord it over the others without appearing to do so or bearing external signs of power; the weaker ones could accept the security offered by the group without feeling humiliated and without having to carry responsibilities for which they were unfit. But for people like myself, who stood in the middle because of their cultural mediocrity and ideological indifference, the collective life of the kibbutz had the attraction of a convent and the repulsion of a discipline deprived of style and spiritual tension. It seems to me, however, that the main reason why so many young people born and reared in the collective villages of Israel today leave them at the end of their military service is that biological links within a self-conceived elitist community are not sufficient to fill the need for new spiritual challenges or compensate for the moral and psychological void of a righteous conformism that has turned into an aim in itself. Thus, many young people who discover that they are not weak enough to identify with the group, nor strong enough to emerge within its façade of false equality, opt for the life of the town. The appeal of privacy and the lure of individual success often seems more attractive to them than the monotony of a disguised upper-class existence in which they have to share the results of their work without obtaining visible rewards for their ambitions.

Nobody I knew at Givat Brenner was more conscious of this tension to come, between idealism and reality, between image and content, between aspirations and daily realities, than Enzo Sereni. Sereni was born to one of the oldest Italian-Jewish families. On the Via Appia one can still see the remains of an ancient shop belonging to a certain Serenus. Possibly one of Sereni's ancestors, he may have sold wine and food to the Roman legionnaires on their way to Judea to put an end to Jewish independence in 67 A.D.

Sereni had come to Palestine at the end of the twenties with his wife, who also belonged to an old Roman-Jewish family, impelled by the same spirit of revolt against Fascism that had made his brother one of the historical leaders of Italian communism.

In Sereni a strong vein of religious passion also colored his philosophical rationalism. Alfonso Pacifici, one of the leaders of Italian Zionism and later an exponent of the strictest religious anti-Zionist orthodoxy in Israel, once told me that Sereni in his youth had gone through a profound religious crisis. He had confessed to Pacifici that he had been on the point of converting to Christianity because of the fascination monastic life exercised on him and his need for inner search. Anti-Fascism and the austerity of socialist Zionism had thus combined to attract him to the pioneering life of the kibbutz. There his political acumen, his socialist faith, and his witty realism made him not only the uncontested leader of the small group of Italian Jewish immigrants to Palestine but also one of the country's emerging labor leaders.

Small, plump, nearsighted, gifted with a sparkling intelligence and a monumental culture, Sereni did not at first sight convey the impression of being a political man. He looked rather like a schoolteacher, slightly inhibited in his movements and permanently uncomfortable in his clothes. He reminded me of the portrait of Silvio Pellico, the Risorgimento patriot imprisoned by the Austrians, whose diary we used to read aloud at school with much pathos and emotion. But as soon as Sereni opened his mouth, in public or in private, this romantic image disappeared, chased away by the immediate psychological tension he always created in his interlocutor. More than by the logic of his thesis, more than by his humanistic culture, one was fascinated by his humanism and his messianic vision of Zionist socialism. Compressed like a coil within a Greco-Christian mold, his Judaism possessed the passion, the rigor—but also the humor—of the neophyte. He himself drew, like Anteus from the earth, renewed strength from the daily contact with the awesome problems of constructing the new Hebrew society in Palestine.

Numerous books and articles have been written about Enzo Sereni. I feel disinclined to read them because of the remorse and sadness I still feel, after so many years, at having developed with him only relations tainted by antagonism. A more serious and deeper contact with this extraordinary person would certainly have enriched me and perhaps changed the course of my life. In part, however, my reluctance to know more about him is due to my desire not to spoil the image—certainly excessively personal—that I have constructed of him and that is so different from the one described in these publications. It is the image of a prism, exposed to the ever-changing realities of a very complex life and reflecting onto others the disconcerting light of an ambiguous personality. This is, as I said, a very personal and probably wrong impression, which I have carried with me since the only occasion I had to talk with him at length, without quarreling or having to listen in enraged silence (because of feelings of inferiority he always induced in me) to his scintillating ideological harangues and his, to me, irritating ideas.

I had recently arrived at Givat Brenner. During the New Year holiday a fit of nostalgia induced me to look for a place where I could attend a service as we did in Italy. I found myself sitting next to Sereni one late afternoon near a wooden shack, which served as kitchen and synagogue for the elderly parents of kibbutz members. They were a small group of decrepit people who, unlike their children, continued to follow the "superstitions" of Judaism and for this reason had permission to cook in a separate kitchen according to biblical dietary rules.

It was sunset, a time that, especially in those circumstances, invited melancholy reflections. We were waiting for the arrival of a few more Jews to make up a minyan for the recital of the evening prayers. Sitting on a wobbly bench outside the shack, with an old Jewish *babushka* wrapped in her Eastern European clothes peering suspiciously at our uncovered heads, we were talking in our native language, trying not to disturb a few old men reciting psalms nearby. All around us, the kibbutz activity, barely reduced because of the holiday, gave us a feeling of temporary exclusion.

Sad and thoughtful, not in his usual optimistic mood, Sereni was quietly thinking aloud about the incumbent tragedy of European Jewry. He had been on a mission to Germany, and only his Italian passport had saved him from trouble. Anticipating the disaster that was about to overtake our people, he felt the immense responsibility that we, the Jews of Palestine, bore for the rest of the nation. He was asking me, or rather he was asking himself in a monologue that I dared not interrupt, in what way we might associate ourselves with the fate of millions of humans trapped by the Nazis in Europe only because they were Jews. It was true that they had not believed in the Zionist message; it was true that they were now paying the atrocious price of their social choices and lack of decision. But we, wiser, cleverer, or just more fortunate, were, in our turn, in danger of becoming the parasites of our national tragedy by remaining spectators of their destruction. What could we tell our sons in the future? That because we were protected by the British we had been able to survive in order to record what European anti-Semitism had done to the Jews? In that case there was a good chance of our young people regarding Hitler and Mussolini just as historical figures detached from reality like Genghis Khan. They might think that our fate was that of just another people, descendants of a race whose destiny was changed by the simple fact that their parents had emigrated to Asia, just as English criminals were deported to Australia, or like the Spanish conquistadores who had gone to America. If we became unable to teach them the meaning of Judaism, they would never really know why their parents were called Zionists.

The working hypothesis of many Zionists was no different from that of the assimilationists, who thought that there was an excess of Jews in the world and an excess of tradition in Judaism. But if the body of the nation was going to be physically destroyed in Europe and if the ancient soul was to become dried up by the passions of the non-Jewish ideologies, what would remain of the fragile Jewish civilization that we wanted to revive? The secularism of socialist Zionism made him fear the creation of ghettos, of Indian-type reservations for the religious Jews in a Hebrew Palestine, in which people would be the object of ethnological curiosity rather than the guardians of one of the most ancient national identities.

In those days Sereni was engaged in an effort of persuasion with the new immigrants from Italy, some of whom wanted to leave Givat Brenner, convinced that life in a socialist kibbutz was a new form of assimilation—a society of Jews who had intentionally ceased to be Jewish. For these newcomers, who were assimilated Jews like me, and mostly former members of the GUF (Fascist university youth), the racial laws proclaimed by Mussolini had brought a sudden need to emigrate and an incentive to search, in Palestine, for the ancient roots practically destroyed by the emancipation for most of the Italian Israelites. They had not yet decided to move to a religious kibbutz, as many of them later did, but Sereni could feel, through the often confused expression of their doubts, that the national-Marxist alternative they offered the socialist movement, and to which he had devoted all his strength and intelligence, could not meet their spiritual needs. He was not interested in gaining more "souls" for his party, being satisfied that these Italian Jews had taken, through their immigration to the ancestral land, the first essential step on the road to "Zionist" truth. What seemed important to him was to convince himself that the ideological road he had chosen was not an erroneous one, that it would not lead some time in the future to a dead end through the creation of a new Jewish Golah (Diaspora) in the Land of Israel.

On the eve of that religious festival, near that decrepit synagogue which, as I said, also served as kitchen and dining room for a miserable bunch of human relics escaped from the moribund ghettos of Eastern Europe and whose sole apparent link with the kibbutz was their biological relationship with some of its members, Sereni argued with himself about the problems that would one day obsess the Zionist state, namely whether the state of the Jews would be able to remain a Jewish state without losing the pluralism that constituted its strength. He was asking himself whether the price of national rebirth might not be paid with the destruction of a traditional collective consciousness, which we would one day increasingly need so that the Land of Israel did not become a land of refuge instead of the promised socialist land. This was, I believe, the first time I heard anyone formulate the idea that the Zionists represented for Judaism what the barbarians had represented for Roman civilization: an instrument of physical regeneration through a process of moral barbarization; a forced passage into normality in order to recover the strength necessary to defend one's uniqueness in a world bent on destroying that embarrassing uniqueness. He hoped, though he did not seem very convinced, that this role could be undertaken by Zionist socialism. He conceived of it like the roots of an old tree from which new shoots of hope, of social and moral progress, would spring up, and not only for the Jews. Jewish socialism, unlike Soviet Marxism and Fascist nationalism, in which Sereni could nevertheless see certain similarities with Zionism, might one day develop the energy of both. It could become, in his view, what Mazzini's version of the Italian Risorgimento had failed to be: a national faith conceived on the basis of man's duties, not of rights; a new approach to old problems; the transformation of the weakness of an ancient race into a new, civilizing force.

The workshop in which this new moral and collective movement should be forged could only be, for him, the kibbutz. But it would not be easy to make the Jewish refugees from Europe, brought to Palestine less by idealism than by the need to escape anti-Semitism, understand that the kibbutz was a kind of new, secular monastery through which the old-new Israel could face the challenges of destruction and rebirth. It would take time, and time was running dramatically short.

I had the impression that afternoon of listening to the abbot of a not-yet-founded monastery, the inspirer of a new monastic order who would have liked to transform Givat Brenner into a Jewish Monte Cassino or a Hebrew Abbey of Cluny. I never had another opportunity to check whether this impression was correct or not. Absorbed as we both became, he in the vortex of political action, I in my romantic dreams, we only had brief and unpleasant occasions to meet afterward. From these encounters I got the impression, probably wrong, that Sereni had developed unfair, preconceived ideas about me. I felt that he despised me for my refusal to remain in the kibbutz and for my emotional attachment to a bourgeois world from which I was still unable to free myself. Among the new Italian immigrants at Givat Brenner, I must have seemed to him the least prepared and the most immature. My ignorance never ceased to astound him. When seated on the grass in front of the "House of Culture," he used to lecture us on socialism, speaking about Labriola and Lasalle, Marx and

Rosa Luxemburg, Engels and Lenin; he could see from the expression on my face how strange and meaningless these names were to me.

He used to explain on those occasions the evolution of the labor movement in Palestine, the moral and political problems created by our coexistence with the Arabs, and—a topic I remember more clearly than the others—the illegitimacy of commercial competition. "We cannot have peace in the world," he argued, "if even we socialists pray for frosts to destroy the orange crops of Spain in order to survive in Palestine." He would then throw himself into complicated explanations on the questions of worker exploitation; of *plus valorem;* on the capitalists who had taken the place of the feudal lords; on the Arab landowners who, without being bourgeois, were assuming in Palestine the historical and political role of the European bourgeoisie; on the British who were liberals at home and imperialists abroad; on the Fascists who, with their secret agents, were trying to persuade the Arabs to support their late colonial expansionism.

I listened to him, often without understanding a word of what he said. The other Italians competed among themselves with questions and comments to prove they knew the texts on which Sereni was speaking and could follow him in his historical and dialectical intellectual games. I kept apart, silent, totally lost and confused, filled with the rancor of the ignorant who would like to discuss something he does not know. At the time I was unaware of the fact that no intellectual and moral idea is more useless than the one offered by others to free one from his doubts. In a confused way I perceived that there was something false, uncertain, unclear in all this verbiage about absolute social values, brotherhood of workers, superstructures, conscious and unconscious complexes, historical materialism, and national myth. It was enough to see how Jews spoke to and looked at the few Arabs who came to the kibbutz to understand that human relations could not be easily categorized. But I could find neither the words nor the ideas to refute them. To my Italian kibbutz comrades, as probably to Sereni, I must have appeared a superficial, aimless youth, reared in an atmosphere politically and socially perverted, who needed to have his "dog's legs straightened," as the Italians say, and his character reinforced by ideological discipline and hard physical work, two things from which, as everyone knew, I intended to escape. In sum, I was, or at least I had the impression of being, a lost cause, on which others in the kibbutz had neither reason nor desire to waste their time. The kibbutz was doing me a favor by letting me pay three pounds a month (a considerable sum in those days) for my food, a daily Hebrew lesson, and four hours of work in the chicken run and, later, in the vegetable garden.

The isolation caused by my violent transplantation into a society so different from that in which I had grown up became deeper day by day because of the indifference and imaginary ostracism with which I felt I was surrounded. When I returned at dusk to my tent, so low that it looked like a dog's kennel (and indeed, I did once find a large bone at the entrance), I was torn by opposing sentiments. I wanted at the same time to adapt myself and to run away from the new society in which I was living. I suffered atrociously because of my ignorance, which made me look childish in front of the others, while possessing an instinctive, animal perception that the perfection of the ideological systems to which I was asked to adhere contained invisible flaws. The less I was able to analyze Sereni's arguments, the more indigestible they were made by these contradictions. I had the constant impression of taking part in a play of the absurd from which I tried to escape, mocking everything I did not understand. The result was a split in my psyche soon manifested by a stutter, which I tried to overcome by going into the fields to declaim Italian poems by Carducci at the top of my voice, or, after I joined the British army, by shouting army commands out loud.

The state of anguish to which this stammering was linked has not yet disappeared. I often find myself speaking aloud to myself or underlining my thoughts with vulgar barracks oaths that I murmur under my breath, hoping nobody will overhear. A difficulty in expressing myself also overtakes me when I have to speak in public, especially in Hebrew. Perfectly normal, my psychologist friends keep telling me. Yet I cannot conceal the fact that the need to repair a crack in my young personality has driven me, and still drives me, to try to find compensation in action for my spiritual and cultural needs. In this prolonged debate with myself, the lure of activism has certainly interfered with an orderly crystallization of habits and a more meaningful accumulation of experience. As a result, I have found myself for years fighting against another, imaginary self, who refuses to accept the realities of life and age and succumbs to the fascination of adventure and change. The dichotomy between my two selves has often made me appear to others and to myself as a bluffer, a "seller of smoke" as we say in Italian, even when time and events have proved me right.

Today I know that my mistake has been to try to force events prematurely, to try to realize projects for which I was not morally prepared or intellectually and culturally ready, though I do not regret that, having just one man's span of life to live, I have tasted many lives. But I also know that this impatience with timetables and realities, this need to overdo things, this passion for change and adventure, is not peculiar to me. It is characteristic of the whole Zionist movement and of the State of Israel, in which, pressed by necessity and inexperience, people have wanted to achieve too much too fast and without being prepared or willing to pay the price that time imposes for what is done without it.

Perhaps there was no other alternative for the Jews of Palestine who survived the Holocaust. The Jewish population, writer S.Y. Agnon makes one of his heroes say, "has suffered so much that it has lost the patience to wait for the Messiah." The result, according to Agnon, has been that in the attempt to build up its own messianic era, the people of Israel have postponed the arrival of the Messiah. This poetic interpretation seems to me an appropriate description of the socialist Zionist epic I witnessed and which is in a way reflected in my own experience. The price we all seem to be paying today in Israel is that of an unsuccessful attempt to catch the Messiah by force. Yet without this arrogant effort, our drama would have turned into banality, a situation in which Jews have never particularly liked to be.

After almost a hundred years, Zionism, a movement supposedly meant to "normalize" the Jew, continues to struggle between exile and the promised land, between the Holocaust and Hitler, between the vulgar and the sublime, without finding a middle path—the path that Maimonides called "golden" and that a famous Hasidic rabbi, the Rabbi of Kotch, "reserved for horses." The break between the real and the fantastic, the possible and the impossible, the serious and the fake, which caused me such great pain in conditioning my character, seems to me today to be part of a larger situation, a reflection of an inescapable condition, a manner no less genuine than others of ultimately sharing the singular fate of the people to whom I belong.

Now that passions and ambitions have been put to rest by age, success, and disappointments, I feel at ease with the fact of having felt, probably earlier than others, in exile in the motherland to which I had chosen to return. I am no longer alone in realizing that the State of Israel—a natural but imperfect incarnation of a splendid ideal—has transformed itself into one of the many Jewish Diasporas, morally distant from, even if physically closer to, the historical and cultural cradle of Jewish civilization. Partly because my familiarity with Italian fascism has immunized me against the more vulgar and grotesque manifestations of Israeli nationalism (which, like the

Italian ones, I know to be the transitory and infantile maladies of an ancient people), I am able today to taste the sweetness that a hard, exciting, contradictory experience offers to people like me: the opportunity to make of the art of living—for lack of other talents—a living *commedia del l'arte*.

6

Smell and Fear

For a long time my relations with other Italian Jewish immigrants to Palestine were determined by my stomach. Even today, when I think back to this period of my existence as a young immigrant, I can clearly recall the smell of the kitchens in the houses that hosted me, the boredom of the conversation and of the prayers that I had to bear before and after meals in order to satisfy my appetite, the irritation that I had difficulty in concealing from those hosts who did not realize rapidly enough the reason for my visit. Two kitchens, however, never attracted me: that of the various kibbutzim in which I happened to stay and that of Mrs. Levi in Tel Aviv—but this was for completely different reasons.

The kibbutz kitchens at that time dished out plates of glued-together spaghetti, probably invented by admirers of the Borgias. They sweetened their poisonous food with vanilla-scented sauce, which I always thought was the product of a sublimation of Jewish suicidal complexes. Meat, in that first year of the war, was rare. Potatoes, which Palestine had just learned to grow, were scarce. However, semolina, olives, and tomatoes were plentiful. Together with slices of black bread spread with margarine and jam, they helped to stay the pangs but left the mouth dry and the stomach empty.

Mrs. Levi's kitchen, on the contrary, offered dishes that had nothing in common with those of the kibbutz. But they were so expensive that it was impossible for me to enjoy them. I still feel melancholic when I remember the hours of unsatisfied hunger I spent in her ground-floor apartment on Karl Netter Street, a street in the heart of Tel Aviv, short and silent even today, and which acted in those years as a welcome harbor for many Jews who had escaped from Italy.

Mrs. Levi was a widow. In 1939 when I first met her, she could not have been very old because one of her sons was still at school. To me, however, she looked decrepit: small, slim, with an angular face, she possessed a shrill, metallic voice that struck fear in my heart. Always dressed in black, tidy, and with a carefully made-up chignon on her head, she seemed to me like the incarnation of a lady director of a reform school. She never offered me anything to eat but showered me with compliments. She had known my mother in her best years, and she used to describe to me her beauty, her grace, and above all her wealth, which had all but vanished. Mrs. Levi, who knew personally almost every Italian Jew in Palestine and a considerable number of those who had stayed in Italy, seemed curiously ignorant of the economic situation of my family. She kept addressing me as though I were an affluent immigrant, impressing upon me, in her own way, my duty not to forget my past. She showed great interest in my agricultural studies, about which she spoke with the respect due to an already famous researcher. In her dining room there was a sofa under a bay window, on which she ceremoniously used to invite me to sit down and accept a lemonade or a small cup of coffee. On these occasions she entertained me with mannered conversation about how painful and unusual it was for her to keep a pension. But she carried on with a dignity that did not allow concessions, economizing on every possible expense but maintaining a culinary standard that on the only two occasions I scraped up enough money to appreciate it, seemed to me miraculous when compared with that of the restaurants I normally frequented. Among my acquaintances she was the only one to assure me that I would certainly reach the top of my military career when I told her of my intention to join the army. She proved wrong, as in most of her other judgments concerning me and my family, but that prognosis at the time gave me tremendous pleasure.

Mrs. Levi had two children. The younger one became in time a respected member of the kibbutz movement and later a teacher of social sciences. The older one, a graduate in agriculture, possessed great talents as a musicologist and a journalist but was destined to suffer increasingly from mental troubles, which finally ruined his splendid brain. At the time his occasionally queer behavior had already marked him as an eccentric among the Italian Zionists.

Many stories circulated on his account. In June 1940, when the British arrested as enemy aliens, for short or long periods, any holder of an Italian passport, this Levi found himself deposited by the British police in the central prison of Jaffa. The place was far from pleasant, but Mr. Levi was shocked mainly by the fact that some of his best friends were missing. He gave the British a detailed list of the people with whom he wanted to share his bedroom, and they were only too pleased to oblige. No wonder that some of these friends remained cool toward him for a long time to come.

Years earlier Mr. Levi had also been imprisoned in the Turin jail on suspicion of being an active anti-Fascist. On that occasion he created some notoriety because of his beard. He had started by refusing the services of the prison barber who had come to shave him on the Sabbath, a day on which, he rightly claimed, Jews do not shave. This happened in September, a month in which the second visit of the barber brought no result, because Mr. Levi, calendar in hand, proved to him that it was not permitted for a Jew to shave on the two days of the New Year, which fell just then. The director of the jail himself, so the story went, summoned Mr. Levi to his office in order to reach an agreed date when, according to the Gregorian calendar, there were no religious Jewish obstacles to the barber's working. Mr. Levi gracefully chose one day, but when the appointed time arrived, again refused to be shaved. "A Jew," he argued with reason and conviction, "is never allowed to shave."

At the agricultural school of Mikveh Yisrael, where I started to study, Mr. Levi acted as instructor, political commissar, educator, and confessor to a group of religious Italian boys brought to Palestine by the Youth Aliyah, the youth section of the Jewish Agency. With these youngsters, we students who had enrolled privately in the school and paid full fees for our studies and keep, had few contacts. They lived in huge dormitories located over the kitchen. We lived four to a room on top of the granaries and the oil press of the school farm in the French colonial style buildings constructed at the end of the last century. They followed a strict religious discipline; we enjoyed the free life of unbelievers. They were all destined to join a kibbutz; we were free to dream of any future activity or career we might choose. We met in classrooms where we shared some of the lessons, in the fields where we worked and, from time to time, on Friday evenings when I used to join them in the school synagogue. I liked the cozy atmosphere of that old building, also in French colonial style, with its red and blue painted ceiling, its stained-glass windows and the marble slabs in the wall commemorating benefactors and fallen students.

But in general the two groups kept apart, also because the quarters of the "private" students were divided according to secular party affiliations. I had chosen to sleep in the quarters

of the General Zionist party because it was the political movement that required the least ideological involvement. The
immediate result of my political choice turned out to be the
stealing of my wallet with many personal mementos I had
brought from home. It was quite a shock, for which the lack
of obligation to attend long, boring political meetings never
fully compensated. The long-term result of this choice was that
I became as separate from the most active elements in the
school as—for reasons of college snobbery—from the Italian
boys belonging to the religious movement. With these estranged schoolfellows one of my only links was our common
fight against bugs, about which we exchanged daily information. We were never completely victorious in spite of the huge
quantities of petrol we sprinkled over our straw mattresses and
the empty bully-beef tins full of kerosene in which we put the
legs of our beds.

Mr. Levi was conscious and resentful of this "class" distinction. Every time we passed each other on the school grounds,
he made pointed remarks about my feudal attitude and that of
my roommates. Sometimes he would sit with me under the
trees that surrounded the grave of the school's founder, Karl
Netter, the father of Jewish agriculture in Palestine. The cenotaph dedicated to him and two little boys who had died,
apparently of typhoid, in the 1880s stood in the middle of
cascades of bougainvillea at the heart of a eucalyptus grove.
The sandy path leading to it seemed to go to the end of the
world: here, silence was broken only by the buzzing of insects,
by the whirring of birds' wings, by the faraway braying of
unseen donkeys, by the rustling of the leaves in a subdued
symphony of nature's orchestra. We used to sit on the base of
the cenotaph and talk quietly with long, silent pauses. I do not
remember what we talked about, and I do not think his
arguments impressed me particularly. But thinking back to
those meetings, so different from those I had later with Pavese,
the great Piedmontese writer, sitting on the slopes of the hills

of Turin, I cannot help being struck by how similar they were, too. I was introduced to Pavese by Professor Monti, an outstanding figure of the Italian resistance movement, soon after my demobilization from the British army. As with Mr. Levi in Palestine, I went on talking for hours in Italy with Pavese about war and God, women and religion, democracy and anti-Fascism, the false hopes the war had raised, and the anguish of people like us, who witnessed the passing of history without being able to take part in the realities borne out in our dreams.

In both cases—with Levi and Pavese—I was struck by the frustrations of two brilliant minds, so different from each other but equally unable to express their talents in the ways they would have liked. Pavese committed suicide; Levi ended up in a psychiatric hospital, where the brightness of his mind slowly dimmed into paranoia. Pavese reacted against the banality of life with the sadness of his writing; Levi brought the impatience of his mind into collision with the inertia of daily life and sought notoriety with clownish actions and eccentricities.

One of the stories, probably apocryphal, that was told about him, concerned his collaboration with a cabalist determined to hasten the coming of the Messiah. This rabbi had conceived a plan to sacrifice an animal on a certain day and in a particular spot in the Holy Land. According to his cabalistic calculations, the sacrifice should take place at dawn and the blood of the animal should be sprinkled on the top of a deserted hill located in the middle of an Arab zone where it would not be safe for Jews to go. The solution was found with the help of a small airplane and the substitution of a strong cock for the sacrificial camel. Mr. Levi was charged to perform the ritual slaughter, while the rabbi coordinated time and space according to his mystical signs. Mr. Levi, however, delayed the arrival of the Messiah by his inability to overcome the reaction of the cock, which refused to keep quiet in the small hired plane, insensitive to the exhortations of the rabbi who, in despair, kept comparing his map with the flight plan of the impassive British pilot. As I said, the story was probably apocryphal, but Mr. Levi's extravagances turned into legends with the passing of time. I witnessed only one of his eccentricities.

On a cold winter's day I went to pay him a visit in the small hut that served as home and workshop for making *grissini*. The hut stood in the outskirts of the town of Ramat Gan, now part of greater Tel Aviv but then separated from the city by a few kilometers of open ground. The idea of introducing this delicate type of Piedmontese bread into the pioneering Jewish society of the time and in the midst of war rationing came from Levi's wife. With her already large family, she was struggling hard to make ends meet by all sorts of activities, among which her handmade bricks were not the most successful. The production of *grissini* was also imperiled at the outset by the smell of petrol acquired in the process of baking them in an improperly functioning oven. The day I went to visit them, the two Levis were about to leave for Tel Aviv, using their children's pram as a means of transport. Mr. Levi, on the basis of his mathematical calculations, had persuaded his wife they could both reach the city with less fatigue if they took turns sitting in the pram and pushing the other along. I saw them leaving on this commercial journey, he with his black beard floating in the wind, his sandaled feet protruding from the pram and the packets of *grissini* in his lap; she, with dignity and energy, pushing the vehicle almost collapsing under the weight, followed by the stupefied eyes of the passersby.

In Ramat Gan there lived a group of Italian Jews whose behavior was the very opposite of the Levis. With few exceptions they had all been members of the Fascist party, out of inertia rather than conviction. This was not their main characteristic. What distinguished them within the Jewish society of the time was the care with which they preserved, in a pioneering socialist country, the life-style of provincial Italian bourgeoisie.

Most had immigrated to Palestine with means, and those who lacked them quickly enriched themselves in the burgeoning war economy and later in the rapid development of a society to which they contributed with hard work. Their numerous sons and daughters participated in the subsequent military conflicts with the Arabs. In their homes, full of solid furniture, bibelots, miniatures, lace runners, and fine table-cloths, there prevailed the same ordered and cautious atmosphere one would find in Venice or Florence: a patriotic mood, devoid of ideology but full of suspicious respect for the establishment. Industrious but mean, dignified but inelegant, they were proud of their newly acquired status of anti-Fascists but strongly attached to the class prejudices that had contributed to the rise in Italy of a regime against which they had never fought. They were boring and banal people, entrenched behind religious rites, concealing a profound ignorance of Judaism; they had transformed the Italian synagogue service into a kind of clannish bond and sign of social distinction. Moderate in every way, from the love of food to political passions, they were happy to have found in Zionism the solution to the problem of their own physical survival and of their own spiritual anemia. Listening to their chatter at the kiddush parties after the conclusion of the Sabbath service in one of their beautiful homes, I wondered how they managed to share in a double, contrasting process of assimilation: that of Italian nationalism, which had betrayed them, and that of the new society of Palestine, which was now called upon to absorb the remnants of a moribund Jewry together with its folklore and liturgy. The result was a switch from one nationalism to another with the same prejudices—the romantic patriotism and the social conformism that they had brought from Italy.

In this minuscule, pretentious, prudent Ramat Gan society I felt at ease only with a Milanese family of Greek origin. Deprived of their own children, they adopted any young person in need of permanent or temporary shelter. At their table, even when their tight budget forced them to cut back the portions, I always satisfied my hunger without shame. In that house I also learned to appreciate, not just understand, the meaning of the blessing for what I had received; I spent here the least sad vacations from school and army. Here I gave free vent, without fear of being laughed at, to my dreams, my hopes, my pains, always finding a comfortable bed, a hot shower, and a clean towel. Only those who have known the pangs of hunger and social uprooting, the shame of a dirty shirt in the middle of well-dressed people, the sleepless rest on a bed without mattress or sheets, the shivers of an icy shower in winter and the thirst of a summer without shade can appreciate a hospitality offered without reservation, understand the longevity of resentment, unjust in my case, borne from help not received because I was too proud and too shy to ask for it.

The house of this Italian-Greek family was built on a small hill, now completely devoured by city blocks, on which a mulberry tree proudly stood for many years. Sitting under its branches in the heat of a summer Sabbath, I would often see a strange person crossing the street below me to enter a wooden hut used as a synagogue. He was a young man in his twenties, tall and suntanned. He wore his hair shoulder length and a long, dirty, white shirt outside his trousers, torn at the hem. He was called the "Messiah" because of his blue, watery eyes looking into infinity and a queer behavior that made him seem like a harmless lunatic. One day, in the middle of the war, he disappeared. Some people said he had been arrested by the British, who had discovered him to be a dangerous terrorist. Others said that he had been run over by a car; others that he had been confined to a mental hospital. In any case, as long as he roamed around in the Ramat Gan streets he attracted me with a strange, inexplicable force.

He was certainly mad. But he shared, or rather epitomized, a type of madness that in various forms circulated during those years like a collective narcotic in the veins of most of the Jews of Palestine. Like them, the "Messiah" seemed touched by a kind of apocalyptic mania. The war that was tearing the world apart was that of Gog and Magog. The Jewish tragedy, of which all the horrors were not yet known, looked like a divine punishment for the assimilation of the Jews to the political and social idolatry of Europe. The White Paper with which the British shut the doors on Jewish immigration and tried to put an end to the hopes of the Zionist movement was a devilish plan; it would eventually be thwarted but at the same time should also be taken as a heavenly warning to the Jews not to misbehave. To the "Messiah," as to many orthodox Jews, misconduct meant the substitution of secular ideology for the Covenant with God, the replacement by human political pride of confidence in Divine Providence. Whatever happened, he preached, the Land of Israel would always remain the land from which God "never turned away His eyes." The faithful Jews, those who—in his words—formed "the personal body-guard of the King of the Universe, Blessed be His Name," would overcome all tests and eventually witness the great portents to come.

England was the ultimate Rome, the "unclean beast" des-tined to die. The Arabs were the enemy brother. Jews must struggle with them not out of hatred but with understanding of the mysterious fate, decided upon in heaven and linking forever the descendants of Isaac and Ishmael, of Jacob and Esau. In every generation, Jews and Arabs would battle for a common heritage, which made difficult, if not impossible, their coexistence in the same territory.

Seated on a shaky bench with peeling paint, his back against the tar-papered wall of the synagogue hut, the "Messiah" threw himself into dissertations of metapolitics, always starting from a particular problem of Talmudic casuistry—for in-stance, whether it was permitted to tie a knot on the Sabbath using the fingers of both hands. From this type of question, for me totally unreal, the "Messiah" went on to discuss—with arguments supported sometimes by the simple displacement of a syllable in a word from the Bible—the duties of man toward animals or the responsibility of the citizen toward the state. I had the impression of standing in front of a political conspirator disguised as a dervish or a prophet's apprentice. His face, surrounded by a thick black beard, turned livid and tense. As he developed his ideas, it looked as though all his blood and the energy of his muscles concentrated on an invisible point of his interior passion. His long-lashed eyelids closed to a slit. From his pupils a sharp, manic gleam darted out, more expressive and frightening than any words. It was the look of a tortured, possessed man, detached from the world and at the same time fully conscious of its existence and totally involved in its reality. A world in which the substance of the body and the substance of the soul—so the "Messiah" explained—were mysteriously joined at their base and their apex with the substance of worlds different from but no less consistent than ours. Man was the crossing point of these invisible junctions that determined the existence of everything in creation. Man could exist only because the Divine has in a way withdrawn into Himself and "left open" a space for His creatures. Only many years later I realized that the "Messiah" was drawing his theories from the Kabbalah. But what I was witnessing then was the running of trickles of ancient, esoteric Jewish thought over the seeds of political messianism, which in time would grow and cover an increased portion of the ground of secular socialist Zionism.

In those first years of war there were no Jewish political successes that would justify the slightest optimism. Everything in Europe and in Palestine seemed to be militating against the establishment of a Jewish national home. It was only natural that in a politicized society like the Yishuv, the Jewish community of Palestine, there began to circulate ideas of national religious mysticism which, forty years later, would openly challenge the legitimacy of secular Zionism.

To this possibility, of course, I never gave a thought. Nor did I understand the meaning of certain news items appearing in the papers and relating to the activities of "fanatical Jews." They were ready, the papers said, to collaborate with the Nazis in order to destroy the British mandatory power, because it had cynically shut the doors of Palestine in the face of desperate Jewish refugees fleeing from Europe. I did not understand why "religious madmen" were joining with "secular bandits" —as the papers said—to reject the authority of the Zionist national institutions and throw themselves into "insane and irresponsible" terrorism against the British government and the Arabs. But in fact I also cared very little about it. So that when I read in 1942 (I had already been in the army for a year) that a certain Abraham Stern, a student of the Hebrew University of Jerusalem, had been killed by the British after having carried out many acts of banditry, I paid no attention to this news. I certainly did not connect it—an event that looked to me like a plain criminal act—with that Jewish resistance movement which, a few years later, would challenge and jeopardize British rule in Palestine.

The "Messiah" was probably affiliated with some of these new secret sects. When he suddenly disappeared, strange things were told about him. But neither these rumors nor the political ideas I heard him propound in the little synagogue in Ramat Gan had any impact on me. Quite the contrary. I was only struck by his theories on angels and devils which, according to him, each of us creates with his own acts and thoughts, sacred or profane.

In some of my waking dreams I witnessed, impotent and terrified, the furious dances of the beings I kept generating with my words and my fantasies, my fears and my repressed ambitions. The angels were few and looked quite feeble; the devils, however, deafened me with their shrieking cries, their accusations of cowardice, and their denunciation of my indifference to the convulsions of our burning world. During these nightmares I had the impression of levitating over masses of tears and blood; they suddenly transformed themselves into papier-mâché figures, similar to the Doré illustrations of Dante's *Inferno* that my father kept locked up in his library. Chased by devils and steered by angels, I floated like a kite on the current of my dream, diving suddenly toward the world of humans, which appeared to me like a succession of sharp edges and pointed angles. All around me people who had called for my help were turning their backs to me, moving away in orderly and disciplined ranks toward a labyrinth of faiths and opinions, of passions and interests, the access to which was closed to me. I saw clusters of people passing by without looking at me, old schoolmates dressed in Fascist Youth uniforms and new comrades from the kibbutz in British military garb. I called them by name, but they did not seem to hear; when they opened their mouths, I did not understand what they were shouting at me. I was standing alone, kept waiting without explanation. Then suddenly I felt condemned by the voice of the "Messiah," who proclaimed that observance of eighty percent of the Sabbath was equivalent to desecration of the Sabbath; or by the voice of a tutor at the agricultural school, who explained why joining the British army was an act of concealed prostitution; or by the voice of the driver who had picked me up at Tel Aviv Port, now murmuring that there was no salvation in political compromise. It was not only a question of nightmares. For someone like me, freshly arrived from a world of compromises and social conformism, the strange behavior of the "Messiah" and the less extravagant but equally rigid behavior of many other people seemed like a spasmodic effort to keep action perpetually aligned on radical ideology.

Nowhere was this more true than at the crossing of Rothschild Boulevard and Allenby Street in Tel Aviv, where I sometimes stopped to buy a glass of orange juice at a kiosk and where one could hear in the street the arguments overflowing from the open terrace of the nearby Café Atara. This was a meeting place of well-dressed gentlemen and shirtsleeved activists. They discussed the future of the world at the tops of their voices in German, Polish, English, and Hebrew, sipping tea and iced coffee. They knew everything, predicted everything, had a ready-made, authoritative, logical answer to every question. They were all prophets, issuing verdicts out of personal beliefs and individual ignorance without listening to other people's arguments.

They were not alone. Discussions of this type often kept me awake all night when, lying on the prickly straw palliasse of my bed, I could hear the aggressive statements of my roommates or those in the adjoining rooms. They went on for hours, usually without reaching agreement: every speaker had his own ideas on how to defend the Jewish people, how to contribute to the war effort, how to win over capitalists to Marxism, how to deal with the Arabs, how to convert the British to the idea of a Jewish state, how to exploit the need of the Allies for our cooperation, how to create a new type of Jew in Palestine.

I found myself immersed in the oppressive climate of these unending discussions without feeling part of them, without sharing in the tension created by continually opposed beliefs, personalities, and cultures. I knew that I should feel involved, if for no other reason than the fact that my family in Italy was by now entangled in the tragedy of the Jewish people. But these impassioned speeches contrasted not only with the memories of the padded world from which I had come but also with the boring routine of agricultural college life, regulated by the sound of the school bell. It woke us up at a quarter of six in the morning and called us to class at eight. It gathered us, famished, at noon in the dining room, dispersed us, lazily, in the afternoon to work in the fields, and invited us to silence at ten at night. That was the time when many of us started talking to ourselves.

The nights I still vividly remember were all made up of skies dotted with stars. A velvety obscurity, refreshed by breezes, caressed my face. The rustle of the eucalypti was broken by the howls of jackals; the sound of a nearby harmonica contrasted sometimes with the call of muezzins from the minarets of Jaffa.

On those nights, when melancholy memories and the pain of work-stiffened muscles joined to make sleep difficult, my mind swung undecided from the knots that could or could not be tied on the Sabbath to the horses I had ridden on the Sabbath in the green fields of Piedmont; from the bullets that we could or could not fire according to the Jewish principle of self-restraint in the case of an Arab attack to my dog Bizir, who was sent to guard my uncle's home in Trieste in the wake of my father's bankruptcy. In those nights I felt my personal dilemma—the inability to forget my past, accept without reservation the present while dreaming of an impossible future—becoming acute and confused. I searched in vain for success among contrasting loyalties, for an escape from our college routine through the uncertain fortunes of war. At the same time I craved for a corner where weeping was honorable, for plains on which to ride silvery steeds. I dreamed of being lulled by the hands of beautiful women, of facing imaginary enemies dressed in full armor, of declaiming patriotic poems in Italian without feeling ridiculous, of playing again with my dog without the constraints of a fatherland, a family, a flag. I dreamed of being asleep for the rest of my life, next to my mother dressed in her red evening gown, the big silk rose on her bosom, her neck adorned by three strings of pearls, with the rest of humanity, the good and the bad, the Jews and the goyim, the living and the dead, evaporated into the air.

During those nights when, perturbed to tears, I got up from my palliasse and sat on the parapet at the top of the granary, I chanced to meet a modest schoolmate one year older than myself. He used to read his poems to me. They were in Hebrew and Polish. They spoke of the vigor of Israel and the forests of Silesia, of the blushing of virgins, and of famished wolves, of glory and of love, of men who turned into gods and gods who turned into men. These images had nothing in common with the earth we hacked by day or the muddy brown water we channeled among the orange trees. It was a language of dreams, of hopes, of repressed fear, which had much in common with my growing sensation of having become a sparrow in a cage. On those occasions, Kantarovitch—that was his name—went on for hours, reading and pausing, reading and staring with me at the starry sky. Once I heard him sigh softly, "Why were we born Jews and not Bulgarians?" Neither he nor I had any answer to questions of this sort. I would have been unable to answer anyone who might have asked me what I thought about the British and the Arabs, the two realities ever present in our daily existence and at the same time distant and hostile, mysterious and evasive, as if they were living on another planet.

Until 1941, when I joined their army, I had no direct contact with the British. A few days after Italy entered the war in June 1940, I had been called into the office of the school director to meet with a sergeant of the British CID accompanied by an NCO of the Jewish Auxiliary Police. They had come to the school to check up on me as a citizen of an enemy country. They probably did not know that a few weeks earlier the Italian consul in Jaffa had sent me a note to inquire whether I wanted to avail myself of the facilities provided by the Fascist government for the repatriation of Italians. As a member of a family that had "deserved well of the regime," I could be included in a list of "Aryans." If the British had known about this they would certainly have interned me temporarily, since they had interned many other Italian Jews with fewer "qualifications" than mine. The British sergeant, after asking me a few questions, polite and sarcastic, allowed me to return, confused and perturbed, to my class. He must have come to the conclusion that I did not constitute a danger to the security of the empire and that as a minor I did not fall into the category of those who had to be automatically arrested.

From this short meeting I derived a fleeting impression of the British mandatory power and of its representatives. Contrary to what the Hebrew newspapers—which I had begun to read—were writing daily, I did not find anything cynical in this behavior of a quasi-colonial administration, which had closed the door of Palestine in the face of Jewish refugees. I realized, of course, that the British were reneging on their promises to the Zionist movement, but apart from the fact that I had no idea what this meant in terms of the future of the Jewish national home and of the Diaspora—since I had not been a Zionist and had no idea of the plight of the Jews in Europe—I did not feel that they behaved toward us as if we belonged to an inferior race. I had never had occasion to meet English people; I had never been an object of their maltreatment or spite. It was also difficult for me to understand how we could—as we were taught at school—fight Hitler as if the White Paper had not been published and fight the White Paper as if Hitler did not exist. Furthermore, what impressed me and attracted me toward them was the feeling of total security and superiority that somehow physically emanated from them even when patrolling the streets. Later, after I came into close daily contact with the soldiers, recruited from all strata of the population of the United Kingdom, I would quickly discover that the British were far from being demigods; they were human beings like anybody else, affected by the same fears, and the same meannesses, and conditioned by the same level of culture as Jews, Arabs, Italians, or French of similar standards of education. However, at the end of the thirties most of the British personnel serving in Palestine still belonged to a generation, now completely vanished, of colonial administrators. They acted at all levels with a great sense of duty and were conscious, sometimes overly conscious, of their imperial responsibility. The fact that they were few—at the outbreak of war the British garrison in Palestine was less than ten thousand soldiers—increased their prudence.

Whatever their feelings toward the Jews, they made a point of behaving, at least outwardly, with great correctness. I was impressed by the distinction of their carriage, by the detached courtesy with which they treated us common mortals when we happened to approach them in the street or in an office to ask for information. The courtesy and authority that were expressed in the way they dressed, spoke, smoked, and behaved became ever more evident when compared with the efforts the "natives" made to imitate them. The social aping in Palestine was then common to all levels: from the "British" moustaches sported by the Jewish and Arab policemen to the smoking of pipes, from the hats of the ladies to the affected pronunciation of those who tried to speak English "better" than the Englishmen. This native version of the language of Shakespeare had become so ridiculous that a special word was created to indicate this type of speech. It was called "Pinglish," a contraction of "Palestine English." A humorous dictionary of this language was compiled by a Jewish lord living in Palestine. What he forgot to tell his readers was that Spanish and French were also languages born out of corrupted Latin, the imperial language of the past. Indeed, when I observed these modern imperial representatives from a distance, it came naturally to me to associate them with the ancient Romans. I realized that in their manner resided part of the secret of their political and moral power, a power that in Italy the Fascist Youth had taught me to deride but that here one could breathe in the air.

Their hidden strength attracted me in a different way but just as strongly as did that of two other groups of inhabitants of Palestine: Arab peasants and orthodox Jews. Totally different, one from the other and both from the British, they seemed equally similar in their social impermeability to foreign influ-

ence, the originality of their dress, their social solidity, and
their apparent indifference to the world around them.

With the Arabs I had no contact whatsoever. I passed them
in the street on my way to the Italian Consulate in Jaffa—as
long as it existed—or to the central post office where one
could buy international postal certificates to be used for corresponding through the Red Cross with relatives in enemy
countries.

At the time Jaffa was, and to some extent has remained, a
kind of municipal rubbish dump. Dirt accumulated on the
sides of unpaved roads, dogs scavenged through the oil drums
full of refuse, horses spilled fodder out of their nosebags, and
animals stood among clouds of flies sucking their blood and
feeding on their excrement. Equally dirty and miserable were
the barefooted Arabs shuffling aimlessly in the streets, badly
lighted at night by electric wires hanging loosely from poles
and between houses built of limestone blackened by smoke.
Jaffa at the end of the thirties thrived on a confusion of trades,
vices, and rivalries concealed behind the apparent idleness of
men sitting in cafes, sucking their water pipes and watching
with bored satisfaction, through half-shut eyes, the passing of
strangers and of women hiding their doubtful beauty behind
their yashmaks.

At the end of King George Boulevard stood a tall building
with two black, cavernous entrances. It served as a brothel, first
for Arabs and later for Allied troops. When passing in front
of this building, throwing quick glances at the women in the
windows—all fat and blowsy—I shuddered with horror and
curiosity. I did not stop or show my face to them, less out of
shame than out of an obsessive impression of being followed
by thousands of eyes. When strolling through Jaffa I always
expected to be met by sudden explosions of violence like those
—we were told at school—that burst out in Hebron and
Jerusalem at the end of the twenties, in the course of which
hundreds of Jews had been massacred. Nothing ever happened

to me, not because of my luck but because the situation was absolutely calm. The British, after three years of guerrilla warfare, helped by special Jewish auxiliary units, had succeeded in defeating most of the bands engaged in what the Arabs called "revolt" and the mandatory government called "disturbances." The main troublemaker, the mufti of Jerusalem, Amin al-Husseii, was thousands of miles away, exiled by the British before joining the Germans. The departure of many German and Italian agents in the wake of the outbreak of war, and the change in political attitude of most Arab governments toward Britain as a consequence of the conflict and of the presence of powerful armies, had put an end to all kinds of violent expressions of defiance against the mandatory administration. I never had occasion to encounter any Arab hostility, and I was always surprised by the kindness with which people in Jaffa answered the queries I addressed to them in my poor English, when asking for directions in the street or how to find a shop where I could buy the sesame sweets I liked very much. Yet I could not help breathing more freely when I saw a policeman appear around a corner or another Jew wandering like myself in the streets of this miserable city, of which Tel Aviv had been for many years a Jewish residential quarter.

I drew a quite different impression from the Arabs who passed in front of the school gates or who used to come inside the grounds to offer us their produce or their services. They were peasants and bedouin and to me looked immensely grand. At night, when I was on guard duty along the school's fenced perimeter, first armed with a stick and later with a heavy Enfield rifle with only ten rounds of ammunition, I watched these Arabs, singly or in groups, swarm on the road to Jerusalem, which passed in front of the school. On foot, on horses and donkeys, in front of their women who followed them carrying bundles on their heads and runny-nosed babies on their backs, they looked like mysterious and unapproachable figures chiseled against a landscape of oriental poverty and exhaustion. We could hear them coming from a distance in the silence of the night. I looked at them, filing past with muffled footsteps without looking at me, aware of my presence but acting as though I did not exist. The black and silver caftans that the men hitched up to their belts, the baggy black Turkish trousers tied to their ankles, the *keffiya*—a black-and-white or colored scarf held on the head by the double ring of the *abbaya* —gave them a noble deportment that Jews, especially those of recent immigration, markedly lacked. Contrary to the debased merchants I saw sitting in their shops in Jaffa, some made more vulgar by their unaesthetic mixture of European and oriental clothing, these peasants, and in particular the bedouin, had the carriage of princes. I envied them their horses, which I would have liked to ride, their way of life, which seemed to me so harmonious and romantic, their apparent imperviousness to foreign influence. This was of course pure imagination, derived from my total ignorance of their language and my absence of contact with them. Yet I felt gratitude toward them for being faithful to themselves.

My feelings toward orthodox Jews were quite different. In Tel Aviv at that time one did not see many of them. At our agricultural college the "religious" people belonged to a youth movement called B'nei Akiva. Their motto was *Torah ve'Avodah* (Law and Work), a slogan that sounded to me like the *Ora et labora* of the Benedictine monks. Monks these companions of mine were certainly not. But they worked harder than the "secular" students, in order, I believe, to overcome a feeling of inferiority toward the secular Zionists, who at that time ruled the Yishuv, and were proud of having succeeded in freeing themselves from the yoke of the Lord.

The problem of the B'nei Akiva in my school (and later of the religious Zionists in Israel) was thus to prove to others and to themselves that they could successfully compete in everything with secular Zionists: they could build collective villages and join labor unions, handle weapons as well as plows, discuss

Marx and Roosevelt no less than the Bible and the Talmud. Yet in their efforts to imitate the others, in the wake, as they were, of the Marxist currents then prevailing in Jewish Palestine, these young religious Zionists felt uneasy, in some way marginal, and in many instances acted with an arrogance equal to their uncertainty.

Not so the orthodox Jews. Their love of Zion was not the result of nationalistic ideas imported from Europe; their presence in Palestine was not a reaction to Fascist anti-Semitism. Their ambition was not to transform the destiny of their people and create a new type of Jew in the land of their ancestors. The Mosaic tradition was the alpha and omega of their existence. It expressed their collective identity; it answered every problem. Tradition was the golden and unchangeable rule to be followed in the service of the Lord. It began before they were born, in their mother's womb, and did not end for their souls after they had shed their mortal coil. The world could persecute them but not make them change their self-righteous, elitist views. Their duty was to improve the unfinished work of creation through an unending process of sanctification of every moment of life, of every gesture, according to a code of behavior that everyone had the duty to learn through continuous discussion but that only their savior could interpret. They did not pay much attention to current affairs, not because they were blind to daily events but because they firmly believed that they understood better than secular people—deluded beings, blinded by earthly passions— the essentials of life. Like true aristocrats who, even if boiled alive by cannibals, cannot help looking down on their torturers, the behavior of these orthodox Jews toward political power—British, Arab, or Jewish—was one of willful detachment and social indifference. A rabbi, invited to give evidence in front of the Royal Commission, which the government in London had set up to inquire into the problems of Palestine after a recurrent outbreak of violence, exemplified the intellectual position of these orthodox, anti-Zionist Jews when he reminded the members of the commission, in Hebrew, that the Israelites had created a highly civilized society in Palestine "one thousand years before your ancestors came down from the trees." This sentence was translated by the Zionist lawyer acting as interpreter as—"The rabbi has expressed some personal considerations of historic interest on the past of the Jewish people."

In spite of my ignorance of Judaism I perceived in these Jews, totally indifferent to the frivolities of the world, piled up in their shabby neighborhoods, overflowing with nervous, animal mysticism, a sense of continuity, a dignity stronger than in any other group in the country. I felt the same about their women, who first shaved their heads out of modesty and then covered them with wigs or ridiculous shawls like the Daughters of Mary congregation in my village, and their children, bundled up into trousers inherited from older brothers and with angelic expressions on faces surrounded by earlocks dangling under stocking caps—all strange, fascinating, repulsive, agitated inhabitants of the orthodox world of Jerusalem. From outside I observed this closed, perfectly integrated milieu with a curiosity made up of admiration and aversion—a milieu from which I felt excluded more than from that of the Arabs, the British, or the Zionist activists at school who enraged me with their ideological atheism.

Between the loyalists of the God of Israel and the modernizing rebels, between the Jews who waited with anxiety for the Messiah and those who, having lost their patience and capacity to suffer, had decided that Jews no longer needed a Messiah, there existed a common denominator of culture that was alien to me. Walking in the alleys of the ghetto-like orthodox quarter of Jerusalem or sitting in a political seminar, peeping through the shutters of miserable Talmudic schools into which I dared not enter, or marching in the fields to the rhythm of a song whose Hebrew words were adapted to the music of

Russian muzhik, I always felt like an intruder, ashamed of my estrangement as well as of the uneasiness expressed by my body language. I knew that I belonged to none of these groups, neither to the Jews nor to the Arabs, not to the religious or to the secular, not to the socialists or to the nationalists, not to the Italians or to the British. This solitude of mine in the lack of privacy of college life, this loneliness, being part of a foreign society in which I could not find a place to retreat, rendered my search for a point of support more pressing and painful than ever.

In this search I switched from feelings of sudden dislike to those of violent attraction for this or that person, from transient ideological enthusiasm to deep reservation about any political trend. This made me suspect, ill-tolerated, and often derided by my schoolmates, better integrated than I in sports teams, youth movements, paramilitary activities, or religious coteries. Forty years later, their faces, some of which have become internationally known, have faded away like the problems that seemed so obsessive to me at the time, leaving only bursts of olfactory memories sterilized by time: the smell of garlic that socialist activists blew into other people's faces with the violence of their argument; the musky smell of charcoal that the Arabs carried in their clothes and that hit the passersby in their villages; the smell of rancid oil frying in the public canteens; the smell of *yash*, the strong eau-de-vie, and of the Sabbath "kugel" in the synagogues at the end of the morning services; the smell of sweat and menstruation of some women on the buses or in the evenings that more piercing and perturbing smell acquired through immersions in the ritual bathwater.

In a hot country where the majority of the women with whom I came in contact did not use any perfume and washed themselves with hard laundry soap, these natural feminine odors that insinuated themselves into my conscience, sexually inexperienced and religiously ignorant as I was, created a permanent tension about which I bragged to my mates and sometimes attempted to speak about in oblique ways with my English teacher.

I was preparing with her for the London Matriculation, which I never managed to complete. I unburdened myself of my dreams and my olfactory experiences through essays, full of spelling and syntactical errors, which she used to correct without ever seeming to notice the allusiveness of these messages. I had established with her—a quiet beauty, much older than I—a halting dialogue made up of broken sentences, rough-cast speeches, and imaginary stories. At the most difficult moments of our lessons, when I tried to conceal the tears in my eyes by looking at the flight of a bird or at a cloud sailing in the sky, I perceived how sensitive she was to my repressed emotions. On those occasions she suggested that I read aloud some poetry or try to declaim some passage from Shakespeare that I had learned by heart. I gratefully complied, aware of the reserve with which she touched the hollow of her throat to make sure that her shirt was buttoned up.

One day, at the end of the summer of 1940, while we were reading a passage of *Othello* together, a solitary enemy plane suddenly dropped a cluster of bombs on Tel Aviv. One fell in front of her apartment, where we had our lessons. It was the first air raid I had ever experienced. I clearly remember the sound of the explosion and the heat of the gust, the rattling of the windows, the crash of the door uprooted by the blast, the sudden sensation of emptiness in my stomach, which afterwards I had so many other occasions to experience. We rushed downstairs where a small crowd of terrified people had already gathered in the basement.

That was the first time I experienced the splitting of my personality, which would accompany me throughout my life at moments of great stress: I saw myself as though from the outside, uttering inconsequent phrases to people from whom I tried to conceal my physical fear and the far greater fear of showing my fear.

My teacher sat in a corner of our improvised air-raid shelter in a state of abysmal detachment, wholly engaged in observing with blissful surprise the cacophonic scene surrounding her. When the sirens sounded the all clear, we rushed out into the streets, which were quickly returning to normal. Lying on the ground was a horse, his gray coat spotted with blood, his tongue hanging out between two rows of long yellow teeth, his body twisted in the harness of a cart, which seemed to look at his death through the shafts sloping down to the road. It was a macabre scene.

People eyed it sideways without stopping. I was fascinated by it because I had never experienced such a vision of violent death. The air was still full of the smell of the explosion, but the birds had started to twitter again in the trees. My English teacher put her arm around my shoulders—many months later she told me that she had noticed my trembling—pushed me gently up the stairs, sat me down in a chair in her blown-up apartment, and offered me a cup of tea. I drank it, leaning on the table from which she had just removed fragments of glass. She stood in front of me. I noticed that my hands were still trembling and that she discreetly feigned not to see. After a long, tense, mute colloquium, she barely opened her mouth to murmur: "There is nothing wrong in being afraid." Her eyes were misted with tears, but perhaps it was only a reflection of the light. I felt a joy mingled with shame when she laid her hands on mine. We stayed like that for a minute. Then I got up, managed an apology and a smile, and turned to the door to leave. She remained leaning on the doorway, following me with her eyes until I vanished down the stairway, her head slightly bent, forgetful of her unbuttoned blouse. That day I began to think seriously about leaving school and joining the army.

7

The Court-Martial

THE court-martial took place in Ramle, in a bungalow built in the colonial style imported by the British into Palestine from India, together with Indian penal law procedures, the topee, and polo. It was a wooden, E-shaped structure, with four rooms in the central row and two more on the wings to accommodate the guard and the toilets. The veranda, its wooden railing coated with burned black oil to keep away lice, had two cascades of red and purple bougainvillea at the corners, giving some color and beauty to this building planted in a landscape of thistles and sand.

Nothing in Ramle was pleasing to the eye. The few administrative buildings erected by the British next to the older ones built by the Turks made the other small, shabby houses —some made of cement, others of clay—look even more miserable. It was difficult to believe that this had once been the capital of an Arab kingdom fighting the Crusaders. Of the old grandeur nothing remained except a high, rectangular tower hidden among the orange groves. Called the White Tower, it rose majestically on the postage stamps of the mandatory administration, but seen at close range its arches seemed to stare at the plain as if through empty eye sockets.

The passing of the train momentarily distracted the flies from their massed attack on the backs of the donkeys and camels. There was a continuous battle between them and the rosy cheeks of the British soldiers, between the sweat of bodies and the starch of uniforms carefully pressed by Sudanese boys, between the rhythmic swish of the animals' tails and that of the command sticks that the officers held clamped under their armpits.

Sitting on a wooden bench near the end of the veranda, I reflected sadly on my military situation, so far from what I had aspired to when I first joined the army. More than anything else I was perturbed by my trousers. While the British wore shorts carefully measured to show off their sporting knees, regimental colors dangling from the elastic bands that held up their long socks, my lower limbs were encased in two degrading tubes of khaki cloth that made me look like a circus clown. These were a type of colonial shorts that the quartermaster's service had designed in one of those flashes of ingenuity encountered only in the military. The idea was to save money and at the same time fight malaria. In order to maintain some kind of uniformity in military dress by day and to protect the legs from mosquito bites by night, we were issued this versatile specimen of military fashion instead of two pairs of trousers, one long and one short. This "divided skirt" was intended to be turned up and fastened with four metal buttons during the day (sewn two outside and two inside the thighs) and let down to the ankles at sunset. The buttons did not fulfill their function. Those on the inside were torn off in the simple process of walking; those on the outside of the thighs resisted longer —with the result that the trousers permanently dangled between the legs. To walk during the day with those swinging tubes continuously falling toward the ground was a spectacle, specially devised, it seemed, to make a visible distinction between servants and masters, between colonial and metropolitan soldiers. I suffered more keenly from this tacit discrimination than from the official prohibition that separated officers', NCOS', and enlisted men's latrines, or, in order not to irritate the Arabs, from the British enjoinders against our wearing the blue and white Zionist colors on our sleeves when serving within the boundaries of Palestine. I was struck by the irony of the situation: my family in Italy might by that time have been obliged to wear the yellow star, while here was I, prevented from displaying the badge of my race on the degrading military uniform I had eagerly donned to fight for freedom and to escape the routine of the agricultural college.

For nine months I had been mounting guard around depots where only the British had the right to enter or escorting convoys of food and ammunition through monotonous, arid landscapes in Palestine, dotted with clusters of miserable houses and the occasional bright patches of orange groves and irrigated fields of the kibbutzim. The great event about which we spoke for weeks in the other ranks' mess had been a trip to Damascus, where once I got a faraway glimpse of the Abbasid capital from a dusty transit camp where we spent a night.

It was not yet eight o'clock in the morning and the air still held some of the dewy freshness of the night. The judges in the court-martial to which I had been summoned as a witness would certainly not arrive before ten o'clock. I had plenty of time to taste my freedom from oppressive garrison duties, at the expense of an accused comrade-in-arms. Opposite the veranda was a small, sparse lawn, on which an Arab soldier squatted on his heels. He had arrived straight from prison, dressed in khaki overalls stained with oil but girded with an army belt and shiny buckle, a side cap dangling on his freshly shaven head. A Scottish corporal, his topee sitting straight on his head, his dark green flannel shirt bright with campaign ribbons, the red and brown kilt of the Cameron Highlanders circling his hips like a peacock's tail, and the leather sporran firm on his belly, asserted all the elegant superiority of the imperial power over my ridiculous colonial trousers and the stained overalls of the Arab.

The Arab was not handcuffed but guarded by two soldiers belonging to his unit. They were moustached and imperious, conscious of the superiority their rifles and their task gave them over another human being. The scabbards of their bayonets shone in the sun. They had, I thought, probably soaked them overnight in a bucketful of urine, then dried the black leather in the shade to avoid wrinkling. They would then scrub them with Kiwi polish diluted with saliva, polishing the scabbards for hours with a red-striped five-by-two-inch piece of white flannel, which I knew was intended only for cleaning the rifle barrel. I had been through this procedure myself and had learned the tricks of the trade upon which our forty-eight-hour leave often depended. This was all that remained of the splendor of a military life that I had dreamed would sweep me away to the battlements of a fort in the Himalayas or to the cloak-and-dagger depths of the heart of Africa. Instead, here I was in Ramle, bored to death and ashamed of my ridiculous trousers, waiting to be called in to bear witness to a sequence of events that I would be forced to lie about.

The idea of swearing on the Bible and then bearing false witness had been tormenting me for a week. It seemed that the act I was on the point of committing for Jewish patriotism and barracks solidarity was the last step along the road of my aborted hopes. My first year of war had not seen one single military action, only a succession of ascents to the corrugated iron roofs that we regularly had to camouflage with mud against improbable air attacks of the unseen enemy. Our Welsh sergeant major, a lanky fellow plagued less by the drudgery of commanding Jewish recruits than by the ulcer that tortured him, liked that corveé the best; the painful contractions of his stomach translated themselves into our Sisyphean work. This consisted of kneading the red earth of Sarafand with water, handing bucketfuls of this mixture to the soldiers on the roof, spreading the mixture on the hot corrugated iron, and then waiting for it to dry and the wind to blow it away so that we could start all over again. The technique must have been invented by the Egyptians for the benefit of our pyramid-building forefathers, although our sergeant major never stopped reminding us that it helped to win the war against the Nazis.

We reaped our revenge by working to the rhythm of impromptu ditties in Hebrew that heaped scorn on our Welsh tyrant. They were usually inspired by a fellow soldier who had trained to be a diplomat in his native Austria. A strange man, this composer; his new Hebrew name, Ben-Yosef, concealed a past that deeply marked his thoughtful face. When we served in the same platoon of the Palestine Buffs, he had not yet grown the beard he wore when he was killed in the defense of Kfar Etzion, a religious kibbutz near Jerusalem, a few years later. A burst of Jordanian machine-gun fire ripped his stomach —so the legend says—as he was playing the accordion. This accordion, carried in a big wooden box, was part of our unit's equipment. On it he composed some of the best-known war songs of that period. Indeed, he was one of the last true bards. I asked him once what the kind of music he composed meant to him. "It soothes the pain of a soul wounded by memories of a beautiful time which none of us will ever know again," he answered.

By now the Arab prisoner had shifted his position. He was standing up in the middle of the lawn, mechanically massaging his thighs as if to rub away the oil stains on his overalls. Like me, he had noticed a car approaching the bungalow and thought it might be the judges. But it was only the duty officer coming to check whether everything was in order for the court-martial. The Scottish corporal brought us to attention. We stood upright for a few minutes and then fell back into our own thoughts and affairs. I left the veranda to go and urinate behind a eucalyptus tree near the railway line. To satisfy my bodily needs without shame, scaring away an ant into a safe crack of warm ground with the stream of my water, gave me a sense of freedom totally absent in the garrison latrines. At the big Sarafand base, as I have already pointed out, status and race were to some extent linked to human metabolism: there were latrines for enlisted men, for NCOs, and for officers. There were also separate latrines for whites and blacks, for men and women, and for civilians and military personnel. Equality was expressed by their identical, long rectangular shape, with the same wooden planks found in the kibbutz, and the occupant's being protected from indiscreet eyes by jute partitions. Since these flapping curtains did not reach the ground, passersby could view a selection of boots and shoes of every type and from every outpost of the empire. Woe to those who entered the wrong compartment; the military police, with their white-painted belts, shiny buckles, and red caps, seemed to have nothing to do but lay ambushes for those who missed the right address. Only the Australians acted as if they lived beyond good and evil. Off duty they did not bother to salute the officers; they ran their own units as if they were autonomous communities of giants in uniform; they were always happy and insolent. After losing a protracted battle against the bugs that infested their barracks, they set fire to a wooden bungalow. When we rushed to the spot together with the army firemen, they told us to keep away. Sitting on the ground, they drank beer, happy as children at the sight of the giant bonfire they had created.

We Jewish Palestinian recruits quickly developed a deep admiration for these Australian soldiers, hoping one day to create a national army as carefree and undisciplined as theirs. Meanwhile we were just a platoon of green recruits waiting for the arrival of additional volunteers to form a Jewish company, which in time would become a battalion of that fighting brigade the Jewish Agency wanted to create as a nucleus for the future Jewish army, and which the British opposed for exactly the same reason.

At the time I understood little of the political problems in which I had become involved. Back on my bench on the veranda of the court-martial bungalow, I recalled ruefully how I had enlisted. It all started on the day the radio announced that the Germans had bombed Belgrade. The news reached us at the railway station of Binyamina, a village near the coast, built by the Rothschilds, where we had been waiting for a train to take us back to the agricultural college. Among my schoolmates was one of Yugoslav origin, who was later to become chief of staff of the Israeli army. He kept explaining to our teachers the reasons for the attack and its probable consequences. The Serbs and Macedonians, he said, would fight against everyone; the Croats and Slovenians, however, would join the Axis. Yugoslavia would eventually be divided among Italy, Hungary, and Germany.

Listening to him, I thought of the valley in the Carnia region where I used to spend my winter and summer holidays, of my walks along the Yugoslav frontier, of the visit I had paid with my father, when he went to inspect the paramilitary units under his command, to the underground defenses that protected the road leading from Tarvis to Zagabria. Names of faraway places well-known to me were now chasing each other around Binyamina railway station like the pieces of newspaper the wind was whirling through the air. Sitting in the shade of a eucalyptus tree, I followed them with my eyes, wondering what might have been printed on them. A stronger gust of wind lifted one piece of paper high in the air, carrying it first in the direction of the vineyards stretching endlessly at the foot of Mount Carmel, then turning it back, first right, then left, and finally landing it on the sandy road to the village. A gray donkey with its head bowed to the ground and its long ears twitching away the flies, waited patiently for someone to pay attention to him. A barefoot Arab, the corner of his tunic raised and tucked into his belt, looked at us with disinterested eyes from the trunk of the dead tree on which he was sitting.

I kept forcing myself to think of the Wild West, trying to imagine myself in a frontier station among cowboys and Indians, waiting for the arrival of a herd of cows announced by their thundering hooves. Everything was still around me, the silence broken only by the voices of my companions, busily refilling their water bottles at the station's water tank, tired and sweaty after the long march that had at last come to an end, discussing the latest war news and the results of our examinations.

With my head leaning on my rucksack, I reflected on the three-day march we had just completed. The hike at the end of the semester was supposed to complete our military training and acquaint us with our surroundings. The British did not like these school marches; twice on the road from the village of Zichron Ya'akov to Megiddo they had stopped us to inquire about the purpose of our trip. As our papers were in order, they let us go, knowing that we would not dare to walk through an Arab area unarmed. The Mauser pistols were indeed with us, dismantled and concealed in pouches tied between the legs of two or three girls, chosen because their demurely braided hair and innocent faces aroused no suspicion. These girls could have been betrayed to a more discerning eye by the fact that they were the only ones wearing "capitalist" skirts. However, the British closed at least one eye. The outbreak of war had created a fragile and turbid collaboration in Palestine among them, the Arabs, and the Jews. It was a peace without social contacts or agreements, full of suspicion—each side knew that the others were preparing for the fight that would inevitably come. However, that was not the only reason why we felt secure and cheeky. It was the thoughtlessness of our age and the unjustified righteousness of our belief that our own strength would ensure us a better fate than that of the Jews of Europe. Their tragedy was a direct consequence of their refusal to come to Palestine when it was still possible; our good fortune was a confirmation of the correctness of Zionism; our self-confidence due to our naive belief in the fact that our strength, not that of the British Empire, protected us from the Nazi extermination machine.

Oblivious to the horrors of war, we swung along, singing to fight off heat and fatigue, on the road of the Apocalypse, which ran from the sea to Megiddo, the site of Armageddon. The acacias and fig trees in the fields bent their leaves toward the hot ground. The wheat stood high and ripe in the small patches of earth, separated by stone walls, in which the Arabs toiled with wooden plows pulled by a mule or donkey yoked together with a small, emaciated cow. The harness, made of rope, often cut ulcerous wounds into the animals' skins, at which swarms of flies came to feast. It was a world real but remote, which met our arrogance with a silence charged with suppressed hatred. This, at least, was how it seemed. I was probably wrong—the Arabs probably felt nothing toward us but fear and embarrassment. They preferred not to look at us. When we met them suddenly at a bend in the road, driving their herds of goats, they squeezed to the sides to let us pass. Those who suffered most from these encounters were the sheep and goats, pitilessly beaten by the shepherds to make them move out of the way faster. Occasionally a goat, less politically sensitive than the others, lost itself among our ranks, refusing to react to the furious barking of the dog. We received it with enthusiasm and mad laughter since it broke the monotony of the march and filled the void of our minds.

We had spent one night at the youth village of Shfeya, perched on top of the only wooded hill in the area. In the afternoon we had been training with wooden rifles, learning to judge distances, to use a compass, to acquire some notion of topography. In the evening after supper we had gathered in the dining room to listen to a speech by the head mechanic of our school. Usually we saw him busy with tractors, his hands covered with grease, his blue overalls oil stained, his sleeves rolled up over his powerful arms, totally immersed in the work for which we all envied him. Here in Shfeya he was transformed into an officer of the Hagana, the Jewish Agency's clandestine military organization. He stood before us dressed in a uniform without badges of rank, but clean and starched, almost as elegant as the British officers, surrounded by a deep aura of respect enhanced by our surprise at the sudden revelation of his true identity.

He delivered a short political speech. We must prepare for the war against the Arabs that would certainly break out once the war against the Germans and Italians ended. The battle of Britain had been won; the battle of the Middle East had not yet started. The Germans and Italians were trying to provoke an Arab revolt against the British, who would not allow any disorder during the period of emergency. If the British could have got rid of the Zionists they would certainly have done so with pleasure, but they could not because of America and because of the moral and political obligations they undertook once they decided to fight Hitler. They had also discovered that they needed us more than they thought. For this reason they had reluctantly accepted our collaboration in fighting against Vichy France in Syria and against the pro-Nazi revolt in Iraq. They appreciated the fact that all over the Middle East Jews were able to collect more information than the entire British secret service put together, but they did not like to admit it. They wanted the collaboration of Jewish individuals without building up a debt to the Jewish institutions. Because of this we had to work together in common schemes authorized by our own authorities. The war would be long—not months but years. Millions of soldiers would pass though Palestine from every corner of the empire. They would need food, uniforms, medical services, and every other kind of supplies from needles to vehicles. Palestine did not possess raw materials, but the Jews were the only ones in the whole Middle

Eastern area who were able to offer the British the fruits of their skills and their agricultural and industrial experience. It was imperative that we exploit this wonderful opportunity the war was offering us to create the basis for a modern Jewish economy capable, once the war was over, of supporting our own fight for political independence. From this war, he said, we would emerge either stronger or with our national hopes shattered irreparably.

It was a serious, precise speech, without rhetoric and without illusions. It gave me a wider vision of what we should do; it showed me that there were possibilities of action other than the agricultural schemes exalted at school. I felt that I could be associated with a task of wider scope with a place and glory for everyone. Lying in the shade of the eucalyptus tree at the railway station, apart from my companions who were, as usual, discussing the prospect of life in the kibbutzim, which they would be entering at the end of the school year, I kept thinking of the Hagana commander's speech, and I was overwhelmed by a sudden secret joy. At last I was going to make the first free decision of my life: to enlist in the British army in order to train for the war of the Jews for the Jews, as the Italians of Garibaldi's legion had done in Uruguay. By leaving the college, I hoped to crack the shell in which I had lived up to that time, to break out of the suffocating atmosphere of boring agricultural studies and of a collective society for which I felt no empathy. By enlisting, I kept repeating to myself, I would fulfill both my national duty and my own destiny. When the train puffed into the station I felt like another person, different from the other inhabitants of my little school world and from the youngster who had left Italy less than two years before without really breaking with his Italian past.

The day the Germans put an end to the Serbian kingdom of Karageorgevich, I swore allegiance to the king of England, emperor of India, and defender of a faith that was not mine.

In exchange he gave me ten silver shillings, a uniform of khaki drill, a topee, a pair of boots, three pairs of woolen socks, a little pouch containing a piece of soap, a toothbrush, a few needles, some thread, a few metal buttons, and a packet of gauze for first aid.

"Ten-shun!" shouted the Scottish corporal. Like an automaton I found myself snapping to attention in front of the three senior officers comprising the court-martial, who were followed by judges, their black gowns over their arms and their wigs in their hands, ready to dispense justice.

The Arab prisoner and his two guards were also standing at attention on the small, yellowish grassy patch. A little further away, a van escorted by military police was disgorging other prisoners, obviously more important than the Arab since they had been granted the right to a defense. Among them stood Corporal Attiah of my company, a twenty-four-year-old brute, looking as elegant as usual in his freshly ironed uniform, his black hair slick with brilliantine. His arrogant smile always irritated me but served him as an infallible weapon for conquering the hearts of shop girls. He passed in front of me, perfectly sure that I would lie in his defense, throwing a glance at me that appeared impudent and scornful.

Since the day I joined his platoon I had hated him for the tricks he played on me as my squad commander and for his jokes. When I was promoted to lance corporal he shouted in the middle of the other ranks' mess that I should replace my stripe with macaroni. Everybody laughed at me. I had not reacted because we were engaged in a war against "macaroni" Italy, and I could not defend her. Now I preferred not to think about it; if I allowed old rancor to overcome me I might not be able to lie convincingly as I had been ordered to do. Attiah disappeared with his escort and the other prisoners into the guardroom. I went back to my seat on the bench, waiting to be called and free meanwhile to plunge again into my reveries.

The British army had not treated me badly. It had not imposed any inhumane discipline on me; it had not given me rags to wrap my feet in, as was common in the Italian army. At the camp in Sarafand we slept six to a room in clean bungalows with warm showers and latrines less smelly than those in the kibbutz. The bed consisted of three movable planks lying on two wooden horses. They were not unduly uncomfortable once one learned how to stuff the mattress cover with straw. True, we had to fight invasions of insects, some of them undoubtedly direct descendants of those brought into Sarafand by the imperial armies of World War I, but they were less annoying than the mosquitoes, against which we vainly fought by spreading eucalyptus oil over our skins at sunset and by using the nets that dangled from the roof over each of our beds.

I loved that net. It was made of a fine white mesh, which allowed me to see what was happening in the room without being seen myself. It gave me a feeling of protection, of privacy and of luxury, which compensated for many of the discomforts of a recruit's life. Neither the physical effort, nor jobs like carrying buckets of excrement or cleaning huge cauldrons full of smelly grease bothered me. What I could not bear was the monotony of colonial garrison life, which killed every dream of adventure and glory I carried in my heart.

In our camp, after half an hour of morning PT, they made us march back and forth on a cement square to train us in close-order, like Napoleon's troops, as if the battles of the twentieth century should still be fought in closed ranks and with fixed bayonets. When we were on guard duty, even in the middle of a sandy waste, we were told to take three steps forward before shouldering arms so that the barrel of the gun would not hit the imaginary roof of an imaginary sentry box. This is what was done in London; this was what all His Majesty's soldiers had to do everywhere in the empire: truth does not change with geography.

Twice during the first three months of our training they took us to the firing range. I was a keen marksman and did not need lessons from my corporals on how to hold a rifle and hit a target. I was complimented by my British officer but offended by the fact that he personally counted the bullets we used, before and after the exercise, to make sure that not one bullet was stolen from the royal armory. In a military camp inhabited by Scotsmen, Australians, Gurkhas, Bantus, Senegalese of de Gaulle, Boers from South Africa, Arabs, and Indians, we, the Jewish members of the Palestine Regiment, were—and felt ourselves to be—more strangers than anyone else in our country, and they, the British, felt that we were not like the other soldiers. The color of our skins placed us among the whites, but the political geography among the colonials; our Jewish race made us natural enemies of England's Nazi enemy, but our origins were in the Axis countries. We were the only military personnel to have a religion as the basis of our national identity and to reject it in favor of a new secular identity, which left the British mystified.

A few days after my enlistment, our Jewish sergeant informed us that we were going on strike. He had informed our British sergeant major that we would refuse all duty, stop eating, and go to prison if necessary, if we were not given bacon for breakfast like the British soldiers instead of other food in the name of "special religious treatment." We were not to be treated like Muslims, or Indians, or any other "bloody natives"; our rations should be exactly like those of the British because we wore the same uniform and fought (at a distance) the same enemy. We were Zionists, not ghetto Jews, and it was not for the British to decide which of our religious superstitions we should follow. Obviously they pretended to respect our religion only in order to deny our national identity as Jews. We would not play their game; we would defend our right to eat bacon as part of our right to be equal—as a symbol, not as a commodity.

The strike lasted a couple of hours. The British did not understand what we wanted, but they realized that it would be difficult to explain why they had to jail a unit of Jewish volunteers because they insisted on eating bacon. The whole thing was absurd, but it could reach London and the House of Commons, where there was always someone ready to listen to the Zionists. Our commanding officer announced that beginning the next morning bacon would be served to the Jewish units as to everyone else in the camp who did not object to eating pork, and we celebrated this achievement in our bungalows as if we had won a political victory. The Welsh sergeant major became more acid and disparaging in his comments. He now accompanied his commands on the parade ground with phrases such as "Heads up, chins in, don't look at the ground: there are too many Jews and Scotsmen around for money to be lying about."

Resting on my barracks bed, I had tried to put some order into my ideas as I watched the movement of the flies on the unattached ceiling of the bungalow. By now only Ben-Yosef and I were left in the room. Throughout the discussion about the strike he had kept quiet, sitting next to his accordion case, and he was now playing on the instrument, improvising a new tune.

"What's the sense," I asked him, "of calling this strike?"

"None," he answered, "but it's the nature of the weak to show that they are stronger than they are. Gandhi, too, believing that the superiority of the British was linked to their carnivorous habits, ate meat, breaking the religious vegetarian traditions of his family. We, too, will mature in time and won't need to demonstrate our national identity by eating bacon, but our problems are much more complicated than those of India."

To win, he explained, Gandhi only had to wait; nobody can control half a billion men and women in their own country. Zionism, however, had to build up a free people and a land at the same time. The strike over the bacon was just an indication of how confused our ideas still were. The Zionist movement, Ben-Yosef continued, had two faces, one turned toward the outside and one to the inside; one looking at political independence, the other at social revolution. "Our trouble is that we don't want to be just like the others; we want to be similar and different at the same time. We are more interested in realizing a messianic dream than a political plan. The religious tradition against which we have just revolted may contain a lot of superstitions, but it also stands at the root of our legitimate rights in Palestine. Those who want to substitute this old Jewish legitimacy with a new, historically and morally debatable one, risk throwing out the baby with the bathwater, as the British say. We no longer have the patience to wait for the Messiah to come and get us out of trouble; Zionists have decided to do the job themselves." Had I ever heard, he asked me, of a writer called Agnon? He lived in Jerusalem and was telling people that the day we got a state we would lose the Messiah forever.

Ben-Yosef did not like to think too much about these problems; they were too big for him. If, as many people believed, the God of Israel was a God who liked to reveal himself in history, the history that the war was now in the process of writing would give him plenty of occasions to reveal himself to his people. We were living in momentous, bestial times; the soul is corrupted less by the evil of action than by the passivity of the individual within the collective action. "Is there anything more unreal," Ben-Yosef asked me, "than the silence of this military bungalow, surrounded by flower beds, in the middle of the military camp in which we play soldiers far from danger, conscious of, and at the same time untouched by, the hell in which the people whom we have the cheek to pretend we are going to liberate are roasting? Is there anything more absurd, more illusory? Is there any greater sin than our beer-drinking parties, our gobbling bacon, while in

Europe millions are dying of hunger, and our own people, the Jews, are literally burning at the stake that the Nazi inquisition has set up in honor of Aryan gods?" He, Ben-Yosef, had a personal antidote to all this—the music he made on his accordion. "A clown remains a clown," he said to me with his sad smile, "even when dressed in khaki."

One day, three or four months after I had joined the army, feeling that I was turning into a clown myself, I decided to go to Kibbutz Givat Brenner to have a talk with Enzo Sereni. I had not seen him for two years. I knew that he had volunteered for British intelligence, but I did not know that he had had trouble with the authorities in Cairo. He was now back in his kibbutz, brooding over his inactivity and planning other daring operations, which would eventually lead him to his death behind the German lines in Italy in 1944.

I found him in the small kibbutz library poring over old European newspapers. I told him at once that I was so fed up with my military service I was ready to desert if I could not get a transfer to a unit where I could do something more interesting and meaningful for the war effort. Sereni listened to me without interrupting but with obvious signs of impatience. At the end he was so irritated by my babbling that he almost shouted at me. There was nothing he could do for me, he said, but even if he could, he wouldn't lift a finger to help me. Who on earth was I to claim special consideration? What had I done in my life to expect more than the others? Who gave me the right to use this terrible war, in which the Jewish people and half of humanity were dying, for my personal satisfaction? What I was looking for, he said, and he was right, was not promotion of a cause but my own advancement. Unable to associate myself with any collective work, I was now trying to run away from the army life for which I had volunteered, in the same way as I had run away from the kibbutz and from my school. I was forgetting that nothing could be built without the patient humility that inspires common action. The cathedrals in Europe did not bear the names of their builders; none of the trees I could see growing around us could be linked to the labor of a particular person; Zionism could not succeed through bombastic speeches or parades, as the Jabotinsky Revisionists—the "orthodox" secular parties of the right—claimed, but only through the ant-like work of devoted people who understood that the Jewish homeland could only be built gradually. This was the meaning of Chaim Weizmann's call for "one dunam at a time; one cow at a time." Better than anybody else I should have known, he concluded, without realizing how deeply he wounded me by quoting Mussolini's famous slogan, that "it was possible to serve a cause even by mounting guard over a petrol can."

I left Givat Brenner full of resentment at Sereni, whom I was not to see again until the night in Bari when he left my unit to be parachuted behind the German lines on a mission without return. In my rage I did not realize what I came to understand years later, that the best way to obtain something is to stop asking for it. In fact, while mounting guard over an oil depot at the Tel Aviv power station, less than two months after my meeting with Sereni, I received a most unusual call from my company commander. He told me that an officer from the Special Intelligence Service had just arrived from Cairo and wanted to see me in private. He left me alone in his office, and after a short while I was faced by a major who spoke perfect Italian. He told me that he was in the process of organizing a propaganda service in Italian (paradoxically enough it was the same unit Sereni had been forced to leave) and was looking for speakers with good Italian pronunciation. He had gone through the list of Palestinian volunteers of Italian origin and wanted to meet me personally. He asked me about my studies and my family, and after half an hour's conversation—which already created a bit of a sensation in my unit—he asked me to go with him to the army broadcasting station in Jaffa for a voice test.

Many years have passed since that day. The officer, a Greek Jew by the name of Nakamuli, a rich paper merchant from Cairo, has long been dead. For me he remains the greatest friend I had in the six years I served in the British army. On more than one occasion after I had left his unit, he helped me without apparent reason. He was not ashamed to invite me to his splendid mansion on the Nile to dine with Egyptian notables and British officers, in spite of my being then a simple NCO. Nothing endears him to my memory more than the way he helped me to read and reread the text for my voice test, making it clear to me that he wanted me to succeed although he knew absolutely nothing about me. He had probably sensed my anguish and my desire to break away from garrison life. I do not know how well I read the article from *Il Popolo d'Italia*, which Nakamuli had brought with him, but I was recruited on the spot, and when I left the studio in Jaffa I knew that I had been touched by the wand of fortune.

However, all these were things to come in the future as I waited to be called in as a witness at the court-martial. Sitting on the veranda, I concentrated my thoughts on the answers I would give to the judges when asked if I recognized the padlock.

A padlock: a piece of iron upon which depended the freedom of a comrade-in-arms whom I hated, and my own dignity, which I knew I was on the point of losing. Not that I had never told a lie before, but to lie on the Bible was quite different from lying about a piece of chocolate cake eaten without permission. And that was exactly what I was on the point of doing, because of the padlock that closed the gate of depot number 6 at Wadi Sarar.

Wadi Sarar was a big ammunition depot. It was reached by the train which ran from Tel Aviv to Jerusalem along the old, winding Turkish line. Our unit had been sent there in the autumn of 1941 to replace some of de Gaulle's Senegalese troops. The guard posts, scattered over a large area alongside big huts full of military equipment, consisted of one tent and eight soldiers, headed by a corporal or lance corporal. Only the British had the right to enter the buildings. Day and night, we colonials were supposed to stop anybody approaching the site by shouting, "Stop! Who goes there?" and pointing our Enfield rifles with fixed bayonets at him. If the unknown person stopped and answered "Friend," we were supposed to shout back, "Advance to be recognized." What happened after that stage we had not been told. If the friend turned out to be an enemy, we would have had to scare him off by our ferocious appearance and our bayonets since we were forbidden to keep our rifles loaded. If, however, the enemy was kind enough to give us time to open the pouches hanging on our battledress, take out the clips and load the rifle, he would still have had a chance to survive because we had to fire the first round in the air. Only with the second round, said the regulations, were we authorized to "shoot to kill," a highly unlikely situation since there was no enemy in sight for miles around. The only really important thing in this game of war was the procedure with which one guard commander handed over the inventory of his post every eight days to his replacement.

During Corporal Attiah's period of guard duty, a few thousand cartridges had disappeared together with the original padlock from the door of depot number 6. Attiah told the British who discovered the theft that the new padlock on the depot gate was already there when he took over guard duty from me. Since nothing was missing from the depot while I guarded it, nobody could accuse me. But if I stated that the padlock in question was different from the one I had observed two weeks previously, the suspicions against Attiah would be much stronger. And since I remembered perfectly well the shape of the padlock that had been broken and replaced, my evidence could be decisive.

From the day Attiah was arrested I had known no peace and quiet. In Palestine at that time Jews formed a closely knit,

state-like community, with their own independent institutions, schools, clandestine military organization, the whole
consolidated by a loyalty based on a highly politicized feeling
of historical experience, discrimination, and persecution. This
cohesion was even stronger in our army units, consisting entirely of volunteers, in which the real authority was vested in
the Jewish NCOs. In fact, back in 1941 the number of Jewish
colonial officers was still very small. Those who completed the
first officers' courses opened to them were sent to join service
units such as transport, engineers, quartermasters, and so on,
which the British needed more than infantry. The few "native" officers in our regiment came from the best local Arab
and Jewish families—Ben-Gurion, Margolis, Nashashibi,
Dajani—and nobody wanted to endanger their promotion in
the military hierarchy by involving them in political problems. They had to be kept out of trouble as much as possible,
while the NCOs, most of whom had joined the army on instructions from the various Zionist political parties of the clandestine military organizations, were charged with the political
guidance of the soldiers. This unofficial but very real authority,
distinct from that of the British, naturally did not manifest
itself every day. The Jewish NCOs carried out their daily duties
according to orders from their British officers, behaving toward us as NCOs behave toward enlisted men everywhere in the
world. We all knew that in matters of "national importance"
they enjoyed an authority far higher than their rank.

When Corporal Attiah was indicted for the disappearance
of ammunition at depot number 6, I immediately found myself
facing the categorical instructions of "the organization,"
brought to me by a "native" sergeant, who was shocked by
the fact that I could raise "moral scruples and objections." As
soon as it became known that my answer to the court-martial
was not certain, a void was created around me. It was not yet
a clear case of ostracism but a sudden unresponsiveness to any
attempt on my part to establish contact with other soldiers.

The human setting around me ceased, so to speak, to exist. It was neither hostile nor provocative, just mute and expectant. Marginal as I was to the Zionist society in Palestine, devoid of Jewish culture, and ignorant of all ideologies, not to speak of being unable to share with others the romantic vision of national revival that I had brought with me from Italy, I was terrified by the idea of living until the end of the war totally isolated in the middle of a society that was itself rejected by the rest of the world. The dread of having to command a squad of soldiers who might refuse to obey my orders in front of the entire unit on parade tormented me no less than the fact that I was being asked to do violence to my conscience. I had nobody in my unit to talk to. I knew that the answer to my questions would be that it was a holy duty to trick the British who had betrayed all their promises to the Jews through the white paper limiting the sale of land to Jews and their immigration into Palestine. "The one who robs the robber is absolved," says an old Jewish adage, and I had nothing against that. What held me back from perjury was the feeling that by swearing falsely in the name of God I would be breaking the very "crystal of my soul," cracking the innermost core of my conscience. Two types of morality, the national and the religious, clashed confusedly in the solitude of my anguish, neither one succeeding in overcoming the other. When I finally received an order to present myself as a witness to the court-martial, and my sergeant asked me what I had decided to do, I was surprised to hear myself answering with feigned confidence, "to lie under oath, of course."

For about an hour the warm approval I thought I read in my comrades' faces made me happy; for the first time I was tasting the strange, sensual pleasure of sinning in full consciousness, the relief of a mind that had decided to leave all doubts behind and accept whatever the future might bring. But it was a short-lived relief. My conscience renewed its constant attacks on my decision, and I could not sleep that night. In the morning, after receiving my travel warrant, I boarded the first Arab bus going past the Wadi Sarar camp and went to see my botany teacher at the Mikveh Yisrael agricultural school. I had not met him since the day I joined the army. His name was Meshiach, and he had studied agriculture at the University of Naples. He wore a pince-nez, and a bow tie on Saturdays, which made him strangely elegant in the untidy surroundings of the school, and he had always received me with great kindness in his home during the months I spent at the school and attended his lessons.

He listened to me with rapt attention. When I had finished describing the morass into which I had fallen, he took off his pince-nez and began polishing the lenses for a long time with extraordinary precision, while I observed the deep indentations that the springs had left on either side of his nose. When he finally replaced the pince-nez, his eyes bore a look of ancient sadness.

"Our sages were asked," he began, "why it is written in the Bible that only the sons of Israel cried at the death of Moses, while both the sons *and* daughters of Israel cried at the death of Aaron. Can we say that Aaron was better or more important than Moses? Certainly not. But Moses had said 'Let justice— if necessary—break the mountain.' He could not accept compromises because only by following absolute justice could he remain at one and the same time the servant of God and the servant of his people. Aaron, on the other hand, accepted compromise for love of peace and for a truth that could not be divine because it was a human truth. Had he not lied to the people when he built the Golden Calf and told them, 'This is your God, O Israel?' He did so because he felt that the idol could serve as a banner, as a rallying point for unity in a herd of sheep left temporarily without a shepherd. Aaron was a great patriot, probably greater than Moses, who could not separate his love for the people from his love for absolute truth."

"You are faced at this moment," he continued, "by the dilemma of Aaron: it is the dilemma with which the devil (remember that for the Jews he is still a divine messenger) faces every one of us sooner or later. The entire Zionist movement, the very essence of our national revival, is a kind of Golden Calf, because the state we want to create is a human construction, with a human morality, not a divine one. We have chosen to come to terms with the devil, with material power, human passions and interests, because we simply no longer have the strength to do anything else. 'The dead praise not the Lord,' says the psalm, and we are on the point of being destroyed.

"If you could ask Moses' advice," he concluded, "he might tell you to break the mountain with your truth. I cannot tell you that, if for no other reason than because while God himself sent Moses to save and guide the people morally and politically lost in the Egyptian exile, he has not sent anyone to bring a message of hope to us and to the Jews whom the Nazi Pharaoh is in the process of destroying in Europe, and here too, with the help of British despots. We stand alone, without guidance, and we have the duty to defend our people. Perhaps we shall have to pay for our arrogance with our lives and those of our sons for generations to come. This, too, may be part of our destiny. I cannot tell you whether you must or must not lie tomorrow; all I can tell you is that the roads that will open before you, whatever you do, will be equally painful, although the covenant with the devil is less difficult to sign than the covenant with God. Free will is the weightiest gift God has made to mortal man in order that everyone may at the end be able to save himself."

Together we left his apartment. We passed in front of the silent synagogue and through the gardens and then started walking down the long sandy avenue leading to the road that links Jaffa with Ramle, between the colonnade of palm trees and amid the uninterrupted buzzing of insects.

When I heard my name called, the conversation with my botany teacher flashed through my mind. Like a marionette I marched into the room of the court-martial at the order of the duty sergeant major. Under my topee, as I stood stiffly at attention, I could not see who was standing to my right or my left. I only felt a score of eyes fixed on me. The colonel, sitting between two other officers, told me kindly to stand at ease. The secretary of the court, an NCO of the Royal Hussars, brought me a Hebrew Bible and made me repeat the formula of the oath. I could feel sweat running down my back and creating a damp feeling in my trousers. At a sign from the president, the military prosecutor walked up to me holding a padlock in his hand. "Corporal," he said, "do you recognize this padlock?" "Yes, sir," I answered, surprised at how simple it was to lie. "Are you absolutely sure of that?" asked the military prosecutor, looking straight into my eyes. "Let me remind you that you have sworn on the Bible to tell the truth, and that God is at this very moment present in this court." "Yes, sir," I repeated, without the slightest effort, with a deep sense of relief, "this padlock is the one that locked the gate when I took over my guard duty." "Very well," said the military prosecutor. I heard behind me the roar of the sergeant major shouting "Ten-shun! About face! Left-right, left-right, halt!" and then a voice tinged with anger, "Dismissed: go back to your camp, Corporal."

With a light step I went out, passing under the cascade of bougainvillea, barely touching the hot sand on the ground with my shining boots. My mind was perfectly clear, my heart totally confused. I felt a strange smile on my lips. I knew I had just signed a pact with the devil, and I was anxious to know what I would get in exchange for my eternal soul.

8

Jerusalem

WHEN I rang the bell at the apartment in Ibn Ezra Street in Jerusalem, I did not realize this gesture would have so many important consequences for me.

It was a three-room apartment on the ground floor with two entrances: the door at the side opened onto a staircase leading to the floor above; the other, at the front, opened onto a veranda. This was separated from the street by a small garden, at that time full of flowers, today overgrown with weeds. Through the veranda a small sitting room could be seen, clean and tidy, with part of the furniture concealed by curtains. A notice in full view, in Hebrew and English, read: TO LET. I crossed the garden in a few steps, walked onto the veranda, and rang the bell to inquire about the rent.

It was six o'clock on one of those summer evenings when a discreet wind waves the cypresses of Jerusalem, wakes people from their siestas, takes them under their showers, and invites those who have the time to get ready to admire the sunset. In less than an hour, the sky would turn red, then violet, and finally enter into the bright obscurity of the night.

I was dressed in civilian clothes, happy to be allowed to shed, after twelve months, my army uniform. I was wearing gray flannel trousers falling inelegantly onto a pair of heavy black boots, a checked jacket, which I carried hanging from my thumb over my shoulder, and a white shirt without a tie —a set of clothing halfway between that of the poorer, untidy dress of the immigrant Jews and the better-cut but climatically unsuitable wear of the British civil servants. It was indeed a hybrid outfit, undefined, like my new status of Italian announcer in the military broadcasting service of the Middle East.

I did not feel in the least embarrassed by it. I had just been promoted to the rank of sergeant; I had ten pounds, which I considered a fortune, in my wallet. In my pay book I carried a card issued by Field Security asking "civil and military authorities" to extend me all possible help in case of necessity. I was nineteen years old and felt free to live like a bird in the middle of a war that raged far away and which would open up, at least to me, the road to fame and success I so much desired.

A middle-aged woman appeared on the threshold. She wore a blue scarf on her head, which disclosed a few faded blond curls. Her unmade-up face revealed a shade of hardness and arrogance behind her delicate features. She wore frayed overalls with a colored apron around her waist. In her right hand, gloved in tan chamois leather, she held a duster as if it were a riding crop. She was obviously the landlady, a typical example of that German-Jewish bourgeoisie impoverished by immigration to Palestine but determined to preserve at all costs the decorum of a past social position.

She looked at me with a hint of a questioning smile on her thin lips. I explained that I was interested in renting a room with half-board and that I was a serviceman authorized to wear civilian clothes because I was temporarily serving with the foreign languages department of the radio. I asked the price and accepted it without arguing since it was below my billeting allowance. She understood this and suggested taking care of my laundry for an additional ten shillings a month.

As we talked, standing face to face, she on the veranda, I on the grass of the garden, I felt her psychological resistance gradually weakening. When she eventually became convinced that I was a Palestinian Jew serving in the British army and not one of those exotic types brought to Jerusalem by the war in the wake of the Allied troops, her face relaxed into a wide smile of agreement and complicity. Months later, when we happened to talk about our reciprocal impressions during that first meeting, she told me that her first impulse had been to turn me down, suspecting me of being an agent of the British Secret Service or, worse, of the Palestine Police. But as I kept talking, I sounded to her so infantile and looked so amusing in my attempts to appear self-assured and important, that she felt the need to offer me "a nest where I could let my feathers grow." Before he met me, her husband had been quite suspicious, asking himself whether it was prudent to allow into the house someone obviously linked with the Intelligence Service. He was convinced that my job as announcer was a cover-up for some more secret operation. But after we were introduced me, he shared his wife's opinion that whoever I might be and whatever I might do, I was, above all, a confused youngster in search of family warmth. Thus, without knowing it, I was accepted from the first moment as a kind of stray dog by two gentle remnants of a destroyed world.

Frau Luise, my landlady, took great care to uphold the dignity of her husband, a doctor from Hamburg who, in 1942, had not yet received a permit to practice because of the great number of Jewish refugee doctors who had flooded into Palestine. Dr. Wilfrid lived by translations and small commercial transactions, the most rewarding of which was the search for British and Arab buyers for the silver, rare books, and miniatures he or his friends had brought from Germany. The rent

I paid for the room and half-board was an important income for him, especially since the whole family could live on the army rations I brought to the house.

Their parental attitude toward me had also been awakened by the fact that their son, an engineer not much older than I, had gone from Germany to England. Their daughter, however, had chosen the life of the pioneers in an extreme left-wing kibbutz in Galilee. Even before knowing her, I thought that she had been right to run away from the padded, conventional atmosphere of her home, to which I, however, found no difficulty in adapting. I was curious to meet this farming daughter who was probably milking cows in her remote kibbutz and whose silver-framed photograph standing on the grand piano attracted my attention by its long, thoughtful face, seemingly absorbed in remote visions. But during the first week I spent in my new dwelling I was too busy with my new work at the broadcasting station to become interested in the life and family problems of my hosts.

They had given me a room at the end of the corridor overlooking the courtyard. Silent and shady, this room offered me, after many months of no privacy, the luxury of a sofa bed with two real linen sheets, freshly washed and ironed, and a table and a chair that did not shake. The cupboard was too big for the one change of underwear I possessed, the two summer uniforms, the winter battledress, my only civilian jacket and trousers, the three striped shirts, and the woolen tie the radio administration had requested me to wear while on duty. The most important thing in the lodging was, however, the bathroom. When I opened the shower tap I was free to let out of the perforated iron rose over my head as much cold or hot water as I wanted. Only those who have slept for weeks in the desert, experienced the hardness of an army shirt disgustingly stiff with sweat under the armpits, and had to face the shame of open-air showers and latrines can value the privacy of a separate bathroom and the exhilaration produced by the myriad water drops on sweaty skin, the indescribable pleasure of the primordial meeting of flesh and water.

In that bathroom, which my landlords took care to leave at my disposal after six in the morning, I sang, dreamed, and enjoyed every instant of the good fortune that the war had brought me, heedless of my future and rarely mindful of my past. If at night I was assailed by melancholy, I usually succeeded in overcoming the pangs of my Italian memories with reveries of my new military career, a psychological process undisturbed by the austere, old-fashioned atmosphere prevailing in the other two rooms of my new residence.

My landlords lived in the dining room, a small space occupied for the most part by a square table and two divan beds. Under the window there was a lace-covered shelf with some porcelain statuettes on it and a vase full of fresh flowers. Under the other window was a cupboard with crockery and cutlery, with the family's Sabbath ritual objects well in view on top —two silver candlesticks, a kiddush goblet, the spice box for habdalah. Hanging from the wall was a Hanukkah oil lamp.

Dr. Wilfrid was an observant Jew, but more in a "conservative" manner than in strict orthodoxy. He prayed alone at home in the mornings, afternoons, and evenings, and went to synagogue only on Saturdays and festivals. He did not usually keep his head covered but presided at the Sabbath meal with style and a feeling of pride that bore witness to the long religious tradition of his family. His wife and daughter were not observant at all. Frau Luise, however, gave the same punctilious care to the laying of the Sabbath table as she did to the ironing of the slightly frayed clothes and the starched shirts of her husband. For me, who had never celebrated the Sabbath in Italy, and who was certainly not particularly impressed either by the sabbatical rites in the kibbutz or by those in the homes of local Italian friends, these intimate Friday evening dinners, always accompanied by excellent food, revealed an unexpected and captivating aspect of Judaism. I enjoyed and relaxed in the peaceful quiet of a dining room in which the golden gleam of the Sabbath candles set at the center of the embroidered tablecloth shone more brightly than the fully lit crystal candelabrum. I was grateful for a tidiness that reflected not only the civility of my hosts but also a larger, ancient order of things to which I felt I somehow belonged in spite of its strangeness. On these evenings Frau Luise always appeared dressed in an elegant, outmoded suit, always wore for the occasion an ancient family pendant round her neck, and before nodding to her husband to start reciting the blessings she threw a last authoritative look at all the objects lined up as though on military parade to "receive" the Sabbath: the gold-rimmed plates laid on the table, the silverware on either side of them, the breadbasket covered with an embroidered cloth, the silver goblet for the blessing, the saltcellar, and, standing in a larger circle around the table, all the other objects in the room.

During these Friday evenings, when the noises had died away in the streets of Jewish Jerusalem and the shadows from the oil lamps quivered in the empty synagogues, Dr. Wilfrid appeared transformed. Impeccably dressed, in summer in a white linen suit, which he exchanged in winter for one of dark English tweed, he sported a silk bow tie under a starched piqué collar, which made him look slightly ridiculous on any other occasion. Now, however, the air of uncertainty and shyness that accompanied him throughout the week was replaced by a proud demeanor, just as the sandals in which he plodded the city streets in search of buyers for his books and miniatures had been replaced by a pair of shiny black shoes. With his head covered by a silk-embroidered skullcap, he recited the Sabbath blessings with an assured voice and a benevolent smile on his lips. This smile must have belonged to the rich and famous Hamburg doctor he had once been, to the director of the great military hospitals in the Great War, to a man who had tasted the comfort of his father's villa in the Black Forest and who now wanted, at least on the Sabbath, to forget his refugee status and his middleman trade.

After dinner we used to move into the third room of the apartment, a sitting room in which nobody slept and which my landlords tried to preserve as an island of culture and affluence. The largest part of the room was occupied by a grand piano. Frau Luise played on it when she entertained friends or when engaged in a harmonious dialogue with her husband at the end of the Sabbath. On those occasions he listened to her, seated on a frayed, brocade-covered armchair, nodding his head in gestures of rhythmic approval and occasionally allowing unashamed tears to roll slowly from his closed eyelids.

Frau Luise, in a way, also talked to me while playing the piano. With her music she was describing to me places and landscapes in Germany, telling me stories of a people whom she had obviously not stopped loving but about whom it was no longer possible to speak except with expressions of hate. I felt the same toward Italy and shared her nostalgia for a country I doubted I would ever see again. Yet this common melancholy did little to melt the layer of indifference that I felt gradually building up in myself—an apathy toward everyone and everything, the result of a destiny that in Italy made of me a Jew in spite of myself, while here it was seemingly turning me into an alien in the midst of so many Palestinian Jews.

Dr. Wilfrid used to gather a few friends in his sitting room on Saturday afternoons. For several weeks I was not invited to join this symposium of good German-Jewish bourgeois. The excuse was that they spoke a language I did not understand. The truth was that they were suspicious of me, not knowing exactly who I was. I had told my landlord of the circumstances under which I had left Italy, how I had enrolled in the Mikveh Yisrael agricultural school, how I had joined, as everybody did in my class, the Hagana. I had described to him my swearing-in ceremony in the wooden hut at the edge of the school's botanical garden, the oath I took while keeping my right hand on a Mauser pistol, my eyes blinking because of the floodlamp that concealed the faces of those who administered the oath. I told Dr. Wilfrid how and why I had left the school at the beginning of 1941 and joined the British army after protracted discussions with my companions and teachers on the advantages and disadvantages, the political morality and the ideological principles involved in serving the king of England instead of the Palmach, the Jewish striking force, which was being organized in the kibbutzim in readiness for a German-Italian invasion. For my schoolmates the choice was simple: those who wanted to share in the Allied war effort but refused to become an integral part of a foreign army enrolled in the Palmach. Those, like me, who were looking for adventure, money, and career could and should serve in the British army.

In spite of my sincerity, my indifference toward ideology seemed suspicious to Dr. Wilfrid and some of his friends, who were emotionally involved in the war even if they did little to contribute to the war effort. They lived riveted to their wireless sets, listening to the news in every understandable language and making the war bulletins the principal subject of their conversations. Under its quiet surface, Jerusalem in 1942 teemed with mysteries, pacts, treason, and plots, imaginary or real. The Jews, the British, and the Arabs plotted against each other and within their own communities, each hating and double-dealing the others in their own particular style and logic.

The unity of the Jews had never been complete. Side by side with the orthodox Jews, clustered in their neighborhoods and hostile to the secular Zionists, there were the "orthodox" secular left-wing parties that hated the "orthodox" secular parties of the right—the Jabotinsky Revisionists. All three maligned the bourgeois, despised the Arabs, and aped the British. The British refusal to open the gates of the country to the refugees from Europe and the first horrendous news that seeped in about the fate of the Jews at the hands of the Nazis, had begun to dissolve the Zionist collective discipline and make it difficult for many Palestinian Jews to respect the Jewish Agency's promise not to fight Arab nationalism and British imperialism as long as the war against Hitler was being waged. There was a lot of talk about groups that had decided to take armed action against the mandatory government. It was even said, in great secret, that some were ready to come to an agreement with the enemy if the Germans would agree to stop the slaughter of the Jews.

The Jewish Communists, who for years had suffered because of the Soviet Union's hostility to Zionism, were now able to defend openly their idea of creating a binational Arab-Jewish state in which Marxism would triumph over the "tribal" Jewish nationalism. All over the country there were political visionaries, military prophets, and ideological parasites; human relics and bureaucratic caliphs; naive heroes and opportunists; charlatans and saints. To me, most of them seemed like hallucinatory figures and recalled to my mind the paintings of El Greco: human beings inhumanly stretched toward unlimited horizons of hope, hate, rancors, and revolts, and at the same time chained down in Jerusalem to the tiny space of a provincial city, aware that in fact they were already witnessing the fall of the greatest colonial empire in the world.

In this gossipy, exalted, mysterious, and parochial atmosphere, palpitating with history and faith, made up of shadows and sudden gleams of light, I could not avoid being an object of suspicion. I represented the "other," although biologically a member of the Zionist "family." At the same time, conditioned as I was by my British uniform, infatuated with my role of "clandestine" speaker, I invited mistrust with my unnatural condescending behavior to the "natives," satisfied with an artificial isolation that so well fitted my immature psychology. Quite often, however, and in spite of this complacency of mine, I felt the need to find someone in whom to confide and with whom to discuss what I was doing in the middle of all these explosive contradictions. Dr. Wilfrid, with whom I often talked, was the person least suited to help me clear my ideas. This good, liberal, German, religious, Zionist doctor dreamed of nothing better than to become a British citizen and to live in a mandated territory.

Sometimes after dinner when Frau Luise asked us to leave the dining room in order to turn the divans into beds for the night, we sat next to the silent piano, he smoking a carved clay pipe, I crouched on the round ottoman near the door. The sliding white muslin curtains at the windows of this quiet sitting room reminded me of the puppet theaters with which I used to play, with one difference; here we were the puppets, manipulated by invisible hands that pulled the strings of our existence, concealed by mountains of words to which, night after night, I added my vocal contribution, reading the war bulletins and the political commentaries of our clandestine radio station. In those few square meters of tidy space, full of fragments and reminiscences of a world destroyed for Dr. Wilfrid and new for me, it came naturally and easily to both of us to speak about the ill-concealed doubts that perturbed our consciences.

For him Zionism was an option, a choice for collective life made by Jews who had lost most of their religious identity and were clumsily trying to build a new one around the idea of a nation that they had picked up piecemeal in the countries of their enemies. In Palestine, Jews were trying to live—so thought Dr. Wilfrid—in a "national home" built according to foreign architecture on our ancestral land, the use of which we had handed over to others throughout centuries of forced absence and which we now wanted to recover in a couple of decades. Under such stress nobody could hope to revive a civilization, a culture of our own. Zionism was a utopia with no moral obligation when turned into a reality. Even if we ignored the Arabs, who after all were an external nuisance and paradoxically contributed to our unity, our problem was how to incarnate our lofty ideas and create a genuinely new Jewish style of life in which our faults would coexist with our follies. The assimilation we had embraced with such enthusiasm in Europe had hastened Hitler's disaster. If we continued to imitate the outside world, the national home we wanted to create for Jews in Palestine risked turning into a vehicle for a new collective assimilation. What new disaster would then befall us?

For him the problem was how to find a way to blend the heritage of Esau, to whom had been promised the world of matter, with that of Jacob, who was chosen to live in the world of the spirit. Zionism wanted to integrate both, not just conciliate them, as for centuries Judaism had tried to do in the ghetto. It was a dangerous exploit, which had never succeeded before and which, in addition, Jews had undertaken in the midst of the chaos in Europe.

Dr. Wilfrid was not particularly worried by the Arab hostility. In World War I he had served as a military surgeon in Turkey and that experience in the East had forever conditioned his mind toward the Orientals.

The Turks had taught him that the Arabs could never be citizens but only subjects. Such, he believed, they should remain within a Zionist state, provided that the Jews would be able to establish with them relations of economic interest stronger than those of political antagonism. The Arab revolt was a beautiful legend created by Colonel T. E. Lawrence, warmed up after the Great War by the romanticism of an English elite touched by moral and political decadence. The Zionists were certainly paying the price of this legend, but in the end the myth of Arabism would produce a flood of words and perhaps of blood, which would eventually extinguish itself in its own contradictions. Arabs, in any case, counted little because they did not know who they were and what they wanted. They possessed a collective political-religious identity as long as Islam had linked them with the other Muslims through the Ottoman Empire and, in a looser way, with the Muslims of other colonial territories. The bedouin of Arabia who created Islam were unable to keep it alive in modern times and inherit the strength of the Turks necessary to impose on all or most of the Arabs a political control based on the collective identity of the Muslims. Once the unity of Islam broke into pieces, the caliphate was abolished, the provinces of the Ottoman Empire were transformed into states without national character, common history, and social or religious equality, what could the strength of the Arabs be? Nothing, since the Arabs would continue to yearn for a dying Europe, clothed in the veils of the Lawrence myth, while incapable of absorbing Western values since these belonged to the Christian world. In the caricature of local imported nationalism, the Arabs would lose the little indigenous creativity they possessed. "You Europeans," a wounded Turkish colonel once told Dr. Wilfrid, "do not want to accept the fact that the Arabs are the fathers, not the sons of the desert, and incapable of creating a state. They are converted Christians who preserved only the shrewdness and the memory of the Byzantine oppression. We, the Turks, coming from the steppes of Asia, have prevented them for centuries from cutting each other's throats as defenders of the legitimizing role of Islam—a faith that befits the believers in it because it is equally accepted by the rulers and the ruled, even when applied in a different manner. The unity of Islam once destroyed, the community of believers will return to being what it had always been in the East—a mosaic of nomadic tribes and masses of peasants exploited by merchants or by robbers masquerading as rulers. The Ottoman Empire will be succeeded by another imported empire, or by chaos. In both cases the Arabs would be the losers."

The Jews, too, would be losers, Dr. Wilfrid believed. "We are not a tribe of robbers but a family of slaves. We have lost the sense of statehood like the Christians who converted to Islam. Our Islam is the European culture. It has drawn from its Greco-Christian roots the poison with which it revenges itself upon us for having given Jesus to Athens and Rome."

The Zionists' error consisted for him in thinking themselves capable of guaranteeing the material survival of the Jews through the creation of a pagan "house" outside Europe. Perhaps one day they might be able to create even an independent state of their own. But it would not last and would be counterproductive. A Jewish Westernized state would look for strength, not for justice; for compromise, not for uniqueness. These were Greek ambitions, not Jewish. Jews had always drawn their energy from the opposition existing between man and God, between the pure and the impure, the sacred and the profane, between pride and piety. Their system of life had developed through the centuries the art of living in balance between stars and dust, subconscious and superego. It worked for a sacred people confined to, but also protected by, the ghetto; it would not work in a modern state in which the "raison d'etat" would replace the "raison de Dieu," because ideology ends in self-destruction. Jews would never be able to put into practice the abstract ideas of human, rational perfection to which they aspired.

The national religion in which Zionism believed was not only alien to Jews, it was the worst of all political beliefs. It had neither limits nor brakes, the interests of the state being above everything. "My country, right or wrong" was a principle totally opposed to the spirit of the Ten Commandments, which were given to the Jews coming out of Egypt and which turned them from slaves into an elitist nation. "If we cannot find a way to turn ourselves from assimilated, pagan Jews into an elitist modern political society," he said, "we run the risk of dying before being born." Dr. Wilfrid was scared of a freedom founded on the principle of self-determination since it implied perpetual opposition to values and ambitions equally valid for others. He was prepared to exchange Jewish national rights for the rescue of as many Jews as possible and the time needed to educate them to statehood. This could be achieved only through the maintenance of the British imperial power over Palestine for the longest possible time. "It may turn out to be like living under a shed that will not protect us from cold or heat," he said, but at least it will allow us to prepare ourselves to face our true enemies: ourselves."

I listened to him, amused and irritated at the same time. I could not share his pessimism or agree with his praise of political immobilism, but I did not find myself in total disagreement with what he was saying about Britain. I did not perceive her foreign presence, as some of my schoolmates did, as fundamentally hostile, as a kind of octopus whose tentacles we had to hack off. For me, Britain represented the sporting field on which I had been invited to participate, the authority that in the sticky confusion of the Orient, projected an image of equity, of order, of fair play. It may all be due to imperial self-interest, but it was more than just exterior pretense. Anyway, Britain was now fighting the worst enemy of the Jews. She had the right to expect our loyalty, and in my case even more than that. After my choking experiences at school, in the kibbutz, in colonial garrisons, my present work in the field of psychological warfare made me dream of a future in which I might rebuild, in a "British" key, the class security I had enjoyed in Italy but without its "Latin" bourgeois straitjacket —a future in which I could take a confused, social, and personal revenge on the humiliations of my past.

To me at that time, Britain seemed the antithesis of provinciality, the opposite of Mussolini's buffoonery and of the cultural banality in which I had grown up. Still fed by heroic films seen in Italy, I abandoned myself to the attraction of the immense red-colored spaces submitted to British power in the geographic atlases; to the influence of a language I was now using more than my mother tongue; to the fascination of an

English style of life that in Palestine was, for the most part, a caricature of Victorianism. My admiration for the British was, as with Kipling, in direct relation to my colonial, psychological marginality, and I was unaware that I was in the process of becoming an "assimilated native" without the shrewdness of the Levantine.

In the years to come, this juvenile experience would help me to understand the mentality and the development problems of the peoples of the Third World. But at the time of the battles of El Alamein and Stalingrad, I did not feel that I was becoming what the French call an *évolué,* parroting what I believed to be signs of English culture and way of life: a moustache, which I found difficult to grow; a sauntering walk copied from some officers; an affected detachment from other people's troubles; a haughty indifference toward the dramatic war events I discussed with the arrogant ignorance of a football expert; and the ill-conceived superiority with which I treated the local "natives," Jews or Arabs, in the streets or in the market. This behavior was not peculiar to me. Jews, Moslems, and Christians competed with each other in those days in aping the British, each in his own way. At the Palestine Broadcasting Station they even had a booklet that explained the secrets of the new language, Pinglish. This mixture of local and Anglo-Saxon words—and especially the adaptation of English syntax to the local mentality—was one of the signs of the cultural disintegration of at least some of those groups of Palestinians, Arabs and Jews, who came in close contact with a foreign society totally convinced of its natural superiority.

Listening to the arguments of my landlord with the foolish righteousness derived from my temporary status as a British soldier and the curiosity of my ignorant exoticism toward a Judaism totally unknown to me, I could not understand the dangers of the pagan rationalism that obsessed him. Zionism was not a ghost that disturbed my sleep. On the contrary, fed as I was by romantic dreams and Fascist ideology, the thought that the state could be an idol, the nation a cruel chimera of which one should beware, never crossed my mind. For me the state was as natural a thing as the air or my mountain vacation. It was the organization that made people go to school, cleaned streets, minted money, distributed medals, gave a meaning to symbols, decorum to churches and uniforms, made trains arrive on time, and protected the legitimate interests of good families like mine in Italy. The state was an institution that had to be defended. Without internal order and protection from external enemies, one could not enjoy the normal pleasures of life, consisting for me mainly in fox hunting, skiing, watching Westerns, and conquering the only thing that at that time was to me of inestimable value—a woman.

And yet my conversations with Dr. Wilfrid made me aware of an aspect of my character that I tried to conceal even from myself. I perceived at the bottom of my consciousness something like an icy spot: I could suffer, hate, enjoy myself with every fiber of my body; I could listen in ecstasy to a piece of music; I could embrace with enthusiasm any cause; I was faithful to friends, sensitive to honor. To lie (as I frequently did) made my stomach ache for days. In sum, I knew that emotionally I was hypersensitive. But I could not help maintaining a selfish reserve even toward those I trusted most and toward the ideas that seemed to me most reasonable and noble. I developed an inability to give myself up totally, as if at the root of my conscious mind there existed a layer of indifference, a core of psychological ice that made it impossible for me to identify myself completely with anything or anybody.

I have never freed myself from this visceral indifference to which I probably owe my capacity to overcome both physical and moral pain. Only with advancing age have I given up the need, slightly sadistic, to have the roots of my teeth treated without an anesthetic. On those few occasions when I broke one of my limbs, I noticed a strange mechanism developing in my brain, a kind of levitation of my consciousness which, without reducing the pain of the flesh, transferred it outside my body.

To this splitting of my senses, I owe my psychological and moral survival in circumstances in which others would probably have gone mad. A word, a gesture of contempt, can still wound me more deeply—as the Arab proverb puts it—than a knife. But even the most terrible burning in the soul quickly cools at the contact with that icy layer. Only the anguish produced by fear of physical danger remains for me a permanent nightmare. To free myself from this I have often committed irrational acts of apparent courage just to overcome, through the fear of fear, the terror I always feel when faced by danger. In these circumstances, just as when confronted by strong physical pain, I feel a splitting of my senses that sometimes lasts for days. I then see myself trembling with fear and shame, pleading for a chance to run away. And opposed to this, another self, who stares from imaginary, empty eye sockets, indifferent and mocking.

A lady friend, endowed with parapsychological powers, told me once that I carried the mark of Cain on my forehead. I was born, she said, with a natural vocation for crime from which I have been saved by my innate animal fear. When I tried to explain to Dr. Wilfrid my occasional splitting into my two selves, he teasingly commented: "It is possible that in you Cain and Abel have not yet separated. You need a woman capable of choosing for you between life and death."

The idea that that was the choice of Faust came to me suddenly a few days later when, returning home late at night, I found Dr. Wilfrid's daughter waiting for me with a book of Goethe in German open on the table. She had arrived in Jerusalem from her kibbutz that afternoon, and her parents, who had gone out for the evening, had asked her to prepare my supper.

Without getting up, she held out to me her long-fingered, warm hand. I felt the two thoughtful eyes, which had been looking at me from the silver-framed photograph on the piano for the past two weeks, scrutinizing me as if I were a laboratory specimen.

"I am Berenika," she said softly. As would often happen to me when with her, I did not know what to answer.

9

Broadcasting
Intermezzo

T HE "CLANDESTINE" Italian
radio of the British headquarters in the Middle East operated
from the studios of the PBS (Palestine Broadcasting Station).
Our office was located in two rooms of the requisitioned
monastery of Saint Peter in Gallicantu on the slopes of Mount
Zion, a long, rectangular stone building, six floors high, with
a queer cement balustrade of a floral design around its flat roof.
From it one could see the entire valley of the Final Judgment
(the Valley of Jehoshaphat), and at the foot of the Mount of
Olives, the village of Silwan, engulfed in the wadi, which ran
down through the Judean Desert toward the Dead Sea.

Beneath the monastery, on the left-hand side and looking
eastward, one could see, partially concealed by two lines of
cypresses, the square stones of an ancient Roman street. After
celebrating the Last Supper on Mount Zion, Jesus had walked
on it to reach the Garden of Gethsemane, where he was arrested—a distance of less than two miles magnified by history
and faith, which the eyes had difficulty in equating with the
images created by legend and religion in the mind.

Mount Zion, at that time, was a silent hill, oppressed by the enormous Teutonic church that Kaiser Wilhelm II of Germany had built at the end of the last century in honor of the Virgin Mary and to please his Catholic subjects, jealous of the favors that German Protestants enjoyed in the Holy Land. The basilica, with its tower-like, copper-plated cupola, would soon become a battered, Jewish advance military position facing the Arabs in divided Jerusalem. In 1942 it was just another religious building whose shape broke the gentle line of the hill during the day and became, like everything else in Jerusalem, just another mysterious shadow in the evening.

From the roof of my office, where I used to go to enjoy the sunset, this tower looked to me like a kind of Tyrolean hat planted on the head of the mountain, a fanciful stone decoration imported into the Orient from the north, a symbol of that metamorphosis of Jewish beliefs which, transplanted from here into the Greco-Roman world, had turned the competition between old and new Israel into a suicide story for Western civilization.

From the monastery one had the impression in the evening of being almost able to reach, with one's outstretched hand, the massive Zion Gate. Through the dark opening of the donjon, orthodox Jews crossed furtively into the street. Bearded and lanky, wrapped in their caftans, their large felt hats bordered by fur, earlocks swinging on both sides of their faces in unison with the nervous movements of their bodies, they moved like shadows to and from the Old City quarters, quickly swallowed up by the stone alleys leading to the Tomb of David. I admired their courage in moving about alone at night in places where we British soldiers were advised not to go for fear of getting knifed. I knew nothing about them, although I was aware we belonged to the same people. They lived in their closed world surrounded by Arabs, keeping apart from the modern Jews whom they considered more impure than the Moslems or the Christians because of their heretical Hebrew nationalism. Only near the Wailing Wall, which at that time consisted of a narrow cobbled corridor, could I perceive the link between me and people so different. Here, swaying and moaning, Jews of all types, orthodox and liberal, native and visitor, young and old, Oriental and Western, felt the weight of the past that united them, often in spite of themselves.

This feeling of unity was strengthened in me by the revulsion I felt for the two British policemen who, at the entry to the passage, watched over our behavior. Their task was to see to it that nobody should blow a shofar—the Jewish ritual ram's horn—to remind the Lord of the promises made to His people. Like the Arabs, the mandatory government did not believe that a Jewish Messiah, let alone the Zionist Jews, would eventually build a Jewish state. But the howl of the shofar was considered political provocation, contrary to the delicate religious status quo. Those two unarmed policemen, looking impassively at the Jews crowding along the wall, seemed to me full of contempt for our native, rebellious superstitions. They stood like mannequins, carefully dressed in their colonial uniforms, probably bored and unaware in their northern, barbarian ignorance of the passions condensed by history in this miniaturized scene of suffering and prayers. To me they were a reminder both of the irritating difference of political status separating us in spite of our common uniform and of the comic marionettes I watched as a child in the theater in Turin, with their angular, wooden gestures moved by invisible strings. Who was the puppeteer activating all these people near the Wailing Wall, each devoted to his own cause and God? I could not find a satisfactory answer. And it was probably this lack of a satisfactory response to a primordial question that would one day push all of us, men and women in search of new roots, to join the fanatics. One day, without really knowing the reason, but moved by a visceral need for action, we would rise up and break all religious laws, demystify all political incantation. We would kill the British whom we admired because they stood guarding us against the Arabs, because they watched us mockingly near the wall; and then we would give vent to our perverse desire to cut off all the beards of the Jews, strip our impossible brothers of their stinking caftans, which weighed so heavily on our Zionist conscience, and start everything anew.

And yet the Wailing Wall was the only place where I felt that our secular national movement, even in its most extreme socialist forms, had a historical meaning; the only place where one could dream of a miracle—without imagining how close we stood to its coming.

In that warm summer Rommel menaced Egypt and Palestine, and people spoke of the inevitable retreat of the British army toward the mountains of Lebanon. These black forecasts did not disturb the sensation of peace and eternity that at nightfall surrounded the monastery where I worked, canceling all traces of the events that troubled the world. In the deep silence, broken by the howls of the jackals, I could let my imagination run wild, as had probably been done before me in these same premises by prophets and thieves, scribes and slaves, Pharisees and Crusaders, Roman legionnaires and merchants, without feeling part of the history that made Jerusalem the crossroad of the world. I was interested in living, in tasting and enjoying the strange adventure that Jewish persecution in Italy and the war in the Middle East had opened up for me. I was anxious to exploit whatever occasion fate offered me and desperate at not being able to explain to anyone why I felt such a need to climb up to the roof of the monastery at night to call my mother softly; to cry without shame over the dog my father had given, without my permission, to my uncle, over the mare on which I had galloped in Italy, and over the tin soldiers I had buried, together with my Fascist Youth dagger, under the cedar in my mother's garden—now probably all waiting, like the dead in the Valley of Jehoshaphat stretched out at my feet, for me to blow the trumpet of their resurrection.

I used to let myself go into these infantile reveries while, under the roof where I was standing, a legion of strange human beings, more unreal than those who inhabited my imagination, were busy, each one with earphones on his head in order not to disturb his neighbor, following the broadcasts of the enemy stations. Their task was to gather the material with which the army's psychological warfare service supplied the many clandestine broadcasting stations, like the Italian one in which I was working.

In those few hundred square meters under my feet there were Bulgarians and White Russians, Frenchmen and Germans; there were Croats who hated the Serbians and Macedonians who hated the Greeks; Moslems hostile to the Jews and Armenians who dreamed of avenging themselves on the Turks. They were tied to powerful receivers for two-hour spells. With one hand on the radio knobs and the other furiously scribbling on paper headed "On His Majesty's Service," these men and women fought against a faraway enemy and at the same time engaged in continuous battles to defend their own linguistic territory, as if it were a piece of the country they served or betrayed according to their own political faith. It was a mosaic of human relics kept together by a war that allowed each one to pursue the illusion of influencing the fate of distant peoples who were probably unaware of their existence and indifferent to their broadcasts. With most of them I had no contact. They were all older than I and belonged to that class of people I considered inferior because of their being "enemy aliens." They seemed to ignore my existence, and I did not realize that for them I was an unexplainable being: the only non-British soldier employed as a civilian speaker, who at the age of nineteen dealt with political questions reserved elsewhere only for senior officers.

With my military superiors I had no special problems. Some of them had come to Jerusalem from Cairo in the wake of the German advance in the Western Desert. Enzo Sereni, who had run the Italian section in Egypt, had clashed with the British HQ and left the Psychological Warfare Department. Of the original group created by Sereni, only one member remained —an officer of the Italian Alpine Corps, captured in Greece by the British and who switched to their side. He called himself de Robillant, drank a lot, pretended to be consumed by TB, and dreamt of—and indeed later succeeded in—becoming a writer. Neither with him nor with the other Italian expatriates, Jews and non-Jews, who had created in Jerusalem an anti-Fascist group affiliated with the movement "Giustizia e Libertà," did I develop close relations. On the contrary, I developed a friendship with the director of the Italian broadcasting section, Renato Mieli, and with his wife, Isa, who worked as secretary of our office.

Their personalities were so different from those of other Fascist refugees or Zionist immigrants in Palestine. Among so many excitable characters, Mieli appeared like an incarnation of common sense, modesty, and courtesy. He spoke softly, accepted philosophically the arrogance of the military administration, and enjoyed making fun of our British controller without his ever realizing it. This controller was an RAF officer who had never been in the cockpit of a plane or near a front line. He belonged to a Hungarian family that emigrated to England and stressed on every possible occasion the aristocratic particle preceding his name. He was also particular about the "y" that ended it (we sometimes substituted a simple "i" in our internal service notes), as if this consonant acted as a phonetic watershed between his Balkan origin and the new status acquired in England.

Renato Mieli had to write a daily political commentary to be broadcast to Italy after the news bulletin. He tried to avoid making use of the slogans with which our British controller wanted to embellish our broadcasts. It was no easy job. "We are a clandestine radio," Mieli used to say. "Theoretically we are operating somewhere on an Italian coastline. To make our clandestinity credible we must give the impression of being constantly in contact with the local population, we must interpret its mentality, be aware of its problems, interest our Italian listeners who have the patience and the courage to tune in. We must therefore supply them with plausible news and only from time to time plant unverifiable items of propaganda and denounce personalities in the Fascist regime. Calumny is useful only if measured, and tendentious interpretation of facts credible only if based on verifiable events." It was counterproductive to conceal the successes of Rommel, or minimize the importance of British military reverses, such as the fall of Tobruk. On the contrary, they should be mentioned whenever possible, to explain the consequences of a war in which Italy, beaten by the Allies or made a satellite of Germany, would in any case become a loser. Mieli looked for every possible item of news on current life in Italy, news picked up from Fascist, Vatican, or Swiss stations, on which to base his political commentary, rather than speculating on major events.

Although monitoring was not my responsibility, I liked to spend hours listening to broadcasts in Italian from wherever they came. I was fascinated by the voices that reached me from Italy, and even more by the little pep talks that the famous "Colonel Steven" gave, in Italian, from London over the BBC. He was a British diplomat who had served for many years in Italy and had an intimate knowledge of the Italian mentality. At a distance of years I perceive how, in the absence of a proper school education, I learned from him, and in general through my work in the monastery of Saint Peter in Gallicantu, the trade of journalism. But it was to Fausto Nitti, the nephew of the former Italian prime minister, whom I owe the reading of my first serious books—Croce's *History of Europe* and *Estetica* —which so greatly influenced my way of thinking.

How this elegant and refined gentleman had ended up in Jerusalem reading daily news bulletins with me for a faked clandestine broadcasting station run by the British, I do not know. I admired him for the way in which he always dressed perfectly, for the free and easy manner in which he carried his Indian walking stick, for the dignity with which he combined an exceptional family past with his present precarious status. Nitti hated speaking about himself; he preferred to listen in silence to others. When we had to present a two-voice program, he reading the news and I the announcements, or vice versa, he took special care in hitting the gong that opened and closed our broadcasts. That subdued rumble of percussed metal, which the microphone was supposed to propagate on the air until it reached the ears of some Italian listener thousands of miles away, seemed to have for him a value greater than any political commentary. I watched him standing near me in the studio, his eyes riveted on the technician through the sound-proof window who had to give us the signal to start the broadcast. In his left hand Nitti held the gong, dangling from a cord tied to two holes on its rim. Bent slightly forward, he raised the hammer with his right hand, waiting like a hunting dog pointing its prey. When the technician gave the sign, with a finger aimed like a pistol, Nitti struck two chimes on the gong, one stronger, one weaker. Then he stretched himself forward, as if he wanted to follow with his entire body the sound he had just produced, as if a tiny part of himself could fly through skies and reach a secure place that none of us knew, where perhaps somebody was waiting for him. Perhaps it was a woman, perhaps an accomplice, perhaps a faithful dog, like mine, now lonely in its kennel, like me, like Nitti, like all those whom the war had uprooted, separated, dismembered. Perhaps it was just the echo of our thoughts thrown toward a faraway, unreal Italy, which we were pretending to help and prepare for its political future, returning deprived of sense to its source in a provincial corner of Britain's cosmopolitan empire.

Isa was the opposite of Nitti. Minute, blond, loquacious, quivering with communist passion, she kept full control of herself in her working relationships but went wild in the style of the bulletins she typed on small sheets of paper. She was indeed quite a strange "comrade": too intelligent and too much conditioned by the Levantine atmosphere of Egypt to insert quotations from Marx and Lenin into her daily conversation, she never let an occasion pass to mention the Red Army without adding the word "heroic." For her every Fascist was a plutocrat, every worker in the vanguard of the people. Cosmopolitanism was doomed, the USSR was saving Europe from the Nazis, and true democracy could exist only in a socialist world. Many of these expressions got lost between the old Underwood on which Isa hammered them out and the broadcast sheets we used in the studio. It was not the British censor who corrected the style of this ardent Alexandrine; it was her husband and sometimes Nitti who expurgated from the text as many of her ideological superlatives as the arrogant banalities of our British controller—one with his modest smile, the other with his impenetrable silences.

In August 1942, when the appointment of Montgomery as head of the Eighth Army had strengthened everyone's courage and faith, the reinforcements the Intelligence Service had requested from its American counterpart arrived in our section. They consisted of two Italo-Americans who, I was told in strict confidence, had been sent by the gangster "Lucky" Luciano to prepare the Allied landing in Sicily. They were supposed to supply us with coded messages to broadcast to Sicilian patriots belonging to political movements that wanted to separate the island from Italy. Our British controller, that RAF officer with the "y" at the end of his name, explained to me that these messages were of two types. There were coded sentences addressed to the Sicilian members of the Mafia, so secret that nobody had the right to know their meaning; apparently they were explosive material that could change the course of the war, if not in the entire Mediterranean, certainly between the towns of Gela and Caltanissetta. Then there were the messages that the captain called "musical accompaniments." These were to be written in a hermetic style supposed to give credibility to our broadcasts in certain Sicilian milieus that theoretically listened to them. These regional-separatist lucubrations would, according to him, prepare the ground for the forthcoming landing and make the inhabitants of Sicily more sensitive and conscious of the history of their island. My captain sincerely believed himself involved in an ideological effort to promote the political consciousness of a pro-British, independent Sicily, even if more controlled than ever by the Mafia.

Ignorant as I was of the history of Sicily, which I had never visited, I could make no sense of the arguments the captain expounded to me, especially in the absence of the head of our station. I was, however, surprised by the fact that the two mafiosi whom we had received from America—one fat and the other thin, lugubrious and comical like Laurel and Hardy—lived an existence totally detached from our section. I do not remember ever having read a message, coded or uncoded, prepared by them. What I immediately noticed was that the two "advisers" spoke a strange, Anglicized Italian that nobody in our section was able to understand. It sounded more like the language spoken by the Bulgarians and Albanians who worked on the top floor of the monastery than the dialect of any Italian province I knew. I also discovered that at least one of these two strange figures (the other soon disappeared from sight) could not write. When I accompanied him—he was the fat one—to the quartermaster's office to sign some administrative forms, I saw him inscribing the paper with scribbling similar to that which my father's illiterate peasants made on the documents he prepared for their signature.

Fortunately for everyone, the two representatives of "Lucky" Luciano knew how to keep their mouths shut. They had been quartered at the American Colony Hotel, one of the most elegant residences in Jerusalem, and there they spent their days, drinking lemonade and beer. Throughout the period of my work at the radio, I do not remember anybody ever making use of their services, partly because—as I said—nobody could understand their language. The British controller of our section had tried to overcome this linguistic difficulty by using sign language which, according to him, expressed fundamental concepts of the ancient Sicilian culture. To me they looked like the gestures children make at monkeys in zoological gardens, but it was probably because I had not been let into this type of state secret. Later, however, it came to my knowledge that, perhaps due to an error of interpretation of languge or of judgment by overly zealous police, the two mafiosi, who were supposed to advance the Allied cause in Italy, had been advancing that of hashish dealers in Palestine. It seems they had no difficulty in making themselves understood in the local Jerusalem markets.

During my time at the radio I never asked to what political or religious creed Mieli and his wife belonged. Only many years later in Rome when I met Mieli (then the editor of an important communist weekly) in the home of a mutual friend —a noble landowner who tortured himself about whether to divide his land among his tenant farmers—did I learn that both of them were Jewish. It was not surprising, since the Communist party in Egypt in the thirties had been to a large extent supported by Jewish intellectuals, the sons of some of the richest families in Cairo and Alexandria. I met one of them during a recent trip to Egypt. He was one of the survivors of the age of Nasser and Sadat, reduced by age, prison, and political failure to a pathetic political relic, rather like one of the characters in Durrell's *Alexandria Quartet*. In retrospect I tend to believe that in Renato Mieli the Jewish strain remained alive even at the time of his active participation in the Communist party. He was, in any case, the only one among the strange figures working at the monastery of Saint Peter in Gallicantu who did not share the general disbelief in the Zionist movement. All the others forecast that Jewish nationalism would die out with the end of the war and provoke a massive return of Palestinian Jews to Europe. Nor did Mieli believe that the British would be able to uphold their White Paper and make Zionists agree to remain forever a minority protected by Britain in an Arab land.

In spite of my work at the Psychological Warfare Department, I was naturally interested in the future of the Jewish National Home far more than in that of Fascism in Italy or in that British-imposed democracy, which I could not even conceive through the lenses of Allied propaganda. My experience with Zionism in Palestine, even if diluted by my Anglophilia, did not help my political and social contacts with the cosmopolitan world in which I worked nor with the larger world outside. If, in "town," I was suspect to the Jews because of my connection with the Intelligence Service, within our "monastery" my status of Jewish Palestinian military personnel among foreign civilians was the object of not particularly friendly comment, usually made in an anti-Zionist key. It was strange how these cosmopolitan refugees, each one strongly supporting the sovereignty of his own native land even when this clashed, as in the case of the Balkans, with that of their neighbor, were unwilling to admit that Jews, too, possessed a nationality of their own and a right to political independence. This debate around the legitimacy of Zionism as a national movement did not cease with the creation of the State of Israel, and it has become more acute since the 1970s with the development of a parallel and opposite Palestinian Arab "Zionism." Going back in my mind to the political discussions of that time, it seems to me that the major difference between then and now does not reside in the topics of the discussions but in their intensity. In whatever language people spoke there was an emotional passion and, I believe, a level of intellect, which in

Israel today remains the patrimony of very limited groups.

I have no clear recollection of how I used my time in the mornings—probably sleeping and making up for the long night hours spent in the studios. I have, however, the impression that from the setting of the sun until dawn, the entire Yishuv did nothing but argue. One of the reasons was certainly the nonexistence of other types of entertainment. Sports were not popular in Palestine; television did not exist; the cinemas screened old films; food was rationed; social life was rigidly divided between those who frequented the British and those (the majority) who shut themselves up in the ethnical, religious, ideological sectarianism of their respective communities: Jews, Christians, Moslems, Greeks, Armenians, socialists, orthodox, etcetera. In the cafés of the new Jewish quarters of Jerusalem, where orange juice, locally produced beer, chicory coffee, and apple strudel were the only edible items, or in the dining rooms, which invariably served as bedrooms, people argued, dreamed, plotted, listened to endless poetry readings, to the music of gramophones, or to foreign broadcasts, without ever looking at their watches. They, or at least those Jewish friends with whom I used to meet, loved, hated, hoped frenetically, splitting hairs over every argument, with impassioned speeches. Fear, hunger, and pain were concealed by a generalized tendency to laugh at the worst situations. We all shared the apocalyptic, messianic, albeit provincial atmosphere of Jerusalem with the ravenous irresponsibility of youth never sufficiently satisfied by action.

The topics of our discussions varied from homemade strategy to the planning of impossible trips; from religious duties to ideological heresies; from the functioning of weapons to free love; from the compilation of subversive posters against the British to the denunciation of some real or imaginary betrayal; from the critiques of books we had learned to the exegesis of the writings of Marx—which most of us had never read. The most stimulating arguments were those between kibbutzniks and city dwellers, between those who rebelled in words against the presence of the British and those who rebelled in thought against the discipline imposed by the Zionist movement. Few acted on their own initiative. Of these I hardly remember the words, but only a troubling succession of faces: faces of young people bronzed by the sun, faces of old people dessicated by sorrow; eyes of women lightened by passion and lust, faces of philosophers and of priests; faces looking at you with slit-like eyes, inhaling their cigarette smoke together with the recondite meaning of their words; faces of youngsters searching for exploits, faces of cowards and faces of saints; faces marred by sentiments toward which one felt attracted as though by an animal force; faces whose expressions said the contrary of their voices, whose eyes turned in the emptiness of anguish; faces of princes and faces of slaves, all of them exposed to the challenges of this land's passionate beliefs.

Among so many different faces, two belonged to the only non-Italian colleagues in my office, with whom I had established a complex relationship. One was Anna, a German Jewess converted to Christianity, living in a convent in the Old City of Jerusalem. The other was Robert, a Christian Arab who had returned from London at the outbreak of war. They had in common a singular hatred for the Zionists and an impelling need to give expression to these sentiments in my presence.

Robert was not gifted with brilliance or culture, but he possessed a sufficient smattering of both to upset me with his political arguments. According to him and—he always added —without the least possibility of error, the Zionist cause was doomed and fundamentally immoral. He proclaimed his certainty with aplomb, choosing in the composition of his sentences as many Anglo-Saxon words as he could, avoiding with care words rooted in Latin, which sounded to him too vulgarly Mediterranean. Impeccably dressed, with jacket and tie even in the most torrid heat, he did not affect an Oxford accent, nor did he try, as so many Arabs and Jews were doing, to imitate the manner of speech and the behavior of the higher British officials. There was, however, in his manner, something as unctuous as his brilliantined hair and as arrogant as the movements of his hands, with which he used to wave away my answers as if they were bothersome flies. My rancor against him was mainly due to the fact that he flirted with Anna with an insistence that seemed to me improper and at times even insulting. I suffered seeing him leaving the office in her company, disappearing in the evenings into the winding alleys of the market leading toward her lodgings, which were impenetrable for me. I imagined them walking in the labyrinth of the native market toward secret, perfumed divans, first arm in arm like two good colleagues, later entwined in amorous struggles in alcoves lighted by candles, filled with oriental carpets and damask cushions, she a ravishing blond, he like the sheikh of Araby, possessing this Jewess, freed by her religious conversion from her tribal loyalties and clutching like an octopus the body of this Arab with all her tentacular complexes.

Anna attracted me enormously. She was older than I by at least ten years, and her feminine charm was blended, for me, with a feeling of motherhood. I looked for every opportunity to meet her inside the office but had not the courage to approach her outside. I felt for her a childish passion and embarrassment, a fear mixed with some familiarity that made me sit next to her in the canteen, wait for her when she left the monitoring hall, accompany her to the NAAFI shop, where one could buy cheaper beer and locally made chocolate. Robert joined us, always elegant and sure of himself, looking for every opportunity to develop his anti-Zionist theories in front of Anna, convinced by my confused reactions that he had succeeded in demolishing my political faith.

Anna preferred to divert the conversation toward religious questions. She seemed to feel the constant need to explain to me why she had converted. She attacked Judaism but never the

Jews, as if she wanted to defend that secular Zionism that had broken with the Jewish tradition and proclaimed the right of the Jews to free themselves from the yoke of the Law. To her this meant a process of collective assimilation, inevitably fated to turn the first Jewish community in history into candidates for Christian conversion. It was a thesis that infuriated her friend Robert, even if he tried to conceal his irritation behind the understatements he formulated in the language of Shakespeare. The Zionists, he believed, even if they converted to Christianity or Islam, would remain somehow Jewish if allowed to exist autonomously. In Palestine their political beliefs would forever remain for him nothing but a new, cowardly form of European colonialism. He turned livid when Anna retorted that the Arabs, too, even when Christians, remained Moslem at heart; that they were men from the desert but incapable of achieving the level of morality that ancient Judaism had developed in the desert. If the Jews had accepted the message of Christ they would have been the true light unto the people. The Christianization of Zionism could herald the final salvation.

Robert and Anna disagreed on everything except the wrongness of the faiths in which they had respectively been born. They both loathed their parents' religions with the passion of a neophyte: she as a convert to Christianity, he as a convert to the British style of life. They took special pleasure in explaining to each other and, indirectly to me, the superstitions of the ancestral religions they had given up.

When Anna denounced her version of Judaism she did it with a detached professorial voice, as if she were describing a fossilized exhibit in a museum—a civilization dead and buried in the depths of time, without any ties with the Jewish life that throbbed so intensely around her, without any connection to the barbarous deeds perpetuated by the most Christianized societies of Europe. She spoke against Judaism with her eyes following a faraway vision, while the hollow of her throat, uncovered by the open collar of her blouse, palpitated more rapidly. At these moments I was struck by her extraordinary beauty, and I was scared by the coldness of her looks, the lack of feeling. There was a frost in her soul, like in mine, which made her sound deeply inhuman.

One afternoon when we stood alone on the roof of the monastery to watch the sunset, I found the courage to ask her what had made her convert to Christianity. I was interested to know, I told her, because my mother had gone the same way. She did not answer me. The sky was already red, the air translucent, a few restless birds flew among the trees. The walls of the Old City reflected on their stones the violet color of the dying day. The tolling of a bell, pulled by invisible hands, reached us from a distant church. I asked her if she saw her conversion as a way to escape from the yoke of her family's Judaism or as a way to be different. Anna remained silent, her thin lips barely open, one hand clasping the railing round the roof, the thumb and forefinger of the other fiddling with a button on her blouse. The very fact that she was listening seemed to me proof that I had at last succeeded in establishing real contact with her, perhaps in warming the ice in her soul. When she finally answered me, she did so with her eyes still fixed on the distance but with a new expression on her face, which reminded me of the portraits of saints on Annetta's bedside table. "I became a Christian because I believe in the purity of platonic thought," she said briskly, before moving away. Years after, reading a page written by Hanna Arendt, I remembered this answer I had not then understood. At the time I had only the impression of having collided head-on with a statue, at the feet of which, like those of an idol, lay my broken feelings.

From that day on, Anna avoided discussing with me questions of religion, directing her arrows against Robert. He was a convert, she kept telling him with the hint of a sneer in her voice, not to a divine faith but to the mundane faith, the cultural values of Europe in which he had been educated. Everything in him, from the way he dressed to the ideas he expressed, was imported from or influenced by the West. He was ashamed of his origins, of his ancient Assyrian Christian family and did not want to be reminded that he belonged to a community that the Moslems had exterminated in Iraq at the beginning of the thirties and the British partially saved by recruiting the surviving men into the auxiliary imperial troops. This was the true reason for his hatred of everything Islamic and his unlimited admiration for everything British. But since he could not be either English or Moslem, he deluded himself with the romantic vision of Arabism he had brought back from England. This allowed him to share in the indigenous nationalism without shedding his hostility toward Islam, while his aversion to Zionism was in inverse proportion to the attraction that British culture exercised on him.

Anna was right, and Robert could hardly bear the truth she was telling him, especially in my presence. I had difficulty understanding how so many complexes could coexist in a single person. But Robert was the Arab counterpart of many Jews I knew: fanatically nationalist and at the same time hostile to their religious traditions, obsessed by the need to express their hate for British colonialism and at the same time fascinated by everything British. His Arabism was a form of exoticism in which he hoped there might sooner or later be a coexistence of the Arab and the English. He could not admit to what Anna kept telling him, that Christian Arab nationalists like him would be the first to suffer from the disappearance of British imperialism from the Middle East. The Moslems would then monopolize all the power and aggress against all the minorities in the lands of Islam. In Palestine common sense and common interests should have united Christians and Jews in upholding the British presence. Instead they were both fighting, for opposing reasons, against their natural ally, Great Britain. Robert laughingly discounted this kind of talk, just as many Fascist Jews I had known in Italy had refused to listen to unpleasant truths.

His relations with Anna, a converted Jewess who tried to fulfill her visions of purity and intellectual clarity in a world of confused, burning passions, probably meant for this Arab-Christian in search of his roots an attempt to patch his broken identity, which later pushed him into joining one of the armed Arab bands during the war against the Jews in 1947–1948. Anna, too, remained on the Arab side, refusing to leave the Christian Quarter of Old Jerusalem. She was found raped and with her stomach slit open on the very day when the Jews surrendered to the British-officered Arab Legion of King Abdullah of Transjordan.

10

Berenika

Berenika was not beautiful, certainly less so in life than in her photograph. Her eyes were wide, her hair cut too short. Her white cotton shirt, which the women of the kibbutz wore on Saturdays, reminded me of the uniform of the Fascist girls youth movement. Her shoulders were slightly bent forward, adding a sinuous curve to her body in contrast to the controlled passion that she expressed in every movement. This slightly concave line of her physique fitted her character: introverted but turned toward action, ready to receive but also to conceal and exclude. The image I immediately formed of her in my mind when I saw her for the first time was that of a cradle in which one could rock but from which one could also fall out at the slightest push of an invisible hand—an image still present in my memory although smoothed by time, passions, and wounds, like one of those silhouettes cut out of black paper by hungry artists on the steps of the Louvre.

I was certainly confused to find her, suddenly, in front of me, waiting to give me my dinner, with the book of Goethe open on the table. I was also overcome by the violence with which her perfume awakened in me the need for a woman. She must have perceived it, and from that very first moment a double dialogue established itself between us made up of banalities and deep, unexpressed feelings, of mechanical gestures and furtive glances. It was, as so often happens between young people, a sentimental ballet of two beings equally attracted but unable to give expression to their sentiments.

Berenika had arrived from her kibbutz, recently established in Galilee, because she thought she was pregnant. Aged twenty, she had thought it her "duty" to accept into her body a "comrade" in need of affection, although she had had no intention of starting a family. She told me this with the detachment of a nurse prescribing the proper use of a medicine to a patient. Her kibbutz in any case was too poor to allow itself the luxury of new children, especially from unmarried couples. Her case had been discussed by the kibbutz secretariat, with tact but without false prudishness. It had been decided that the best thing would be for her to have an abortion. She had agreed. She would not have known what to do with a baby—even if raised communally in a kibbutz. The war was transforming the country and, more important, would certainly change the whole world. In such circumstances men and women did not have any more right to dispose freely of their bodies, of their lives, than millions of soldiers locked in battle, or the myriad human beings, reduced to an animal existence, who were enduring the war. The body of a healthy young woman like hers should serve some more useful purpose than turning out babies, many of whom would probably be killed before being weaned. The idea of having an abortion seemed logical to her because of its very brutality: it was part of the general atmosphere of violence in which we had to learn sooner or later to live.

The doctor who had visited her was not, however, fully convinced of her pregnancy and had advised her to wait. Out of this involuntary pause emerged her unexpected vacation, a brief period of life she was spending in a kind of moral and biological limbo. But this state of uncertainty had persuaded her to break off relations with her boyfriend and come to stay with her parents in town. She was not particularly suffering from the break. She had rather the impression of having abandoned a patient in the middle of treatment. She felt toward the human wreck with whom she had copulated a strange maternal feeling, an instinct of protection stronger than toward the being who perhaps was already growing in her womb. Both appeared to her weak, naked, skinned alive. She imagined them as shapeless masses of blood, sinews, and ganglia, exposed to the indifference of the world, easy prey to predators, in need of delicate care, of bandages, of baths, but differently related to her. Her comrade was something physically detached but ever present in her mind; the other—she did not know what to call it—was ever present in her body and in her deepest, irrational consciousness but intellectually alien to her and in possession of a selfish vitality over which she had already lost all control.

I listened to this talk with a shameful, confused, and at the same time tense and excited mind. From the very first moment we met—I do not remember whether it was the same evening when I found her waiting for me in her parents' apartment or the following day when we went out together for the first time to walk along the crenellated walls of old Jerusalem— she had explained to me the reasons for her coming to town with such a simplicity and frankness that I felt my own feelings for her were becoming wrapped in aseptic thoughts. When, in the quiet of my office, I thought about her, I tended to compare her with certain booklets of military instruction that I carried in my knapsack. These manuals aimed to prepare soldiers to face the most violent events. And yet they described them in the same tone Berenika had used to narrate her personal story: front lines where people were dying were translated into colored graphs; battlegrounds into maps dotted with arrows; mortal weapons into mechanical toys. Everything was made one-dimensional; existence was a simple matter of causes and effects, of variable solutions, of schemes. Everything was clear and simple, "like a printed book," my uncle's cook—who was illiterate—would have said, and yet everything was so obscure, mysterious, convulsive.

Behind Berenika's cool logic stood passions and humors clothed in a nurse's apron, and I was unable to link them with the man from whom she had just separated and the creature who might be growing in her womb. I was disconcerted in front of this girl, only one year older than I but who seemed so experienced, who had drunk to the dregs the poison of the senses and uninhibitedly answered the animal call that often kept me awake at night. Walking at my side along the walls built by Suleiman the Magnificent, she unveiled to me the secrets of a body equally attracting and repelling. From her eyes and from the curves of her shoulders I received both inviting messages and signals of icy detachment. I was divided by the desire to throw myself into her, forgetting myself, the war, and the past, and the anxiety and fear of losing myself in the obscure meanders of her dangerous character. But all the time, in spite of my confusion, I felt that something secret, unspeakable, and strange existed in this woman, concealed behind a cool shamelessness of logic. I imagined, for lack of a better idea, that her strange manners were dictated by her political ideas or that she might be involved in some clandestine affairs that imposed on her this complex behavior.

Imprisoned by my doubts and fantasies, I believed her to be involved in sordid affairs with Arab beys or British officials from whom she probably stole secrets. Or that she ensnared some local effendis ready to sell to the Jews land in the areas forbidden by the British White Paper. Everyone at that time, in any case, was plotting, counterplotting, and had some private or public secret to conceal. Only I was living in the grotesque clandestinity of a radio station broadcasting in Italian from Jerusalem, trying to make probably nonexistent listeners believe that we were located somewhere in Italy. There was nothing really to brag about. With shame and sadness I kept telling Berenika what I was doing, why I had joined the British army, about my boredom at performing guard duties in the middle of nowhere, dreaming of the battles in which I never took part. Now at least I had become, by mere chance, an announcer in a camouflaged broadcasting station. But I still felt alien in my new country, estranged from the queer cosmopolitan people who populated my office, unable to rebut Robert's arguments on Zionism and Anna's ideas on Judaism, while looking for fame and adventure through the cracks that the British administration, the war, and my knowledge of Italian had suddenly opened before me.

Berenika listened to me with her ironic smile and her absorbed eyes. She let me talk for hours without interrupting me, without asking questions, curious only to know some details of my mother's personality, of our village home, or of my dog, Bizir. She never asked me what I did in the office, and I carefully avoided asking her about her political activities. I knew that as a member of a collective settlement she must have belonged to some clandestine military organization. But I could not imagine what task could have been given to a woman of her age, free from family ties, attractive, educated, and fanatic.

There was another aspect of her behavior that intrigued me. Like her mother, Berenika was not observant. But even more than Frau Luise, she showed great respect toward her father's religious beliefs. I wondered where she had found the courage to tell Dr. Wilfrid, so prudish and strict in his moral principles, the reason she had come to town. Yet it looked as if her troubles had brought her closer to her father. She, a member of the Hashomer Hatzair, the leftist pioneer movement, which never lost an occasion to attack rabbinical Judaism, took greater care than her mother to make the apartment ready for the Sabbath: she spent hours polishing the silver; she arranged the flowers; she made sure the tablecloth was smooth and the table settings were perfectly aligned. With great concentration she lit the Sabbath candles, and when in the kitchen, she—who outside her home ate every kind of forbidden food—was more particular than her mother in separating the pans used for cooking meat from those used for milk. This, I thought, must have been her way of thanking her father in silence for his understanding. But beyond her feeling of gratitude, I sensed something deeper, an intellectual and moral engagement, devoid of religious conviction, but meant to make of every gesture an act of devotion, a family, daughterly prayer.

When I caught her making my bed I laughed at her for the precision with which she made hospital corners. Once she allowed me to help her. She made me turn the woolen blanket three times in order to make sure that the factory label was underneath and in the top left-hand corner. That was its place and there it must stay. For those who could understand it there was an order in everything, she told me, just as there was a language for everything created: flowers, stones, furniture. The dignity of things should never be violated. When I asked if this were not a kind of ritual of her personal religion, she avoided answering. She insisted that her passion for reading the Book of Psalms was purely literary and wanted me to listen to the rhythm of the Hebrew language. When she read them for me, her harmonious voice became metallic, stressing ancient words as if they were square stone. But in order not to mislead me about the spirit in which she read the psalms, she never failed to add: "Goethe and Schiller, too, have written verses as beautiful as those by David. Pity you don't understand German."

Quite different, however, was her behavior in political matters. She vehemently discussed the progress of the war with her father. She exalted Russia and had doubts about the sincerity of the British military effort now that the fear of a Nazi victory had receded. She did not have clear ideas about the war aims of the United States. Italy did not interest her, or perhaps she avoided talking about it in my presence after what I had told her about my Fascist past and that of my family. However, neither with her father nor with me did she ever express any opinion on the Zionist movement and its ideological trends. As to her experiences in the kibbutz, she spoke like somebody telling stories to innocent children: the work in the chicken house, her adventures in the kitchen, her problems in keeping milk fresh. Simple facts of life that any Italian farmer's wife could have told a visitor without ever touching on the ideas, the psychological and moral problems that united or divided the inhabitants of these egalitarian communities, usually made up of uprooted people of bourgeois origin, trying to reconstruct their lives in the framework of an idealistic, collective family, free from biological constrictions.

When I sometimes questioned her about the policy followed by her party toward the Arabs and the British and its postwar program, she looked at me with a strange smile without answering, as if to say, "You can't understand these things." Only once, when I told her that in my view the kibbutz, in spite of its pretensions to equality, was a collective aristocratic institution, whose members would sooner or later behave like "feudal collective knights," did she throw me a look full of anger and answer me almost in a hiss: "Only someone who grew up in a Fascist milieu could reason like that." But her face soon softened, and her smile became coquettish and inviting.

As the days went by, I found my situation more and more ridiculous and unbearable. I was full of desire for this woman, so attractive and physically so near me, and at the same time I behaved like an elderly friend of the family, spending hours listening to her personal situation. I wanted to make her share my life, my thoughts, my anguish, and, instead, I spent most of my time with her discussing literature and philosophic subjects totally unknown to me and which, on top of that, did not interest me at all.

One day Berenika mentioned to me the financial difficulties she might have if she were forced to have an abortion. I immediately offered her fifty pounds sterling, a fabulous sum at that time, which represented all my savings. She accepted the offer without a word of thanks. I felt so deeply offended that I spent an entire night fantasizing how I could revenge myself, furious at having given away my money in a fit of generosity dictated solely by my need to appear what I was not, namely rich and generous. In the morning, with heavy eyes and my head more than usually confused, I got up with the stern intention of informing her that our relationship could no longer continue, at least not in the way it had developed up to that moment. I had had enough of playing the "squire of dames" to her and of being treated like a schoolboy. Sitting at the breakfast table, where toast waited to be spread with the margarine of my military rations, I searched in my mind for the most offensive phrase with which to wound her.

Berenika entered the room with a mug of steaming milk in her hand, put it on the table, sat down next to me, and in silence took my hand, accompanying the gesture with a look full of sweetness. I felt a sudden void in my stomach and was overtaken by an uncontrollable fit of coughing, which sent me running to the kitchen for a drink of water. When I returned, my eyes were still watering and I had difficulty talking. Berenika was still seated at the table, stirring the sugar in my coffee cup. She did not give me time to open my mouth. She took a slice of toast, started to spread it with margarine, and staring at it as if it were the most important object in the world, she said, almost talking to herself: "Something happened to me last night. I don't need to go and see a doctor."

I could not find a more intelligent reply than to say—"You see? In the end everything turns out all right," and I was happy that my coughing gave me a pretext to conceal the emotion that now really made my eyes water. Berenika must have noticed it, although I kept rubbing my eyes with my knuckles. This was the first time I realized that the eyes are sunk into the hollows of the skull, and by running my fingers over my cheekbones I could feel the shape of my face and perceive the reality of my "impersonal" skeleton concealed under the skin. Thus, my first, vibrant impulse of love came accompanied by an equally violent sensation of death and the taste of a slice of toast covered with Australian margarine.

Now that she was no longer preoccupied with her biological problem, Berenika decided to return that morning to her kibbutz in Galilee; she wanted to get involved in activities that would take her out of the chicken run and make her forget the anxieties of the last few weeks. Probably, she said to me, she would ask her comrades to authorize her to volunteer for the British army. Whatever the case, she would return to Jerusalem as soon as possible since there were a lot of things we now had to talk seriously about with each other. A short break was necessary for both of us. She needed a few days to look inside herself; I should do the same. I agreed and told her that I would wait for her return with great impatience. At that moment Dr. Wilfrid entered the room. Berenika told him that she had decided to leave Jerusalem. "Does your mother know?" he asked. "Not yet," Berenika said, smiling softly. "Then it's better that you go and tell her about it." And there was that air of naive complicity between the two.

By the time Berenika returned I must have been well on the way to my office. At one corner of the street I bumped into an old lady who was taking her dog for a stroll. Both looked at me with a stupefied air as I bowed to them and went on my way whistling, euphoric.

From the morning she left Jerusalem until her return ten days later, I did nothing but think of her, of her body, and of what I would tell her about us and our future. There were moments when I was so deeply immersed in my erotic thoughts that I must have given the impression of a sleep-walker. One evening, when dressed in uniform, I was followed by a patrol of military police while on my way to the radio station. They stopped me, believing I was drunk since they had heard me talking to myself. I told them I was reciting a piece of poetry I had learned by heart for a party we had organized in the mess. They checked my pay book, made no comments, and let me go, happier than ever.

In the office, too, people realized that something had happened to me. I showed little interest in the news bulletins they prepared and I read every day; I did not discuss the progress of the war. I spent most of my time looking out the window of our monastic office, looking at the flight of birds and at the changing colors of the Mountains of Edom beyond the Dead Sea.

Those were days of great tensions and hopes. The British were dashing toward Tripoli, the Americans had landed in North Africa. The end of the war seemed suddenly near and the defeat of the Axis powers inevitable. In our section there was a lot of talk about the political system that would replace the Fascist regime in Italy. Names of persons unknown to me were continually bandied about. Our commentaries mentioned political groups such as the Partito Popolare, the Communist party, Giustizia e Libertà, names that sounded to me as unreal as those of the Longobards or the Bourbons, who ruled Italy centuries before and about whom we had learned at school. Only Isa Mieli, who looked more excited by these political events and speculations than anyone else in the office, took an interest in my emotional state.

One afternoon, while walking along the path from the Church of the Last Supper to the Zion Gate, she suddenly asked me: "Does your girlfriend bother you a lot?" I blushed to my ears, but I was grateful to have at last an opportunity to talk about Berenika and confide my pains to somebody. I felt a growing need to share my anxieties, my fears, the passion of this first love and at the same time to explain my anger toward her. As I started to answer I realized how difficult it was for me to describe her: not because I knew so little about Berenika's life but because of those strange, enigmatic aspects of her personality and the mystery that I felt surrounded her. I had the impression that Berenika had gone through experiences that had split her character, clouded her soul, and made it impossible for her to live at the pace of the rest of humanity. All I could say to Isa was that indeed I was involved with a girl who was making my head spin as never before.

We had just gone through the Zion Gate and ascended the high steps leading to the top of the bastion to admire the sunset. Sitting in the niche between two massive battlements, the fragile figure of Isa, already undermined by the illness that would soon lead her to her death, faded into the shadows of the advancing night. Without questioning me, she urged me by her silence to talk. I told her how I had met Berenika, what I knew about her kibbutz, and the problem she had had with her "fiancé." I tried to explain why she seemed to me so different from other girls, especially from Annemarie, of whom I suddenly realized that I had not thought since the day I first set foot in Palestine.

Annemarie was a student I had first known in 1937 at the tennis club in Alassio, owned by an Englishman—Bennett, I think was his name—who had not been persuaded, either by the sanctions imposed by the League of Nations against Italy for the invasion of Ethiopia nor by Fascist propaganda against *perfide Albion,* to leave Italy. I did not like tennis particularly; I preferred fencing and riding. But it was considered quite fashionable in Fascist times to play tennis, and in that particular club two things attracted me—buttered toast and Annemarie, who had initiated me into many secrets of that sport: how to hold the racket at the proper angle; how to pronounce correctly certain English words that sounded ridiculous to me, such as "play" and "ready," without which the game was not supposed to begin.

Annemarie was easy to be with. She laughed at everything I told her about my schoolteachers, the horses I rode during my vacation in the Alps, Annetta's pretended fright when I suddenly jumped out at her from behind a door in the hope of making her drop the plate or glass she was carrying. With Annemarie, sitting on the green benches of the club in the shade of the hedge, caressed by the Mediterranean breeze, I could talk about everything without feeling embarrassed or bored.

A year later, in 1938, after the racial laws against the Jews had been published, I went back for a week to Alassio as the guest of an aunt of mine who lived nearby. Quite naturally I ran to the tennis club to look for Annemarie and to play in a place where Jews were still admitted, since it was private ground.

Annemarie had arrived in Alassio a fortnight before. She looked quite happy to meet me and her company became, for me, quite indispensable. I waited for her in the mornings when she returned from her swim and in the afternoons when she came to play tennis. She herself seemed indifferent to my changed status. I did not discuss the matter with her, but I thought it impossible that she could not be aware of it, and the fact that she continued to deal with me in such a straightforward manner made her friendliness to me more dear. When I told her, for instance, that my family had moved from Friuli to Piedmont and that I would stay with my grandmother in Turin in order to continue my studies, she looked truly happy and suggested we should continue to play tennis at the Fascist headquarters, which had the best grounds in Turin. I did not react, telling myself that either she was not aware of the anti-Jewish laws or did not realize that I was a Jew. I was too afraid to upset our relationship by explaining to her the situation to which the Fascist laws had relegated me in Italian society. So I went on behaving until the end of my vacation as though nothing had changed, hoping that her ignorance would continue forever. The day before I left, we were resting on a bench after a fierce match, panting and sucking a lemonade with a straw.

"Do you think people like Mr. Bennett would have been able to defend the British Empire against an attack by the Italian Army?" I asked.

"Why do you ask me such a question?" she replied, surprised.

"Because," I said with perfect nonsensical logic, "I may leave next year for Palestine, and Palestine is part of the British Empire."

"And what on earth are you going to do in Palestine?"

I told her that I was a Jew, that I no longer had the right to study in an Italian school, that my father had lost his job, and that I was forced to emigrate. I thought, therefore, that the best place to go would be where nobody could reproach me for the crime of having been born a Jew.

Annemarie had heard about the racial laws in her home, but she did not link them with me or with any other person she knew. She could not understand what "those people in Rome" wanted from me. Nobody in Italy was able to distinguish between Jews and non-Jews. Her father had explained to her that it was a problem that had never existed in Italy and that Mussolini had been obliged to invent it to please Hitler. In any case, she could not see how the laws could influence our relationship. We had nothing to do with politics, we were both members of the Fascist Youth, and it seemed absurd to her, in fact impossible, that I should not be allowed to go and practice at the Fascist headquarters in Turin. If this was indeed so, we could find some private tennis court to continue playing. She said these things, a bit angry, with her legs drawn up to her chin and her heels on the bench, the empty lemonade bottle held between her knees, into which she blew bubbles of air through the straw. We promised to meet each other in Turin. She lived at the side of the station; I, in my grandmother's apartment just a few hundred yards from there.

Not long after, a few days after the beginning of the school term, I decided to phone her. I was attending the Jewish Secondary School established in a great hurry by the Turin Jewish community to accommodate the scores of young Jews suddenly expelled from public institutions. She answered, seemed quite embarrassed, and told me that she was very busy. I insisted, and she finally agreed to meet me under the portico of her house early the same evening.

I had forced her hand and was sorry and a bit ashamed about it. But all I wanted was to tell her that this should be our last meeting because I realized the difficulties it would cause her to maintain relations with a Jew. I wanted to part as good friends, to let her know that I had decided to go abroad. I wished to take with me the memory of our nice friendship and the image of an Italy that, at least among young people of my age, made no distinction between Jews and non-Jews and did not share the view of "those in Rome." I wanted our friendship, which was obviously beginning to turn for me into a romantic love, to be an expression of secret, common revolt against the injustice that separated us: a token of hope I could carry with me in order to remain linked with my past wherever I went.

It was a rainy, melancholy evening that forecast disaster. I was walking into it, pushed by the desire to see her again as much as by the need to face a Jewish destiny that up to that date I had been able to avoid.

I saw Annemarie come out of the doorway of her house, hesitate a moment, look around, and then proceed straight toward me. She was accompanied by a man. I noticed that he wore a black overcoat, a felt beret, and a pair of yellow shoes on which fell the cuffs of a pair of badly pressed trousers. He held Annemarie closely with his right arm as though he were pushing her forward against her will—a reluctance that probably existed only in my imagination. When they got close to me I noticed that he had a small moustache.

"My father," Annemarie said. "Pleased to meet you," I replied shyly, stretching out my hand to him. He kept his own under his daughter's arm.

I felt my throat become dry and my face pale. I thought of the day when a schoolmate of mine had hit me on the chin and knocked me backward onto the ground. I had not felt any pain but only the sensation of leaving my body and entering into a kind of black cave full of fluttering birds. This time, if I had fallen on the ground, nobody would have come to my help. I was alone, standing under the portico, my brain emptied of ideas and blood, unable to react, while another part shouted at me to disappear from there, to be swallowed up by the earth.

Annemarie was switching her alarmed, sad gaze from her father to me. I caught in her eyes more embarrassment than compassion. Suddenly her father started to talk. He had a slightly raucous voice marked by a strong Piedmontese accent. "You are a Jew," he said, without resentment or any particular spite. "I and Annemarie are Italian. I understand that you are on the point of emigrating. You are right to do so, but it would not be good either for you or for my daughter if you two continued to see each other. I preferred to tell you this personally, as man to man. Do you understand me?" "I understand perfectly," I answered. Later I hated myself for not having been able to find a more offensive reply. Perhaps it was the trembling I spotted on Annemarie's lips that prevented me from doing so. Perhaps it was the fear that had overcome me together with blind rage. I should have turned my back haughtily on them; instead I stood there immobile, under the portico, until father and daughter had gone back into the house, then pushed my hands into the pockets of my overcoat with such force that the lining tore.

I caught myself doing the same thing with the pockets of my battledress trousers while I was telling Isa the story of Anne-marie. She noticed it and said: "A girl of that type is not worth tearing your trousers for. Time, you will see, will soothe the pain. There is an Egyptian story that says that when God created the world he made everything small so that it could grow up with time: the grain into the wheat, the baby into the man, the bud into the flower. Only sorrow was created fully grown, so that it might decrease with time and man be able to live with it."

We climbed down from the wall, and I accompanied her through the narrow alleys of the market up to the Damascus Gate, along the old Roman street that crosses the entire walled city of Jerusalem. We passed Arabs pushing donkeys laden with sacks of flour in front of them; Jews going to the Wailing Wall, their eyes riveted to the ground, their bodies shrouded in black. On the corner of the Road of the Cross, a Franciscan friar passed us with a great billowing of his brown habit. On both sides of the street merchants were closing their shutters; in the cafés young Arabs played *shesh-besh* while older ones, wearing red fezzes, inhaled, dignified and absorbed, the taste of their water pipes. At the Damascus Gate a police patrol— the British constable with his elegant blue peaked cap, the Jewish and the Arab auxiliary constables with their imitation astrakhan cossack hats—eyed with indifference the passersby. It was a world full of life, in which everyone went about his affairs absorbed in his own thoughts, indifferent to my feelings as they were indifferent to the slabs of paving stone worn smooth by feet and history.

Berenika returned from her kibbutz on a Sunday afternoon. She told me that the community secretariat had agreed to her request to join the British army. She was now waiting for the announcement by the British military authorities of the formation of a new company of volunteer women drivers in order to report to the enlistment office. Then, after two months of training at Sarafand, the same camp where I spent my time as a recruit, she would be posted to Transport Command in Egypt. The war, she said, had at last reached a decisive turn: after El Alamein and Stalingrad the destiny of the Axis powers was sealed, whatever their capacity to carry on fighting. It was the destiny of the Jews that remained unknown. No one could forecast how many of them would still be alive in Europe at the end of the hostilities. All the survivors would be in need of help, and the British would be the last to extend it to them. The Jewish Agency hoped that London might allow the creation of a "Jewish Legion" to take part in the fighting and eventually be allowed to rush to rescue the remnants from the ghettos. These were pious illusions, Berenika said. A large Jewish fighting unit would acquire political rights on the battlefield that the British had no interest to grant. So, she continued, the men had to be patient and prepare themselves for the struggle that would certainly take place in Palestine against the British and the Arabs once the war was over. The women in uniform, especially if they were in charge of transport, would, on the contrary, be more free to move around within the liberated territories and probably be able, without arousing suspicion or opposition, to bring concrete help to the Jewish survivors. This was the reason the Jewish authorities in Palestine had decided to speed up the recruitment of Jewish women. Berenika felt herself more available than her "women comrades" after all that had recently happened to her. In any case, if she did not join the army she would certainly have felt obliged to leave the kibbutz, and most of her friends were against her doing that. So she had returned to Jerusalem to wait for her call-up, but she did not want to stay in her parents' apartment. There was not enough space, she told me with an understanding smile, for both of us. She would rent a room in the neighborhood by the end of the week. Meanwhile she would go to Tel Aviv to prepare her "military accoutrement."

In the few days that followed I did nothing but think about how and when we would meet. Even when reading the news bulletin I could not take my thoughts away from her face, her body, and stop asking myself how I would tell her that I wanted to make love to her. I could not, obviously, go straight to the point. I had to create an appropriate "ambience"—for instance, to go and see a boring film in order to have an excuse to leave the cinema in the middle of the screening. Or to invite her to a cozy restaurant for dinner, or for a trip to the Dead Sea, or better, to go horseback-riding, this last scenario looked more romantic but certainly less comfortable. The only scheme I did not conceive was the quite unpredictable one that eventually took place.

Berenika returned, happy and suntanned, from Tel Aviv. We dined with her parents and then went out for a walk along the old battlements of Jerusalem.

It was a warm autumn evening, when the stars of the East shine so brightly that they look like iridescent butterflies, palpitating in their efforts to break away from the sky. Along the path from Jaffa Gate toward the Zion Gate we did not meet a soul. I walked next to her, carefully avoiding touching her, clutching in my left hand the handle of my pistol, my right hand sweating in my trouser pocket. She walked absorbed in her own thoughts, turning her face toward me from time to time with an oddly sad smile.

I suggested we climb to the top of the Zion Gate and look at the darkness of the Jehoshaphat Valley, spotted by the trembling lamps in the Arab houses. She agreed without demur, and I understood that it was quite unnecessary for me to look for a pretext to tell her what she obviously already knew: that I desired her, that I had not had the courage to say it before for fear of a refusal, that I was not quite sure of really loving her since I had never loved anyone before, that I had nothing to offer her but was even prepared to join a collective settlement to be near her.

She listened to my confused talk in silence, and when at last I found the courage to put my hand on her shoulder, she bent her head toward it, inviting me through that gesture to kiss her. Then she asked softly whether I had ever been with a woman. I told her, blushing, that I had not and she, with her detached, sweet, and cruel way of speaking, explained to me that people could be caught in the nets of sex more easily than by the nets of religion. The only way not to fall prey to sexual instincts was to treat them with indifference like any other bodily need, without trivial fantasies. The bourgeois world in which I had grown up had replaced godly religions with the religion of money but had preserved many taboos of the past. Among them sex was still predominant. She had freed herself from them for quite a while. There was nothing wrong in my desire for her; she also felt a strong attraction for me. She would not let my hunger for a woman go unfed, but I had to be rational in my passions because our physical link could not expect ever to enjoy the space and the time necessary to transform itself into a permanent link. Consequently, there was no need for me to engage in a romantic walk or other types of reveries in order to satisfy my biological aims. She had a room, we could go there straight away, if, of course, I wanted it and was not afraid to face the experience with her.

I was not just afraid, I was trembling, and I continued to tremble for the whole way back, which seemed to me much longer than the way we had come. I do not remember what I said to her, walking next to her, and I think I did not even embrace her. But I still clearly remember most of the details of the apartment, of which Berenika gave me the key so that I would be the one to open the door.

It was a wooden door with a slit in the middle for letters. Behind it there was a step from which one entered a small hall.

Fixed to one side of it there was a bronze rack, and on the other side a shelf. The kitchen opened to the right of a small corridor, the bathroom to the left. The corridor led to a large room with two bay windows, protected on the outside by iron bars. There were no curtains, and cases full of books stood everywhere. In the middle of the room on the square table covered by a sheet of glass, there was a large basket full of fruit—oranges, dates, nuts, and raisins. A big box served as a cupboard without a door, and under the windows an iron bed was covered by a crude, floral bedspread. On the floor, on the old gray tiles, was a mat. All was still.

Berenika looked at me in silence. I, more embarrassed than before, did the same. "I'll go into the bathroom," she finally said. When she came out she was completely undressed. "Naked as a worm," I thought to myself, quite disenchanted. But that was not quite an appropriate moment for aesthetic speculation. When we parted, she said: "You see, the whole thing is not very important." I answered that it was not true, that it had been a sublime moment for me, but I knew, as much as she knew, that I was lying. What, in fact, I could not get out of my mind was an advertisement for padded brassieres I had seen in a local newspaper that read: "In any case, when they fall, it's too late." What she did not realize was that once more I felt that I had killed something in me.

The emotional anticlimax provoked by this meeting, so long awaited and then revealed as so disappointingly aseptic, created a break between us that deepened with the passing of time. It sharpened the contrast between the trepidation of my senses and the icy core of my soul. I probably exaggerate in attributing to that single event a state of mind that was obviously part of my nature. Be that as it may, after that night my relations with Berenika became increasingly atrocious. I sought her body with fury, and she tore my soul to shreds. I told her I loved her, and she replied that love, as physical enjoyment, was a delinquency at a time when our people and the Western civilization were dying. I told her that once the war was over I would take her to Italy to introduce her to Annetta who used to hold my hand until I fell asleep. She insisted I should read Freud and Marx to understand to what extent human sentiments are the product of the economy. I talked to her about my village in Piedmont, about my father's horses killed in the Great War, about the streams along which we played cowboys and Indians. She urged me to abandon these infantile dreams and remember that true nobility is the fulfillment of collective obligations. I meekly suggested that Marxism was a populist aristocracy that often forgot the individual. She held that the state of Jews to be created in Palestine should be unique in its nature—planned by men and women who looked for a perfect model society in a promised land, not born out of chaos as in the case of other nations. I retorted that she was deceiving herself in believing that an uprooted people would turn into a nation of saints by virtue of socialism. As soon as the British relinquished Palestine to the Arabs, they would engage in an all-around, cutthroat battle among themselves and with the Arabs.

We kept on arguing even when we went out riding. It was possible to hire good horses for a shilling an hour at stables near the Jaffa Gate and in less than ten minutes to be out in the fields, leaving behind us the city, which at the time was much less extensive than today. I liked to gallop, to make the sheep and goats I occasionally met on my path scatter amid the barking of dogs and the swearing of shepherds. She, on these occasions, walked her horse and kept me waiting for her in the sun, full of reproaches for my "arrogant" style. There was no way of convincing her that if the Arab shepherds had been mounted and I on foot, they would have acted in exactly the same way as I did, for the pleasure of showing off; or that the galloping of a well-ridden horse, even if it scattered a flock, possessed a beauty of its own, which an Arab in particular would appreciate. This kind of argument made no impression on her. As long as social distinctions were not abolished, she would patiently explain to me, linguistic expressions and styles of life would continue to reveal the inequalities of men. I was a typical production of class relations, unaware of acting according to the superstitions created by economic relations. If we, the Jews of Palestine, did not become conscious of this in the country we wanted to build, we would become worse than other people. It had always been the fate of the Jews either to rise up to the stars or to eat the dust—never to lead a life of mediocrity.

For me, these talks—apart from being boring and inappropriate for a ride—made little sense. I listened to her while making my horse prance at her side, looking with desire at her open shirt. When she became aware of my inattention she used to shake her head with the mocking expression of a schoolteacher who had lost all hope of educating a stubborn boy. I would then dismount, take her horse by the bridle, lead it under the nearest tree that offered some shade, help her dismount, and make her sit down on a stone or an old olive root protruding from the ground. I asked her whether the Crusaders, who perhaps had tied their horses to our same tree, entered into her economic system; if the knights of France and Germany who had come to die in the stony valleys of Judea had been moved only by economic motives; if the women who for years had waited for them, had done so out of economic superstructures. I asked her where she put the adventurer who had searched for the sources of the Nile, the desert hermits who had searched for the message of God, the Zionist youth who left Russian universities to drain swamps. Who forced the orthodox Jews to live in their ghettos in Jerusalem? Were they not obeying an "economic" determinism quite different from the one the Marxists wanted to sell to the world? If it were true, as she kept explaining to me, that the class that controls the means of economic production also controls the means of spiritual production, how did it happen that in Rome, slaves and freemen educated their masters, and in Europe the priestly commoners educated the noblemen?

Irritably throwing pebbles at the horses' hooves, I sometimes found myself almost shouting my questions, asking her whether it was so difficult for her to understand that a person could abandon home, treasure, and power for the sake of a woman; whether it had never passed through her mind that it might be easier for someone to fight for a lady than for a party. As for myself, I would have no difficulty in joining her kibbutz, but for her sake, not for Marx or Freud. In any case, I was not alone in the world in needing a woman to overcome the fear of the dark, the shame of poverty, the fear of war, the dread of facing people stronger than I. After all, a perfumed handkerchief could be more encouraging than a party card.

Berenika listened to me patiently. Sometimes she would make a brief comment, such as "How stupid your Crusader knights must have been"; or "What good does a hermit bring to the world?" On other occasions she would explain to me, kindly, why I was dreaming and gently scold me for being unable to realize that I was living in the twentieth century. Once she almost shouted at me that it was high time I remembered that I was a Jew whose duty it was to demand justice and vengeance from the world, not a squire in a feudal court searching for occasions to impale a Moor on his lance. If we wanted to continue our relationship I must learn to remember that she belonged to her kibbutz, to her party, to her people, before she belonged to herself. The war was not the same war our fathers had fought. It was truly the war to end all wars because it would end only when the tree of Nazism and Fascism, both fruits of capitalism, had been uprooted. The sacrifice that humanity was now making would be useless if an entirely new society did not emerge from all the horrors of the war.

Our state would also be different from the others. The true strength of the Zionist movement consisted of the fact that most of its members were uprooted people who searched for a land in which to strike new roots. In this sense the fight against the British and the Arabs was a secondary aspect of the Zionist revolution, which had broken the centuries-old traditions of Judaism and in so doing had released an energy choked by millennia of prayers and submission. Our transition from a situation of passive objects of history to active factors in history was something unique. We were indeed our own ancestors, building from the very beginning the life of an entire people, creating a new race of Jews, free from the cultural chromosomes of secular suffering. The spirit of the people could—and indeed should—become stronger through the macerations of the flesh of its members.

In pronouncing these phrases, Berenika's voice became sharp and metallic. I perceived in it a dry hatred of material things, including the body that encased, or rather kept, her spirit in shackles, and a desire for vengeance against her own senses, whirling in a black hole of passions. She always startled me with her suppressed, inexplicable anger, and at times she scared me. Our conversations then turned into monologues that made me feel I was standing alone in the peace of the olive trees, the beauty of which Berenika seemed unable to taste, just as she seemed oblivious to the buzzing flies that made the horses paw the ground.

Meanwhile, day followed day rapidly, and we both knew that the time of our separation would soon arrive. The newspapers announced the formation of a new ATS (Women's Transport Service Unit) company. Berenika volunteered for it, and I was posted to Cairo, no longer to a clandestine radio outfit but to an intelligence unit preparing the Allied landing in Sicily. We both felt sorry and relieved at these developments. Our relationship had become too complicated, artificial, and unreal, our physical relations shrieking and painful. I proposed to her that we should say goodbye with a last horseback ride.

At half past seven in the morning, the two horses I had ordered the day before from Abu Selim at the Jaffa Gate stables were waiting for us, fed and saddled. They were two white mares, spotted with black, unable to walk quietly, already profusely sweating after a few minutes of cantering. Rain had fallen during the night; every clod of earth, thirsty from the long drought, glistened. The unshod hooves of the horses caressed the wet paths, crushing here and there the weeds and the stalks of dry wild oats.

We were trotting in line, enjoying the fresh air, the early sun, the flight of birds, casting around handfuls of thoughts in the silence of a morning as young as our bodies. At the entrance to a wadi I let Berenika ride ahead of me, so that she should not have trouble in controlling a horse anxious to run. She put her mare at a gallop and I looked with passion and sadness at her mass of brown hair flying in the wind.

Suddenly I saw her mare swerve and Berenika, jerked out of her saddle, clinging to the neck of the animal, which fortunately stopped immediately. Not far from her an Arab shepherd stood, arms upraised, waving a stick menacingly in his hand. In a second I caught up with him and, without thinking, raised my riding crop over his head and hit him violently, I believe on his back. Only then did I realize what had happened: Berenika was about to ride into a flock of goats, which she had been unable to see because of a rise in the land, and the Arab shepherd had moved forward to warn her and try to stop the horse. He had had no evil intentions, and I had hit him without reason. I could not even apologize because he had run away in fear.

Berenika, meanwhile, had got up from the ground, fuming with rage and indignation, her horse, unaware of her tumultuous feelings, already grazing peacefully nearby.

"I'm sorry for what happened," I told her, trying to help her to remount, "but I thought he was going to hurt you." She looked at me with a tense face, her eyes almost closed with

rage, screaming two words that still burn me: "Nazi! Nazi!"
Turning her horse, she trotted back to Jerusalem without
looking at me.

When we returned the horses to the stables we were like
two strangers. Abu Selim sensed it and did not insist on our
drinking the usual cup of coffee he had prepared for us. He
followed us with a curious gaze as we walked into town.

A shower is a wonderful remedy, I thought to myself as I
stood under the hot water and sponged away the perspiration
of that disastrous ride. I was quite decided not to request an
explanation from Berenika for an insult I felt I had not deserved. The incident, I told myself, would make our break
easier, if not less painful. The convoy I had been attached to
was leaving for Cairo in the late afternoon. I would return to
the apartment at three o'clock, an hour I was sure Berenika
would not be there, take leave of the doctor and his wife, settle
my account, and drink the cup of tea that they would certainly
offer me. I felt full of energy, and I thought of my schoolteacher in Italy who had once explained to our history class
that the Romans had conquered the world because they practiced water therapy. From alternate hot and cold baths, he said,
the Romans drew the energy that modern Italians had lost
because they did not bathe themselves enough. In fact, especially in summer, there was always a smell of young bodies
insufficiently washed in our classroom.

Thinking back to that good old man as I vigorously tow-
eled myself, I burst out laughing. I felt a sudden urge to sing
and started to hum the march of the Alpine troops, as I did
when returning from the lake where I had been fishing for the
trout still wriggling in my creel.

How far away that lake was now, with its pine-tree forest;
Luza, the big old mare I was allowed to ride; my father's
mountain cottage where he used to read the Book of Jonah on
the Day of Atonement; the sleigh rides over the snow; the
Indian tepee; the old gramophone that I wound up while my

sister and her friends danced with the army officers during the summer maneuvers. Almost without my being aware of it, the tune of the Alpine soldiers froze the smile on my lips, and two big tears started rolling down my cheeks. How shameful if anybody had surprised me crying in such a shameless way. It was a good thing I was leaving that same day without having time to see Berenika again.

But she was there, waiting for me outside the bathroom, leaning on the jamb of my bedroom door, thoughtfully nibbling at her thumbnail. Her hair was still untidy, her unbuttoned shirt showing two wet patches under her armpits. "Come," she said, "we must not leave each other like this."

The room was fresh, shady, and silent. The bed was too narrow for us both, but we lay enlaced as though we would never part. Her body was cold, and her voice sounded altered —raucous, not out of passion but out of pain mingled with fear. She was talking softly, with her face half buried in my shoulder, and spoke as though I was not present.

It had all happened, she said, on a summer afternoon, the last she had spent in the Black Forest. The house was big. One entered it through a glass door that opened into a hall, from which a wooden staircase led to the bedrooms upstairs. Three men came in; she did not recollect their faces. They looked like three carnival masks, their cheeks red with perspiration, and their mouths smelling of beer. They wore brown shirts and boots against which one of them continuously snapped his whip. Frau Luise had faced them first, with considerable courage. Her father, on the contrary, had immediately lost his head and his countenance. He started to shout that he had fought in the war, that he had received the Iron Cross, First Class, that they had no right to enter his house. They just laughed at him, spat in his face, shouted all sorts of insults at him, and then knocked him to the ground. This was too much for her mother; she started to scream and call for help. Berenika rushed down the stairs. In her agitation she forgot that she was only half dressed. It was probably this that gave them the idea. Two of the men dragged her father into his study and locked him in. The third grabbed Berenika in front of her mother. Now Frau Luise had stopped shouting; she watched the whole performance like a statue, her eyes and mouth wide open. She did not even move when she saw that they were throwing her daughter to the ground.

"It was very painful," Berenika sobbed, "very painful, especially at my back when they pressed me against the first step of the stairs. From that moment I have no longer been in possession of my body. These arms, this stomach, these legs are strangers to me. For this I am unable to love, only to render some service. But at least I am no longer the prisoner of my flesh. I am free. No one can ever do me more harm. No one can affect my spirit. Only memories wound me; and the whips that hit human beings. They are all Nazi whips. Even if handled by someone like you, like you."

It was the first and last time I saw her crying without shame.

II

Bitter Fortune

T<small>HE</small> E-BOATS of the Royal Navy dashed along at full speed on the glassy waters of the Adriatic. In the fresh April morning I tasted a deep, satisfied peace. The sun's rays, the wind, the smell of the sea became part of me together with my new fantasies about the future.

The war was nearing its end. With this operation I would gloriously complete my military service, canceling out the disillusions of the past. Once more the gates of chance were being opened to me. With childish satisfaction I touched the two brand-new pips of a second lieutenant on my shoulders. It was a temporary rank, given me for the duration of this operation. They did not change my status as warrant officer, and with the imminent surrender of the German troops in Italy, there would be no time to turn them into a permanent rank through that Royal Commission about which I had dreamt for so long. Between going to an officers' course in England and a quick demobilization, my choice, after four years of war, was irrevocably made. But on the ship taking me to Yugoslavia, I was what I appeared to be from my army papers. The way the first mate had offered me a double ration of rum from the ship's earthenware jar left no doubt about it —like the pass I still have in my files, tattered by time, delivered to me by the HQ of Tito's Fifth Army. It explicitly states that on 9 November 1945 I was authorized to circulate freely in every zone held by the Partisans. It bore the signature of a political commissar, a certain Major Branko Mamula, clearly written under the only sentence in Serbo-Croatian that I knew by heart: *Smaart Fascismu-Sloboda Narodu* (Death to Fascism—Freedom to People). If the major had been aware of the true purpose of my mission he would certainly not have granted me this permit. My orders were to report to the HQ of a unit of British rangers stationed in Zadar and continue with them into Istria. Officially our task was to harass the retreat of the troops of General Vlassov, the Russian officer who had linked his destiny with that of the Germans. But in fact we were asked to contact the X MAS, an elite unit of the Fascist Republican army, commanded by Prince Valerio Borghese. According to certain reports, the prince was ready to surrender south of Trieste if the Allies could reach him before Tito's Partisans. Even today I still do not know how reliable our information was. We never made contact with the X MAS because the Partisans, who wanted to reach Trieste ahead of the Allies, stopped the rangers north of the town of Pola. Here we got the news of the surrender of the Germans in Italy and went back to Zadar.

Anyway, what counted for me on that morning when I was rushing toward a new horizon of my life, was not the surrender of Borghese, but the fact that the task I had received and the temporary promotion that went with it soothed the feeling of shame I had been carrying with me since the day I refused to parachute behind the German lines.

How that refusal burned in my soul! And how easily I could have avoided getting into trouble. It would have been enough to explain to the medical officer what I felt after my harrowing jump from a plane at Gioia del Colle. Instead, out of pride and out of fear of admitting being afraid, I had kept quiet, like the beadle of the Jewish school in Turin, whom I had gone to take leave of before my departure for Palestine. "I will kill myself," he told me, "because I am too afraid to die." I had laughed in his face, without thinking then that one day I would find myself in the same situation.

At the field hospital near Bari, where I had been lying in bed for two weeks after the night jump that had broken my ribs, the nightmares had become more violent and more frequent than ever. I had tried to overcome them by persuading myself that statistically it was less dangerous to jump from a plane than to travel overland in a military convoy. I tried to raise my morale by repeating to myself the stories I would be able to brag about once my mission was over. I imagined the face of my father seeing me suddenly appear in his study, hundreds of miles behind the enemy lines. I imagined myself hiding behind one of the big, black-and-white pillars in the church of my village in Piedmont, ready to scare Annetta as she came in to pray early in the morning. I shut my mind to the dangers waiting for me on the ground, convinced as I was that the war would remain for me a beautiful adventure. Yet I could find no remedy for my nightmares.

I kept seeing myself sitting on the edge of the hole in the bottom of the plane, flying in the night toward unknown destinations. I felt my legs dangling in the void, frozen inside my padded overalls less from the cold than from fear of the jump. I could not take my eyes off the green light, which by changing to red would signal me to throw myself into emptiness. Then there was the fall: a long, interminable descent, in darkness, with a parachute that refused to open and the blood that rushed ever more violently to my head. All around me was the silence of the grave, as if the entire universe, while watching my fall, was holding its breath. In my dreams, the violent jerk, just above the ground of the airfield, which had made me yell with pain and relief, never came. In them, no one asked me whether I was all right, no one carried me like a bundle to a jeep and rushed me half-fainting to the hospital. In my dreams there was only the thud of my body hitting the ground. It woke me up each time I tried in vain to extricate myself from the black embrace of the mud.

Why didn't I go and talk to the doctor of my unit? Nobody, after all, forced me to parachute behind the enemy lines; it was only my desire to play the hero. But the fear of seeming afraid had been stronger than common sense. I had kept quiet until the very last days before my mission—after I had drawn the operational equipment, the belt with two hundred gold sovereigns in it, discussed the code and the area of landing with the intelligence officer, and waited with growing anxiety to be called by the CO to learn the date and hour of my jump.

When I entered his office I was convinced that one way or another I would leave it unscathed because I would certainly lack the courage to tell him that I was afraid. Instead, the confession came out by itself, in short, broken sentences. I was dismissed with a dry "Very well," which still feels like a knife in my stomach. I gave back the belt with the sovereigns, the equipment, the code, and went to my room on the roof of the villa where we were stationed to collect my personal effects before returning to my intelligence unit. From the military kit bag I took out an Italian revolver, which I had stolen from a captured enemy depot. I laid it on the edge of the bed. The weapon, falling on the ground, fired a shot. The bullet grazed my forehead, burned a lock of my hair. I looked at myself in the mirror, my ears still deafened by the explosion, which no one else in the building had apparently heard. At that moment I told myself that it had been a fortunate accident.

Here, on the deck of the boat that sped toward my beautiful future, I knew that it was not true, that on that evening in Bari I had seriously wanted to die. An invisible hand had diverted the bullet, as when my father, cleaning a pistol in his study, had fired a shot at my head by mistake. Obviously I was not yet destined to die. In this war, which had swallowed millions of men and women and children, it was written that I had to pursue my military masquerade, going on drinking barrels of beer in the messes while my people were dying. That evening in Bari there was only one thing for me to do: disappear, throw my uniform away, take back my original name, which I had changed when I joined the army, and thus close twenty-two years of existence and try to start one totally different. I had to change my looks and my soul, do away with what I was, become a different person.

With these black, determined thoughts, I walked out of the villa, convinced of having passed the point of no return. But I had walked less than five minutes in the direction of the fields when I bumped into Francesca.

How different was Berenika from Francesca. Not in her general appearance, although there was some resemblance between the two women in spite of the fact that Francesca was more than thirty, but in her face, as I remembered it on the top of the stairs of Kasr el-Nil barracks in Cairo.

After my transfer from Jerusalem to Egypt, Berenika had followed me as an ATS driver in a transport company. For weeks I had hunted for her without success, as I was not aware that she had changed her name. When I finally saw her again it didn't occur to me to ask her why she had done so. It was quite common for Palestinian Jewish volunteers born in Germany or Italy to change their names when enlisting in the army, in order to ensure their safety if captured. I had done it myself. Only when I found myself standing in front of her with a bouquet of flowers in my hand and told her of my firm intention to marry her, did I understand from her embarrassed answer that her new name was that of her husband.

It was a rude shock, but at the age of twenty, and in wartime, nobody ever died of love. Still, I continued to feel

rancorous and could not cancel from my memory the enigmatic expression on her face. There was in it something tragic
and dark, like an appeal to death, an incurable sadness. It was
a kind of inexplicable anxiety I noticed also in the eyes of some
of the Jewish soldiers who had arrived in Italy from Palestine.
They somehow lived, like Berenika, in the world of the Holocaust. I, on the contrary, in spite of the fact that all my relatives
were in places occupied by the Germans, had never connected
their lot with the news that was reaching us with increasing
frequency about the systematic extermination of the Jews by
the Nazis. This was probably due to the fact that I could not
imagine them dead, and that the few Italian Jews I had met
in Bari had told me about the dangers they had run in crossing
the lines, but also of the help they had received everywhere
from the local population. The tales of their escape sounded
like adventure stories, often punctuated by humorous anec-
dotes. The idea that my father or mother could have been
deported thus never crossed my mind. And in fact, as I have
already related, they saved themselves, my father by playing
the itinerant peddler for eighteen months along the streets of
Piedmont, and my mother by taking refuge in a convent with
my sister.

Francesca, unlike them and unlike Berenika, was neither
Jewish nor Italian, but Yugoslav from Dalmatia, and did not
carry on her face any trace of her tragedy. I had met her several
times on the tramway passing in front of our HQ. I had noticed
her less for her refined features framed in a mass of Titian hair
than for the contrast between her elegant bearing and the
vulgar atmosphere prevailing in the town.

Every corner of Bari at that time exuded humiliation and
sadness. The war had spared the center of the city but the
harbor had been torn up by the explosion of an Allied ship full
of ammunition. The old palaces, run down by time and ne-
glect, looked much the same as the houses of the poor in the
ancient parts of the town. Everywhere mud turned into dust

when the sun dried the street, and dust turned into slippery mud when the rain mingled with the sewage from the broken drains. Tangles of telephone wires underlined on the longest walls of the town the historical pronouncements taken from Mussolini's speeches, which now sounded grotesque, fading away under the effect of the elements.

The Italian civilians, with whom we Allied soldiers had not yet received permission to fraternize, looked like ghosts. On the Teatro Petruzelli Square long lines of horse-driven carriages waited for customers. The skinny horses slept on their feet with their ears protruding from holes cut into straw hats. They looked as miserable as the drivers. Only in the open country, where the Allies concealed their guns and lorries under camouflage nets among the olive trees, did the ancient people of Puglia, who had passed within a few months from the Fascist regime to a foreign occupation, seem capable of retaining some dignity. With these silent and surly people, whose dialect I did not understand, we soldiers had no contact. The cooks who prepared our food; the women who cleaned our offices; the few clerks who knew enough English to run the gasworks, the slaughterhouse, the telephone exchange, and the harbor were all refugees. They came from all over: Italians from the north; Yugoslav monarchists fleeing from the communist soldiers of Tito; Yugoslav Partisans who came to collect their rations and cure their sick and wounded in Bari; Greeks and Albanians who crossed the Adriatic, transporting in their boats men, animals, spies, and explosives.

Each group had its own internal and external hierarchy, created by the changing fortunes of war, by misery, and hate. The Jews stood one step above the Italians; the Partisans one step above the soldiers of the disintegrating Royal armies of Italy, Greece, and Yugoslavia; the British officers felt superior to any minister of the new, provisional Italian government. And then there were the black marketeers with their wobbly carts, their shaky tricycles, with some old, gas-operated vehicles, who traded in everything—from women to currency, from soap to weapons. With or without permits, one would find them in the middle of military camps, inside political offices, offering real or faked influence. Despised by all but compromising everyone, these black marketeers represented new channels for the energy of a people who had lost the structures of their traditional authority. Finally, everything and everyone was submerged by the masses of soldiers coming from overseas, whose conquest of an ancient European land seemed to have gone to their heads.

There was neither hatred nor violence toward the local population among the Australians, the Scots, the South Africans, the Indians, the British, the Palestinian Jews, the Cypriots, and the Canadians, who walked aimlessly in the streets of Bari. Few of them were able to appreciate the artistic treasures of the city; none had clear ideas about Fascism, especially since the signing of armistice with Italy the war was being fought only against the Germans. But to this flood of uniformed men and women coming from the deserts of Africa, accustomed to dividing the world into white men and colored, the Italians who shined their shoes and sold them whatever they possessed gave a feeling of vulgar pride, of petty domination, and of certainty in a victory that the humiliation of a defeated people made at last palpable after years of war.

In this atmosphere of arrogance and misery, the healthy, modest beauty of Francesca shone with particular vividness. She was sitting on the wooden seat opposite me in the tram, her legs clamped together and her knees showing under her short, clean skirt. She wore a simple but elegant black-and-white striped blouse, tied at the neck with a velvet ribbon, and her posture roused in me feelings of admiration and respect. I would not have dared to approach her if, on a particular afternoon, I had not noticed two large tears rolling slowly down her cheeks from behind her dark sunglasses.

When she got up and moved toward the exit, it came

naturally to me to ask her whether I could help her in any way. A question of this kind, put by an unknown Allied soldier to a woman on her own, could at that time be easily misunderstood. She looked surprised, but either because I spoke to her in Italian or because she could not bear alone the trouble that oppressed her, she did not hesitate to answer me. Her daughter, aged four, had been struck by meningitis. The doctor had told her that the Allies possessed a new drug that might save her. Penicillin was the name, or something like that. She had spent the whole morning looking for somebody who might find it for her. She was now on her way to the doctor to tell him that she had had no success.

Without any certainty of being able to help her, I told her that I could probably solve her problem. I was ashamed at my showing off but happy to have established contact with such an attractive woman. Not knowing what to do, however, I went to the Jewish Soldiers' Club, she following me closely with the uncertain trustfulness of a lost dog that has suddenly found a protector.

The major attraction of the Jewish Soldiers' Club, theoretically open to military personnel of all religions, but in practice frequented mostly by Palestinian volunteers, was the cheese sandwiches. A number of Jewish refugee women, more hungry than ourselves, prepared these cheese sandwiches in enormous quantities from ten o'clock in the morning to ten in the evening. There were a couple of local Italian youngsters who did nothing but clear the tables of coffee cups and empty bottles and refill the urns with water for tea and coffee. These drinks were considerably more tasty than those offered by other military canteens since nobody in the Jewish Soldiers' Club poured into the urns packages of soda bicarbonate, which was supposed to dampen the sexual urges of the soldiers. Unlike other canteens, beer was consumed in relatively small quantities and was replaced by soda water, the most popular drink of the Jews in Palestine. A current joke claimed, in fact, that it was also the best way to locate wounded Palestinians on the battlefield. The Italians, the British, and the Germans could be identified by their asking for "acqua," "water," and "wasser," respectively, and Palestinian Jews by their call for "soda."

The Jewish Soldiers' Club was poorly furnished. There was a silent radio by the side of one window, an out-of-tune piano that came to life under the hands of transient musicians usually playing the songs of the Jewish pioneers who had dried the swamps of Zion and other nostalgic Eastern European tunes. On those occasions the Palestinians clustered around the piano singing arias that Jewish soldiers from other countries tried to follow with affectionate humming. But this happened rarely. The great sport in the smoke-filled rooms was to discuss politics, to revive, in Bari, the ideological quarrels of the Zionist movement, to embroider on the gossip from the Tel Aviv cafés and from the kibbutz general meetings, which reached Bari after weeks of delay. The discussion always ended on the question of what would happen in Palestine after the war, a subject on which everybody held a different opinion.

At the far side of the club's larger room was a brown door, always half open although nobody dared go through without some very specific reason. It led into a room even more sparsely furnished than the others, which served as an office for "the committee."

Nobody knew how many members made up "the committee." They were NCOs belonging to the various Jewish units stationed in the area, occasionally joined by mysterious civilians coming from far away. They represented the various political currents of the Yishuv and the different clandestine military organizations—the Hagana, the Irgun, and the LEHI. At home they could fight and betray each other; in Bari they worked together in an atmosphere of suspicious concord, dictated by the need to act in unison for the benefit of the Jews who had escaped from the Nazis. In that room people sat up late every night. Decisions were made that caused military vehicles full of food and blankets to run up and down the roads of southern Italy, and plots were made to trick the British, on the principle that the Zionists had to fight the Germans as if the white paper did not exist, and fight the white paper as if the Germans did not exist.

I did not belong to any of these groups. The badge of the Intelligence Corps that I wore on my beret and the parachutist wings that I had recently added to my uniform made me, if not suspect, at least unclassifiable to the club habitués. But on two or three occasions I had brought to the "committee" sums of money I had confiscated from German or Fascist agents. This now authorized me to ask for help, or at least for advice. To my surprise, help was given on the spot by an elderly member of the committee in the form of a scribbled note addressed to a nurse at the field hospital located outside Bari on the road to Barletta. "Her name is Sara, Sara Bauman," he told me with a wink, and then added: "Best wishes for the health of the daughter and for your success with the mother." I blushed to the roots of my hair.

It was not possible to ask for a lift for Francesca on a military vehicle. I hired a carriage pulled by a horse more sleepy than his driver, who must certainly have been surprised by our destination and by the strange silence of the couple behind his back. We arrived at the hospital after half an hour of slow trotting and embarrassed conversation, made more difficult by the onset of a cold, rainy evening. Francesca had married a Yugoslav engineer in 1938 and had had a daughter just before the German invasion in 1941. One year later they had gone underground. The husband, surprised while hunting for food by a band of Ustachi (the Croat nationalists who collaborated with the Italians and the Germans), had been tortured and then shot. Francesca and her daughter were transferred by the Partisans first to Tito's headquarters on the island of Lissa and then to the mainland. Knowing Italian and English well, she worked as a secretary at the Allied office running the harbor. Hers was a war story like many others, full of the usual violence and sorrow.

The field hospital on the road to Barletta consisted of a big house surrounded by Nissen huts used as wards. Somebody pointed out to me the hut where I would find Sister Bauman. I had no difficulty in recognizing her: small, with her hair pulled into a bun under the starched cap, obviously a non-Anglo-Saxon, with her nose slightly squashed. Nobody would describe her as a beauty queen, I thought to myself, and quickly classified her: spinster, thirty years old, Russian origin, formerly employed in a kibbutz kitchen, ideologically involved.

As if she had read my thoughts, Sister Bauman answered my Hebrew greeting icily. She threw a suspicious glance at the chit I held out to her, and with eyes that pierced like a gimlet, asked me what I wanted the medicine for. I told her the truth. With a raised eyebrow she asked: "Yehudia?" (Jewish?). "No," I answered, and felt at once that I had ruined my chances.

Without saying a word, Sister Bauman turned her back on me and disappeared into the ward. I was left standing next to her table, miserable and furious, waiting for her reappearance. I did not dare to leave before speaking to her again because I wanted to have something to tell the woman who was waiting outside in the carriage. I had kept her away from her sick daughter for hours, had raised her hopes, and now had to find an excuse to explain why I could not help her. But what enraged me even more was the idea of having to stand there like a pillar, exposed to the spiteful judgment of a nurse who, from her point of view, had every right to treat me like a black marketeer. She was certainly thinking that the medicine was going to be used in some dirty business that had nothing to do with Jewish or Zionist solidarity. Ashamed and impatient, I stood at the end of the ward, cursing the moment I had offered my aid to an unknown woman, asked the help of the "committee," and now exposed myself to the contempt of this insensitive and ugly woman who clearly enjoyed punishing me by letting me stew in my own confusion.

After an eternity of time, Sister Bauman reappeared. She held in her hand a tray full of gauze and thermometers and a round, metal box, similar to the mess tins in use in the American army. She laid the tray down on the table, took her navy blue cape off the hanger, threw it over her shoulders, covering the round box in the process, and signaled me to follow her. "I've taken four vials," she whispered to me. "I put them in a thermos—they are double-size—distilled water and powder—you will have to mix them—they must be kept in cold storage. I'll give them to you outside the hospital; here there is a danger that some doctor might stop you. They are worth more than gold."

Only then did I realize how unjust my thoughts about her had been. I prayed silently that the driver would have moved the carriage away from the hospital entrance so that I would not have to show her that I had a woman with me. Instead, he was standing, with his horse asleep, in the same place where I had left him, some twenty yards away from the gate, with Francesca barely visible in the depths of the carriage, crouched in a heap, her arms crossed around her shoulders to keep out the cold.

As if she had understood my embarrassment and the careful behavior of the nurse, Francesca did not move, looking at us with eyes full of uncertain hope. When we came closer to her, Sister Bauman asked me in Hebrew, "Does she understand English?" I nodded my head, and she started babbling to Francesca, still seated in the carriage, in a tone completely different from the one she had used with me. She asked what the illness was, the age of the child, her general condition. Shaking her head in a movement of sympathy, she repeated, stressing every word, the instructions she had already given me. "Now go straight home," she finished, "and look for a doctor or for a nurse to give the injection. You will see, everything will turn out all right." Francesca stretched out her hand to take the thermos. There was an instant of uncertainty between them. Then, to my astonishment, they embraced each other. After a moment she smiled at Francesca, turned her back to me, and with a brisk "Shalom," returned to the hospital.

I went back to Bari with Francesca in the carriage. She refused to let me pay the driver because, she said, she wanted to go straight on to the doctor. We parted like that at the entrance to the city—she, moved but in a great hurry; I, happy to have been able to help her but full of desire to see her again. We had not disclosed our family names to each other, nor our addresses, only our first names. We had both felt the need not to ruin the beauty of a disinterested happening, which had given hope to her and had helped me for a moment to forget my nightmares. Now, after more than two weeks, and at the very moment when I was grieving for myself and on the point of doing something rash, I found her in front of me, as if she had been sent by destiny.

Francesca greeted me with a big smile. She had been looking for me for quite some time to thank me. The medicine had saved her daughter's life, and she was now convalescing in a Yugoslav Red Cross home for children. She had noticed at which tram stop I used to get on and off and decided to try and find me. She wanted to know the name of the nurse, to send her at least a bunch of flowers. We had not only saved the life of a child but also given her back faith in a world in which human beings had changed into beasts. But here she stopped abruptly. She looked into my face and asked, "Don't you feel well?" Since I only answered by shaking my head, she said in a kind but firm tone, "I don't live far from here. Come with me. I'll make you a good cup of tea or coffee. It will do you good."

Rocked by the movement of the ship, I was smiling to myself, thinking back to the room in which Francesca had received me on the day when, unable to kill myself, I had decided to disappear from this world. Without her I would certainly have got myself into great trouble. Also I would not have been transferred from Bari to Rome; I would not have seen my uncle again; I would not have reestablished contact with Italian society; I would not. . . . Once more I felt protected by my little star, asking myself why things happened to me so differently from others; why an angel or a devil kept rushing to my help every time I got myself into trouble. For others, life was a drama; for me, just a game. Was it still the result of the Faustian pact I had signed by perjuring myself on the Bible at the court-martial to save a fellow soldier whom I hated? Would there never be a final price to pay?

The Dalmatian coast began to emerge on the horizon out of the quiet sea. The first mate, his face framed by a black beard straight out of a packet of Players cigarettes, kept explaining to me the route we were following. Neither from him, nor from the sea, nor from the land far away did I get an answer to my questions. I decided to give myself up to the pleasure of living without thinking of the morrow, without trying to understand why there are those in the world who suffer and those who are happy.

That decision, however, came straight from the room of Francesca. Located on the first floor of a house inhabited by refugees, the room was connected to others by an external passageway on which a common latrine let out a feeble smell of urine. While she was looking in her purse for her key, I noticed the eyes of two children, of an old woman, and of a man peering at me curiously and enviously from doorways in which glass panels had been replaced by cardboard. An Allied soldier meant tinned milk, cigarettes, laundry to wash, and some other minute chances of making money. I paid no attention to them; that evening I felt only a great need to hide, to sleep, to forget, and to confide my pain to someone. With great relief I heard Francesca closing the door behind us.

The room was big, poorly furnished and lighted, with a red brick floor and a ceiling held up by crude wooden beams, badly whitewashed. Opposite the entrance, on a bed covered by a red bedspread, the whiteness of two pillows stood out. At the foot of the bed was a chest with a swinging mirror on top, a few toilet articles, and a candlestick. Between the chest and the chairs, a rough table covered by a red-and-white-checked piece of oilcloth. Next to the bed there was a big peasant cradle, a bowl, and a small, enameled baby's bath. In a niche was a grate for a wood fire with some pans on it. Behind a curtain one could discern a washbasin and a tap. There was a deep silence, a sense of peace, of order—a smell of woman and home.

Francesca drew two chairs up to the table and made me sit down. She took out of the cupboard a tray, a tin with biscuits, and from behind the curtain, two cups. Then she started lighting the fire to boil water. She moved with controlled gestures, without making any noise. Her actions, both intimate and unembarrassed, filled me with infinite melancholy. Rocking myself backwards and forwards on the chair, I ended by leaning against the wall, closing my eyes, and falling asleep. When I opened them again, Francesca was standing in front of me with a steaming cup of coffee in her hand and a worried expression on her face. "It seems to me that something serious has happened to you. If you want to tell me, you can speak to me without fear, just as I did to you that day on the tram. We live in a cruel world, but human beings can still help each other sometimes." She looked at me with great kindness while I slowly drank my coffee, slightly bitter and not of the best quality. But it was hot, like the atmosphere in the room. My first words were: "I have committed a shameful act." She, thinking in wartime terms, replied with a mischievous smile: "I find it difficult to believe. Anyway, certainly not with me." Her sentence made me laugh and freed me a bit from the oppression that had been tormenting me since the morning. It was not easy to open my mouth, but once I started speaking —I do not know whether for half an hour or an hour—I was no longer able to stop.

I spoke in disconnected sentences; memories sometimes preceded the words and sometimes followed them. I spoke of my village in Piedmont, of my school years at Udine, of my dog, of the chickens in the kibbutz, of the court-martial in Ramle, of the Jews whom I had had no courage to go and save behind the lines, of my joining the army, of my night parachute jump. I spoke about my dreams, my solitude, my fears, about the red flowers my mother wore on her evening dress. I explained to her why I had wanted to kill myself; why I had decided to desert, disappear, to go around in the world with the mark of Cain on my forehead, which marked twenty-two years of wasted life; no, only sixteen, because those of my childhood did not count; indeed, only nine, because we Jews become responsible people only at the age of thirteen. I spoke, I spoke, without really knowing what I was saying, and she listened to me almost without blinking, without moving a muscle of her face, her chin supported on her clasped hands, her elbows on the oilcloth of the table, intent, very beautiful, clean, maternal, with only her nostrils quivering.

We sat like this, facing each other in the quiet of the room, even after the disconnected flood of my words had exhausted itself. When her turn came to speak, she did so with a voice that sounded detached, as though she were talking of a third person.

"If I had married at the age of eight, which happens to some Moslem girls in Yugoslavia, I could now, at more than thirty, pretend to be your mother. But with the millions of minutes that I have lived through, full of fear, shame, tears, broken hopes, I really feel at this moment like your grandmother. Not just tired . . . decrepit. And I have gone through so much that I don't feel I can judge anyone anymore—certainly not you. I have known you for too short a time to be able to do so, even if I wanted. But I will tell you something that still gives me, too, a lot of nightmares.

"You know that the Ustachi captured my husband. They tortured him and killed him, together with some peasants who had nothing to do with the Partisans, out of sheer cruelty, vengeance, out of their need to show their own authority through the suffering of other human beings. Before I left for Lissa, the Partisans attacked a German convoy. They took some prisoners among whom was a Ustachi leader and his woman —wife or mistress, whatever she was. They ordered me and other people of the area to go and witness their execution because, they said, these were two human beasts and had to be executed in an exemplary way.

"They kept the two locked in a house at the edge of a wood. There were flowers under the windows, a small river running limpid between the trees, grass, and moss. A place where death looked unreal. The Ustacha and the woman waited with resignation, their faces swollen by beatings, he with a torn uniform, she ridiculous in a dress that once upon a time must have been quite elegant.

"The woodcutters arrived. They carried their axes on their shoulders. One of them told me that the Ustacha had killed two sons of the old man who was leading them. In Indian file, with the other local inhabitants the Partisans had rounded up, we went into the wood. It was a wonderful day, with the sun penetrating through the pine trees in bundles of golden rays and with birds singing. When we arrived at the sawmill, the old man who led the march activated the circular saw. The blade turned, gleaming in the air, emitting a sound of strident metal that tortured the eardrums. When they grabbed the Ustacha by the shoulders and tied him onto the sliding bench in place of a log, the man, who up to that moment had maintained a dignified countenance, started screaming like a wild beast. They quieted him with blows on his head. Then it was the turn of the woman to be tied up, about a yard away from him. She kept quiet. She did not open her mouth even when the old man, lowering a handle, started the sliding platform moving toward the blade.

"The two bodies tied astride the platform looked like rolled up carpets on the railing of a balcony. People around me held their breath; I had the sensation of having turned into a block of stone. When the blood of the Ustacha spurted onto the sawdust there was a shriek of wounded flesh that almost immediately stopped. Now it was the woman who was moving toward the blade. She continued to keep silent. Half a meter from the blade, she succeeded in twisting herself to one side and turned her head toward us. Her mouth was wide open, her eyes fixed, and her body agitated by a kind of repulsive orgasm. A Partisan went up to the old man and raised the handle to stop the movement of the bench. Two men, walking on the sawdust soaked in blood, untied the woman. On the other side of the blade, two pieces of the man's body looked like marionettes whose strings had been dropped.

"The woman, raising herself, leaned first on the bench, then bent her knees and started vomiting. With a kick, they made her stand up. She staggered away into the meadow. Among the trees, the sun continued to throw its rays in a cascade over the grass, the birds went on singing. When the saw stopped turning, there was utter silence, full of the scent of pine trees and moss. The woman staggered and fell face forward onto the ground. They left her there. They told me afterwards that she had gone mad."

Francesca had placed her arms on the table. She convulsively contracted her hands while continuing to talk with her detached manner, as if she were relating an event of no importance. "I told you this story," she said, "because even around the most horrible things, life goes on. God has given to every being the gift of fear, and the animals have learned to use it better than men. If my husband had been afraid, he might still be with me. If that Ustacha had been afraid, he would not have committed the crimes that made him tremble at the moment of death. How can you know how the adventure you wanted to embark on, in order to show other people that you were not afraid, would have ended? Perhaps the fear you are so ashamed of today will one day appear to you like a virtue. But that is not the main thing I wanted to tell you: the essential thing is that this rotten war is coming to an end. Those who have come through it, like us, alive, have the duty to live as long as possible to repair the disasters that men without fear, small and great, have caused, believing themselves in the right to change the face of the world. If we have sinned, our punishment will be to atone for our sins by living, not by looking for death. Otherwise there would have been no reason or sense for you and the nurse to steal penicillin for a child you did not know."

She spoke softly, with warmth, and with a light in her eyes. I sensed her perfume and followed with my eyes the rising and sinking of her blouse, tightly buttoned at the neck. I had a great desire to touch her, but I could not find the courage to do so. "It's late," I said, "and it's time for me to go. It did me a lot of good to speak with you."

She looked at me and murmured: "If you want, you can stay." The sudden change from the formal *lei* to the informal *tu* in the Italian had the effect of a punch in the stomach. My head was empty and my face, I believe, very pale, when I put my hands on her shoulders. We remained for a long moment immobile, standing at arms' length. Later, when, lying next to her, I measured the passing of time by the beats of her heart, I heard her whispering into my ear: "Don't be afraid, little soldier; life is stronger than evil."

The Friday Cage

Andrew Diamond

This is a work of fiction. Names, characters, and events
are the products of the author's imagination. Any
resemblance to actual persons or events is purely
coincidental.

Cover design by Lindsay Heider Diamond. Woman's
silhouette licensed from Stock Unlimited. Thunderbolt
and fingerprint licensed from Deposit Photos.

ISBN (Paperback): 978-1734139228
ISBN (e-book): 978-1734139211

For Lindsay, who is every bit as hardheaded as Claire.

1

Am I paranoid to think someone is following me? And if they are following me, why would they be so obvious about it? A 1971 burgundy Lincoln Continental sticks out, even on a busy avenue in Washington, DC.

She could see it in the rearview. The knocking engine and the blue smoke from the tailpipe—it was the same sound, the same acrid smell of burning oil she had noticed in front of her house that morning, and the morning before.

As they waited for the light at Wisconsin and Calvert, Claire studied the driver's reflection in her mirror. He was a big man, tall and fat, with light brown hair and enormously broad shoulders. Was that why he drove the old Lincoln? Because he wouldn't fit into a smaller car?

He was stuffing what looked like the last bite of a sandwich into his mouth, licking his fingers greedily, like a dog devouring its treasure before anyone could snatch it away. The pale January sun flashed in his blue eyes and lit the golden stubble on his fat cheeks. Eyes that close together, Claire thought, in a face as broad as his, made him look crude and thuggish, like an enforcer or a goon.

The impatient honking of the cars behind told her that the light had changed. She hit the gas.

Is he following me just for fun, she wondered. A stalker, or a perv? Or did someone hire him?

She looked again in the rearview. He was tearing the Subway wrapper from a new sandwich, stuffing it into his mouth as fast as he could get the paper off.

Peter wouldn't hire anyone to follow her. If he wanted to know what she was up to, he would call, as he had done so many times in the weeks since she'd left. She didn't answer, and she didn't listen to the messages. The sound of his voice would cut too deep, and she would resent his wounded tone because she knew she had caused it. It was easier to delete the messages unheard than to acknowledge her guilt. After four weeks, the calls stopped. He'd given up.

She turned her eyes back to the road just in time to avoid rear-ending a taxi.

Maybe it was the cop, she thought. Maybe the cop assigned the goon to follow me. But wouldn't a cop just send another cop? I mean, a professional? Someone who knows how to be discreet?

Cops usually keep a low profile, don't they? Unless they want to pressure you. When they think you've done something wrong, they *want* you to know they're watching. But what have I done wrong?

She glanced in the sideview and thought back to her interview with the police detective. He was neither professional nor discreet, showing up at her door, giving her *the look*, and then peppering her with questions about the circumstances of Gavin's death without first telling her that her friend had died. She had to glean that bit of information from his questions, and when she did, it was a shock the detective did nothing to soften.

The thought of that encounter still angered her, even now, six days later. First of all, a man doesn't look at a woman that way when he's coming to talk about her friend's death. Though she did nothing to encourage it, she received that look from men old and young. The look that lingered a little too long, that took in the chestnut brown hair and eyes, the fair skin, the splash of pale freckles across the bridge of the nose, the look that approved of the face that was objectively pretty even as it coldly discouraged familiarity.

The detective had shown up on the doorstep of her grandmother's house on Oregon Avenue as she was getting ready for work. Backlit by the sun rising through the bare trees of Rock Creek Park, he was a dark silhouette in a cloud of steaming breath.

"Can I help you?" Claire asked.

She wore a simple grey pants suit, her bare feet washed in the flood of cold from the open door. Without shoes, she was five foot six, a deficiency she corrected with heels that brought her closer to eye-level with the men at work.

The detective was a big man. Six two or six three. Over two hundred pounds, probably in his early thirties, with close-cropped reddish-blond hair, a red pock-marked face, and small ears that stuck out like clay pinched from the sides of a child's sculpture. He wore civilian clothes, black sweater and slacks, with the black jacket of the Prince George's County Police department. On his belt was a golden badge but no gun.

He hesitated a second, giving her the familiar, unwelcome look that first registers attraction and then searches for a sign of reciprocated interest.

"Miss Chastain?"

"Mizz," she corrected.

"Did you receive a call from Gavin Corley last night?"

"Excuse me," she said coldly. "You are?"

"Darrell Gatlin. PG County Police." He peered over her shoulder into the living room strewn with packing boxes, books, papers, photos, and old vinyl LPs—remnants of the life she was dismantling now that she had moved her grandmother into assisted living.

His curiosity was intrusive, a desire he was going to satisfy regardless of her wish for privacy. She pulled the door against her shoulder to prevent him looking in.

"Did Gavin call you last night?" he asked.

"What business is that of yours?"

3

The expression she wore in this encounter was one she had cultivated during her years in the corporate office in New York, when she was often the only woman in the room, usually the youngest, and always the least powerful. Her business face showed an unmistakable edge of hardness that quietly told the men who needed to be told exactly where her boundary was, and that they would always be on the other side of it. After so many years of putting on that face, she had become the person it projected.

Still, there were some, like this one, who just wouldn't get it. They kept searching for a way in, for an indication of interest or some weakness to exploit.

"You're the last person he called before he died," the detective said.

Died?

He didn't register her shock because he wasn't looking at her face. His eyes went first to her hand, checking for a ring, then to her thighs, which no longer filled out the pants she had bought just last fall. Stress and anxiety had prevented her from eating in the six weeks since she'd left New York. At her normal weight of one-thirty-five, Peter could still see in those pants the curve of her muscle. If this cop saw something he liked in the slacks that now hung loosely on her, it was a projection of his own desire.

Three weeks ago, when her weight dropped to one-eighteen, she stopped weighing herself. She was several pounds below that now. What kind of man is attracted to a woman who isn't well? Fixers, she thought. Caretakers who want to heal you. And stalkers. Creeps looking for someone they think they can dominate.

She took him for the latter.

"I'm sorry, did you say Gavin is dead?" Dismay and anger stirred in her voice.

"You didn't know?" He sounded almost annoyed, as if death were a technicality, a distraction from some more important point.

4

What kind of response was that, Claire wondered. What kind of detective starts hurling questions without first informing you... without offering condolences... Her eyes were already narrowing. The crease between them was beginning to show, the one her friends knew to look out for.

"He passed away last night. In an accident."

Passed away? Is that the term police departments train their detectives to use?

She glared at him as her heart sped. Her blood pressure was rising quickly.

"This is how you tell me? This is how you tell me my friend is dead? Who are you? How did you even find me? This is my grandmother's house. How did you know I'd be here?"

"Miss Chastain." The conciliatory tone meant to soothe her sounded condescending.

"Mizz."

"What did Gavin say to you?"

"Fuck off." She shut the door in his face.

She read about the crash later that day on the *Washington Post* website. *One Dead in Single Car Accident.* Gavin's Chevy Equinox had run off a wooded road in Prince George's County, flipping down an embankment before coming to rest upside down. An early-morning commuter had spotted the car around 5 a.m.

At work that afternoon, she rehearsed in her mind how she would have described the detective to Peter, if Peter were still around to talk to. First was the issue of professionalism, or lack thereof. Can a police detective show basic courtesy? Or is it beneath them to try?

Second, how could that cop have expected her to know at 7:30 a.m. that Gavin was dead when he'd only been found two hours earlier?

And third... Third...

This was what chilled her now as she approached the entrance to the garage on 18th Street. A quick glance in the sideview showed that after two miles and half a dozen turns, the fat goon in the old Lincoln was still behind her.

5

Third, how did the cop know Gavin had called her? Even if he had Gavin's phone, he couldn't have unlocked it to look at the call history because Gavin, the ultraparanoid computer security expert, used a six-digit passcode.

The Lincoln didn't follow her into the underground lot. She checked her mirrors as she descended to the second level, checked them again as she pulled into her spot. She cut the engine and sat quietly for a moment, listening for the knocking of the old Continental. When she was satisfied there was no one else around, she got out.

On the solitary walk from her parking spot to the elevators, a chilling image flashed in her mind—that rude cop pressing Gavin's dead finger against the phone, scrolling through the call history, finding her name.

She pressed four inside the elevator, watched the doors slide shut, and wondered again what had led the detective to look for the owner of a New York phone number, area code 646, in a house on Oregon Avenue.

If they know he called, she wondered, do they also know what he said? And if they know what he said, why haven't they been back to follow up?

She had deleted the message, but she remembered it verbatim. His last words to her:

"I'm pretty sure I screwed this up, so I'm passing the torch to you. If worse comes to worst, I know you'll see this through. Love ya, babe. Sorry for the trouble."

2

Her boss was standing at the reception desk when she left the elevator on four. He tried to look like he wasn't waiting for her, a ruse she had bought last Friday.

"Claire!"

"Good morning, Anoop."

She brushed past him without breaking stride, and he followed her into the carpeted hall. Long-limbed and thin, with a black mustache and an easy manner, he struggled to keep up.

"Li tells me you're almost done."

Almost done with a month-long assignment, certifying the year-end financials of a generic pharmaceutical manufacturer.

"I'll have it to you tomorrow," Claire said.

"It's not due till the end of the month." He held his coffee high as he dashed along behind her, as if an extra foot of altitude would prevent a spill.

"Then we're ahead of schedule." She turned left into her office, sliding her shoulder bag down her left arm as she entered.

"*You're* ahead of schedule," Anoop said. "After tomorrow, you take a few days off."

"I didn't ask for time off, and I don't want it." She dropped her bag on the desk and pulled off her coat.

"You've worked twenty-eight days in a row."

She pushed the door halfway shut, forcing him to step back into the hall, so she could hang her coat on the hook. It was an act of simple efficiency. Her coat was off and she had to put it somewhere, and if he happened to be in the way of what she had already decided to do, that was just bad timing on his part. If her action had the added benefit of keeping him outside the office, where she wanted him, he was too good natured to suspect it, and too polite to call her out on it.

"And you're complaining?" she asked impatiently. "That I get things done?"

"You worked on Christmas day. *In the office.*"

Because I didn't want to spend the whole day alone with Leona, Claire thought. You would have done the same thing if you had a grandmother like her.

"This is how people burn out." Anoop pushed the door open.

He would have stepped in if she hadn't stood in his way with that look of impatience that made him feel he was wasting her time. It was a useful look that almost always had the intended effect.

"I've worked a lot harder than this."

Anoop understood that when he interviewed her for the job. He knew she was overqualified, that she belonged a rung or two above him on the ladder, that someday he might be reporting to her. He had hired her because she was the kind of person he would *want* to report to—sharp, competent, to the point. The only thing that bothered him was why a woman as intelligent and ambitious as Claire Chastain would take a step down from the complexities of corporate valuations and due diligence to certifying numbers in a revenue report.

"You have degrees in business and accounting?" he asked in the interview.

"It's all there on my résumé."

"This is more like the work you did early in your career. Straight numbers. You OK with that?"

"I read the job description."

When he asked her why she left New York, she told him she needed to care for her grandmother. That was partially true. She needed to move Leona into a facility before Leona assaulted another grocery clerk, tore up another month's bills, smashed up another car. Beyond the move and the visits to help her grandmother make the transition, there would be no caretaking. Leona wouldn't let anyone help her, and Claire was not a caretaker.

The answer had satisfied Anoop. She started the job nine days after moving to DC, a week before Christmas, and hit the ground running.

"After tomorrow," Anoop insisted now from his place in the doorway, "you'll take the rest of the week off."

She looked him in the eye and shook her head. No.

Anoop hadn't known her long enough to be able to read her. Peter would have understood the anxiety that underlay her defiance. He would have known that with a few gentle pushes, given at the right time, in the right way, she would relent. The report that she had already completed, that she was reluctant to turn over, represented the end of an assignment into which her troubled mind had retreated from the spiraling chaos of an unraveling life. The thought of time off, of days during which her mind would have no external focus, no deadlines, no objectively measurable goals, worried her.

Peter would have seen the worry, would have recognized it as the root cause of her refusal. He would have addressed it directly.

"There comes a time when you have to slow down," he would tell her. "You have to look at the questions that don't have easy answers."

"Leave me alone."

Her face hid every emotion but anger and annoyance, the two that were most useful in getting people to back off. If there was more to her inner life than that—and there was—she would choose whom to show, and how much they could see.

When people can't read you, can't understand what you're feeling, Claire thought, they can only guess what's going on inside. And from their guesses, you can figure out who they are, how they think, because they fill in the blanks by projecting what they would feel if they were in your shoes.

Anoop, she knew, was a fundamentally decent person. So was Peter. Anoop was easier to get along with because they had a simpler arrangement: do good work, do it on time, and all is well. Anoop was also intimidated by her just enough to accept the boundaries exactly as she defined them. She could see him calculate now and then the cost (high) and the potential benefit (uncertain) of trying to develop a more personal relationship.

Peter, on the other hand, was more difficult. Sharing a bed entitled a person to more intimate access. She was willing to accept that. But she often found him looking into her, and she felt the person he saw was not the one she wanted to project. The thoughtful looks that had once flattered her as signs of his infatuation had, over time, come to feel intrusive. He was prying behind the façade, trying to gain some insight into her, some understanding of who she was, and that, to her, amounted to taking something without her consent.

Worse yet, her anger didn't intimidate him.

"Listen," Claire told Anoop, softening her tone and posture. "I know you think you're doing me a favor, but I need the work."

"You need rest," Anoop said. "Have you looked in the mirror lately?"

Wrong response, she thought. When a woman is struggling, you don't ask her how she feels about her looks.

She had stopped looking at her reflection during the week between Christmas and New Year's, when her ribs had begun to show. Now when she got out of the shower, she left the steam on the mirror.

"I understand you're concerned for my health," she said. "But I need something to do. I can help Li with whatever she's working on."

"Li's working on entry-level stuff. She doesn't need your help."

"I'm telling you what I need," Claire said. "I'm being very clear, and if you don't start listening, I'm going to lose my temper. Try to get the message before that happens."

She had him on his heels now, so she pressed her point.

"Li needs a mentor, and I'm going to be that person. Now are we done?"

Anoop stepped back and let out a sigh of frustration. She turned to the desk and kept her back to him as she slid the laptop from her bag.

When he left, she picked up the two letters beside her keyboard. The first was from her old firm in New York. She opened it to find another letter inside, a reminder from a professional organization to renew her membership. One more thing that had slipped through the cracks during the upheaval of the past six weeks.

The second letter was from a bank, addressed to Claire C. Chastain. She wondered what marketing list they had gotten her name from. She never used her middle initial. The name of her firm was on the second line of the address, and she could feel the rigid outline of a credit card inside. That would be her company MasterCard for business expenses. Anoop must have ordered it.

She felt someone else standing behind her now as she dropped the letter onto the desk beside her bag.

"Claire?"

She turned to see Li in the doorway, open laptop in hand, wearing the same anxious-to-please smile she showed to every person she considered her superior.

You don't have to take that submissive attitude, Claire thought. It only works against you in the corporate world. And don't stand at the threshold waiting for permission to enter. Walk in. People give you only as much respect as you demand, so aim high.

Li seemed to sense her annoyance, and to shrink from it.

"Yes, Li?"

"These numbers do not make sense." She overenunciated each syllable of her textbook English, inadvertently drawing attention to the Taiwanese accent that made her self-conscious.

You're a project, Claire thought. When I was twenty-two, in my first job out of college, I didn't take shit from anyone. And I certainly didn't invite it. You have to set the tone from the get-go, or people will walk on you.

"What numbers?" Claire asked.

Li nodded her head—a little bow, Claire thought—and smiled. "In this spreadsheet you sent me."

"Jesus, come in, will you?"

Li stepped in and nodded again. "Thank you!"

She set the laptop on Claire's desk and pointed to the columns on the left of the sheet.

"You see here? These are raw materials. And here..." She slid her finger to the right. "These are outputs. The outputs don't match." Li looked at Claire to see if she was following.

"What are these numbers?" Claire asked. "I need some context."

"Manufacturing. Amount and cost of materials in the left columns. Output units on the right. They are measured in doses."

"Why is that in a spreadsheet?" Claire squinted at the numbers. "PharmaCore tracks manufacturing in a central database."

Li shrugged.

"Where did you get this?" Claire asked.

"From you."

Claire vaguely remembered receiving it, not wanting to waste time on it, forwarding it to Li for vetting.

"Look." Li pointed to the left. "Enough inputs for twelve million doses, but only ten million units produced."

"OK, we don't need to get into that level of detail. All we have to do is certify the year-end numbers for the Securities and Exchange Commission. Cash in, cash out, assets, and liabilities."

"But they are trying to be acquired, yes?"

"Yes, they're considering that."

If Claire were still in New York, she might be working on behalf of a prospective buyer, a multibillion-dollar corporation, uncovering details of the target company's manufacturing processes and facilities, its management structure, intellectual property, market position, products in development, jobs that could be cut after the acquisition—every aspect of the giant, multidimensional enterprise that could be classified as value, risk, or opportunity. Compared to that, the financial auditing she was doing now was boring and one-dimensional.

"Their prospectus says their manufacturing process is the most efficient in the industry," Li said.

"That's not our concern."

"It says less than one percent of raw materials are wasted in production."

You are very sharp, Claire thought. And thorough, for even bothering to read the prospectus. You need to *make* people listen to you instead of *asking* them to listen. I know what you're going to say next.

"These numbers show they waste sixteen point six-seven percent of raw materials in production. That is a large discrepancy."

Thank you for getting the numbers right, Claire thought. Thank you for being precise.

"OK, but it's not our concern," Claire said. "If a buyer comes along, they'll discover that information on their own during due diligence. Our job is just to double-check accounting and certify the numbers."

"Then why did they send us this?" Li asked.

Now that's how you ask a question, Claire thought. Direct and to the point. Don't leave the person any way out other than a direct response. Why can't you talk to Anoop that way? Or any of the other men? So much mindpower goes to waste because women like you and me are taught to doubt ourselves before we even speak. We hold our tongues for fear of being wrong and half the world's truth goes unsaid. Trust your mind, speak your piece, and if you're wrong, make whoever disagrees with you prove you're wrong. I'm going to toughen you up, Li Ming, whether you like it or not.

"I don't know," Claire said. "We're just about done with this audit, and whatever's in that spreadsheet is beside the point. Don't waste your time on it."

Claire could see Li's relief. Li thanked her—a little too profusely, Claire thought—with a nod and an anxious smile.

Ten minutes later, when she was seated at her desk with her laptop plugged into the big monitor, Claire emailed her copy of the spreadsheet back to the PharmaCore manager who had sent it. "I think you sent this to the wrong person."

She studied the message for a moment, then removed the two words that weakened her assertion. "You sent this to the wrong person."

3

At noon, she told Anoop she'd be out for a long lunch with her grandmother. She knew Anoop wanted twenty-four hours' notice before such an absence, but when he hired her, she told him she wasn't a nine-to-fiver. She would meet her deadlines on her own schedule, as she had done in New York.

Now she wanted to see how he'd react when she asserted the privilege they'd agreed upon. She knew he wouldn't openly object, because he was scared of her. But if his tone or his body language showed any hint of discomfort with the arrangement, she would confront him and make sure they both explicitly understood the nature of their relationship. This was the kind of boundary she had to enforce clearly and early, and she knew she could because she was always ready for a fight and he wasn't.

"I'll be gone at least three hours," she said.

"Take the rest of the day off if you want. Get some rest."

Good, she thought. I don't have to waste energy on that battle. I can save it for Leona.

Half an hour later, her blue BMW arrived at the home in north Bethesda. The original Rollingwood had burned in the 1980s, and the rolling woods had been replaced by rows of million-dollar homes for the lawyers and lobbyists who didn't want to put their kids into the DC public school system.

The new Rollingwood, a three-story brick colonial at the apex of a long, curved lane, looked like an oversized realtor's office or a suburban bank, with wings on either end to house the elderly inmates who couldn't remember what offense had landed them there. The elaborate winding paths in back pleased the firm of mind and confused the residents for whom the facility was designed. In summer, birds flitted in the fountains, and the pathways were bright with roses, hydrangeas, and peonies. In winter, the dry fountains and cropped stalks reminded the occupants of what they had once been and where they were going.

"How is this better then where I am now?" Leona raged when she first saw the place.

January wasn't the best time of year for this kind of move, Claire realized. But what was the alternative? To let Leona kill herself on the road? Or kill someone else?

She parked and went to the psychiatrist's office first. She had met him twice before. An even-tempered, reassuring man with greying hair and photos of the twins—one boy, one girl— in their high school graduation gowns. A widower not yet old enough to stop noticing a pretty face.

"The combativeness," said the doctor, "the aggression and abuse—those are all symptoms of the disease."

Claire shook her head. "No. She's always been like that. Has she hit anyone yet?"

"A little smack when one of the nurses annoyed her. Not too bad compared to what we sometimes see. Why did you ask about hitting? Did she—"

The doctor trailed off, but she knew from his look where this was going.

"Used to hit me?" Claire said. "Is that what you were going to ask? Is it really any of your business?"

Don't look at me like that, she thought. You must be over fifty. I'm thirty-two. This is business. This is your job. Keep your mind on the patient. That's what we're paying you for.

"I'm more concerned about the bewilderment," Claire said. "She can be lucid for two or three hours at a time. Then all of a sudden she doesn't know where she is."

"That's only going to get worse."

"And she tries to hide it. She's too proud to admit it, even when it's happening."

"That's not unusual."

"You have to be stern with her," Claire said. "Gentle doesn't work. She doesn't respect that."

You could tell that just by looking at the woman, Claire thought. Scowling and rail thin, with razor-straight bangs she cut herself and that crease of anger etched permanently between her eyes, she's a model of severity.

She's worn the same coat for twelve years, and not because she likes it. Some people who grow up poor want everything money can buy as soon as they have the money to buy it. Others, like Leona, internalize their poverty. They continue to inflict it on themselves and their household because they know no other way of being. Try growing up with *that*.

Gavin knew what she was like. Gavin's father knew too. Old Ben Corley. That's why Claire was always over there. To remind herself that not everyone in the world was as mean as Leona.

One Saturday morning when she was sixteen, she hovered in the Corleys' kitchen as Ben cooked breakfast for her, Gavin, and himself.

He didn't ask what was bothering her. He just puffed at his cigarette, stirred the eggs, turned the bacon, and waited until she was ready to speak.

"I hate her," Claire said at last. "I fucking hate her!"

"Don't."

"Why shouldn't I?"

"Because she's your teacher. She's a model of everything you must not be in this world, and you'll never find a better teacher than the one who makes you feel the lesson to the bottom of your soul."

"I never want to be like her."

"You won't be."

Ben Corley's vote of confidence was a memory she turned to in times of doubt to reassure herself that her heart wasn't as cold as the persona she projected. But lately, she had begun to doubt his assessment.

I'm exactly like her, Claire thought. I don't trust anyone. I'm always on guard. How could Peter have tolerated me? Why would anyone want to marry a person like that? It's like living with a porcupine.

The only difference between Leona and me is I don't attack people who don't deserve it. I don't go after the ones who can't defend themselves.

But I have just as much anger, just as much hostility, and sometimes I find myself hoping someone will come along who deserves to be on the receiving end of all that rage, just so I can let it go.

She stopped her train of thought when she felt the doctor's eyes on her. My thoughts must be showing on my face. She touched her cheek, as if to check. Stop looking at me, will you? It's intrusive.

"You have some issues to work out with her?" the doctor asked.

"I'm not your patient."

"No, but this is a difficult time and a difficult process. You have to remember you're dealing with a person who's not all there. She'll continue to fade, and you're going to have to come to terms with the fact that you may not be able to resolve all of your..."

"My what?" Claire asked. "Differences? Issues? Grievances? Which word were you going to choose?"

"Why don't you choose the word, Claire? You don't have to tell me." He turned and picked up the iPad from his desk. Pulling up the record of his next patient, Claire assumed. Without looking at her, he said, "She's in her room. It's kind of you to take her out. I think it'll do her good."

He sat on the edge of the desk scrolling through the iPad, pretending not to notice her lingering at the door.

After a long moment, he asked without looking up, "What is it, Claire?"

"I'm sorry I'm such a bitch."

"You're not a bitch."

"Oh, but I am."

"Well, like I said, this is a difficult time."

* * *

At lunch, Leona's first jab came as soon as the maître d' had seated them.

"Why did you leave New York?" she barked.

"Can you please speak in a civil tone?"

"Answer my question!"

"I hated it," Claire said flatly. "It was all about winning. That's all anyone cared about."

She had explained this to Leona several times, but she didn't mind saying it again for her own sake, to reassure herself that she had made the right decision.

"You didn't hate it when you got there. What changed?"

"I don't know, Gran. I honestly don't."

When the waiter came to take their drink order, Claire asked for water while her grandmother insisted it wasn't right to order until Peter was seated.

"Peter's not coming."

"Why not?"

"We're not together anymore. I've told you that a dozen times."

"What did you do to him?"

"I didn't do anything, Gran."

I left him.

"If you two are having a fight, call him and make up. This is stupid. Us sitting down to lunch with no Peter."

"I'll call him, Gran." She wouldn't, but Leona would forget in a few minutes and drop it. To the waiter, Claire said, "She'll have an iced tea."

When the waiter left, her grandmother stared at her, confused. Claire raised the menu to avoid looking at her. In Leona's more contentious moods, a simple look could provoke a fight.

After a few seconds of silence, Claire lowered her shield and watched as Leona scanned the faces at the surrounding tables. She seemed to be trying to place them in her memory. Leona Chastain, in her lucid days, had been a journalist on Capitol Hill. She seemed to know everyone—congressmen, senators, lawyers, and lobbyists—but had had no friends that Claire could recall.

Her mind had been sharp enough to carry her to the top of her field, but her abrasive manner and bitter cynicism offended enough people over the years to assure she'd never be more than a mid-level information gatherer. She could dig facts out of people, but she couldn't make them comfortable enough to open up and spill the meaningful story.

Her failure to rise, Leona used to proclaim proudly, was due to her uncompromising honesty. "People in power don't like people who speak the truth."

No, Claire thought. People in general don't like people who are rude.

"How can you stand living with her?" Gavin used to ask. "She's always accusing you of things you didn't do. She never stops picking on you. She's just downright mean."

"What am I supposed to do?" Claire asked testily. "I deal with it, OK? That's all I *can* do until I get out of here."

"Well, if you can defend yourself against her, you can defend yourself against anyone."

Now as Leona struggled to pick out an acquaintance in the sea of strange faces, Claire could see the bewilderment in her eyes, the welling sense of defeat. She found no joy in seeing the tyrant of her youth humbled.

No, humbled isn't the right word, she thought. It's humiliation. She's humiliated, and no one deserves that.

"What are you looking at?" Leona growled.

"Are you going to order?"

"I would if I could read the menu. Why is the print so small? Do they think we're leprechauns?"

"The curried chicken looks good."

"Then I'll have that." Leona dropped her menu on the table and turned to look behind her.

"Where's the waiter?" she barked. "Waiter!"

"Gran!" Claire laid her hand on Leona's. "Keep your voice down."

"How can you want to take care of her?" Gavin had asked on the day Claire returned to DC.

"Who else is going to do it?"

"She never took care of you."

"So what am I supposed to do? Abandon her? You don't do that to someone who needs help. Besides, I have things I want to ask her."

"About your father?"

"I want to know who he was."

"Good luck digging that out of her."

On a good day, Leona would answer questions if she liked the topic. Claire's parentage wasn't a topic she liked, and today wasn't a good day.

All that knowledge is going to the grave with you unless I dig it out, Claire thought, but how do I even broach the topic without setting you off?

Leona looked at the empty place beside her.

"Where is Grace?"

Claire rubbed her temples and took a deep breath. Her mother, Grace, had died twenty-seven years ago, when Claire was five. Drunk, in a car with an even drunker married man fifteen years her senior. "Slutting around with someone else's husband," as Leona put it.

She was with a lot of men, Ben Corley had told her. Looking for the love she didn't get at home.

"Grace isn't here, Gran."

"Why hasn't anyone set a place for her? What's going on? Where is the waiter? Why are we here?"

Oh, God, Claire thought. Her stomach began the familiar churn of the past six weeks, her headache was coming back, and she wasn't sure she wanted to eat anymore.

4

On her way back to the office, Claire stopped at Staples in Bethesda, and then at the house on Oregon Avenue. She passed the half-packed boxes in the living room, threading through stacks of books and photos and old LPs. She set her shoulder bag on the kitchen counter. The kitchen was *her* space, for *her* things, which were not to be mixed with Leona's things, which were all on their way out.

She fished a dime from her coat pocket and fit it into the slot on the bottom edge of her phone. One twist and the back came off to expose the electronic innards.

She took the battery out. The chip beneath it said SanDisk 64GB. She marveled as she pulled it from the phone. No larger than the nail of her index finger, it had once held two years' worth of photos and videos, plus data for half her apps.

Is it a sign, she wondered, that it went bad now? That I lose all my photos right after leaving New York? Was this whole chapter of my life meant to be erased?

She tore open the package of the replacement chip she'd bought at Staples.

She pushed the new chip into the slot, replaced the battery and the rear panel, then flipped the phone over and turned it on.

New storage device detected. Format now?

She tapped yes, laid the phone face-down on the counter, and left it to do its work.

An animal rustled the leaves out back. Probably a deer from the woods across the street. They had been a rarity when she last lived here, fourteen years earlier, but now they wandered out from Rock Creek Park to forage in people's gardens. She took off her coat, laid it on a chair, and made a mental note to have the yard cleaned up.

She walked down the hallway to the second bedroom, the one she had grown up in and swore she would never return to. On the floor beside the dresser she found a second pair of heels, ones that didn't dig into her Achilles tendons. They were a quarter-inch higher than the ones she was wearing. She took off the one pair and put on the other.

It was strange to be in that house alone. Even with the clutter of what remained to be packed, it seemed impossibly empty in the absence of the hostile spirit that had once dominated it. The echoes from the bare floors and walls reinforced the feeling of emptiness, and the memories came trickling back.

"You fell because why?" Leona asked, her bony fingers digging into the flesh of Claire's six-year-old shoulders. "Because you went up on the wall where I told you not to go, and you were twirling around like a fool, and this is what happens to stupid people. Go clean yourself up, and then go to your room where you can't get into any more trouble. I'll call you when dinner is ready."

In her room, she vowed that the next time she got cut, she would clean herself up without telling her grandmother.

In the last year of grade school, when the boys started noticing girls, she provoked feelings they didn't know how to express. She was the pretty one who didn't try to be pretty, the quiet one who had a lot to say but didn't say it. She didn't understand their crude attempts at flirtation, and didn't respond. Some of the boys began to hate her.

When she complained about the way they teased her, Leona's unsympathetic response was, "Why do you *let* them be mean to you? Weakness invites abuse. You have to make them understand they won't get away with it."

When her teacher assigned her to a group project with those same boys, she stayed after school and asked to be put in another group. The teacher called Leona and explained the situation, and when Claire got home, Leona laid into her.

"Why do you bother that woman with your complaints? Why do you make yourself look weak and make me look like a fool?"

"I don't like those boys, Gran. I don't know why they pick on me."

"Boys are assholes," Leona replied. "They're practicing to be men. I told that teacher to put you back in the group."

"Why?"

"So you can figure it out for yourself."

Claire folded her arms across her chest and said defiantly, "Then I'm not going. I'm not going back to school."

She recognized that was a mistake half a second too late to avoid the bony backhand on her cheek. Leona put everything she had into that one. The strike knocked Claire off balance, and the fall hurt worse than the blow.

She spent the evening stewing in her room, angry with herself for forgetting the fundamental lesson Leona had drilled into her. Weakness invites abuse. She had asked her teacher for help. That was a show of weakness, and Leona had delivered the punishment.

The lessons repeated over the years. She learned to close herself up, to hide everything from everyone. She told herself that when she graduated high school, she would leave the city and never come back.

And now here she was.

She looked at the suitcase atop the dresser, the one she hadn't unpacked, because putting her clothes away would mean she'd settled in, and she wasn't going to do that.

"Why don't you use the drawers?" Leona had snapped as she watched, eagle-eyed, from the hallway the day after Claire returned. It wasn't a real question. The point was simply to convey how strongly she disapproved.

"Mind your own business," Claire shot back. That was the tone that made the men back off at work. Growing up with Leona had taught her that defense didn't work against bullies. Offense did. Meet aggression with aggression.

Along with the toughness she had intended, Leona had unwittingly instilled in her granddaughter a hatred of cruelty, intimidation, and oppression. Since she had moved her grandmother out, Claire had thought more than once of burning down the house, but instead of allowing herself to indulge in a cathartic daydream, her practical mind went straight from the fire to the fire inspector to the police and lawyers. The fantasy ended with the insurance adjustor denying her claim and the fire department handing her a bill for putting out the flames.

Get out of this house, she told herself. It poisons your mind.

On her way back to the kitchen, she felt a draft wafting through the crack beneath the basement door. She opened it and was surprised to feel how much colder the air was on the other side. When she flipped the switch at the top of the stairs, no light came on. She went down anyway.

She had visited the basement frequently enough in recent weeks to navigate it in darkness. Why, then, did she bump into something in a passage that should have been clear? And what was it?

She extended her hand and felt the rigid surface. A suitcase.

If she had had her phone with her, she would have turned on the flashlight. But her phone sat on the counter in the silence upstairs, and she stood alone in the silence below. The air began to move. The draft came from the rear of the house, from the window in the northwest corner, where the dim winter light filtered through the dried spatter of heavy summer rains.

On her way to the window, her foot thudded against something else she hadn't remembered being there. It was heavy and soft, like a body. The direction of the draft reversed, sucking the door shut at the top of the stairs. She pressed her foot into the long, semi-soft thing she had almost tripped over. The rug from the living room. She had rolled it up more than a week ago, leaned it against the wall, and now it had fallen.

She stepped over it and examined the window. It was open at the bottom. The wood casing around the latch showed someone had pried it with the flat edge of a screwdriver.

She shut the window and secured the latch. Then she turned again into the darkness and stood listening, wondering if the heartbeat she heard was her own or someone else's. The more quietly she tried to breathe, the louder and faster came the beat, until she decided at last that she was alone, listening to her own fear.

She thought back to when she'd put her phone down in the kitchen. Was that really a deer she'd heard in the leaves out back? Or was it a person crawling out of the window she'd just closed?

She stood the rolled-up rug against the wall, made her way back to the suitcase, pushed it back into place. She ascended the stairs with a slow dignity, as if someone might be watching and she wanted them to see she wasn't scared.

Upstairs, she checked the windows and doors. Her iPad was where she had left it, beside the stove. Nothing in Leona's office had been disturbed. Her mother's bracelets were in the box beside her bed.

On the nightstand, she found the diamond studs Peter had given her. She sat on the bed and put them in and was surprised to find they still had the power to comfort her, to make her feel less alone.

At the thought of Peter, the emotion came too strong and too fast. Shame, regret, uncertainty, confusion, longing. She stood abruptly, cut off the unwanted feelings, and marched to the kitchen, her heels clomping in the empty hall. She picked up her bag, her phone, her keys, and headed to the car, to work, where all the world's problems were reduced to numbers neatly aligned in rows and columns, numbers that either added up or didn't. And when they didn't, it was someone else's problem because she was just the auditor.

On the step outside, she locked the door, tested it to make sure the deadbolt was set.

The mailman was walking up the driveway with a handful of letters. They met by the door of the BMW, and he handed her Leona's mail.

"Only five?" Claire asked.

The mailman pulled his headphones off. "Only five. How's she taking to life in the new place?" He looked to be sixty or so, a light-skinned black man with a full head of grey hair. His walk had the bounce of a fourteen-year-old.

"Not too well, but it's only been a couple of weeks. Is this all there is?"

"That's all. You tell Leona old Bernie says hello."

"I thought there'd be more," Claire said. "Water, gas, electric. Nothing's come for days."

"I've filled that box every day but Sunday. Gas came Saturday for the whole neighborhood. Electric was Friday. You should have a pile."

Claire shook her head. "I check it every night when I get home. The box is empty."

He told her which papers to file if she suspected someone was stealing her mail. "Or you can do it online. It's faster."

He pulled his headphones back on and walked across the lawn to the next house.

The clock on the dash of the blue BMW said 3:15 when she backed onto Oregon Avenue with her phone to her ear. Anoop picked up on the third ring.

"I'm taking the rest of the day off."

"Relax," he said. "Get some rest."

"Yeah. I'll see you tomorrow."

She passed Daniel Lane and Dogwood Street. At Chestnut, the old Lincoln idled roughly by the stop sign to her right. She was too preoccupied to notice.

The mail. The basement window. Your mind is starting to slip, she told herself. You have to stop believing everything is a threat. This is how you ruined it with Peter.

When she turned left and headed into the woods, the rumbling beast sprang into line behind her.

5

Gavin Corley had grown up around the corner from her, a few blocks south, on the DC side of Western Avenue, which formed the city's border with Maryland. They had played together as children, catching crayfish in Rock Creek and pretending to hunt foxes on the woodland trails.

His paranoia began to appear in high school. Where she saw coincidences, he saw conspiracies, outlines of a hidden order by which dark forces controlled the world.

"The campaign to control us is a carefully orchestrated two-pronged attack," he told her when she returned to DC. "The media distracts the mind with *entertainment*"—he put the word in air quotes—"to keep us from thinking about what the politicians and corporations are really doing. That's the first prong.

"The second prong is a physical attack against our bodies. The foods they push are killing us. Look how fat everyone is. Look how many people have diabetes. Then there's alcohol, tobacco, and opioids, legal corporate-manufactured toxins. The pharmaceuticals have turned the medical profession into their private distribution network."

"Come off it, Gavin."

"Look how many people they kill! The government's in on it too."

"I'm sorry. No. How is the government in on it?"

"The DEA!"

"Their job is to stop the drugs."

"But they also approve the amount of opioids the pharmaceuticals can legally produce."

"I thought that was the Food and Drug Administration."

"No. The DEA sets the numbers for controlled substances, and those numbers go up every year."

"Why would the DEA or anyone in the government want to kill us?"

"People who drug themselves are easier to govern. If they happen to kill themselves, well, that's their own fault."

"Oh, come on, Gavin!"

That was their conversation over morning coffee six weeks earlier. He'd been saying similar things since high school. The targets of his paranoia had evolved over time, but his general outlook hadn't wavered since his father had checked him into a psychiatric hospital a week after 12th grade graduation. He'd hacked into the public school system's central computers to expose... God knows what. Some kind of conspiracy or corruption. He couldn't remember himself after the meds kicked in.

Gavin stood an inch under six feet, thin, with a wiry blond ponytail, an unruly beard, and piercing ice-blue eyes. You could have mistaken him for a 1960s counterculture crusader, or the kind of hacker the FBI would parade before the cameras to show off a major bust.

Since his high school episode, he had worked on the right side of the law, securing computers against cybercriminals, analyzing breaches in compromised systems, uncovering hackers' methods, and hardening servers to withstand attacks.

"Thank God for computers," Ben Corley once told Claire. "Thank God he found something as rigidly logical as his own mind to engage him and give him a paycheck."

"The hackers," Gavin told her in the coffeeshop six weeks ago, "are always looking for weaknesses to exploit. The only way to beat them is to think just like them. You look at a system and you ask yourself, how would I break into this thing? Then you break in. Then you backtrack and close up every hole you just exploited."

That's exactly how I think, Claire thought. The method you apply to defend machines, I apply to defending myself. I meet a person and I think, how could they hurt me? How could they screw me? Then I make sure they can't.

"What are you working on these days?" she asked.

"Setting up secure servers. Hardened systems."

"For whom? The government? The NSA?"

"Companies."

"Really?" she teased. "You've gone over to the dark side of corporate America?"

He shrugged. "I have a skill and there are only two ways to make money from it. Hide secrets or steal them."

"Don't companies have their own system administrators to do that work?"

"Companies have sys admins for their *internal* systems. But internal systems are subject to compliance audits and discovery requests from lawyers. A company's not going to keep anything incriminating on the systems the law can reach into."

"So, you're like the guy who sets up the private email server for Hillary Clinton?"

Gavin smiled. "That whole fiasco worked in our favor. That made people understand that when you set up a shadow system, you have to do it right. You're building a vault, not a cardboard box. It takes a lot of vigilance and expertise to secure. Not everyone is good at it."

"Well it's nice to see you coming out of your depression."

"What depression?"

"Come on, Gavin."

"I haven't been depressed."

"You don't have to be embarrassed about it."

"I've never been depressed. Ever."

"After you got t-boned by that truck, you were laid up and couldn't work. I'm not blaming you. I'd go crazy too if I couldn't work."

He looked away, irritated.

OK, she thought. Drop it. He hasn't fully shaken off the dullness and lethargy of the past few months. He's not totally over it. He still has the sniffles, that perpetual cold. Depression weakens the immune system. Maybe in a few weeks, when he has some distance, when it's not so raw, we can talk about it.

Before they got to talk about *that* again, he was dead. And in the intervening weeks, he'd been irritable, edgy, his paranoia rising to the point that she had begun to wonder whether he needed another hospitalization.

The crash that killed him occurred sometime between 9 p.m. on Monday, January 13 and 5 a.m. on Tuesday the fourteenth. She knew that because his final voicemail came in at 8:57 Monday night and the news articles said a commuter had spotted his overturned SUV around 5:15 Tuesday morning.

In a smaller town where a local death would be more newsworthy, the reporters would have published a follow-up piece with more detail. But this was DC. The story had been forgotten as soon as it was published, like a cloud of breath dissolving in the winter air.

It took Claire forty-five minutes to reach this stretch of road from which her friend had departed this life. She wasn't sure she was in the right place until she saw the bright pink spray paint that marked the trajectory of Gavin's Chevy Equinox as it left the road. She passed it once, slowing to glance down the embankment. She drove half a mile to a crossroad, turned around and drove back, parking on the grassy shoulder.

The Lincoln had followed her through the U-turn. When she parked, a flash of panic shot through her. She was alone on a rural road with no witnesses. She gripped the door handle tightly, watched the big car slow in the sideview. As it passed, the broad-faced driver looked in on her with an unexpected expression. For a second, she thought he was going to ask if she needed help.

He passed slowly, lingering as if to see what she would do. She picked up her phone, pretended to dial 911. The ancient Continental lumbered on, a thin blue cloud trailing behind it.

When it rounded the bend and was out of sight, she got out and crossed, examining the surface of the road. There were no tire marks near the pink paint lines. Gavin had run off the road without skidding. Why? Was he on his phone, not paying attention to where he was going?

Maybe he was having a paranoid episode, thought someone was chasing him, came around the bend too fast.

She remembered another meeting, just before his death. Sunday brunch beside the Potomac, in the loud chatter of Founding Farmers.

"Look how many decades the government allowed tobacco companies to sell their toxic, addictive products." He spoke loudly above the din.

Tobacco was personal because of his father.

"You know how many people they killed? More than all the wars this country ever fought. And now the pharmaceuticals are doing the same thing."

"Keep your voice down," she whispered.

"Why should I?"

"Everyone's looking at you."

"That's what I've been telling you my whole life." There was a glint in his eye, a playful smile as he made fun of his own paranoia. He leaned in and whispered, "They're watching you too, Claire."

She rolled her eyes, knowing he had already queued up another rant. The only question was who was on his shit list today.

"Go on, Gavin. Get it out of your system."

"Facebook turns on the mic on your phone and records your conversations."

OK, she thought. Today he's mad at the tech companies. "I don't use Facebook."

"So does Instagram. So does your smart TV. Alexa and Google Home are trojan horses that people bring willingly into their homes to spy on them. And now those Ring doorbells surveil the whole neighborhood."

"Do you ever get tired of being the victim?"

"When I get tired of it, I turn the tables."

"What's that supposed to mean?"

"It means fight the power."

"Can we please have a meaningful conversation?"

"Yeah, I'm done."

"Thank God. How's your father?"

"Not good."

Claire followed the spray-painted lines down the embankment. The weather had gotten cold, and the ground that was soft when the Chevy tumbled over it was frozen now. She knelt and pressed her fingers into the indentation that might have come from the top edge of the SUV.

Farther down the slope, at the edge of the trees, a flattened patch of dead weeds showed where the Chevy had come to rest. A broken sapling leaned forward, indicating the direction of the vehicle that had hit it.

There's nothing here to cause a crash, Claire thought, and there was no ice that night. It was almost balmy.

She looked back toward the road. It's a gentle turn. He couldn't have been speeding. If so, he would have gone farther into the woods.

A few feet ahead, atop the fallen leaves, a flat white cardstock box rocked gently in the wind. Claire picked it up and read the label. Triptan. A migraine medicine. She took it herself on occasion, when she first saw the aura, the harbinger of the headache to come.

If the aura appeared while she was driving, she pulled over, took the meds, and waited until her vision cleared. Had Gavin been driving half-blind? Had he simply not seen the turn?

The box was dirty and sticky, as if it had been pulled from the garbage. The blister pack that held the pills was missing.

The wind picked up, dry and cold in the waning light. Since she had left New York, she had grown thin. The frigid air seemed to bite into her bones. She put the box into the pocket of her wool coat, tied the belt tightly around her waist, and made her way back up the grassy slope.

6

The Continental was waiting for her around the bend. The acrid scent of burning oil stung her nose. She passed without looking, heard the rumbling engine roar to life, saw the leviathan in the rearview, noted the number of the DC plates.

"All right, you fucker," she said as she watched the headlights flip up—the beast opening its ancient yellow eyes on the frigid night. "You want to follow me? Follow me here."

She picked up her phone, opened the maps app, and said, "Prince George's County police department."

She chose the office on Rhode Island Avenue in Hyattsville. It was on the way back to the city.

"Come on," she coaxed, glancing in the rearview. The Continental's yellow headlights pointed outward toward the edges of the lane, giving the behemoth a cockeyed look. "When we get to the station, we can talk this out with the cops."

She drove south along the Baltimore-Washington Parkway, then west on Riverdale Road and south again on Baltimore Avenue.

The station was in view when her phone died. She checked the mirror and saw him sixty feet behind. "Thank you for not tailgating," she said as she pulled into the parking lane. "I wish all DC drivers were as polite as you."

He slowed behind her, and she wondered if he'd stop.

He didn't. The old beast crept slowly past. He didn't peer in at her this time.

Claire rested her head against the wheel and let out a deep breath. Then another, and another, draining the tension from her body. She didn't realize, until the rapping at the window startled her, that she was about to fall asleep.

A cop was tapping the butt of her flashlight against the glass.

"You OK, ma'am?"

Claire looked up to see a black woman whose gold badge matched the one on the rude detective who had questioned her after Gavin's death.

There was something reassuring about the woman's broad shoulders and stern expression. This was a person who could take control.

Claire rolled down the window. "I want to talk to you."

The cop motioned with her flashlight. "Pull your car in straight."

7

At a desk inside the station, Patrol Officer Sharice Greer asked for her license. She seemed to sniff Claire's breath as Claire handed her the card.

"The way you pulled into that parking spot and left your tail out in traffic..." Greer trailed off. "Just doing my job. You want some coffee?"

"No thanks."

Greer scanned the license and stared into the computer.

"You're a long way from New York," she said. "You lost?"

"No, I..."

How do I explain this, Claire wondered. I think I made a mistake. I should have stayed in New York. But I ran, and I didn't know what I'd done until I was here. Back in that... In that awful bedroom.

Greer looked her in the eye and asked slowly and clearly, "Are you OK?"

"I'm fine."

"You're fine?" Greer repeated in a tone that struck Claire as unintentionally condescending. This was how teachers addressed schoolchildren who told lies.

"I just want to be clear," Greer said. "No one is hurting you?"

"No."

"No one is harassing you? Following you?"

"Um…"

Greer picked up the cue immediately. "You want to talk in private?"

"Sure." Claire hugged her purse in her lap. She was beginning to doubt whether this was a good idea. She would feel foolish explaining her paranoid thoughts to this woman who took everything so seriously.

It sounded stupid. A big fat guy, out of nowhere, in an old smoking Lincoln.

You're making this up, she told herself. You're making it up because you don't want to deal with your real problems. You overthink things, come up with imaginary problems to… Then she reminded herself that her disappearing mail wasn't imaginary. The mailman had confirmed it.

Greer led her to a room with three chairs and a table. She shut the door and stood for a moment studying the license, then smiled and shook her head. "Last time I weighed one-thirty-five was in middle school."

That made her feel even more self-conscious. She was well below one-thirty-five. Greer would see that if she removed her coat, which she now decided she wouldn't do.

She felt the persistent anxiety of the past few weeks as a tightness in her chest, in her shoulders, face, and stomach. Foods that didn't used to bother her made her feel ill. Busyness was the only antidote to worry. She had to be productive in some objectively verifiable way, with a tangible product to justify every hour of her waking life. She feared slowing down, feared seeing clearly the person who might have made a huge and terrible mistake.

She wanted to tell this cop who was so observant, so attentive, so willing to listen: It's not just Leona I distrust. Everything is a threat. Everyone. That's why Gavin and I got along so well. We had the same view of things, even if on the surface we looked nothing alike.

I understand why I am this way. Leona was full of spite and malice. A kid learns to defend herself against a person like that. It's a matter of survival. But you have to understand, there was no malice in Peter. None. He understood me, and that was the most threatening thing of all. Everything provokes me, don't you see? And please—I don't know how to undo who I am.

Greer slid the license across the desk. "What are you doing down here from New York?" The gentleness in her tone was encouraging.

"I live here. In DC, I mean."

"So you're not lost?"

Claire could see her watching closely, assessing her tone and body language. Greer's perceptiveness reassured her. She was dealing with a competent, intelligent person. But looking at herself through Greer's eyes, she saw a woman who was weak and uncertain. She couldn't bear to be perceived that way.

"No," Claire said, straightening her posture to appear more confident. "I'm not lost."

Not in terms of roads, she thought, not in terms of north and south.

"What did you want to talk about?"

If I tell her some strange man in an old car is following me, she wondered, how long will we be here? And what would be the point? I live outside her jurisdiction. She'll tell me to talk to the DC cops who will say I can file a restraining order. Against whom? I don't even know who he is.

"I uh... A friend of mine died."

"I'm sorry to hear that," Greer offered.

"In a car accident."

"Here? In PG County?"

"Yeah. That's what I wanted to ask about. One of your detectives came by my house."

Greer blinked and said, "Came to your house in DC?"

"To ask about my friend."

"OK." Greer nodded, but her tone asked where Claire was going with this.

"Is that normal after a car accident? After a fatal accident?"

Greer watched her carefully but showed no intention of answering.

"I mean, because it seems like you'd send a detective to investigate a homicide, but not a run-of-the-mill accident."

Claire felt foolish in the face of the other woman's silence.

Greer shook her head as if snapping herself out of a train of thought. "I'm sorry, tell me your friend's name and the name of the detective who came to question you."

"Gavin Corley was my friend."

"Corley." Greer screwed up her eyes as if trying to recall the name. "OK. That was last week."

"Six days ago."

"He flipped his car," Greer said. "I remember. Who came to talk to you?"

"Um... His name was..."

"He didn't give you a card?"

"No."

Claire walked through the scene in her memory. She could see his face, pale with red-rimmed blue eyes and translucent lashes. Pockmarked cheeks, reddish-blond hair, short military cut. Military... war... gun, Gatling gun. Gatlin. That was his last name. His first name also reminded her of guns. Barrel. Like barrel.

"Darrell Gatlin," she said.

Greer seemed about to say something, but hesitated as if unsure of herself. "I'm sorry, what was that?"

"Darrell Gatlin."

"Darrell Gatlin came to your house?" Greer's tone said she didn't believe her.

"Yes."

"When?"

"Six days ago."

Greer watched her in silence for a few uncomfortable seconds. "What did Darrell Gatlin ask you?"

"He wanted to know about a phone call. Gavin called me the night before the accident. I didn't answer because I was working. The message didn't make any sense"—or maybe it did, she thought—"so I deleted it."

Did Greer catch that? Her moment of uncertainty?

"I figured I'd talk to him the next day," Claire added.

Greer stood and began to pace. "Darrell Gatlin asked you about a phone call?"

"Yes. And I have to say, he wasn't very polite."

"No," Greer said thoughtfully. "No one ever accused him of being polite."

"He didn't even tell me Gavin was dead. He just launched right into an interrogation."

"It's called an interview," Greer corrected. "Interrogations are for suspects."

"Well it felt like an interrogation. But he didn't tell me Gavin was dead. I had to infer from his questions what had happened. Don't you train your officers—"

"Detectives."

"—your detectives to show compassion in cases like that?"

"Yes, we do." Greer nodded, looking troubled as she paced. "We train them very carefully, so they don't make people feel the way he made you feel."

"So he is a detective? Like, homicide? Because you do go out and interview people for homicides, right? You would send a detective into DC for that."

Greer took a deep breath and said, "Miss, uh..."

"Chastain."

"Miss Chastain, you mind stepping out here with me?"

She opened the door. Claire followed her back toward the station entrance where Greer stopped and waved come-here to a male cop. As the man approached, Greer said to Claire, "Can you describe Darrell Gatlin again for me please?"

"About six foot two or three. Probably two hundred pounds. Light reddish-blond hair, cut short like a Marine. Blue eyes..."

She trailed off as Greer and the other cop stared at her.

"What?" she asked.

Her eyes followed theirs to the photo on the wall five feet away. Patrol Officer Darrell Gatlin was a black man, apparently well under six feet, and definitely not two hundred pounds. The plaque beneath his photo was engraved with the date, almost two years ago, on which he had been killed in the line of duty.

"Did this man show you a badge?" Greer asked.

"It was on his belt."

"Gold, like this one?" She pointed to the badge on her chest.

"Yeah, but I didn't look too closely at it. I was sort of in shock. I mean, I had to piece together from his questions the fact that my friend was dead. I was too busy processing *that*."

"Miss Chastain."

"Mizz," Claire corrected.

"I want you to come back to this room and tell us about Darrell Gatlin."

She told them the whole story. Greer took notes. When Claire was done and the male cop had left the room, Greer got up and shut the door behind him. She looked quietly at Claire for a few seconds, then said, "Tell me why you came here."

Claire hesitated.

"Tell me why you came here tonight. What was happening *tonight* that made you come in?"

Again, she hesitated. Then finally: "Someone's been following me."

"How long?"

"Two days."

"You have a description?"

"I have the number of his license plate."

"Let's look it up," Greer said.

8

Ezekiel Timmons lived just off Georgia Avenue in the Brightwood neighborhood of DC. He had a history of minor infractions: drunk and disorderly, disturbing the peace, urinating in public. Numerous fines, but no felonies and no jail time.

The mug shot from his last booking showed a bedraggled black man of sixty-one years. He was bald on top and grey around the edges. He had food in his beard.

"This him?" Greer asked.

"No."

"You want to come with me and take a look? See if there's anyone at that address you can identify? It's not far."

They took Greer's patrol car.

With a pot belly, full grey beard, and puffy bloodshot eyes, Ezekiel Timmons looked like a wreck more than sixty years in the making. He was drunk when he answered the door, and neither he nor the woman in the background, whom Claire took to be his wife, invited them into the house. Greer made sure he noticed the baton in her right hand.

"Who's that?" asked the woman in the house.

"Rollers," Timmons barked. "Y'all ain't even DC heat. What the fuck you want? I didn't do shit."

"You sell a car recently?" Greer asked.

"That's my business. Who's this?" He eyed Claire warily, unsteady on his feet. "A lawyer? I told you I ain't done shit."

His breath reeked of liquor.

"Watch your tone," Greer said. "Who'd you sell the car to?"

"Big fat peckerwood. Y'all two can go fuck him in the back seat."

He tried to shut the door on her, but she stuck her baton between the door and the frame.

"That kind of talk can get you arrested for assault."

Timmons pulled the door open and shot back, "Stickin' your weapons in my house can get you arrested for illegal entry. Police fuckin' brutality."

"I haven't touched you. Yet. He give you a name?"

"Who?"

"The guy who bought the car."

"No," Timmons snapped.

"When's the last time you saw him?"

"When he put the cash in my hand."

Timmons shut the door.

In the patrol car, Greer told Claire the Lincoln was still registered to Timmons. Whoever bought it either hadn't gotten around to filing the paperwork, or wanted to avoid leaving his identity in the public record. "That's why he paid cash," she added.

Greer told her to file a report in DC, and warned her that there wasn't much a big city police department could do.

"They can roll by your house a few times a day. If they catch him out there, they'll run his license, get his name. You can ask for a restraining order, but realistically..." She shook her head. "No police department has the resources to guard a private citizen around the clock."

The light at Eastern Avenue, the city line, was red. They rolled to a stop, and Greer turned to Claire.

"What kind of work you do?"

"Financial audits. I certify the numbers on the earnings reports of publicly traded companies. It's not as interesting as what I used to do."

The light changed and they crossed into Maryland.

"What was that?"

"Valuations. Due diligence for corporate purchases. Company A wants to buy company B. Before they fork over fifty million dollars, they send me in to do a thorough investigation. I look at the numbers, the health of their processes, their products and services, internal corporate structure, morale. I have to figure out things like will this manager still fit in with the new structure after the acquisition? Which employees would take too much knowledge out the door with them if they left? What kind of incentive will make them stay? Are processes documented? Are they repeatable? Scalable? I go in there, dig through records, interview people, uncover all I can, and write up a report."

"Sounds like detective work."

"It is. It's corporate-social-economic detective work. You do any investigations?"

Greer shook her head. "No. Detectives get fixated on the cases assigned to them. That's not my style. I like to be out in the flow of things. Scan the horizon, see what's popping up, go contain it before it becomes a bigger problem. Patrol officers are the janitors of civilization. We clean up the little messes before they become big messes, so people like you can go about their business in peace. That's what I like to see. People living their lives without a lot of hassle."

Greer glanced at her. "Why'd you switch to doing just numbers? Sounds like due diligence was more interesting."

"It was. I switched because—oh, that's a long story. This job is temporary. They like me at the company. I can tell they want me to stay. But the work isn't challenging enough. It doesn't fully engage me."

"Think you'll go back to what you were doing before?"

"It's funny. Now that you ask it, I'm pretty sure the answer is no."

"Why not?"

"It's not the best use of my mind. The last couple years, I felt like all I did was help rich people get richer. They'd buy a company and gut the staff. Put a lot of people out of work so they could line their own pockets. I feel like, if I have a skill, then I have a responsibility to put it to good use, to help people. God knows there are enough people in this world who need help."

"Amen to that."

Greer slowed behind a line of cars at a red light. "So what's next?"

"I have no idea," Claire said. "None at all."

"Tell you what I would do if I were you."

"What?"

"Sit down with a piece of paper like an accountant, list all my skills in one column, put what I want out of a job in the next column, list what kinds of jobs are out there, and see what matches up. You feel safe going home?"

Claire wanted to say yes. Saying no would be admitting weakness.

"OK, your hesitation tells me no," Greer said.

She hit the gas as the cars ahead proceeded through the green.

"You have anywhere else to go? Any friends? A boyfriend?"

Claire winced.

"No. I haven't lived in DC in fourteen years."

"Can you go to a hotel?"

"I can," Claire said. "But for how long?"

"Until we ID the guy. If he hasn't registered the car in his name, he couldn't have insured it. Driving without insurance is a violation. If the car's that old, it may not pass inspection. If he paid cash for it, he might not be able to prove it's his. The more you start poking at a case like that, the more things you find to harass a guy about. We can make him uncomfortable. And if this guy—you say you don't know him?"

"I have no idea who he is."

48

"A stalker you don't know... Might be mentally ill. We arrest him on a violation, he might not be able to post bond."

Greer dropped Claire off on the street in front of the station.

"You file that report," she said, handing her a business card with her name and phone number. "Go in person."

"I will."

Claire unlocked her car and got in.

* * *

She followed East-West Highway to Silver Spring. In a few minutes, she would turn on Beach Drive, cut through Rock Creek Park, and...

No. She wasn't thinking. She wasn't supposed to go home.

She sat at the light at Colesville Road, debating whether to head into the city, to a hotel that was closer to the office, or out to the suburbs, where they were cheaper.

Either way, she thought, I still need to stop by the house to pick up a change of clothes, a toothbrush.

Then came the familiar knocking sound. He rolled up right beside her. When she turned to look, the driver turned on the interior light so she could see his broad stubbly face and close-set eyes. The pointed, angry expression told her he didn't like her checking up on him, didn't like her bringing the police into this.

"Shit!"

She panicked and gunned it through the red light. A white pickup blared its horn as it swerved around her.

She saw the light turn green in the rearview, and the big cockeyed Lincoln came after her at its leisure.

She pressed the pedal to the floor, hitting sixty-five before slowing to turn right on 16th Street. The Continental had no trouble keeping up on the straightaway, though it careened out of its lane on the turn.

Claire picked up her phone to call Greer, but the screen wouldn't come on. She remembered it had died just before she reached the station.

She gunned it up 16th Street, hoping a cop would notice and pull her over. Lincoln, as she now called the giant driver pursuing her, followed comfortably, a few car lengths behind.

The light at Georgia Avenue was green, and they both took the left turn too fast.

If he wants to hurt me, Claire thought, why doesn't he just do it? Why does he have to keep stalking? Maybe that's the part that turns him on. A long foreplay to build the fear. Fucking perv. Fucking psychopath!

Racing up the onramp to the Beltway, her mind turned to where she had tried to stop it from going all day. She thought of calling Peter in New York. Not that he could defend her against a man that size. Even if he were here, he didn't know how to fight. But he did make her feel safe.

That's a good summation of my life right now, she thought. Wanting to call someone who won't talk to me on a phone that doesn't work.

The Continental trailed fifty feet behind her past the DC Temple in Kensington. As they approached the Connecticut Avenue exit, it began to drop back. The old battleship jerked unsteadily as it receded in the rearview. She saw the hazards go on as the car drifted to the shoulder.

He's out of gas, she thought. That old tank can't get more than eight miles to the gallon.

Claire continued past Connecticut Avenue, then turned north on Wisconsin, toward Rockville. She couldn't remember what hotels lay up that way, but there had to be dozens.

9

At 12:48, her eyes opened to the red digits of an unfamiliar alarm clock. She startled, thinking, I have to clean the kitchen before Peter gets home. The pots and dishes are piled so high, he won't be able to fill a glass of water.

The senselessness of that struck her when her feet touched the carpet. The floor should have been bare wood. She sucked in a breath. Where am I?

In front of her was another bed.

A hotel, she remembered now. You're not there anymore. You're here. There is no there. *There* is all gone.

When she found the engagement ring in his sock drawer, she was flooded with terror. He had talked of children in those last few weeks, and she had let him go on as if he were talking about some other couple, some future she had no part in. She seemed to withdraw from herself when he spoke, observing the scene not through her own eyes, but from across the room. From her position beside the door, she watched two characters in a play.

She had moved in four weeks earlier. She had brought a few pieces of her own furniture into his apartment and had sublet hers, even though she had told herself since middle school that if she ever consented to live with a man, it would be in her place, not his. Leona had drilled into her the certainty that she would never be safe unless she were in a position to end things at any moment and still be on her feet, still in control and in possession of all that was rightfully hers.

"You're pretty, like your mother," Leona told her, "and that's not a thing to be proud of. It makes you a target. Don't be weak like her. Don't be a fool, unless you like being used and abandoned. It's the men who made her drink, and she wouldn't have died if she hadn't been drinking that night."

Claire disagreed with that last part. It was Leona who made her drink, but Leona had arranged her blind spots to prevent her from seeing her own faults.

Leona had the world all figured out: Men were only too happy to oblige the women who asked to be victimized. She said it outright, and she said it implicitly in her criticisms of Claire's mother, whose ruined life was proof that she was right.

In high school, when Claire's first boyfriend proved that one of Leona's favorite assertions was correct—that the act of sex required only one consenting partner—Claire told no one. But somehow Leona seemed to know, seemed to infer the cause of her sudden loss of confidence, her sullen withdrawal and need for isolation.

"Better you learn now than make the mistakes your mother made," Leona said at last. She seemed to feel vindicated, perversely pleased.

When Claire got sick of stewing about it and confronted the boy a few days later, he smiled, said he was happy she was over whatever was bothering her because he liked her. In his mind, they had both had a good time.

When she told him her side, he listened. Then he said, "You have to understand, there's a point of no return. You can't just lead a guy right up to the edge and then change your mind. It's like, once you cross that line, you're committed."

No words could express her fury at those remarks, so she punched him in the mouth.

"What?" he said, trying to catch the blood pouring from his lips. "I'm just telling it like it is."

"So am I."

The fact that he thought his response was reasonable or even acceptable told her they were worlds apart, on opposite sides of an unbridgeable gap.

The question Claire kept coming back to was, How could I have walked right into that? Why did I not see it coming?

Your mistake, she told herself, was wanting something in the first place. Desire is need, need is weakness, and the more weakness you show, the more you invite people to walk on you.

Her conclusion—that Leona was right, that she had to be ever on her guard—was the most bitter part of the experience. The feelings she had had for her first crush, the fact that he liked her too, the way they had gotten along at first—all that was supposed to refute the cynicism of Leona's worldview. Instead, the outcome just confirmed it.

Men inhabited the other side of the great divide. If a woman wanted to be safe, she had to be able to infer what they were thinking, predict what they might do next. If you couldn't see someone's intentions, then you had to assume the worst, keep in mind all the ways they could hurt you, and prepare your defenses accordingly.

To one so guarded, intimacy was not a process of opening up and letting go; it was one of ever-increasing vigilance, of worrying how close a new man was getting to that point of no return, physically or emotionally. Physical intimacy was something she watched from the outside. Another man doing something to another woman while Claire looked for signs of things going wrong and kept one eye on the exit.

She had no interest in weak men, or in men who weren't as smart as her. By her reckoning, that disqualified ninety-nine percent of the applicant pool right off the bat. The ones who were smart and strong were often aggressive, at least the lawyers and financial professionals she'd met in New York. After growing up with Leona, she despised aggression.

What did she like? A combination of intelligence, confidence, and kindness.

And where does one find that?

It walked right up to her one day in The Strand on Broadway. She'd run into him before, she couldn't remember where, but his face was familiar. Blue eyes, light brown hair. Five foot ten, tall enough, with a medium build and an unfortunate tweed jacket over an even more unfortunate checkered shirt.

Wardrobes are fixable, she thought. Personalities are not. Let's see what he has to say.

He was buying Robert Caro's biography of Robert Moses.

Claire had read Caro's biography of Lyndon Johnson at her grandmother's insistence. "This is how it works," Leona growled as she handed over the first volume. "The most ruthless asshole wins, and Johnson was the master."

Had Peter read it? Yes, all three volumes. He wanted more of Caro.

They had lunch at Gotham. Walked in and got a table. How was that for a sign?

He was an administrator at an educational nonprofit. Weak, Leona would have said. The only thing worse than a person with no ambition was a do-gooder. A willing fool. Claire worked hard to push that voice aside.

He was clearly infatuated with her and incapable of hiding it. That flattered her and made her uneasy. You're putting yourself too far out there, she thought. It would be so easy to cut you down. You'd be crushed, and you'd show it. Cover up a little. Show some dignity.

Still, there was something fascinating about the way he expressed his feelings so openly, how he had accepted in himself emotions she had taught herself to hide.

Over the weeks, she tested him. Because he lacked aggression, she looked for weakness. A man had to have one or the other. She found he was as firm in his belief and as confident in his opinions as any of the blustering corporate climbers she had worked with. He just didn't force his opinions on others. He asked questions, too many at times. He listened, and he didn't try to change her.

If he has a weakness, Claire thought, it's me, and I'm not sure I like that. Growing up with Leona had taught her that at the core of all close relationships was a battle for control. The controller—Leona, Peter, or whoever—was constantly trying to impose their will on the victim, her, and her job was to thwart them. Helpful suggestions and friendly advice were merely disguised attempts at manipulation. They provoked the same combative reaction as someone telling her what to do. If conflict was the essence of human relations, then the fiercer the conflict, the tighter the bond.

She could not have explained this in so many words. She merely felt it, and it was why the relationship with Peter always felt lacking. They got along too well. Intermittent arguments couldn't reassure her of the strength of his commitment. Only persistent conflict could do that, so she manufactured it, picking fights she didn't need to pick.

Some part of him seemed to understand she didn't want to be fighting. He could always talk her down, and even as she was grateful for that, part of her still saw the peaceful ending of their disputes as weakness in both of them. Part of her still believed that defusing a conflict, even an unnecessary one, amounted to less than winning it, and a peacemaker, even when he was right, was inferior to a victor.

In her more sour moods, the fact that he put up with her at all was a strike against him. I wouldn't tolerate someone picking baseless fights, she thought. I'd tell them to fuck off.

Before she had made peace with her decision to move into his apartment, before she had accepted how much of her prized independence and self-sufficiency she'd relinquished, Peter started talking of children, those needy creatures that would emerge from her own womb to trap her in a life of smothering duty. She watched from across the room as the man on the couch spoke dreamily of a future that terrified the mute woman beside him.

Nothing damages people like family, Claire thought. The root of all injustice in the world is that children cannot escape their caregivers. Except to die. To die drunk in a crash, as her mother had done after years of slutting around in search of someone who would really love her. Who *could* love her, or could at least go through the motions of love.

And her father, whoever he was, had run as fast as he could from that scene. That's how she thought of it in her lowest moods. But even in the best of moods, she still couldn't deny that he had abandoned her. Maybe he had his reasons. Maybe Leona had made his life a living hell. But the betrayal was a gaping hole in her life.

When Peter spoke of children to the woman on the couch, she watched from beside the door, the exit that was her only safety. He's telling her he wants to set the ultimate trap, she thought, the ultimate failure scenario. He wants to risk another generation, perpetuate the cycle of cruelty and abandonment. There are so many ways for this to go wrong. He's telling her cheerfully, like he doesn't get it. He just doesn't get it.

There it was again. Man on one side of the chasm, woman on the other.

How can he not see how much he's upsetting her, Claire wondered.

Because she doesn't show it. She hides it, like she hides everything. She doesn't speak because these are feelings she's not supposed to have: not wanting to please the one who loves you, not wanting to bear children, resentment at being expected to love them when you're not sure you can.

When she found the ring, she understood that he'd interpreted her silence as consent. She had watched him approach the point of no return against which she was ever on her guard and she had watched him cross it. The whole mess was her fault for not stopping him sooner.

She didn't realize what she had done until two days afterward, when she awoke at Leona's with two suitcases from the life she'd just abandoned.

She remembered that, in her panic, she hadn't put the ring back in the drawer. She'd left the note beside it, written in a violent, slashing hand. "I'm sorry. This has to end."

Recalling it now, in the middle of the night in a dark hotel room, a wave of nausea rose from deep in her gut. She saw stars when she stood from the bed, clapped her hand over her mouth to stop the puke from going on the carpet, but the heaves were dry. She hadn't eaten in hours.

At 2:36 a.m., she turned the alarm clock on its face, so the glowing numbers would stop mocking her insomnia.

At 4:30, she awoke again, sweating, staring into the broad face of her stalker, trying to pry his huge hairy hand from her mouth.

She sat up disoriented, her heart pounding, surprised once more to find herself in a hotel. In the dream, she'd been at Leona's.

At five, when she knew she wouldn't get back to sleep, she turned on the light and sat at the desk.

I can't change the past, she told herself, and the present isn't working, so let's look forward.

She took Greer's advice, picked up the notepad beside the lamp, and made three columns: "Strengths and skills," "What I want out of a job," and "Available careers."

In the first column, "Strengths and skills," she wrote:

- Bitch
- Good with numbers
- Persistent
- Not easily fooled
- Can manage details & big picture simultaneously

Under "What I want out of a job":

- Variety and challenge
- Help people
- Make the world a better place

Under "Available careers":

- ~~Doctor~~ (Ten more years of school?? NFW!)
- ~~Lawyer/prosecutor~~ (Can't stand lawyers. Plus, law school.)
- ~~Nurse~~ (Sick people are cranky and I barely have patience for normal people.)
- Cop?

Hmm... Sharice Greer was the first person she'd met in months whom she respected right off the bat. But Greer had a physical presence Claire lacked, a look that commanded respect on the street, not just in the conference room.

Claire chewed the back of the pen, pictured herself writing a speeding ticket while some fat suit in a hundred-thousand-dollar Mercedes stared at her tits and tried to explain why he was above the law.

She pulled the pen from her teeth and added a final note.

- ~~Cop?~~ (I'd shoot someone.)

OK then what, she wondered. You burned all your bridges, maybe because you needed to. This is the perfect time to start over. All you need is to find the right field. You have plenty of skills and all the ability in the world, so... So, what, Claire? What's next for you?

She pondered the question in silence for several minutes and came up with nothing.

Enough of my own thoughts.

She stood abruptly, picked up the TV remote, stabbed the power button, and watched the colored clouds sweep across the map.

The Weather Channel said a storm was coming.

10

She reached the house at 7:10 a.m. Her plan was to shower and change, but she didn't want to arrive before daylight.

She drove two rounds of the neighborhood, looking for the burgundy Lincoln, and didn't pull into the driveway until she was satisfied it wasn't around. She rolled down her window, sniffed for the scent of burning oil but smelled only dry leaves in the stinging winter air.

When she walked in, she left the front door open, in case she had to run back out. She stepped loudly on the bare wood floor, keeping her keys in hand in case she met an eye that needed gouging. She made a mental note to go to the DC police and file her report, and to pick up a can of mace. She had lost the old one in the move from New York.

The house was cold. She went from room to room, turning on all the lights, checking to see if anything had been moved or taken. She checked the closets and the bathrooms. When she was satisfied that everything was in order, she considered checking the basement to make sure the window was still closed, but the thought of going down there scared her.

She went through the back door and checked the basement window from the outside. It was locked.

She went back in, bolted the back door, and then the front. She double-checked the windows and slid the lock shut on the basement door. A determined attacker could break it with a good hard push, but not without her hearing.

She got a knife from the kitchen, and the hammer from under the sink, and took them to the bathroom with a change of clothes. She locked the door before running the water and showered with the curtain open. So what if the floor got wet? If anyone came through that door, they'd get a hammer to the head, and when they tried to pull that away from her, she'd grab the knife from the soap dish with her other hand. Aim for a soft spot in the throat or below the ribs.

The thought of the big man in the Lincoln coming through the door scared her. She pushed it away and thought instead of the men she'd known and hadn't liked, the ones who talked over her at work, the ones who'd underestimated her, the ones she'd seen mistreat her friends. She stoked her anger with thoughts of injustice. The injustice of not feeling safe in the house she'd grown up in, of Leona's cruelty, of that gargantuan fat-faced stalker in his old piece-of-shit car, of how law enforcement and the whole legal system were set up not to prevent people like him from hurting people like her, but to come in after the fact and assess penalties for the damage that could not be undone.

The thoughts drove her adrenaline to such a peak that by the time she turned the water off, she was fantasizing about catching big fat Lincoln unawares and putting the hammer through the back of his head.

At 7:30, she was in the car. One of the benefits of not wearing makeup.

On the drive downtown, she asked herself what kind of life this was where she had to worry in her own shower. How long would she have to live this way? How many others lived this way, with no way out?

At 8:05, Anoop caught her on her way out of the elevator.

"A nurse called about your grandmother."

Claire stopped. "Is she all right?"

"She's being difficult. They called twice."

Great. Twice already and it's only eight a.m. "Why didn't they call me?"

"They did."

Right. Her phone was dead and she had no charging cord at the hotel. She'd charge it at her desk.

"Where's Li?" Claire asked.

"I put her on another project."

"That's not what I asked. Where is she?"

"In the conference room. Will you just sign the audit and go home? I reviewed it. It's flawless."

"I need to go over it again."

"No you don't."

"It's my work, Anoop. Not yours. I'm going to review it before I sign off."

She pushed past him, ignoring his advice to take the day off.

After dropping her bag at her desk and plugging in her phone, she found Li alone in the conference room, four bankers boxes open on the floor, papers strewn atop the table.

Li stood staring at her laptop, biting her bottom lip.

"You're working with paper?" Claire asked.

There was that smile, the nervous, accommodating smile Li couldn't seem to suppress.

"They are old records," Li said.

"You want some help?" Claire asked partly to have an excuse to spend more time in the office, partly to see how Li worked, so she could guide and mentor her.

"It would bore you," Li said.

"Is it boring you?"

"No."

"You don't have to lie."

"I am being polite." Li pronounced each syllable slowly and clearly.

"There's a time and a place for that," Claire said, "but you don't need to be polite with me."

"Yes, ma'am."

"I'm not ma'am. You can speak plainly with me."

"This work would bore you," Li said.

"You want to grab some coffee?"

"If you would like coffee, I would be honored to join you."

Claire let out a breath of frustration. How do you teach assertion to someone so deferential?

"Let's go then," she said.

Claire didn't need coffee. The caffeine would push her nerves over the edge, and the acidity would aggravate her knotted stomach.

At Gregory's on 19th, she ordered chamomile tea and a croissant filled with spinach and feta cheese, an old favorite from New York. The smell of it revolted her, even though she had craved it when she ordered it. She pushed it away without taking a bite.

"I'm bringing you in on my next assignment," Claire said. "Next week. It's like the last one, certifying the numbers, but this time I'll be able to walk you through the steps from beginning to end."

"Thank you," Li said. "Thank you. I look forward to it."

"Don't say thank you twice. A little gratitude is always welcome, but overdoing it makes people think you're too eager to please."

"Sorry."

"And don't say sorry unless you've actually done something wrong—"

"Sorry."

"—or people will walk on you."

"I'm sorry," Li said.

"Stop saying that."

"I'm sorry for apologizing."

This wasn't going as Claire had hoped. She decided to change tack.

"When you walk into a presentation, have all your numbers straight."

"Of course."

"Because men in particular will argue when you say things they don't want to hear. They'll try to make it personal. They'll try to make it about you. Don't let them. Stick to numbers and facts. Make them argue against those."

"I am grateful for your advice," Li said with a polite nod.

"You don't have to bow your head."

"I respect you."

"OK, but you have to be able to tell people things they don't want to hear. I really think that's something you need to work on."

"Thank you. I will tell everyone as many bad things as I can."

"That's not what I— Look, in this business, you have to be able to tell *men* what they don't want to hear. I mean, as long as those things are true."

"You are too thin."

"What?"

"It is something you don't want to hear. If you disagree with me, I will put you on a scale and we can talk about the numbers."

Claire smiled.

"Also," Li said, "you are too picky. There is nothing wrong with your croissant."

"I don't like the way it smells."

"The fact that you are arguing tells me my words make you uncomfortable."

"No, I just don't like the smell."

"You are too picky, Claire."

"OK, that's enough."

"Sorry."

On the way back to the office, Claire told herself that Li would be a bigger project than she'd thought. She didn't grow up here, Claire reasoned. She didn't set foot in this country until she started college at eighteen. She was raised in a culture of respect and rigid roles. You can't just undo that. You need to listen to her more. Listen and find out how she sees things. Don't expect to turn her into a brash American. Don't even assume it's the right thing to do.

Maybe, she thought, as she held the building door open for Li, maybe she's the mentor and I'm the project. I mean, she doesn't have any of my hang-ups, none of my wariness or chronic suspicion, and she seems to get by just fine.

The oddness of those thoughts struck her suddenly. She could not have thought them a year ago, or even a month ago. The idea of voluntarily letting down the defenses she had spent a lifetime building would have made no sense. Something in her was shifting.

At her desk, she finally got around to listening to the messages from Rollingwood. Two different nurses said Leona wanted to go to the zoo. She was dressed and waiting in the lobby.

Why the zoo? Leona had no interest in animals. She always said they were to be eaten and not heard. Was this sudden interest a quirk of dementia? A regression to her rural upbringing in Frederick County?

Claire called the home. "Tell her I'll be up around one."

She spent the rest of the morning reviewing numbers she didn't need to review. The audit was clean. At 11:45, she looked for emails to answer, but nothing in her inbox required a response, except the reply from the manager at the pharmaceutical company.

"You sent this to the wrong person," Claire had written in reference to the spreadsheet she and Li had puzzled over.

Now the man wrote back. "I didn't send that."

Claire would have let it go, but she didn't like the presumption of a man who would contradict her when she was plainly and verifiably right.

She tapped out a quick response: "Um... Check the from address and tell me it isn't yours." She thought about adding, *Would you have written such an obnoxious and condescending reply to a man?*

No, she thought. Too provocative. How about something a little more friendly? *It's OK. We all make mistakes.* But why try to make him feel better? And we don't all make mistakes like that, blatantly contradicting the obvious truth. How about *Fuck you*. That was clear and to the point.

In the end, she left it as it was, hit Send, and then signed the audit. She put yesterday's letters in her shoulder bag, and was about to slide her laptop in as well. But she decided to leave it on the desk. It would give her an excuse to come back later.

She dropped the signed audit on Anoop's desk and told him she'd be out the rest of the day. She had it planned out already. Lunch with Leona, then the zoo, which she was sure wouldn't last more than ten minutes, once her grandmother woke up and realized where they were. Drop Leona off, then go to Second District Police Headquarters on Idaho Avenue and file the report about her stalker. She had thought about doing that first thing in the morning, but then she would be letting Lincoln dictate her schedule. Screw him. He'd have to take his place in line behind her other responsibilities.

After the police station, she'd come back to the office, check her email, maybe get a head start on the next assignment.

"Take the rest of the week off," Anoop said.

"No."

"You need to relax."

"Relaxation stresses me out."

11

The burgundy Lincoln didn't follow her out of the lot, or up Connecticut Avenue. It wasn't behind her at Friendship Heights when she crossed into Montgomery County, but still she checked her mirrors every few seconds, expecting it to appear.

Maybe he's off the clock, Claire thought. Maybe I'm too boring to stalk. Or maybe I'm too thin and he got tired of looking at me.

When she pulled up to the entrance at Rollingwood, her grandmother was bundled up outside, pacing and ready to go.

"What the hell took you so long?" Leona barked. She yanked the door open and elbowed the attendant who was trying to help her in.

"I told you I'd be here at one," Claire said in the calmest voice she could muster.

"That was yesterday!"

"That was this morning, Gran. Close the door. It's cold out there."

To Claire's relief, Leona had already eaten, so they could skip lunch.

As they drove down Bradley Lane toward Connecticut Avenue, Leona yanked the mail from Claire's bag and tried to tear open both envelopes at once.

"What are you doing?" Claire snapped.

"Why don't you open your mail?"

"Give me those." Claire pulled the letters from her bony talons and threw them in the back seat. "What's the matter with you?"

"What's the matter with *you*?" Leona asked. "Why'd you lock me in that shithole? Am I that much of a cunt? Or is it you? You're the cunt!"

"Jesus, Gran, I hate that word."

This was not going well. Claire's only hope was to get her into the zoo as quickly as possible. The smell of the animals would remind Leona of the manure in the pastures of her youth, and that would make her want to leave. The old woman never had a single good thing to say about her childhood, or the countryside in which it unfolded, though she still owned the house west of Frederick. It was an investment property, a rental to supplement her Social Security.

That reminded Claire—the tenants had left three weeks ago, the day before the New Year, and she needed to check in with the rental agent to make sure the house was clean so they could get new tenants in. One more thing on her list.

As they headed down Connecticut Avenue toward Cleveland Park, Leona seemed to settle into a better mood. She talked about ham and fish or something Claire could safely ignore. Claire would park behind the apartment buildings on Connecticut near the top of the zoo instead of driving all the way down to the lot at the bottom. Then she could get Leona in, let the smell of the animals trigger her, get her back out, and take her home.

As she pulled into a parking spot, she realized her grandmother was talking about Hamilton Fish, the congressman from New York, one of many she'd interviewed during her days as a journalist, and one of the few she seemed to like. She was going to have lunch with him next week, she said, to catch up. Claire wondered which decade Leona was reliving. Ham Fish had died in 1996.

In the zoo, Claire traced the path that old Ben Corley had taken her and Gavin on a dozen times in her childhood. Start with the pandas near the top, then make your way down. If Claire had had a father, she liked to imagine he would have been as patient with her as Ben had been.

The pandas didn't interest Leona, nor did the elephants, giraffes, orangutans, or gorillas. And the smell didn't deter her. She seemed to be in search of a particular animal. She was calm and focused throughout the walk. On what, Claire couldn't guess and didn't care to know. All that mattered was that she had entered one of her docile periods, and that could last for twenty or thirty minutes, as long as nothing triggered her.

In this period of calm, Claire made the mistake of letting her guard down. She was thinking ahead to the police station, to what she would tell the cops at Second District about Lincoln and his big piece-of-shit car.

And she thought back to a conversation she'd had with Gavin a few weeks earlier. It didn't make sense at the time. They'd been talking about her work, about how much less challenging it was to certify numbers than to do the full archeological dig of a due diligence investigation.

"I needed a job right away," she said. "So I took the one that was open."

She could see at the time that his mind was elsewhere. She could see the glint of paranoia in his eyes as he stroked his beard.

"What, Gavin? Where are you now?"

"Some people think the safest way to pass secrets is through encryption," he said.

"Who's talking about encryption?"

"But even that leaves a trail."

"Gavin?"

"There's still a record of the communication between two parties, though you may never know what was said."

"Hello? Why are you telling me this? We were talking about my job."

"If you want to be really secure, you pass a message in a way that no one would know it had ever been passed."

"Ooh, I don't like the way you're looking at me. Like you're cooking up one of your plans. Keep me out of it."

"You know, it's like magicians do. Sleight of hand." He showed her his empty palm, turned his hand over and then produced a golden Sacagawea dollar out of nowhere. "They make every motion in plain sight. They just trick you into watching the motions that don't matter instead of the ones that do."

"Jesus, Gavin! Are you like, on drugs or something? Can you come back to the real world? We were having a conversation. At least, I was."

"Sorry. You were telling me about an audit. What was the company?"

"It's a pharmaceutical. There's nothing all that interesting about it."

"Really? I never thought I'd hear you say that." He stroked his beard. "I mean, you look so deeply into everything, it all becomes interesting. That's why you're never bored. You always somehow find the heart of the matter, even where other people wouldn't know the matter had any heart at all."

That was a strange thing to say, an unexpected compliment she took to heart. The grief came in a sudden wave. She missed him deeply.

She and Leona were nearing the tiger's enclosure at the bottom of the hill. Leona stopped abruptly at the leopard's cage. "Aha!"

She turned and pointed down the path toward three small girls chasing each other in circles and shrieking. "That's you," she hissed.

Then she pointed to the agitated leopard pacing in its tiny prison.

"And that's me. And *you* put me there, you harpy!" She banged the side of her fist against Claire's shoulder. "You ingrate! You frigid little witch! No wonder Peter left you!"

The attack stung because Claire hadn't seen it coming, hadn't readied her defenses. It also hit a nerve.

She turned and walked quickly away to avoid exploding with anger. Part of her wanted to protest, to explain that she had let her grandmother live independently as long as possible, and was now performing her duty to the woman who had raised her. And, Claire wanted to add, she had left Peter, not the other way around.

"Where are you going?" Leona demanded. "Why are you running away?"

I'm going to kill her, Claire thought. She's had it coming for thirty-two years, and now I'm really going to hurt her. Doesn't she know I have enough going on in my life right now? Can't she be decent for one day? For one fucking day?

As the figure of her granddaughter receded down the path, fear crept into the old woman's voice.

"Claire, don't you leave me here! I want to go home. Claire! You nasty little bitch! Take me home! Now!"

Claire turned and folded her arms across her chest. Leona watched her come back, then watched her turn and walk away again. Claire wouldn't allow herself to walk far enough away to lose sight of her grandmother, nor close enough to hit her. She paced back and forth, knowing that to Leona's muddled mind it must appear as if she were coming and going, coming and going.

"Make up your mind," Leona shouted, "or I'll call a cab."

Claire pushed back her anger and hatred by force of will, took her grandmother firmly by the arm, and began to march her back up the hill toward the zoo entrance.

"Stop pulling me," Leona said. "Where are we going?"

"This is why I won't have children," Claire said, and the words brought tears to her eyes. It was the first time she had ever said it aloud, and somehow, announcing it in public made it feel final and irrevocable.

"Because they act like you! They act like you, and I know my patience and I know my temper, and I'm afraid I'll hurt them. I'll hit them, like you used to do to me." She gave her lagging grandmother a violent yank. "It's not fair to treat people like that, and I won't ever do it. Not to anyone. Not even to you."

"Listen to yourself, Claire," Leona said scornfully. "You sound like a child. Stop pulling me!"

Claire let her go and said with forced calm, "I'm going to walk two steps ahead of you at a speed I know you can keep. If you want to get home, you'll have to follow me."

That plan worked out well.

In the car on Connecticut Avenue, as Claire ground her teeth and felt the beginning of a violent headache, Leona said in a pleasant, cheerful voice, "Well, I think you'd make a wonderful mother."

After I strangle you, Claire thought.

She had another problem now. The Lincoln was on her tail again.

"I'll deal with you after I get rid of her," she groused.

"Who are you talking to?"

"You can follow me to the station on Idaho Avenue." She watched the rearview. "Then I won't have to tell them what you look like. You fat bastard!"

"Claire? Are you angry?"

"Why can't it be just one thing at a time? Why?"

She understood now how people reached a breaking point, why sometimes they just snapped.

12

After dropping Leona off, Claire got a call from Officer Greer.

"I pulled your friend's case file."

"Gavin's?"

"Yeah. You have a minute?"

Claire looked at the Lincoln in the rearview. "Actually, why don't I come out there?" One police station was as good as another, she thought. It would make him go away.

When she arrived, her relief at the sight of Greer made her realize she had been more tense than she'd thought.

"You OK?" Greer studied Claire's face and hands as if looking for signs of abuse. It made her feel small, like someone's charity case.

"I'm fine."

"Come back here," Greer said.

They went to the interview room they'd been in the night before.

"Cause of death for Gavin Corley," Greer said when they were seated, "was alcohol poisoning, not blunt force trauma, which is usually what you see in a fatal accident."

"Um..." Claire left it hanging, and Greer could hear the doubt in her voice as she tried to process information that didn't make sense.

"Was he that much of a drinker?" Greer asked.

"He didn't drink at all. He had a bad reaction to alcohol."

"Death is certainly a bad reaction," Greer said. "His blood alcohol was point four-six. Also had hydrocodone in his blood. That's a bad mix. He have a drug problem?"

"No. He was in an accident about nine months ago. They gave him painkillers. He may have had some left over. Maybe his injuries were acting up."

"But he didn't use regularly?"

"I couldn't imagine it."

"Look at the car." Greer turned her laptop to Claire. "It's not badly damaged. There was no impact. The top crumpled in when it flipped, but not far enough to cause a head injury."

Claire could see the silhouette of her friend hanging upside down, suspended by the seatbelt.

"That's disturbing."

"It's disturbing to me," Greer said. "That car was on a wooded road, two miles from anywhere. How does a man with a blood alcohol level of point four-six manage to drive a car more than two feet? Most people can't even stand at that point. And why, if he's that drunk and he's hanging upside down, why didn't he throw up?"

Greer looked curiously at Claire. "The coroner said his stomach was empty. Did he drink half a gallon of liquor on an empty stomach?"

Claire shook her head. "He never drank hard alcohol."

"Well, those pain pills can make you do funny things."

Greer turned the laptop back toward herself and clicked the trackpad. "Now the coroner's photos—" She stopped and checked herself. "I'm not going to show you these, but I'll describe them to you."

"I don't mind seeing them," Claire said.

Greer shook her head. "This is your friend. You will mind seeing them. I'm going to show you just one." She squinted at the screen as she clicked. "OK, here." She turned the laptop back toward Claire.

"The coroner photographs all the injuries. Your friend had none, because there was no impact, except for this."

The photo showed Gavin's forearm, white and over lit by a bright examination light. The ruler beside a rough gouge showed it was about two inches long.

"The coroner said he probably cut himself on something jagged before he got into the car," Greer said. "There was nothing in the car that would have done that."

"What does that make you think?" Claire asked.

Greer shrugged. "I don't know. I'm still stuck on how a guy with a point four-six drove two whole miles before going off the road. And why didn't he have his lights on? If they'd been on, someone might have found him while he was still alive. Instead, he was out there for hours."

"Can you investigate?"

"Not this one. Coroner already ruled it an accidental overdose."

"Can you get the coroner to reopen the case?"

"And assign it to a detective with a four-year backlog?" She shook her head. "Even if I could, this would go straight to the bottom of the pile. Unless someone's raising a stink, and that would have to be a family member or a politician."

"I don't know any politicians," Claire said. "And as for family, all he had was his dad, and he's not long for this world." She thought about old Ben Corley, wheezing in his wheelchair with his oxygen tank and fentanyl patch. "I don't think I could even tell him about the alcohol. Why upset him again? Let him leave this world in peace."

But it wouldn't hurt, she thought, to pay old Ben a courtesy visit.

13

She took her time after leaving the station. With no grandmother to harass her and no Lincoln stalking, she pulled into Panera for a sit-down meal: coffee and a grilled chicken sandwich. She told herself she would eat the entire thing, but after thirty minutes, she could only get half of it down.

She wasn't sure if eating triggered her anxiety or simply made her more aware of the anxiety that was already there, but her stomach tightened and churned whenever food was in front of her. At night the tension crept into her shoulders, up the back of her neck and turned into a headache.

In daylight, that same tension drove her forward at work and helped her make the final push to move Leona into Rollingwood. Stress and anxiety kept her moving forward despite the lack of food. Since leaving New York, she'd been running on fumes. Running and running, trying now and then to think about what she was running from.

When she got up at 2:00 or 3:00 or 4:00 a.m. for aspirin and chamomile tea, she sometimes sat at the kitchen counter and began her letter to Peter. Trying to sort out all that had gone wrong in her mind and heart, trying to explain that it wasn't his fault, all she could ever come up with was, "I'm sorry."

Sorry she left, sorry she didn't return his calls, sorry she had to work so much, sorry Leona needed her. She knew those were all excuses.

These major life changes aren't supposed to happen all at once. She could only give her attention to the most immediate need. Her grandmother was in the room with her. Peter was not. So she packed and sorted Leona's belongings, curated the remnants of someone else's life, deciding what was important and what was not. She fled to the office when she could, and she didn't think about Peter until the middle of the night when she couldn't sleep and couldn't find anything else to distract her.

She pushed away the remains of the chicken sandwich and returned to her car, feeling overfull from a meal that wouldn't have sustained her through a normal morning in New York. Funny, she thought, how your stomach contracts when you stop eating.

On her way out of the lot, she checked her mirrors. It was a habit now, one more in the pattern of defenses she had evolved. Look out for threats, ahead, behind, and all around. Prepare, so that when the threat appears, you have a plan of action. Today's plan was to go to Second District—if the Lincoln reappeared.

For now, it was nowhere in sight. For now, the plan was to visit Ben Corley.

She regretted lingering so long in the restaurant. The sky was dark, and rush hour traffic was heavy.

14

It took over an hour to reach Western Avenue. Halfway between Pinehurst Circle and Oregon Avenue, she pulled the car to the curb on the DC side. Looking at the dead moss on the roof of Gavin's childhood home, she remembered how weak and ashen Ben Corley had looked at his son's funeral.

The old green Ford Explorer parked in front of the house was spattered with salt residue from the last snow. That was four weeks ago. The rear driver-side tire was low, and the tabs on the license plate had expired in November. The shaggy grass in front of the house was tangled with leaves. The wood casings around the windows had begun to rot.

A flat-bed truck carrying Gavin's grey Chevy Equinox pulled up in front of the Explorer. She watched the driver, a burly, bearded white guy in a blue jumpsuit, get out and unfasten the straps. He climbed into the Chevy. What was he doing? Releasing the parking brake. Shifting into neutral. He climbed down and worked the lever that tilted the bed, then he unwound the winch and lowered the SUV into place in front of the Explorer. Two vehicles whose owners would never drive them again.

Society's machine continues through its motions, Claire thought, even after the people who are supposed to benefit are gone. The cops had the Equinox towed. Insurance paid the shop to replace the broken windows, pull the dents out of the roof, return it to the next of kin.

The driver of the flatbed squinted at his clipboard beneath the streetlight. When Claire approached him, he said, "You Gavin Corley?"

"Do I look like a man?"

The driver looked her up and down. "You live here?"

"No."

"I need a signature for the Chevy."

"I would hope so. You'll need to get that from Ben, inside."

"Ben?" The driver wrote the name on the signature line of the paper. "What's his last name?"

Claire's frustration at his stupidity showed in her look. "Corley."

He finished the signature, tore off the yellow carbon copy, and handed it to her, along with the key fob that must have been in Gavin's pocket when he died.

"Have a nice day, lady."

"It's night," Claire said. Inwardly, she added, And I'm not a *lady*. This isn't Victorian England.

She glanced over the work receipt as the driver pulled away in a cloud of diesel smoke. Then she peered into the Chevy. She couldn't see much inside, but she had the key.

She opened the driver's door and the interior light came on. She looked for the jagged edge that might have gouged Gavin's forearm. Nothing stuck out.

She checked the repair receipt again. There was no mention of work on the interior driver's door, so if it had no sharp edges now, it probably had none at the time of the accident.

She looked over the front and rear seats. The interior was clean. The shop must have vacuumed it before they returned it. In the back, though, she saw something on the floor. She closed the driver's door and opened the door behind it. There on the carpet was another box of migraine medicine, like the one she'd found at the crash site. It must have slid out from beneath the seat when the flatbed tilted back.

The box was empty. Like the other one she'd found at the edge of the woods, it was dirty, as if it had been pulled from the garbage.

Behind the passenger seat were two white plastic bottles. She reached in, pulled them out to the light of the street. These were statins, medicines to control blood pressure. Two huge bottles of a thousand pills each. Who buys that many pills at once?

Pharmacies, Claire thought. That's why there's no prescription label, no patient name.

She closed the door, put the box and the bottles into her car, and then went in to see old Ben.

15

A heavyset woman in a nurse's uniform answered the door.

"Is Mr. Corley in?"

"Yes, ma'am." She had a faint Caribbean accent. "In the living room."

The house was stuffy and overheated. Probably, she thought, for the comfort of a frail old man with poor circulation.

She was taken aback when she saw him. He looked even worse than he had at the funeral, nodding in his wheelchair with deeply lined ashen skin. The clear plastic tube strapped beneath his nose came from a green oxygen tank mounted on the back of the chair.

He raised his head slowly at the sound of her approach and didn't seem to recognize her until she spoke.

"Mr. Corley?" She knelt in front of him so he could see and hear her.

He smiled and said in a labored voice, "Claire! How have you been?"

"Busy."

"Mmm." His eyes blinked slowly. "I remember being busy. Always waiting for life to slow down. And now it has."

"I wanted to express my condolences. Again," she added, wondering whether he remembered seeing her at the funeral. He had been nodding then too, from illness or from fentanyl, she couldn't tell. "Gavin was a wonderful person."

"Wasn't he?" Ben smiled feebly. "Somehow you two are always twelve years old in my mind. Always just coming in from the woods."

"I remember those days," Claire said with a pang of nostalgia.

"He started getting a little kooky near the end."

"Gavin?"

"That's who we're talking about, right? He always had that streak of paranoia. It came and went, but he had it bad near the end. I was worried about him."

Corley ran out of breath and shut his mouth. Claire watched him inhale deeply through the tubes, reoxygenating himself before he could speak again.

"Would you like a cigarette?"

Claire hesitated, unsure if he was joking.

"If you do the whole five-decade regimen like I did, two packs a day, you'll come out looking as pretty as me." He smiled and so did Claire.

"They say a man will give his life for his true love," he wheezed. "My sweetheart was a nicotine weed."

Claire remembered him looking unhealthy even at fifty: thin, high strung, preoccupied with work, and always with a cigarette between his lips.

"Mr. Corley, I was wondering. Was Gavin in any trouble before he died?"

The nurse standing in the doorway seemed to perk up at the question.

"Mmm..." Corley's head dropped, and for a couple of seconds Claire thought he had fallen asleep.

"Hard to tell," he said at last. "He certainly thought he was in trouble. But that came and went with the paranoia."

"Did he say there was anything unusual going on?"

Corley took a deep breath of oxygen. "Just that he had left his job."

"Where was he working?"

"Oh, some computer place. Voyage?" He closed his eyes and thought. "No, Voynich." He opened his eyes again. "Voynich Systems. Computers for the paranoid."

Ben lifted his head higher to look at her, see if she got the joke.

"High security stuff," he said. "They ran servers for sensitive data. Stuff people wanted to lock down. You had to be a top security engineer to set up those systems."

"Did he say why he left?"

Corley shook his head. His chin dipped toward his chest, and Claire looked to the nurse as if to ask whether it was time to go. The nurse nodded back toward Corley as if to say, Just give him time.

In a moment, his head was up again.

"Do you know if Gavin was planning to leave his job?" Claire asked. "Or was it a sudden thing?"

He stared at her quietly, fondly, sadly.

"I always felt sorry for you, Claire. Your grandmother was such a mean, hateful person. So bitter and combative. And your mother, do you remember your mother?"

"Barely." Her mother was a feeling and a voice. The womb of love from whom she had been delivered too soon into the claws of the witch.

"She was a beautiful woman, Claire. And I don't mean pretty. She had a warmth to her."

Let's not go there right now, Claire thought.

"You look like her."

Silently, to herself: I know.

"It was her warmth that attracted people. She was such a generous spirit. She would give anything to anyone."

And she did, Claire thought. At least, according to Leona. Though give wasn't the word Leona used because Leona didn't know anything about giving. She "put out." Put out for whoever she thought might love her. Whoever was willing to take advantage.

"You're *her* child, Claire. Not Leona's."

Oh, Leona never let me forget that. She made sure I wouldn't suffer the same fate, wouldn't be taken advantage of. Everyone has an angle in Leona's world. Everyone is out to take something from you. Trust no one and give nothing. Generosity is foolishness. Love is the ultimate foolishness. An open heart is complicit in its own victimization. It begs to be exploited.

"All the beauty that was in your mother, I see in you too. Always have."

Well, I'm glad someone does, Claire thought. But you're probably just projecting. I don't blame you. Illness and old age look for comfort, and if you can't find it, you invent it. Did you know I put a knife through my boyfriend's heart? Walked out on him for no reason? Because I was scared. Because *he* thought I was beautiful too. He thought I was worth a lifetime of devotion, and I couldn't understand how anyone could see me that way, how I could ever live up to that. So I panicked and I ran. Is that beauty? Is that kindness? Generosity? Love? To abandon someone? However much I look like her, I am not my mother. My father, maybe. He was a betrayer too. An abandoner. Or maybe I'm just Leona in a prettier package, faking courtesy half the time, and the other half being a bitch so no one can say I didn't warn them.

She stood abruptly from her crouch. "Jesus!" she blurted. "Where are these thoughts coming from?"

"Claire?" Ben Corley looked concerned.

She pushed her thoughts aside and changed the subject to practical matters.

"Did a man come by here after Gavin died? Did a man come and ask you questions?"

"Mmm," said Corley quietly. "About two days after. A very rude man. I didn't care for him at all."

"What did he look like?"

The nurse chimed in behind her. "Tall man. Blue eyes, light hair and face pocked all red. Nosy and rude. No hello, how you doing. Him walk right past before I asked him in. Went to Mr. Corley and give him the third degree."

Claire turned to the nurse. "What did he ask?"

"He asked if Gavin had been by recently," Mr. Corley said. "I told him no. I hadn't seen him in about three weeks."

"I tell him to leave," the nurse said.

"Then he wanted to know if Gavin mailed me a package," Corley said.

"'e was right up in your face," said the nurse. "Rude and threatening."

"I told him no," said Corley.

"And I tell him again to get out," said the nurse.

"He said Gavin stole something," Corley added, "and he wanted it back. But Gavin was no thief. I thought the man was deranged."

Corley was breathing hard. The nurse went to his side, took his hand.

"Through the nose," she reminded him. "Deep breath."

She nodded no to Claire, as in, No more today.

Claire whispered, "Goodbye, Ben." She went to the door but didn't open it.

She waited as the nurse calmed the old man in the other room.

When at last the nurse came to see why she hadn't left, Claire whispered, "You have something to tell me."

"If you want to talk to him more, come back tomorrow."

"No." Claire shook her head. "Something else."

"Ma'am?" The nurse seemed nervous.

"A few minutes ago," Claire said softly, "when I asked if Gavin had been in trouble before he died, you perked up. Why?"

"Ma'am, I don't want no trouble."

"What kind of trouble was Gavin in?"

"Not in," she whispered. "Causing."

"He was causing trouble?"

"I had to keep him out. Away from here."

"Why?"

"The fentanyl," she said softly. "He steal the patches. Mr. Corley didn't know."

Suddenly, the change Claire had seen in Gavin made sense. It wasn't depression that had dulled his eyes and slowed his mind. And it wasn't a cold that had made his nose drip. She thought back to Gavin's accident nine months ago. He'd been broadsided by a pickup. The doctors reset the broken arm, braced his neck. The ribs and collarbone would have to heal on their own. They gave him painkillers. He was still taking them a month after the accident, even though he'd been healing well.

With opioids, a month was all it took.

"If I tell my employer we need more patches," the nurse whispered, "they ask what happened to the ones we had. I get blamed. They think I sell them. So I stretch out what we 'ad left. I didn't change them as often as I should. He was in pain." She nodded toward the living room. "He didn't know why he felt so sick. The next time Gavin come, I try to send him away. I tell him he make his father sick, but he look sick himself. Ashamed too. The drugs, you know. When they have you, it's all you think about. He was sick, that boy. Dopesick."

16

Claire ran the heat in her car in front of Ben Corley's house as she reassessed her last few interactions with Gavin. Why hadn't she recognized it? The way he drifted off and lost the topic of conversation. His increasingly strange voicemails, culminating in that last one: "I'm pretty sure I screwed this up, so I'm passing the torch to you. If worse comes to worst, I know you'll see it through." Screwed what up? Maybe he was high then. Maybe he was delusional. The coroner said he had died with drugs in his system.

But he couldn't have been that far gone. He had returned to work sometime after the accident and had managed to hold down a job. But there's such a thing as a functional addict, she reminded herself. How many celebrities had announced they'd gone to rehab to kick a pill habit no one guessed they'd had. They were still cranking out movies, TV shows, radio programs as if all was well. They fit their addictions into the schedule of their lives until they couldn't anymore. Maybe Gavin had reached that point. The breaking point. Maybe that's why he decided to drink himself to death.

No. She rejected the thought. If he really wanted to die, he wouldn't have done it with liquor. He hated alcohol. But I don't think he wanted to die. I don't think he ever would have done that to himself.

She picked up her phone, found the Voynich Systems website, and skimmed through the front page. *Highly secure systems for your most sensitive workloads.* Farther down the page, *24/7 service.* She had to visit three more pages before she found a phone number.

A man answered on the first ring. "Voynich. Collins. Can I help you?"

"Hello?"

"Account number?"

"What?"

"Who's calling?" he asked.

"My name is Claire Chastain."

"You have an outage?"

"No. I'm calling about Gavin Corley."

"Gavin Corley?" His tone was curt, as if she had offended him.

"Yes."

"What about Gavin Corley?" There was an edge of hostility in his voice.

"He worked there until a couple of weeks ago..."

Long, tense pause.

"Who is this?" the man demanded.

"I told you, my name is Claire—"

He hung up, and she sat staring at the phone, wondering, What the hell?

She put the car in gear, drove to the end of Western, then right onto Oregon. No Lincoln in sight. The light above her front step was on, as well as the light in the front room. All good.

She drove around the block on Daniel, then again on Dogwood, then again on Chestnut. No scent of burning oil. No sound of the knocking engine.

When she pulled into the drive, she slid the hammer out from beneath the driver's seat. One side of the head had a steel point to shatter a window that wouldn't open, the other had a blade to slice through a seatbelt. It was the kind of gift an anxious husband might give to a wife whose daily commute took her over a decaying bridge. "If you fall into the water, cut the belt, knock out the glass, and swim up toward the light." Only Claire had bought it herself. The blade was useless right now, but the hammer point could penetrate a skull.

She would go in, pack a few days' worth of clothes, then go to Second District to file her report. Then maybe go to the office to pick up her computer. Then to the Hilton on Connecticut, or the Embassy Suites on 22nd, where she could use her points for a few free nights.

That was the plan, anyway. That was what she was thinking when she got out of the car.

17

The door was the first sign something was wrong. She had left it locked. Yellow light from the front room leaked through the open crack, a slashing line across her shoes. She took half a step back and nudged the door with her left hand, the hammer cocked in her right.

The chaos inside was worse than the mess she'd left. The boxes on the living room floor had been overturned, their contents kicked everywhere. Farther back, the kitchen drawers and cabinets were open.

She turned, dialed 911, and walked to the end of the driveway. When the dispatcher answered, she told him someone had broken in. She was afraid to go inside.

Two and a half minutes later, the first patrol car arrived. The cop, a short black man with a friendly, reassuring air, asked if she was OK, when she'd arrived at the house, whether she thought someone might still be inside.

The last part was what worried her.

"I'm not going in there," she said. She had already begun to shake.

Two more patrols arrived in the second car. A woman who seemed too young to be on the force, and a man of thirty-five or so, burly, dark skinned, with a grumpy manner. The woman stood outside with Claire while the men went in.

"When were you last in the house?"

Claire paced nervously. "This morning, for half an hour or so."

"Do you have a burglar alarm?"

"No."

"Any valuables in the house?"

"Nothing that would be valuable to anyone else. Have there been other burglaries in the neighborhood?"

It would have been reassuring if there had been. She'd feel less targeted.

"Not recently," the cop answered.

When the men called them in, they asked Claire to lead them on a tour. Where did she keep valuables? What was missing?

The only valuables, Claire told them, were the diamond studs in her ears. She had packed up most of her grandmother's belongings. The good stuff went with her to Rollingwood. The rest would go to Goodwill, except some furniture, which she would sell.

There was a TV in Leona's bedroom, unplugged on the floor beside some other items to be sold. It was too big to carry out, at least in broad daylight, which seems to have been when the burglary occurred.

Every closet had been opened, every drawer, even the cabinets beneath the bathroom sink. The suitcase she had stumbled into in the basement the day before had been thoroughly searched. They had even ripped out the lining.

"Sometimes when these addicts can't find things worth stealing," said the burly cop, "they get desperate and tear through everything. This wasn't a professional job."

From the top of the stairs, the woman cop called down. "Ms. Chastain?"

There was something in her tone Claire didn't like. She was going to show her something she wouldn't want to see.

"Can you come up here for a minute?"

She led her to the guest bathroom, the one in which Claire showered and brushed her teeth.

She didn't say anything, just pointed the beam of her flashlight at the toilet, an unnecessary gesture, since the overhead light was already on.

The water had overflowed the rim. The bottom was clogged with her bras and underwear.

"Oh God." Her knees went weak.

"Has someone been harassing you?" the woman asked.

Claire closed her eyes, put her fingers to her temples, and let out a long breath. "Yes."

She gave her report in the kitchen. The burly cop asked the questions and wrote down her answers while the rookie observed. He occasionally pointed out notes to the younger cop, things to be sure to record in a burglary report, details about domestic incidents and stalking.

"It's not a domestic incident," Claire said. "The guy who's following me—I have no idea who he is."

She gave them the license plate number—she'd memorized it—and a description of the car. The shorter cop, the one who'd arrived first, showed her his laptop.

"Is this the guy? He's got a few priors. Drunk and disorderly."

"No," Claire said. "That's the guy who sold the car. The guy who's been following me is white."

"Have you done anything to offend anyone lately?" That was the burly cop asking.

"Not that I know of."

"Any prior boyfriends? Obsessive types?"

"Peter, but he's not obsessive. Or aggressive. He doesn't have a mean bone in his body."

"Does he have any reason to be upset with you?"

"Plenty," she said. "He wanted to marry me, and I left him."

"You had a fight?" asked the woman.

"No. I just walked out."

The young woman stared at her as if waiting for further explanation.

"God, please don't look at me like that," Claire said. "I don't know, OK?"

"How long ago?" the woman asked.

"Six weeks."

"When did the stalker appear?"

"A few days ago."

"Have there been any other unusual events recently?" asked the burly cop.

"Gavin."

She explained his death. Alcohol poisoning. He didn't drink. And apparently, he didn't turn his lights on either when he drove at night, or someone would have found him before 5:00 a.m. And Gavin had a drug problem. She just learned that this evening.

The burly cop: "He have any friends? Drug friends looking for money? Looking for a fix?"

"I wouldn't know."

They took another tour of the house. What was missing?

An iPad. And the disk drives from Leona's office drawer.

"Any idea what was on those?" asked the woman.

"Backups of her writing. She was a journalist. Maybe some photos. Her taxes."

Burly wrote it all down.

"Do you have someone you can stay with?" the woman asked.

Claire shook her head. "I have hotel points. I used to travel a lot for work."

"Stay at a hotel then. We'll have a report ready in the morning so you can get the ball rolling with insurance," said the woman. "If you want, we can do another walk-through tomorrow and see what else is missing. The more we document, the more insurance will pay."

"Yeah..." Claire was shaken and numb.

"You want a ride?" asked the thin cop. "To the hotel?"

"How about to my office?"

That was the closest thing she had to a home in this city. Someone might still be working at—she checked the time on her phone—9:57. Some of the consultants were workaholics, like her. If no one was there, she'd pick up her laptop and go to the Hilton or the Embassy Suites. Maybe have a drink, or two, or three, to calm her nerves and get to sleep.

She wanted to pack for a few days before leaving. She found her toothbrush on the bathroom floor, but decided to leave it after she pictured the intruders dunking it in the toilet.

She picked up a jacket from the bed and found it had been torn at the seams. Same with the pants on the nightstand.

Except for the shoulder bag she had walked in with, she left empty-handed.

On the ride down to 18th Street, she sat in front, beside the skinny cop who seemed to sense she didn't want to cry in front of him. They drove in silence.

When he dropped her off at the office door, he gave her his card for the second time. A reassuring gesture that didn't require words. The wrong words, even with the best intentions, might have triggered her, sent her over the edge.

18

When she left the elevator on the fourth floor, she couldn't remember how she had gotten there. Had she really been in that police car? Or had it been a dream?

The double glass entry doors were locked. Two overhead spotlights illuminated the reception desk. The rest of the area was dark, like a theater set before the characters walked on stage. She touched her key card to the chip reader and went in. Beyond reception, motion sensors lit the halls at her approach. In the silence of the corridor, she heard the spongy imprint of her shoes on the carpet. She stopped before her office door to listen for the steps of others as the motion sensors behind her told the lights one by one to go back to sleep.

She flicked on her office light, dropped her shoulder bag on the desk beside the black laptop. There was a note from Li thanking her for coffee that morning. Who writes thank-you notes for coffee? Claire debated for a moment whether this was a practice she should discourage in her protégé or one she should adopt herself.

She sat, opened her laptop, and typed her password as if it were 8:00 a.m. The feeling of routine gave her a momentary sense of normalcy, a retreat from the events of the day.

Twenty-six unread emails. None of them important, except the one from Anoop marked "Urgent." She clicked and read.

"Turn off the screen and go for a walk. Your health is more important than your work. Eat, rest, and you'll come back a better Claire."

She deleted it and skimmed over the subject lines of the remaining items.

Then she checked her personal email, which was empty except for what the spam filters had missed. She had no use for cheap Canadian Viagra and no interest in replying to Evgeniya who "had saw from your profiles you are more handsome than all Russian bad husband."

Does the internet really think I'm a man, Claire wondered, or do the scammers target men because they're easier to bait?

She considered for a moment responding to the Nigerian prince whose fortune was being held for ransom by a corrupt government. What should she tell him? It was thoughtful of him to have chosen her out of the seven billion people on the web, and generous of him to offer ten million of his captive dollars in exchange for a mere ten thousand of hers. But as a prince, he might want to read up on politics and human nature. Any corrupt regime that would impound a few million of his dollars would happily steal a few thousand more.

She went back to her company email, scanned the subject lines again. The response from the PharmaCore manager caught her eye. The man who had sent her the spreadsheet. She clicked and read.

"I know it came from my email," he wrote. "But I didn't send it. My account was hacked while I was out of the country. Will you please delete that? It's company confidential and not relevant to your financial audit, or whatever you're working on over there."

How does he know what's relevant to my work, she wondered, with a tinge of hostility at his presumption. How does he know what's relevant to anything?

She got up and stood at the floor-to-ceiling window behind her desk, looking down on the empty street. This part of town was dead at night. The restaurants and bars were a few blocks away, to the east on Connecticut Avenue, to the north at Dupont Circle, and to the west in Georgetown. This strip of 18th was all business. The coffeeshops and restaurants were bustling at breakfast and lunch, then closed up when the nine-to-fivers went home.

She watched a cab roll up the street toward M, followed by a little blue Chevy with a glowing Uber sign on the dash. The two lone figures on the sidewalk moved in opposite directions, their heads cast down against the cold. She instinctively reached for the string that controlled the blinds, but there were no blinds. Other than a tinted film to dampen the heat of the morning sun, these windows had no mechanism for privacy.

She suddenly saw herself from the perspective of the street. A solitary woman framed in a rectangle of light, like a character in a television show, trapped in a box to be watched. The trials of her life were entertainment for an audience she couldn't see.

Is this what Gavin felt like, she wondered, when his paranoia flared up?

After the first episode, when he was eighteen, she stopped trying to tell him it was all in his head. It didn't matter if it was in his head. It *felt* real to him, and if it felt real, you had to treat it as real.

She wondered now whether paranoia was contagious, whether he had passed it on to her when he died. "I'm passing the torch to you."

Was this the torch? This anxious mental illness? This perpetual state of unease? If so, she marveled at what strength he must have had to endure all those years without cracking up.

"They watch everything you do, all the time," he said, *they* being the security cameras in public spaces, the phone companies that know your location, the cars that know your movements, the smart TVs and social media apps that know what you like so they can feed you more of it, the ads that follow you from site to site across the internet.

Is this what he felt like? Like he was the TV show everyone was watching?

She watched the Uber pass again—it must have circled the block—then she returned to her desk and sat. The laptop screen was dark. She'd been standing at the window five whole minutes.

Claire slashed her fingers across the trackpad. "Wake up, you slacker! I didn't say you could nap."

The screen flicked on. She typed her password and reviewed the message she'd been reading.

"It's company confidential and not relevant to your financial audit, or whatever you're working on over there."

"Whatever I'm working on here," she repeated softly.

She found the spreadsheet, opened it up, scanned through the numbers. Her company's agreement with PharmaCore said they would retain documents required to back up the results of the audit. They would delete everything else once the audit was complete. The manager was right. The manufacturing data in this spreadsheet wasn't relevant to her financial report.

She was going to delete it and send—what was his name? She checked the email again. Robert Spolsky. She was going to send Robert Spolsky a reassuring message that she had got rid of his stupid spreadsheet and he could stop worrying.

She closed the document, dragged it into the trash, and as she began to type her response, a new message from Spolsky appeared.

"Delete the damn spreadsheet!"

Claire stopped typing and stared at the message.

She checked the time. 10:39. She looked at the message again, and then another one appeared.

"You're looking at it now. Delete it!"

She shook her head. How could he know I'm...?

She stood quickly, turned to the window, and reached again for the blinds that weren't there.

She looked up and down the street. If anyone was out there watching, she couldn't see them.

Then she remembered something Gavin had told her, a trick he used to track hackers who tried to break into his servers. Leave some documents in a place where they could be easily stolen. Hide URLs—links to web pages—inside the documents. When the hackers opened the documents, the documents would send a silent request to a server that Gavin controlled. His server would record where the request had come from. Armed with that information, Gavin could stalk his attackers.

The hidden URL was called a beacon. Advertisers used them on the internet to know what websites you visited and what articles you read.

Claire dragged the spreadsheet out of the trash and opened it. She clicked on the second tab and saw a message in one of the cells that should have contained data. *Unable to retrieve data. Server replied: 401 / Unauthorized.*

That would explain how Robert Spolsky knew she was looking at the spreadsheet, but why did he care?

She shut the laptop, closed her eyes, and took a few deep breaths.

She had always prided herself on her ability to control her feelings by sheer force of will, but tonight she was faltering. Her house had been robbed, her mail stolen, a big man in a Lincoln was stalking her around town, and now someone was watching her across the dark reaches of the internet.

At least the cops knew about it. At least they knew some of it. Cops in two jurisdictions. But what could they do? Wait for someone to kill her and then assemble the clues to figure out what they should have seen coming?

Claire opened her eyes. You don't have to be so dramatic, she told herself. It's not as bad as all that.

She turned her mind to practical matters, where emotion held no sway. The Embassy Suites was an easy walk, just five blocks west. But she didn't feel safe walking. The Hilton, farther up Connecticut, had a nicer lobby, warmly lit. They also had a restaurant and bar with plenty of people inside. People were witnesses. Stalkers didn't attack people in front of witnesses. She would go to the Hilton.

She slid her laptop into her shoulder bag, turned off the light, and left the office.

In the hallway, the lights flicked on one by one ahead of her, as if they knew where she was going and wanted to help her get there.

At the elevator, she unlocked her phone, clicked the Uber app, and pondered the address that Uber considered Home. Oregon Avenue might have once been her place of residence, but it had never been home. Not in her childhood, when Leona was in it, and not now that Leona had been moved out of it. Home, she realized in a flash of emotion, was Peter and the apartment in New York. Home was the place she had destroyed in her panic.

The elevator doors opened. She tapped the screen. Take me home.

A call came in as the doors slid shut. Li's number showed on the caller ID.

"Hello?"

"Ms. Chastain?"

It was a man's voice, serious and somber. In the background, a woman was sobbing violently, unable to catch her breath. Claire's heart skipped a beat, then raced.

"Yes."

"You're a friend of Li Ming?"

Heart in throat. That was Li sobbing. "Is she OK?"

"She's OK." The man identified himself as officer something or other, Metropolitan Police. "Hold on."

The sobbing diminished, as if he'd walked away from Li to speak in private.

"She lost a couple of teeth, and her left eye is swollen shut."

"What happened?"

Claire stepped out of the elevator, phone pressed to her ear.

"She got mugged and took a pretty bad beating. Can you come sit with her? Help her calm down?"

"Where are you?"

"Washington Hospital Center."

"Shit." She tried to remember where that was. Off North Capitol. She'd tell the Uber driver when she got in. "Tell her I'll be there as soon as I can."

"You work with her?"

"Yes."

"She thinks the company will be mad at her for losing their laptop."

"Oh, God. That should be the last thing on her mind." Claire could see the blue Chevy waiting at the curb outside, the bright Uber sign lighting the window. "I have a car waiting. Tell her I'll be there in twenty."

She ended the call.

What the *fuck*? Seriously, what the fuck is going on?

In the cold, sharp air outside, the scent of burning oil put her on high alert. She heard the rumbling engine off to her left, turned, and saw the taillights of the massive Lincoln heading away from her, rounding the corner onto M.

"You missed me, fucker." She said that aloud as she dashed to the waiting Chevy. She yanked the door open, ducked in quickly so she could get out of there before he circled the block.

"There's been a change of plans," she said as she pulled the door shut. "I need to go to—"

Then it hit her. The Chevy with the Uber sign was the same one she'd seen circle the block twice. That was fifteen minutes ago, and it was still here. Why?

The door lock clicked. The driver craned his head around, his steel-blue eyes lit with the satisfaction of a stalker that had captured its prey. She recognized at once the red-blond military cut, the pockmarked face of the rude inquisitor.

"Hello, Claire."

19

He turned forward and hit the gas. That was his third mistake, which was three too many against a woman who had spent her entire life on guard.

Claire pulled her shoe off and smashed the heel ten straight times into the side of his face. She was aiming for the eye, and had managed to hit all around it, drawing blood and a couple of screams. She tore the cartilage on the back of his ear and may have broken some of the fingers on the hand he tried to protect himself with.

The car hopped the curb and rolled to a stop on the sidewalk.

Claire unlocked the door, jumped out, and ran. Her bag was still over her left shoulder, her right shoe still in her right hand as she dashed into the narrow lane of Desales Row.

The second mistake of Fake Darrell Gatlin had been showing his face before she had her seatbelt on. The first was thinking he could take her alone.

As Claire hurried through the narrow alley-like lane, she saw two figures approaching. She was going to ask for help, but they seemed to speed up at the sight of her. They were coming for her too, she realized. And behind them limped a third, much larger man.

She turned and walked quickly back toward the blue Chevy. It had rolled backward off the sidewalk into the middle of 18th Street. Was Fake Darrell still a threat? Had she blinded him, or would he be able to see her coming? Could she even make it to the street before her pursuers caught up? Clutching the right shoe as her only weapon, she cursed the heel of her left that hobbled her as she tried to sprint.

Before she reached the light of 18th Street, one arm grabbed her, then another. A hand clapped over her mouth.

"Give it up, Claire."

Her heart pounded into her throat as they dragged her back into the dark. The hand that covered her mouth and nose cut off all her air. Her heart beat wildly as her lungs desperately struggled to draw breath.

The big man was still back there somewhere in the dark, and God only knew what he was going to do to her. He wasn't as fast as the other two. His size and his limp seemed to slow him, but he would be there any second, and he was large enough to crush her in his arms or break her in half.

As she tried to wrench free of the men holding her, all three of them spun at once. Her eyes widened in terror at the giant silhouette in front of her. He was a good foot taller than her, and probably two hundred pounds heavier. There was a split-second of silence before the man whose hand was smothering her exclaimed with a shock as great as hers, "What?"

A huge meaty fist thundered into his face with a freight train of an arm behind it, knocking him backward six or seven feet. The giant flung the second man against the wall of the building. His head thudded on the stone and he slumped to the pavement. The first man staggered forward into an uppercut that nearly lifted him off his feet, then fell face-first into a swiftly moving knee and crumpled to the ground.

The big man grabbed Claire under the arm and pulled her toward 19th Street. He was hustling now, limping more quickly than he had approached. She could barely keep up with him, tripping over the heel of her left shoe as he dragged her sideways.

"You wore the wrong damn shoes," he said as they emerged into the light of the street. His words had a southern drawl. "Never wear heels when people's tryin' to kill you."

The burgundy Continental was parked on the far side of 19th. He pulled her around to the passenger side, let go of her arm, and opened the door. Then he limped to the driver's door and watched as she stood frozen in confusion.

"Well? You gettin' in?"

She thought of running, taking off the left shoe so she could sprint, but which way? There was no one on 19th Street to help her, and the only other option, the alley, had two assailants in the middle and Fake Darrell at the end.

The big man kept staring at her, mouth slightly open in an expression of confusion.

"Claire," he said. "You know if I was out to hurt you I woulda done it by now. It's not like I ain't had the chance."

Her posture relaxed from deathly terror to high alarm. Her face showed her bewilderment as she tried to make sense of the situation.

"Come on," he said softly. "Get in."

When she didn't move, he added, "'Less you want to wait for your friends over there to come back and get you."

She got in.

20

The engine sputtered and knocked when the big man hit the gas, then it seemed to catch all at once and the car lurched forward with a roar.

He patted the dashboard and cooed, "Atta girl."

Claire watched him wide-eyed, eyes dilated, nostrils flared, senses on high alert.

He turned to her and smiled. "That's four hundred and sixty cubic inches. Ain't got the same pickup she once had, but then neither do I."

She kept her right arm cocked, right hand gripping the shoe as she scanned his face for targets. She didn't want to have to think when it was time to attack. Know ahead of time where to aim the blows so you can put every ounce of energy into them.

She estimated he was in his midthirties. Six and a half feet tall. Over three hundred pounds, and curiously at ease.

His right eye was closest. And his head was tilted slightly back, exposing his throat. But all the meat on that thick neck was padding. One blow wouldn't hurt him. She would have to go for the eye.

The whole car leaned to the right as they turned left onto L Street.

"She ain't so nimble," he said. "But she is a beast."

"Who are you?" Claire demanded.

"Your guardian angel," he said.

"Someone hired you to follow me?" That was a guess.

"Obviously. Hey, if you don't mind me saying, you need to lighten up."

"Don't tell me what to do."

He looked at her face, then at the heavy heel of the shoe cocked in her right hand. "You're like a crouched panther ready to strike, aintcha?" He turned left onto 18th.

"The shoe ain't gonna do you no good, but I like your spirit. This here's what you need." He pulled a stun gun from beneath his seat and handed it to her. It looked like a mini hair dryer with a black rubber grip and two sharp metal prongs at the business end.

"Hold it by the grip with your hand up close to the front. If someone tries to take it, the metal plates on the side will shock 'em just as bad as if you'd pulled the trigger."

He slowed the car and watched her examine the device. "Don't test it on yourself. I already made that mistake so you wouldn't have to. Now put your seatbelt on. You're gonna need it."

When she didn't do it, he brought the car to a full stop in the middle of the street.

"Listen, Claire. You want to get out, be my guest. I don't care. I already been paid for this job—"

"By whom," she snapped. "Who paid you?"

"Hell, I don't know."

"And for what?"

"Protection. Keep an eye on you."

"Protection from whom?"

"You tell me, woman."

"I don't know," Claire said.

He shook his head. "Now that's a problem. A person don't know who their enemies is, they's in real trouble. Buckle that belt so you don't go flyin' into the dash."

Without taking her eyes off him, she did as he said, holding the stun gun as he had told her, the sharp metal prongs within striking distance of his huge neck.

The car rolled forward toward the blue Chevy from which she had escaped a few minutes earlier.

"Your buddy right there…" he began in his slow drawl—then he punched the accelerator and aimed the giant Continental at Fake Darrell's rear bumper. On impact, the little Chevy shot forward thirty feet and came to rest against the back of an SUV.

"… is a nasty piece of work."

He steered the Continental into the middle lane and sped past the wrecked Chevy. "My feeling on him is he ain't gonna tell the cops about this. 'Cause a guy like that"—He laid on the gas to make the light at M Street and kept accelerating toward Connecticut Avenue—"he ain't working on the right side of the law. You know how I know?"

He turned and glanced at Claire.

"I saw him stealing your mail."

At Connecticut, he turned left, aiming the massive hood toward the tunnel beneath Dupont Circle.

"You tell me where we're headed," he said. "'Cause it ain't safe to go back to your place, and I ain't got a place."

Claire pointed the stun gun toward the windshield, pulled the trigger, and watched the crackling blue lightning dance between the steel prongs.

"Yeah, it works," the driver said.

Claire looked at him again, saw how he watched the road, untroubled, completely at ease, as if nothing had happened.

Then she looked at the floor, covered with Subway sandwich bags, each one stuffed with wrappers and napkins and other bags.

She opened the window as they pushed through the tunnel.

"Sorry I smell," said the man. "Happens when you live in a car too long."

"Who hired you?"

"Hell, I don't know."

"What do you mean, you don't know?"

"What do you think I mean?" He turned for a second to look at her as they emerged from the tunnel. "Long as I'm on the protectin' end of the job and not the hurtin' end, I don't need to know who hired me. Fact, I prefer not to. Them fellas escorting you through the alley back there might try to beat it out of me, and I feel better having nothing to tell 'em."

"How do you get paid then?"

He stopped at the red light at R Street and smiled at her. "You're like a—what is it you do? Some kind of accountant? It's always about the money with you people, ain't it? You don't need to concern yourself with my business. You look out for yourself."

"I do."

"I can see that." He hit the gas half a second before the light turned green and the car lurched forward.

"Do you have to take off like that?"

"Four hundred and sixty cubic inches, ain't no other way to do it."

"You were paid in bitcoin, or some cryptocurrency." That was a guess. The only other way money changed hands anonymously was in cash. She wanted to see his reaction.

"What? How'd you know— Listen, lady, you keep your speculations to yourself."

"From some soldier-for-hire site on the dark web? Is that it?"

When she saw his shoulders go up, she knew she was on the right track.

"Shit, woman. Keep your mouth shut, will you?"

"So it was Gavin. Gavin hired you to protect me because he did something wrong."

"Stop talking."

"But why would I need to be protected?"

"Well, you ain't too big. Got about as much meat on you as a starved dog."

"Shut up. I'm thinking."

"I wish you wouldn't have told me that name," he said. "Now they got something to beat out of me."

He punched the gas and rocketed through the light at Florida Avenue as it turned yellow.

"The less we know about each other, the better. And by the way, Miss Nosy—"

"It's mizz," Claire corrected. "Mizz."

"—I didn't like you checking up on me, talkin' to that fella that sold me Ole Bessie here. I didn't like that one bit."

"I never would have known," Claire said, remembering the angry scowl he had worn when he pulled up beside her last night. "You have a real poker face."

"Shit, lady, no wonder you ain't got no friends." He slalomed around a slow-moving car as they approached the Hilton. "With a mouth like that."

"Just drive."

"Where to, Claire? Where we gonna go?" He shot her a quick questioning glance. "Not your house. And not a hotel either, 'cause you need a credit for that, and if someone's after you they could be watching your accounts. And turn your damn phone off. They can track that too."

"I know a place," Claire said. She pulled her phone from her bag and turned it off. Then she clammed up at the thought of the isolated country house her grandmother had grown up in. It was more than an hour outside the city, far enough from the nearest neighbor that no one would be able to hear her scream. She looked warily through Leona's distrusting eyes at the giant beside her.

He seemed to read her thoughts. "If it makes you feel any better, I'm married."

She sat in silence as they passed California Street.

"And I want my wife back."

His own words seemed to wound him, and he repeated them softly under his breath. "I want her back."

When Claire showed no interest in pursuing the topic, he added, "She's talking to me now," glancing at her as if for approval. "She's warming to it. All I gotta do is not fuck it up, so don't you worry about me touching you 'cause it ain't gonna happen. My army buddies, we had a name for girls like you."

"I'm not a girl."

"O-M-L," he said. "Outta My League. I wouldn't mess with the likes of you even if I was single. When we get where we're going, I'll sleep in the car. Just tell me which way to point the wheels."

"North," said Claire. "Straight up Connecticut to the Beltway."

"All righty then."

His relaxed posture and easygoing manner puzzled her. The violent confrontation a mile back didn't seem to bother him at all. His temperament was the opposite of hers, she observed. She wanted to be certain of every outcome while he seemed to roll with whatever came his way.

As they passed Kalorama Road in silence, Claire thought back to what Ben Corley had said. Fake Darrell Gatlin, during his interrogation, had accused Gavin of stealing something and had asked if Mr. Corley received a package.

What would be in the package?

Gavin built and monitored secure computer systems. The kind people set up to guard secrets.

What people? What secrets?

Whoever they are, they're not very bright, Claire thought, being so obvious and clumsy in the way they had questioned her and Mr. Corley. If they truly suspected that I or old Ben Corley had what they were looking for, they would have sent their A team to try to retrieve it. God, I hope that's not their A team. I've seen so many poorly run organizations. So many incompetent—

Crap, what about Li? She's still in the hospital, traumatized. What's she going to think when I don't show up? But I can't go there. Those people have been in my house. They know where I am, even when I'm at work in the middle of the night. If they're the ones who attacked Li, would they be waiting for me to come see her? Would they attack me again?

I want to get out of this city. I want this all to be over. I want to sit with Peter in front of the TV and not think about anything.

"Got two daughters," the driver said proudly.

"Shut up, I'm thinking."

"Aw, come on now! I been alone in the cold for days with no one to talk to."

"So have I."

"Then you oughta have some sympathy."

"Just drive, Lincoln."

He slammed the brakes with all his strength, and the rusty rotors dragged the old tank to a lazy stop.

A panic flashed through her—what have I done? Enraged the giant.

Quick as lightning, she raised the stun gun to his chin. Zap that big fat face, burn his fucking eyes out of their sockets.

But he made no effort to attack her. He just stared, mouth agape in wonder and surprise.

"What?" Her eyes were wide with suspense and the stun gun shook in her hands as her finger tightened on the trigger.

"How the hell did you know my name?"

21

Lincoln proved to be quite a talker. On the drive to Frederick she learned more about him than she cared to know. He hadn't always weighed three hundred and twenty pounds, a fact he repeated no fewer than four times. In his fighting days in Iraq, he weighed two thirty-five. He wasn't no hero but he wasn't no slacker either. He woulda done a second tour if he hadn't injured hisself getting throwed from the back of a truck, and it wasn't even in combat, so it didn't count toward a purple heart.

Some of his friends came back all busted up and had good reason to be depressed, but old Lincoln was doing pretty well, except for not being able to get around so fast, and not being able to do some of the plumbing work he used to do, and crawlspaces was a problem now, and once he had to be dragged out of one because his hip locked up and it took three guys to haul him outta there and I tell you that was humiliating.

He hired an assistant who was skinny and nimble like a monkey to get into the tight spaces, but then customers started calling the assistant to do the work and leaving him out of it, and what kind of thanks was that for giving a man a job?

Old Lincoln wound up sitting around the house half the time and there wasn't nothing to do but eat and wait for someone to call about a busted pipe, so he got fat as hell and his wife made him sleep on the couch on account of his snoring.

It's a slow slide down that hill to where the only joy in life is another cheesesteak or two whole pizzas, he told her, and you gotta be on the lookout for the little things you start letting go, because you let go of them and pretty soon you let go of the big ones too. One day you wake up three hundred and twenty pounds and your wife is telling you to get out and you're standing there wondering what the hell happened.

Claire thought back to what Lincoln had said earlier, that he wished she hadn't mentioned the name of the person who had hired him, because if the bad guys caught him, they could beat it out of him. The way this guy blabbered, they wouldn't have to do much beating. Just sit him in a chair and wait five minutes.

Now he wasn't complaining about the state of his life, no sir, because he rekkonized he was responsible for his own damn self, and he'd patch things up with his wife, and he'd lose the weight because he was eating healthy now. Subway—that was the ticket to shedding the pounds—only it didn't work when you ate twelve of 'em a day, but he already had a plan to get that under control, and it was dead simple. Eat less.

Near Gaithersburg, he pulled to the side of the highway and cut the engine.

"What are you doing?" Claire asked.

He unbuckled his belt and was about to open the door. "This old girl burns oil. You smell that? I gotta top her off."

"Why didn't you just rent a car?"

"What? You mean, with my credit card? And my driver's license? That has my home address on it? Hell, why don't I just paint my name and phone number on the side of this one here?"

"So—what? You're like some secret agent? Covering your tracks and hiding your identity?"

"I don't need whoever's chasing you to come after my family."

"At least you could have gotten a decent car."

"Now why would I settle for a *decent* car when I could have a seventy-one Continental? This here is nineteen feet and five thousand pounds of American engineering glory, built right in the heart of the US of A." He stroked the dashboard. "Four hundred sixty cubic inches and the pride of Wixom, Michigan."

Claire let out a sigh.

"Hertz and Avis can keep their damn Hyundais." He got out, taking the keys with him, and opened the trunk. In a minute, he had the hood up and was pouring in a quart of oil.

"There now," he said as he got back in. "That didn't take but two minutes, and listen to her purr when I start her up." He turned the key and the old engine chugged to life.

"That sounded more like a hairball than a purr," Claire said.

He checked the side mirror and was about to shift into gear when his phone chimed.

His face lit up when he checked the screen. "Got another comment on my story."

"Why didn't you turn your phone off?" Claire asked. "You made me turn mine off."

"They ain't trackin' me. 'Sides, this here's a burner."

He told her he had contributed a story, "Gut Feeling," to a soldiers' blog called Zero Hour Survivor and all the reader comments were forwarded to his phone.

"People like this one because it's positive," he said, showing Claire the phone. The comment said, "Nice to come across one that isn't a horror story."

"Check this out. See this number?"

"I don't care," Claire said.

"That's his IP address. Gets forwarded with every comment. I can click on it and see where he is." He tapped and when the map showed Ansbach he turned the screen back to her. "That's a base in Germany. He's active duty. I can drill down right to the building he's sitting in." He zoomed in to show her. "Am I talking too much?"

"If this is how much you have to say," Claire sighed, "then you're talking just the right amount."

"I know, right! It's like the words got all backed up after all them days alone. And now I got a friendly ear, I just can't help myself."

She didn't mind him talking as much as she would have minded him asking questions. She always felt comfortable knowing more about the other person than they knew about her. By the time they reached Hyattstown, Claire was satisfied that he had no interest in harming her.

Lincoln's daughters, eight and twelve, were his pride and joy. Even though his wife was angry with him, she let him call each day to talk to the girls.

"Now I don't blame her for wantin' me out," he said. "I understand it ain't no picnic living with a depressed person. I was dragging her down every time she had a happy thought. She got fed up, said why don't you go back to Iraq? You talk about it like it was Disneyland."

He looked at Claire and said gravely, "It ain't no Disneyland, just in case you're thinking of going."

Then he proceeded to his war story. She knew it was coming, and she hoped it would be brief.

"You hear about these guys coming back with PTSD," he said, "well I got lucky. The guys who's all messed up, they didn't see it coming, didn't know what hit 'em till it was too late. Me, I had the opposite happen. I was driving back to base with my boys and I checked in with a buddy on routine patrol about a mile away. I picked up the radio and I says, 'How's it going?' And he says 'All quiet on the western front.' And, Claire, I can't tell you why but them words just made my guts churn. I knew something bad was gonna happen. I turned off the road and headed over to where he was. Me and my boys got there just in time.

"There was an ambush waitin'. It would have been four of their guys against two of ours. But we showed up just in the nick of time. Made it four of them against six of us, and they didn't have a stomach for them odds. They squeezed out a few shots then turned tail and ran. We musta pumped out a hundred and fifty rounds. Wounded three. The other one got away."

He turned to see Claire's reaction.

"You want this exit," she said, pointing ahead. "Route fifteen."

He nudged the wheel and the battleship drifted right.

"OK, it ain't the most exciting war story, but it got me thinking. Why'd them words turn my guts like that? Why did I know something bad was going to happen?"

"Stay right," Claire said. "Go into the shopping center."

"You know why?"

"Why?"

"Angels," he said.

"Head over to CVS. We need some things for the house."

"Angels reached into my gut and gave it a twist to tell me I had to get over there and help my buddy."

As they approached the drugstore Claire said, "We need water, toothpaste, soap, shampoo. I want you to shower when we get in."

"I smell that bad?"

"Yup."

"Well thank you for not complaining the whole way."

"You're welcome. Thank you for helping me out back there. Now turn that phone off."

He did.

22

The one-story bungalow west of Frederick where Leona had grown up sat atop a cinderblock foundation thirty yards off the road. To the east was a small wood. Rolling pastures surrounded the other three sides.

It was cold when they entered the main room—a combination living room, dining room, and kitchen—their footsteps echoing on an old plank floor as bare and hard as Leona Chastain herself.

Claire turned up the heat on the baseboards. Lincoln set a bag of Chinese food on the stained Formica counter beside the stove, then carried the soap and shampoo into the bathroom.

The recently departed tenants had left a sagging grey couch that reminded Claire of an old swayback mule that once inhabited the neighboring pasture. An upside-down wooden chair and a folding card table leaned against the far wall. One bedroom was empty, except for an ironing board with broken legs and a set of blinds crumpled on the floor. The other bedroom had a broken lamp, two empty beer cans, and a futon mattress hemorrhaging bright white stuffing through a footlong gash. Claire inspected it for stains and bedbugs before returning to the living room.

The smell of the Chinese food, usually so appealing in the cold of winter, made her feel anxious and tense.

When Lincoln returned, "all fresh and pretty," as he put it, he went straight to the food. Claire noticed that he winced when his weight was on his right leg, and that he favored his left.

Seeing the food unopened, he said, "You didn't have to wait for me."

"I'm not hungry."

"You gotta be hungry. Unless those guys scared away your appetite." He opened one cabinet and then another. "Hey, uh... There ain't no plates in here."

"Nope."

"Chinese tastes better outta the box anyway." He opened a container, smelled it, and seemed to approve.

"You ain't got no meat on your bones, and I can tell by your skin you don't eat enough."

Claire touched her face. "What's wrong with my skin?"

"It's dry and pale."

"It's winter."

"Uh huh. Which explains your defensive tone. Just sayin' some food'll do you good. I ain't judgin'. In my family, everyone eats too much, like me, or not at all, like my sister. It's a soul sickness. Means something ain't going right in your life."

He reached into the bag and pulled out a plastic fork. "Hope you don't mind sharing from the box."

"Go ahead and eat it all. I'm really not hungry."

Something clicked in her mind. She pulled her laptop from her bag as Lincoln carried his food to the couch. She watched as he stood looking at the sagging relic.

"Think it'll hold me?" he asked with a smile. "One way to find out."

He aimed his immensity toward the left side, avoiding the slumping middle. The couch groaned but didn't collapse.

"Now there's a good sign," he said cheerfully. "If I'd a fell over, the food woulda gone over too, and that woulda been a tragedy."

Claire picked up the chair by the far wall and set it beside the couch.

She opened her laptop while Lincoln ate.

"There Wi-Fi in here?" he asked through a mouthful of food. "We gonna watch Netflix?" He stabbed the tiny plastic fork into the box and frowned as the tines bent on the cashews.

"No."

"I was kiddin'," Lincoln said, watching the oily food slide off the fork. "Why they make these forks so slippery? Whole point is to pick *up* the food. What are you doing anyway? Work?"

She ignored him as she examined the spreadsheet the PharmaCore manager had asked her to delete. She scanned the rows that showed the quantities of raw materials and the number of doses produced for each of the company's drugs.

Why was this information in a spreadsheet on some manager's computer and not in the central database?

She remembered what Li had said, how the company's prospectus had bragged that it wasted less than one percent of raw materials. But the spreadsheet showed it wasted over sixteen percent of materials for—-which drug was it? Oxycodone, their generic version of the opioid painkiller. The numbers showed enough raw material for two million doses more than had been produced.

She scanned the rest of the data. The only other medicine that showed such waste was hydrocodone. Another opioid. There was virtually no waste in the production of non-opioids.

She remembered the angry message from the manager. *Delete the damn spreadsheet.* And the beacon, the hidden link that tried to load data from a remote server. It would have alerted the PharmaCore manager that Li had the spreadsheet as well. Whoever had mugged Li had taken her laptop, but not her phone. The cop had called from Li's phone.

If the muggers wanted money, they would have taken the phone. But they wanted the laptop. And they had beaten Li. Claire was sure that wasn't necessary. Li would have handed over whatever her attackers demanded. But they wanted to send a message, just as they'd wanted to send a message when they'd ripped apart the house on Oregon Avenue and clogged the toilet with her underwear.

She remembered the PharmaCore manager's other message. *I know it came from my email. But I didn't send it. My account was hacked while I was out of the country.*

Now it all fell into place. Gavin, with his hacking skills. Gavin, who had hired Lincoln to protect her. Gavin, who had stolen something that Fake Darrell wanted back.

"I can see your mind whirlin' like a tornado," Lincoln said through a mouthful of food.

She stood abruptly from the chair, set the laptop on the counter, and pulled the boxes of migraine medicine from her shoulder bag. She knew now what had seemed off about them. A quick look confirmed it. The blank white space on the rear of the boxes had no expiration date and no lot number.

When she was certifying PharmaCore's earnings statement, she came across a line item: four hundred thousand dollars to overhaul their track-and-trace compliance system. She had looked up track and trace from her desk at work. Every medicine container the company shipped was stamped with a lot number. If they shipped any bad meds, they knew which lots to recall, which pharmacies they'd been sent to, even which patients received them.

The Drug Enforcement Administration used lot numbers to track controlled substances like oxycodone. They knew exactly how much was produced at each facility, where the pills were shipped, and when.

But what if PharmaCore was producing pills off the books, with no lot numbers and no record of production in their central database? Who would know the drugs had ever been made? What if they were sending doses out the back door, packaged as migraine meds, blood pressure meds, pills the DEA didn't care about?

What if the only record of their existence was in a spreadsheet that belonged to some anonymous manager?

Still, she thought, the drugs had to be distributed. Getting two million pills onto the streets, funneling the money back to the producer—how would you coordinate all that without being discovered? Especially a pharma company whose whole production process, whose every transaction was tracked by federal regulators and compliance auditors?

You couldn't manage the logistics of an opioid racket on the company's internal systems. No way.

You'd set up a secure server somewhere outside to handle encrypted communications, track inventory and cash flow. Maybe that's what Gavin had stumbled into. Just the kind of conspiracy to trigger his I-told-you-so paranoia. He was already convinced Big Pharma was an organized drug cartel. Why not expose them when he had the chance? He could have even set the servers up himself. Wasn't that what Voynich Systems did?

If Gavin had been hooked on opioids after his accident, hooked to the point that he was stealing meds from his dying father, maybe his annoyance with this particular conspiracy was more than just a matter of principle. Maybe he took it personally.

She remembered his paranoid breakdown at the end of high school, hacking the public schools' internal network, stealing data, his father committing him to the psychiatric hospital.

When she had visited him there, he was calm and rational. "I can't right every wrong in this world," he told her. "But when it's personal, I'm going to stand up for myself and make them sorry for screwing me."

She looked at Lincoln across the counter.

"Shit," she said. "He would."

Lincoln pried open a box of fried rice and licked his fingers. "What in the world is chuggin' through that brain of yours?"

"Remember what you said to me? That a person who doesn't know who their enemies are is in real trouble? Well I think I just figured it out."

She explained everything she'd just thought through.

"Well I'll be damned," said Lincoln.

"I don't think I'm in any less trouble for knowing who's after me," she said. "In fact, I'm more nervous now than I was before. Right before Gavin died—"

"Whoa!" Lincoln exclaimed. "He died?"

"Seven days ago. No, eight? I can't keep track of the days."

"How'd he die?"

"Alcohol poisoning."

"I'd be a drinker too if cheeseburgers didn't taste so damn good. He a vet?"

"No, listen. Before he died, he lost his job. Apparently for stealing something. And that guy whose car you smashed up back on Eighteenth Street—"

"What's his name?" Lincoln asked sharply.

"I don't know. He came to my house pretending to be a cop. He told me his name was Darrell Gatlin. But he's Fake Darrell. Well, Fake Darrell also paid a visit to Gavin's father. He asked whether Gavin had dropped anything off or sent a package. Now if Gavin stole something—"

"A server or a hard drive," Lincoln said. "Full of evidence. Them drug companies is pushers. A couple of my buddies got hooked on them pills when they come back from Iraq. I was on 'em myself, for my hip. Turned me into a zombie. They constipate you too. I didn't want nothin' to do with 'em after a couple a days."

"Slow down," Claire said.

"You want some chicken?" He was opening another carton.

"I need time to think."

"'Bout how you're gonna overthrow a big corporation? Good luck with that. You like General Tso's? This one's a little sweet, but it hits the spot."

"No thanks." She thought about Gavin's last message. *I'm pretty sure I screwed this up, so I'm passing the torch to you. If worse comes to worst, I know you'll see it through.*

You screwed up all right. Why'd you have to drag me into it?

Thanks, Gavin. Thanks for passing the torch of your paranoia. Now I have to look over my shoulder all the time like you did. Now I have to doubt everyone, suspect everyone, look for hidden motives, second guess my every move. Thank you very much for that. Someone should have listened to you. Someone should have paid attention to the red flags, put you on meds for your own good.

She thought about the burglary. The only things she was sure were missing were her iPad and Leona's hard drive. They were looking for files. If they had found them, they might have left her alone.

Lincoln stabbed the plastic fork into a chunk of chicken. "I understand now why your friend paid me so much."

"How much did he pay you?"

"Never you mind, Miss Accountant."

"It's mizz. Get it straight, will you? Mizz!"

"But I'm starting to think it wasn't enough," he said as he chewed. "With him dead and you being chased by that fake cop, and them two in the alley. You're in some kinda trouble, lady."

"I'm not a lady."

"OK, princess. Don't get snippy with the help. I'm here to protect you and I got two more days on my contract."

"Two days?"

"If your buddy's dead, I don't expect he'll be paying me for the second week."

"What happens in two days?"

"I go home. Get back with the wife and kids. She's the one said I needed an adventure. She said go ahead and take one of them soldier of fortune jobs you keep looking at on that website. Go play tough guy again so you can feel like a man. Snap you outta your damn depression."

"Do you feel like a man now?"

"A hungry ass man. Big fat ass bottomless pit of a man. You better eat some of this 'fore you shrivel up and disappear."

"I don't want any."

"I'll make you a box, good and healthy to put some meat on your bones. Mizz Claire."

23

In the morning she felt the vibrations of Lincoln's footsteps through the cold wood floor. She was on the futon mattress in the room with the broken lamp, her mouth and throat parched by the dry baseboard heat.

When she heard the couch groan and the crumple of paper, she knew he was eating. In a moment she smelled steak. He must have made a food run while she was sleeping. She checked her phone for the time, but it was still turned off. Judging by the height of the sun, it was past nine o'clock.

She had been up late listening to Lincoln snore. She didn't have the heart to make him sleep in the car, so she told him to take the couch. She wondered how a woman put up with that kind of noise in her bed. Peter didn't snore.

She found Lincoln in the living room finishing a steak sandwich. He pointed to a Subway wrapper on the baseboard heater. "Got you spinach and egg whites on a flatbread. I figured you was finicky. The oven don't turn on but the heater keeps it warm. There's coffee on the counter."

To her surprise, she was hungry. She ate standing at the kitchen counter. The sandwich tasted good, and the coffee quickened her mind, but her thoughts made her feel anxious and ill: Fake Darrell and his comrades; her grandmother, needy and thankless; Peter all alone; and herself, the betrayer.

"Nice to sleep on a couch," Lincoln said, "after all them nights in the car. After the automobile, the couch is the finest invention ever made. You can eat on it, sleep on it, watch the Super Bowl, make babies, have babies. Our second was born on the couch 'cause my wife didn't think the contractions were close enough together until... Well I don't want to get too graphic while you're eatin'. 'Sides, you look like you're ready to puke anyway. You OK?"

"My stomach is off. It's stress."

Lincoln crumpled his sandwich wrapper and dropped it on the card table.

"She didn't want to talk to me this morning," he said.

His leading tone told Claire he wanted her to ask him about the call so he could unburden himself. She gave him an encouraging look and he continued.

"Passed me straight off to the girls. Ella has a science test today. She was nervous. Always does well, but you gotta remind her she's smart before she starts to doubt herself. You like that sandwich?"

"It's OK."

"That's the kind of thing I'm s'posed to be eating if I want to watch my figure. But it just don't hit the spot like a big old pile of beef."

Claire sipped her coffee as he continued.

His wife was mad at him, he surmised, because she had to run the household alone while he was away, which was a problem of her own making, because she's the one who told him to get out in the first place, and he could fix that just by going back, but not till she quit being so damn angry, which wasn't gonna happen because she was stubborn, and (he suspected) she liked being mad at him because it kept her from having to think about her own damn problems.

"You're quite the psychologist," Claire observed.

"You have to be when you're married."

"Hey, um..." She looked around for a towel to wipe her hands and finding none, she wiped them on her pants. That drew a smile from Lincoln.

"You're loosening up," he said.

"What's it like? To be forced out? To be apart? I mean, how does that feel from your perspective?"

He gave her a strangely knowing look that made her uncomfortable.

"What's it like to have your woman reject you? Is that what you're asking? It hurts is what it's like. It makes me angry and it makes me wanna fix the problem, 'cause I'm a problem solver is what I am. Only, like I said, she's stubborn, and she don't seem to want the problem solved as bad as I do."

The couch groaned as he leaned back, his eyes fixed on her. "You know that's the first real question you've asked me. First time I saw any genuine interest in your eyes. Now I got a question for you. What is it makes a woman not want to eat?"

His bluntness made her uncomfortable.

"When it's cold out and you're too skinny to keep warm, it ain't natural to avoid food. It's like you're trying to shrivel up and disappear."

"I'm not anorexic, if that's what you're saying."

"I didn't say that. I just said maybe something's eating *you* instead of you eating something, which is the way things is s'posed to work. You want to talk about it? 'Cause you got a nice pair of diamond studs in your ears that I know didn't come from that grandma of yours."

Claire startled at the mention of Leona.

"Yeah, I seen her," Lincoln said. "I'm following you, remember? She don't strike me as the generous type, so who gave you the diamonds? 'Cause, you know, every time you get that sad lost-in-thought look, you start twisting 'em around like you're tryin' to wind yourself back up."

Claire thought about that unconscious action. She knew she did it sometimes, but she hadn't remembered doing it on the car ride from DC, or while they talked last night. She hadn't noticed that he'd been observing her closely enough to pick up on that.

"Who gave 'em to you?"

Claire took a breath and girded herself. Opening up was not her specialty, but if this man could talk so freely about himself and his life, why shouldn't she be able to do the same? She saw it as a challenge and the only way to know whether she could meet it was to try.

"My boyfriend," she said softly.

"What's he like?"

"He's sad. I left him."

Lincoln waited for her to go on, but she didn't. She just looked down at her coffee, lost in thought.

"You feel bad about it," he said.

"Very. It makes me not want to eat."

He waited again, but she would say no more, so he sat quietly and watched the emotions register on her face as she thought.

I made a mistake, she told herself. I acted out of panic. I can't even say I acted. I *reacted*. I didn't think because I couldn't. He wanted to give his life to me, but I wasn't in a position to accept it, and I couldn't tell him that. I couldn't even have told myself, because there were no words, just panic. If I had it to do over again, I would tell him I need more time. But I don't have it to do over again. He cared enough to ask the most important question of his life. He trusted me enough to be that vulnerable, and I abandoned him. I can't forgive myself for that. They say that when everything is on the line, you find out who you really are. Well, I never thought I'd be a coward, but that's what I am.

Lincoln leaned back, picking at his teeth. He pulled his index finger from his mouth and said, "You're being too hard on yourself, Claire. It shows in your face."

"You think?" she asked testily. "Well I don't think so. He'll never speak to me again, and I don't blame him. I did the worst thing a person could ever do to another person. If someone abandoned me like that, I would never forgive them."

"You sure about that?"

"Of course I'm sure."

But it struck her now that she wasn't sure. Hadn't her own father abandoned her? And hadn't she fantasized her whole life about meeting him and patching things up? About developing a real, healthy relationship? Hadn't she wished a thousand times that that wound would heal, would grow into something positive, something beautiful and good?

"You're like a poker player who likes to hold his cards close," Lincoln said. "Don't wanna tip your hand to nobody. But I can tell you're thinking about it. You better ask yourself again. You sure there's no forgiveness?"

Claire shook her head.

"Is that no, there's no forgiveness, or no you're not sure?"

"I don't know. What am I supposed to do? Call him? Show up at his apartment?" It was *his* apartment now, not theirs.

Lincoln shrugged. "If that's what it takes."

"And what would I tell him?"

"Tell him you're sorry. You made a mistake. What's holding you back? Pride?"

"Shame."

"Then tell him you're ashamed. You said you already did the worst thing a person could ever do. So what's the harm in talking to him? You afraid he'll reject you?"

"I'm afraid he'll tell me I'm every bit as horrible as I think I am."

"Then you two will be a little closer to even, a hurt for a hurt, and maybe you'll feel less guilty. But are you sure he'll reject you?"

Claire shook her head. "I don't let myself think about it. I'm afraid he won't take me back, and I'm afraid he will."

"Now that's a quandary," Lincoln said. He sat forward and rubbed his chin as he thought through the matter. "What did you like about him?"

"He's patient and easygoing," Claire said. "He gets me. He calls me out when I'm not being honest with myself. Little things bother him, but big things don't."

"What's a little thing?"

"Him cutting his finger. Scuffing his shoe. Being late for work. Not having enough time to brush his teeth."

"What's a big thing?"

"Me losing my temper. Me being a bitch. When I found that ring..."

She didn't say the rest out loud.

I was paralyzed with fear. And then I was angry. At him, for making me so scared. I wasn't over moving in yet. I wasn't ready to give up the next piece of my independence, my identity. I packed two bags, wrote the note, and left. What did he do when he got home? When he saw the drawers I'd left open? The mess? The ring on the dresser with the note? How did he react? What kind of person would do that to another person? What is wrong with me?

"Claire?"

Looking up at him, she knew he had seen everything she'd just been feeling.

"You all right?"

She shook her head silently.

"How long were you two together?"

"About a year."

"Living together the whole time?"

"Just the last month."

"Hmm." Lincoln tapped his fingers on his knees and thought. "What if you told him everything that was just going through your head?"

"I couldn't."

"But what if?"

She shook her head. "I'm too ashamed."

24

After breakfast, she had to get out. The old couch, the broken ironing board, the torn mattress were the castoffs of people who seemed to have left in a hurry, as she had done when she fled Peter. The house reeked of abandonment. The coldness of the place, the emptiness, made her think of Peter in the apartment without her, of Leona's bare, unfurnished soul, of the sense of absence that had clung to her throughout her childhood.

She asked Lincoln if he wanted to walk with her, knowing he'd refuse. The way he limped on that injured hip, a five-minute stroll might be too much to ask, and she knew she'd be gone longer than that. But she wanted him to know she wasn't just walking out on him.

"You go," he said. "Seems like you got some things to think about."

She walked along the road past horse and cow pastures, moving to the frozen shoulder when cars passed. Clouds had crept in over the western hills, and her breath steamed white in the moistening air. She turned her collar up against the wind and felt the lack of flesh on her bones in the penetrating cold.

She thought through her problems as she walked, wanting to solve them intellectually so she could return with a plan of action, but her life was a tangle of unsolvable troubles. Peter was a bridge permanently burned. Her grandmother's hostility would likely get worse. The house on Oregon Avenue was unsafe, a place she could neither stay nor leave. Her future was a big empty question mark.

Peter knew me, she reminded herself. He knew which parts of my life I had together and which parts I didn't. He knew why I worked all the time. At work, everything went right. They kept giving me tougher assignments, more hours and more responsibility. And he was always trying to pull me away from that. "Shift gears, Claire. Slow down. Life isn't all about work." I didn't like him telling me what to do. Even if he was just asking, it felt like telling. I was succeeding at something, and he wanted to take it away. That's how it felt at the time. But I know where his heart was. When I'm not angry, not in the moment, I can see it all more clearly.

He would say, "You're never content." And I would say, "You're too content."

She bit her nails as she walked.

He'd say I had too much ambition, and I'd say he had too little. He'd say, "You need balance in your life. Working eighty hours a week isn't healthy. You don't even spend all the money you earn."

"Yes, but I have it. If there ever comes a day when I can't work, I'll have the money."

"Why would you worry about that?"

"Why wouldn't I?"

"One day you're going to wake up and find that that job can never give you back all the emotional energy you poured into it. It'll give you money and prestige, but it won't give you an emotional life."

"I don't want an emotional life."

"That's what you think. But I know you. You can't hide everything from everyone, as hard as you may try."

"Don't tell me what I want."

And when I talked to my friends, they all seemed to take his side. At least, they weren't one hundred percent on my side, which is what I needed, because he was starting to make me feel uncertain.

Thinking back now on her twenties, she remembered how annoying her friends had been with all their dating dramas, all the emotional energy they had sunk into relationships with men. If they had put that energy toward something productive, some career with measurable progress, they could have gone so much further.

But now she saw it from a different angle. Working out trust issues takes time and effort, more for some people than for others. Her friends had done the hard work in their twenties. She hadn't.

Her mind went back to Peter. God, if I couldn't get along with him, who *can* I get along with? I'm going to end up like Leona, alone and bitter, if I don't do something now.

I have to change. Because it's not just about me anymore. I've already hurt one person. I'll hurt more if I don't fix myself.

But what can I do? My life is a mess. What can I do *now*? What problems can I solve *today*?

Her mind drifted back to her job. Next week would bring a new project, a new set of numbers to certify, and she hoped it would involve travel. She hoped their books would be a mess, their internal documents hopelessly disorganized, requiring long hours and deep absorption.

She thought of Li, whose public face needed hardening. No—Li needed consoling. She had forgotten about that. Li needed to feel safe again first. Then she needed a mentor.

And she thought of how, if she by chance encountered Lincoln's wife (purely a fantasy) she would gently lecture her on the corrosive effects of pride and stubbornness and poor communication in relationships, on how ill will, anger, and resentment can destroy even the strongest bonds. Love, Claire would tell her, is not to be scorned.

When the snow began to fall and her nose was red and her hands were freezing in the pockets of her woolen coat, she stopped and looked in bewilderment at the road behind her.

How far did I walk?

Over an hour, it turned out. The walk back seemed to take twice as long, and when she arrived at the house, the old Continental wasn't there. A note in the kitchen said he had gone for food and would be back soon.

By the time Lincoln returned, it was past two. He brought her another sandwich, an apple, and an orange.

"I want to go back," she said.

"Where?"

"DC. I can't stay here. This place is depressing."

"Yeah, but where are you going to sleep? You can't go home. Not with those guys after you."

"I have a friend in the police department in PG County. I can call her."

"But you don't live in PG County. What could she do anyway? Assign a guard? You already got one of them."

Claire wasn't listening. "Or I could stay with a friend." That was a lie. In the fourteen years since she'd graduated high school and left the city, she had fallen out of touch with the friends of her youth.

"And put them at risk?" Lincoln asked.

"Li needs help."

"Who the hell is Lee?"

"Look, I have to *do* something, OK? I can't just sit around and think about problems that have no answers. Take me to the office."

"That's where those guys tried to pick you up last night."

"They wouldn't try that in the daytime. Not with all the people around downtown. And I can talk to the cops. They know my situation."

"But then where are you going to go?" Lincoln asked in a tone that told her she wasn't being reasonable. "When the workday's done, where you gonna lay your head?"

"Goddamnit, what the hell do you care?" She had already run as far as she could, and now he was trying to corner her, to push her back against the wall, and that was something everyone who knew her knew not to do, because when she couldn't run, she fought.

"You need to go far away," Lincoln said. "Till this blows over. Why don't you go back to New York?"

"No," she said flatly. "Absolutely not." She eyed him angrily, as if he'd been trying to shove her into a fire.

Lincoln sighed in frustration. "Alright, lady. It's your life."

The snow had been falling lightly for two hours, leaving a dusting on the roads. The old Lincoln with its worn tires and rear-wheel drive didn't do well on the slick surface. Until they reached the salted interstate, they had to proceed at a maddeningly slow pace.

Approaching Gaithersburg, Claire decided it would be safe to turn on her phone and check her messages. To her disappointment, none of the two dozen emails in her inbox required action. The one from Anoop said, "Stay home and relax! Your work will still be here when you get back." She deleted it.

She called Li, who didn't answer. So she left a message. "Hang in there, Li. Take some time to rest. I'll come by and see you as soon as I can."

Lincoln gave her the side-eye and muttered, "Try taking your own advice."

A voicemail from a nurse said Leona was being difficult, asking why her daughter kept failing to show up for their dinner dates.

Her daughter, Claire thought. Was that a mistake on the nurse's part, or had Leona forgotten again that her daughter was dead? Did she now think Claire was her daughter?

Claire called the home.

"Tell her I'll be there in an hour. I'll take her somewhere nice."

She told Lincoln to aim for Bethesda, to drop her off at Rollingwood.

"And where am I supposed to go?" Lincoln asked.

"Take a few hours off."

"And do what?"

"I don't know. What do you do with your free time?"

"Turn that phone off," Lincoln snapped. "All the way off."

25

The snow fell fast and thick on Rockville Pike. An accident south of White Flint blocked all but one lane, backing up traffic for over a mile. The flashing red and blue of emergency vehicles lit the glittering flakes like Christmas lights in a snow globe.

When they finally reached the site of the collision, Lincoln let out a whistle. "They musta slid out. That Mazda got her whole side kicked in. Hope there wasn't no one in the passenger seat."

It took thirty more minutes to reach the curving lane of Rollingwood. By then the snow was four inches deep. The storm had hit harder here than up north in Frederick. The road was blocked at one end by a plow whose driver was in the street arguing with a man whose car he had just plowed in.

"Drop me here," Claire said.

Lincoln came to a stop fifty feet behind the plow. "You gonna walk?"

"It's one block." She pointed forward. The colonial bricks of Rollingwood were just visible through the swirling flakes.

"In those heels?"

"I'm not going to sit here and wait for those two to work out their problems."

She opened the door as the plowman and the motorist continued their dispute.

"How you gonna get to a restaurant?" Lincoln asked. "You ain't got a car."

"Ever heard of Uber?"

"I'll drive you."

"Give yourself a break." She closed the door and he watched her fade into the thickening snow, determined to do something, it seemed, anything but sit passively and feel like she wasn't in control.

In the fading light, her head tilted down against the pelting flakes, she wasn't looking where she was going, didn't see the idling black car, the men getting out of it. Men who knew where her grandmother lived.

Lincoln laid on the horn, letting out a long uneven wail. In the gray distance, she turned as if to ask, What?

Her back was to them now. The big man who had emerged from the passenger door took her by the throat. The short man grabbed her arm. They seemed to pull in opposite directions, yanking her half out of her coat as they forced her violently into the back seat.

26

This time, there were three of them. This time, they took her coat off and stuck a needle in her thigh. When she awoke, her hands were bound with plastic police ties.

The small man beside her, the one holding her shoes, was grinning.

"Next time I stick you," he said with a creepy glint in his eye, "it'll be with something bigger. And we'll see if you're as frigid as you look."

"Shut up back there." That was the driver. Claire looked up to see him glaring in the rearview.

She recognized his voice and his short, reddish-blond hair. He wore a rigid neck brace—from getting rear-ended by the Continental last night, Claire thought—and the right side of his face was bruised. The swollen wounds beside his eye strained against the butterfly stitches, oozing a shiny liquid. His ear was bright red, lumpy and inflamed.

"Don't tell me to shut up," the little man barked.

"Shut up!" slurred the big man in the passenger seat. He was the source of the foul alcohol odor.

"Both of you shut up," said the driver. "Her friend is still on our tail."

Claire looked at the man beside her. He seemed to be shorter than her, probably by two or three inches. His dark hair was thinning on top. His round nose and thick strong shoulders made him look like a stocky little Napoleon.

"Why'd you let him catch up?" he asked in a smart-alec tone.

"I didn't *let* him catch up." The driver looked again into the rearview. His right eye was bloodshot. "He's damn persistent is what he is. I'm surprised he hasn't wrecked yet, the way that old boat fishtails in the snow. How you doing, Claire?" He seemed to try to turn when he addressed her, but the brace prevented him. "You ready for your payback?"

A glimpse of the Lincoln's cockeyed yellow headlights flashed in the mirror.

"If I was driving," said Napoleon, "I would have shaken that guy twenty minutes ago."

Twenty minutes, Claire thought. He's been following for at least twenty minutes. Maybe forty or sixty. We must be far from Bethesda. She looked out the window but saw no signs or streetlights, just snowy woods beneath a starless sky.

Why hadn't Lincoln just rammed them, she wondered. Maybe he worried about hurting her. In this snow, the car would go off the road, the men would get out and it would be three on one. The driver with the neck brace, the big drunk, and Napoleon against the limping giant. And what if they had guns? What if there was a shootout?

"The reason you're not driving," Fake Darrell said to Napoleon, "is because we don't have a booster seat high enough for you see over the dash."

The little man drew a gun from his coat and pointed it at the back of the driver's head.

"You *are* stupid enough to shoot me, aren't you?" Fake Darrell said. He glanced in the rearview. "Let me tell you what'll happen if you pull that trigger. We'll run off the road and hit one of those trees. Then Claire here will kick the shit out of you."

"Like she did to you last night?" Napoleon taunted.

"Shut up," snapped the driver.

"Stop saying that." Napoleon's sulky tone told Claire the driver was getting under his skin.

"Then her redneck boyfriend," Fake Darrell continued, "the human garbage disposal, will finish you off."

"You're right," said Napoleon, leaning forward with the gun. "For once in your goddamn pathetic life, you're right. I'll wait till we stop, then I'll shoot you."

"And what'll you do about André the Giant back there?"

"I'll make him sorry he ever tried to mess with the likes of me."

"Uh huh. You see what he did to your buddies in the alley last night?"

Napoleon didn't respond. He slid his gun back into his coat and looked out the window.

"Because if you had, you wouldn't be shooting your mouth off."

The man in the passenger seat began to snore. "Goddamn drunk," the driver muttered. "I tell him it's a work night and he shows up with a flask."

Napoleon turned to Claire, leering at her with deliberate creepiness to make her uncomfortable. When she refused to show discomfort, he pushed her folded coat off her lap and put his hand on the inside of her thigh, still with his taunting eyes fixed on hers.

She elbowed him hard in the throat. He let out a grunt and started to cough.

"Serves you right," said Fake Darrell. Claire could see his grin in the rearview. "This is work, Pee Wee, not date night. Keep your hands to yourself."

"Bitch hit me right in the throat."

"If you had tied her hands behind her back," the driver replied, "like a professional, she wouldn't have been able to do that. So who's at fault here? Huh?"

"Just drive, you fucking ape."

"Shut up."

Again, Claire caught a glimpse of the headlights' reflection as the Lincoln bobbed over a bump. The car she was in had gone over the same bump a second and a half earlier. She did the calculation in her head. One and a half seconds at thirty miles an hour—an unsafe speed on a snowy country road—would put the Lincoln about 75 feet behind.

Why such a distance, she wondered. Then she remembered how the brakes had barely managed to stop the car on Connecticut Avenue, even when he slammed them.

"Look at him slide!" the driver crowed, watching the rearview. "Those tires have no tread."

Claire heard the Continental's giant engine knocking and sputtering as it got closer. Then it began to choke.

Please, she thought. Please don't tell me he's out of gas.

The old tank had driven from Frederick to DC earlier that day, with lots of idle time in snarled traffic. And then it followed them from Bethesda to wherever they were now. She thought back to the previous night, to their stop at the CVS in Frederick. He hadn't filled the tank then, after the long drive up from DC. He had to be running on fumes.

"Here he comes," Napoleon said with a smile as the knocking engine roared. "In for the kill."

"Face front, you dumbass!" barked the driver. "Unless you want to be wearing one of these." He meant the neck brace.

Fake Darrell hit the gas and the car rocketed forward just before the charging Continental could make contact.

It never did hit.

Claire's heart sank as she heard the old engine sputter out.

"Well look at that," Napoleon gloated. "Your buddy's dropping back. He's giving up!" He turned to Claire with a grin. "Your buddy quit! He just up and quit on you!"

Claire closed her eyes and said silently to herself, "He didn't quit. He wouldn't leave me. He wouldn't." As if his loyalty were more important than the fact that she now had only her wits to protect her.

27

"That was too damn close," Fake Darrell said.

"Lighten up," said Napoleon. "We lost him a mile and a half back."

"Did you just tell me to lighten up?"

"You heard me."

"Great. If he shows up, I'll send you out to fight him." The drunk passenger let out a piggish snore and Fake Darrell added, "You and gin blossom here."

Claire had noted every detail of her surroundings since the old Continental gave up the chase. They had turned right off the road less than two minutes after dropping Lincoln. She calculated they had covered a mile or so in that time. Then they had gone right again, straight for half a minute, then left. After one more minute, they made a final left onto a dark narrow road. She could tell from the bumps it wasn't paved.

They descended through the woods and came to a stop before a small brick house in a clearing.

"Wake up!" Fake Darrell snapped. He shook the shoulder of the man beside him. "Wake up, you goddamn sop!"

The man grumbled, turned, and slumped against the door.

"Fucking drunk." He tried to turn to Napoleon, but the brace stopped him, so he said into the rearview, "Take her shoes off."

"I already did." Napoleon held up the shoes so he could see them in the mirror.

When they forced her out, the cold snow stung her bare feet. The two men walked on either side of her.

"You're not getting those heels back," Fake Darrell said. "You crafty little bitch."

"I wouldn't have let her hit me like that," Napoleon said. "I don't take shit from women."

"How could you? They don't even give you the time of day."

"What's that supposed to mean?"

"Shut up, Pee Wee."

"Stop telling me to shut up, goddamnit!"

The small brick building had a single door, lit from above by a bare bulb. To the left was a tiny snow-covered car. A Mini or a Fiat. Light green doors, the color of the Vespa scooters she'd seen all over Italy. It had to be a Fiat. Did that mean another person was waiting inside? Her fear continued to rise.

Fear won't help you, she reminded herself. Thinking will. Observe. Think. Prepare.

She looked again at the building. The windows were protected by crosshatched steel screens, like a chain-link fence, with spaces just large enough to put your fingers through. They were bolted into the brick, probably to keep people out, Claire thought, though they'd serve just as well to keep people in.

The building was too small to be a residence. Claire had seen structures like it belonging to the power company or the water utility. They contained pumps or switches, or at least so she imagined. The doors said Keep Out and no one but utility servicemen ever went into them.

She noted the wires at the top right corner of the building. They ran off into the woods. Two of them. One for power, since something had to supply the burning bulb, and one, perhaps, for communications.

She quietly tucked these observations away with the others. Napoleon had her shoes, her bag, her coat, and a gun. Her hands were tied in front of her, not behind. Fake Darrell stoked Napoleon's inferiority complex. They didn't like each other. Fake Darrell was disabled by his neck brace. The snoring drunk in the car would likely be asleep for some time.

Watch quietly, she told herself, note their weaknesses and blind spots, their interpersonal dynamic, their exploitable flaws, and every aspect of the environment. Build an arsenal of facts to arm the one power they cannot restrain, the mind that men always seem to underestimate.

28

Her mouth went dry with fear before they got her through the door. When she saw the chair, her arsenal of facts went out the window and there was nothing left but terror. It looked like an old barber's chair, chrome armrests topped with leather pads, a footrest to tie her ankles to. They would beat her, she was sure, torture her. That glowering little Napoleon would make good on his threat to stick something into her, see if she was frigid.

Napoleon pushed her into the chair and fastened her wrist tie to the right armrest, forcing her to sit in a sideways twist. She didn't kick when they tied her ankles. She spent her energy instead trying to calm her breathing, slow her racing heart, push back the terror and regain control of her mind.

After they tied her, they stood behind her speaking in low voices. She picked up little snippets as she pushed back at her fear. *Get the info and get rid of her.*

She heard them unpacking something. The rasping lid of a cardstock box, the tearing of a paper wrapper.

Were they going to kill her?

"No evidence," Fake Darrell warned in a stern whisper. "You hear me?"

He appeared in front of her with a needle.

"You see this?" He pointed the needle at his neck brace. The bottom of the brace flared out to his shoulders while the top pressed up beneath his chin, immobilizing his neck. "This is what your fat fucking friend did to me last night. I can't pay him back for it, so I'll pay you."

He jabbed at her face with the needle, a threat rather than a real stick, and she winced.

"You wouldn't like that in your eye, now would you?"

"Stick it in her eye," Napoleon said gleefully.

"Shut up you ignorant midget."

"I'm not a midget."

She closed her eyes and breathed. Pull yourself together, Claire. Fear won't help you here. There's something you can do. There is *always* something you can do. You just have to find it. Stay alert. Watch and think.

"Did you measure this?" Fake Darrell squinted at the syringe.

"I used the whole bottle," Napoleon said.

"Which is exactly what I told you not to do, you fat little dwarf. She's not a fucking horse. How much do you think she weighs?"

"Do I look like a bathroom scale?"

Claire opened her eyes.

"You look like something else you find in a bathroom," Fake Darrell replied. "Something you *leave* in the bathroom."

The color in Napoleon's face and neck was rising. He's razzing the little guy too much, Claire thought. He thinks it's funny, but the little guy's going to lose it if he doesn't stop.

"Remember which one of us has a gun," Napoleon said.

Claire made a note. There was only one gun, and it belonged to Napoleon.

She watched Fake Darrell squirt a jet of brown liquid from the needle, then she scanned the room.

To the right was a table with an open laptop. She wondered if it was connected to the internet through the wire that ran out of the corner of the house. To her left, on the other table, was her coat and bag, Fake Darrell's jacket and Napoleon's too.

145

Between her and the door, a small camera angled down from the ceiling to record whatever they were about to do to her. The green light said it was watching.

What was behind her, she didn't know. She had been too terrified to register the details when they brought her in.

"Hold her arm down," Fake Darrell said.

"Why do I have to do it?"

"You seem to like touching her."

"Just stick it in her eye."

"Quiet, Pee Wee."

Napoleon glared at his partner as he pressed her bound arms against the chair. His hands were hot and hairy. And they shook. Anger, she thought. I can hear it in the way his breath quivers when he breathes in through his nose. He's a ticking bomb.

Fake Darrell thumped his forefinger against a vein in her arm, trying to make it swell. He stuck the needle in and pushed the plunger down half an inch.

"Just a little to start her off. I don't want to put her to sleep."

Put her to sleep? What was in that needle, she wondered. If he didn't want to put her to sleep, then he probably wanted her to talk. Sodium Pentothal was supposed to make people talk, but veterinarians used it to put animals to sleep. Forever. Claire wondered how carefully he had measured the dose. *She's not a fucking horse.*

He seemed about to withdraw the needle. Then he gave the plunger another push.

No, Claire thought. No. I am not a horse. Do not put me to sleep. I know I've been miserable, but please don't put me out of my misery. My life will get better. I promise. Give me one more chance. I'll fix myself. I'll do it right next time. I swear I will. I swear!

She felt the drug ooze into her brain like a venomous serpent. She tried to push it back like she'd pushed back every other feeling she didn't like, but the poison seemed to go right to the root of her power, strangling her will itself. She felt something infinitely stronger than her was pushing her underwater. Her mind spun desperately through all the defenses that had carried her this far in life, but none of them could help her now. She was watching herself die.

Her head slumped to her chest.

She whispered, "Peter, I'm sorry."

29

The world faded back in phases. Sound first, distant and muffled. Then light, dim and blurred. She wasn't sure if she'd been asleep or just drifting somehow. Some part of her remembered being with people. Talking.

Her back was sore from her twisted position in the chair. The binding around her ankles was too tight. Her feet tingled and her toes were numb.

She was adrift in a sea of nausea as she listened to the men talk behind her. Her will returned. She wanted the motion to stop, the motion of the waves that made her feel sick. She ignored the dull ache in her head and focused on stillness.

Someone was approaching. Fake Darrell, not little Napoleon, she guessed from the footsteps. She closed her eyes and pretended to be asleep.

"I told you she'd have nothing," Fake Darrell said. "That's why they partnered me with a midget and a drunk instead of someone competent. She's a low-value witness."

"How do you know that shit works?" Napoleon asked.

"You heard her."

"I heard her slurring on about Peter and her old bitch grandma."

"And the spreadsheet."

"What's the point of letting her go on about all that?"

"Get her flowing," Fake Darrell said. "You know how women are. You gotta let 'em blabber for twenty minutes before they say anything useful. But she doesn't have anything."

"You wouldn't recognize useful if it bit you on the ass."

She kept her eyes closed, remembered the dark road, the light above the door. She remembered walking in, her terror at the sight of the chair, being tied down, injected.

"I told them we were barking up the wrong tree," Fake Darrell said.

"What tree are we supposed to be barking up?"

"How the hell should I know? But it's got to be someone else in the organization."

Organization, Claire thought. Do they think I'm part of some organization?

She opened her eyes and looked down. Her vision was clearer now. She saw no blood. Her clothes hadn't been disturbed. She closed her eyes again.

"She's listening," Napoleon said.

"She's not awake."

"Yeah she is. She's faking it." He slapped her face and her eyes shot open. "See?"

"Don't leave any marks," Fake Darrell barked.

"What difference does it make where she's going?"

"Think about it, you fucking dumbass. They find her in an icy pond with no marks on her, it's a drowning. They find her all bruised up, it's a murder. You want to take that rap?"

Napoleon looked at him with smoldering hostility.

What makes them think they're dealing with an organization, Claire wondered. It was just Gavin, wasn't it? Gavin stole their data and—what? Threatened them? Tried to blackmail them?

"Don't fucking touch her again," Fake Darrell said. "I'll be back with her car, if that damn drunk can follow me back here without crashing. You get her set up. And don't fucking kill her, you dumb shit. She has to be breathing when she goes into the pond so the coroner finds water in her lungs."

He pulled his jacket from the table and went out through the door. Napoleon pointed his finger like a gun at his back and pretended to pull the trigger.

While the door was open, Claire noted every detail of the scene outside. The light above the door had been turned off. It didn't seem to be snowing anymore. There was no sound of a nearby highway, no glow in the sky of city lights. Above the tops of the bare trees, on a ridge less than a quarter mile away, a pair of ancient yellow headlights prowled the snowy road like a beast in the night.

30

How long has he been out there looking for me, Claire wondered. How long have I been in here? Hours?

Had Lincoln flagged a passing motorist for help? Or had he pulled a gas can from the trunk of the Continental and limped through the snow of an unlit country road? How far would he go for her?

"My friend isn't as smart as he thinks he is," said Napoleon. His tone was sulky and aggrieved.

She watched him as he stood by the table with the open laptop. He's got a complex, she thought. No one recognizes him. No one gives him his due. Poor little guy. Someone should pat his head. Give him a hug.

"He should have followed up on some of those things you said," Napoleon continued. "Like that bit about passing the torch in your buddy's last voicemail. What did he really pass you?"

He looked at her as if waiting for a response. "I mean, you know what we're after, right? So why do you have to be so damn stubborn? You could have made all this go away a long time ago. Could have gone back to your quiet life."

"I have no idea what you're talking about," Claire lied. She could have said she didn't have the hard drive Gavin had stolen, but then she'd be useless to them. She already knew they were planning to kill her. As long as they thought she *might* have what they wanted, she'd be worth keeping around. She could lead them on, buy time, figure a way out.

"Maybe you don't," Napoleon said. "But I don't know why he'd leave you that message."

"How do you know what his message said?"

"You told us. And when we pressed you on it, you said he didn't pass you anything, which I believe. We went through your whole damn house. That was a shitty thing for your friend to do. Get you caught up in all this trouble and leave you no way out. What's a Nupe?"

"What?"

"You said you had to report to a Nupe. My friend should have dug in on that one, because obviously you're not the one in the organization we should be going after."

There's that word again, she thought. Organization.

She scanned his body for a sign of the gun. If it was on his hip or in a side holster, she would see a bulge. But his black sweater was so baggy, it might not show. It might also be tucked under his belt in the small of his back. Or in his jacket on the table to her left. If she could get it...

If she could get it, then what?

The Fiat. The little green Fiat parked out front. If she could find the keys...

"Why don't you outline the organization for me," he said.

"I don't know what you're talking about."

"Come on. What's the point of lying now? You're not going to live long enough for it to matter."

"What did I say about Anoop?"

"You don't remember?"

"No."

Napoleon pulled a butterfly knife from his pocket and flipped it around in his hand, opening and closing, opening and closing.

"You said a Nupe told you to stay away. What is a Nupe?"

Claire watched him quietly and said nothing. Keep talking, she thought. I want to understand how you think.

"Some kind of code name?" he asked. "It wouldn't surprise me. Your buddy Gavin, fucking thief, thought he could blackmail us. He was a smart guy in some regards." He stuck the knife into the table. "Smart enough to know what to steal and how to get it. But he was using. Did you know that?"

Claire watched and said nothing. The knife had drawn her attention back to the laptop on the table. A wire ran into it. A network cable. She remembered the line that ran from the corner of the building, up through the woods and back to civilization.

"A junkie's a junkie," Napoleon said, "whether they're shooting, snorting, smoking, or just downing pills. They're all slaves to their addiction. He wanted a shit ton of money and five thousand pills. Pills! No one asks for pills. Fucking dumbass. Just ask for money, then you can buy all the pills you want. I don't know what he was thinking anyway. We'd just pay him off and let him go?"

He looked at her as if awaiting comment.

"You're a very pretty woman, you know that?"

She eyed him coldly.

"Yeah, you know it." He pulled the knife from the table and flipped it closed. "You damn well know it, and you lord it over the guys who want it but can never have it."

He took a step closer so she could see the hatred in his dark brown eyes.

"Does it make you feel powerful? Being the thing desired? The thing withheld?"

"I'm not a thing."

He turned and started flipping the knife again.

"Your buddy Gavin made it sound like there was more than one person involved. He made out like someone else was holding the files, like someone else would handle the return of our property."

He turned and glared at her. There was something pathetic in his sullen look, like he really wanted the approval of a woman he found attractive. She wondered for a moment if she could sweet talk him, seduce him, but the thought revolted her. She couldn't fake interest in him even when her life depended on it.

"Makes sense, right?" he continued. "I mean, if it was a one-man operation, just him with the files and he comes trying to blackmail us, well... All we have to do is kill him, and problem solved, right? So he tells us there's others involved. Whether that's true or not, I don't know. We have to play it like it is."

"There are others," Claire said calmly. If he believes that, he might think twice about killing me.

"Who?"

"Obviously, I'm not going to tell you that."

"You want to die?"

"I'm going to die anyway, according to your friend."

"He's not my friend."

"He doesn't think very highly of you, does he?"

"Guy's a prick. Who else is in your organization?"

Claire shook her head.

"You don't think we can beat it out of you?"

"Remember your instructions. Leave no marks. You don't want to anger your friend."

"Fuck him." He stepped toward her, flipped the knife open, and pressed the flat edge against her nose.

"A woman can go from pretty to ugly in a second." He made a slicing motion, pretending to cut off the end of her nose. "One fucking second. You see what I did to your little Chinese friend?"

"Li?"

Napoleon's eyes glinted when he smiled. "Li," he repeated fondly. "She's a screamer. You know, it turns me on when a woman shows real fear."

"You're disgusting."

"Yeah, I get that a lot from women. After a while, it starts getting under your skin. All those little slights." He kept flipping the knife—open, closed, open, closed. "The worst insults are the ones they don't even say. It's just a look, you know? They size you up in one quick glance and you're just some piece of shit they want nothing to do with. They look away, like just the sight of you is gonna soil their precious eyes."

"Maybe if you behaved better..." Claire let the suggestion hang and made no effort to hide her disgust.

"Yeah, see." He stabbed the knife into the table again, this time with the force of rising anger. "Now that would be fair. Judging someone on their behavior. But it never gets that far. It's like they hate me as soon as they see me, so I never get a chance. And if people are gonna hate me no matter what, why should I behave?"

Oh, how you pity yourself, Claire thought.

"See?" He pointed at her. "You're doing it right now. This is what I'm talking about. I know that look." He pulled the knife from the table and put it to her throat.

"You don't think I'll cut you?" he hissed. "You don't think I'm serious?"

"I'm sure you're as serious as an angry little man can be, but your friend told you not to, and he seems to have you on a leash."

"You goddamn fucking—"

She looked at her phone on the table to the left.

Napoleon's eyes followed hers. "Oh, you want the phone?" He crossed to the table and picked it up. "Here you go." He turned it on, typed in her pin, and put the phone into her bound hands.

"How'd you know my pin?"

"You told us. We've been all through that thing and—wait. Anoop! Anoop is one of your contacts."

"Mind if I call him?" she asked.

"Don't bother. This building is a Friday cage."

"A what?" Claire saw the phone had no signal.

"A Friday cage. Means it blocks radio signals. Nothing goes in or out."

"You mean a Faraday cage," Claire said. "It's lined with wire mesh to block electromagnetic radiation."

Napoleon looked at her stupidly for a second. "It's a Friday cage."

"Faraday," Claire corrected. "Look it up." She said those last words out of habit. It was a challenge she used to throw at the men in New York when she had her facts straight and they didn't. She wasn't expecting a reaction, but Napoleon couldn't let it go.

"All right," he said defiantly. "I will." He crossed to the table on the right and typed at the laptop.

Claire saw a page of search results load onscreen. So there is a connection out of here.

"Well I'll be damned," he said. "You're right. It is a Faraday cage. Nice work, Miss Smartypants."

"It's mizz," Claire said. "Mizz."

Napoleon yanked the phone from her hands and tossed it onto the table with the coats. "How does Anoop fit into this organization? You take orders from him?"

"I was supposed to check in with him earlier this evening." The plan was now forming in her mind.

"Well that's not going to happen."

Claire's fear rose as he walked behind her. She didn't like him being out of sight. He was moving things, making rustling noises. Then he returned with a coiled plastic tube and some items she couldn't identify, wrapped in what looked like sterile white medical packaging.

"It would be fun to keep you around, beat some information out of you, see if you scream and cry like your little Chinese friend..."

He tore open a package and removed a needle with a port. Claire recognized it as the kind hospitals put in to run an intravenous drip. The coiled tubing, she now understood, went with it.

"But my pal is calling the shots here and he thinks you have nothing to tell us. You're just a low-level witness that needs to disappear."

"According to him," Claire said. "But as you said, he didn't follow up when I mentioned Anoop. You did."

Prey on his inferiority complex, she told herself. On his resentment of Fake Darrell. On his certainty that he's smarter than his partner.

Again he stepped behind her. Again he returned.

"Now this," he said, showing her a bag of clear fluid, "is what hospitals call lactated Ringer's. It's a saline solution they drip in to keep patients hydrated."

"Your friend thought I had nothing to say," Claire said. "But as soon as he left, you uncovered a new fact about a new person in the organization. And you didn't even have to beat me."

"And this..." Napoleon stepped behind her and returned with a bottle. "Is Everclear. One hundred and ninety proof. Goes in the drip, the drip goes in Claire, and Claire and her car go into the pond. Nice and neat. The best thing is, you can't throw it up because it never even touched your stomach."

So that's how they did it with Gavin, she thought. That's why he had that gash on his arm. The coroner would have noticed the needle puncture. The gash looked like the kind of cut a careless drunk might get, and it hid the puncture.

"The game is still on," Claire said. "If I don't report to Anoop, he'll start turning the screws."

"What's that supposed to mean?"

"He'll release some documents to the media. Enough to hint at what you're doing. Enough to turn up the heat on whoever's running this show."

"You're full of shit." He uncoiled the tubing that would go into her arm.

"You think?"

She left it at that, left it hanging. An old negotiator's tactic. Casually plant the idea of a potential threat, leave it vague. Let the other person think it through, let them fill in the blanks, see where their mind goes with it.

As he straightened out the tubing he seemed to lose interest in what his hands were doing. She could see he was thinking. He didn't notice when the tubing coiled up again.

"Does it ever bother you," she asked, "working for someone stupider than you?"

"All the time," he said. "All the fucking time." There was the anger again. She had hit it dead on.

"You want to save your bosses some trouble? I don't mean the red-haired guy, I mean the higher-ups."

"They can fuck themselves." He straightened out the tubing again. "They dug their own damn graves. Let them lie in them."

Claire looked up at the video camera on the ceiling.

"Yeah, it's recording," Napoleon said.

"When they review the video," Claire said, "they'll see your friend got nothing out of me but you did."

"Loyal fucking soldier," he muttered. "That's me." He removed the protective plastic cover from the needle, then said to the camera, "You see that, you stupid fuck! I told you not to let that Nupe thing go!"

"Let me check in with Anoop," Claire said.

"Shut up." He unscrewed the top of the Everclear bottle, sniffed it and winced.

"I'm overdue. He's going to release the documents."

"I said shut up."

"Remember you're on camera." Claire nodded toward the ceiling. "You're going to have to explain to your boss why you didn't prevent the release of information when you could have. Especially when they see me telling you straight up how to do it."

Claire addressed the camera. "When the news starts to leak, you can thank Pee Wee here for not doing his job."

Napoleon stepped between her and the camera, his face reddening with anger. "Shut the fuck up!"

"You're too short to block me from view."

His face twisted in rage. The first blow landed on her solar plexus and knocked the wind out of her. She doubled over against the right armrest to which her hands were tied and he dug three hard rights into her lower back, grunting like an enraged savage.

"I'm sick of hearing that shit," he yelled. "I told you I don't take shit from women. But you had to test me, didn't you? You fucking cunts always have to cross the line." He punched her a fourth time in the same spot. Everything flashed white, then went black.

For a long time, she couldn't draw a breath. Her eyes filled with tears and the black world swam with stars.

When she could breathe again, she wanted to sit up, but she didn't want him to see the tears. She stayed folded, slumped forward and to the right as the pain in her lower back radiated through every part of her body, carrying waves of nausea with it.

She tried to take deep breaths to calm herself, but full inhalations were too painful.

Now he was pacing in front of her, his own phone to his ear, forgetting with his loss of temper that there was no signal in the little house.

"Goddamnit!" He slammed the useless phone onto the table beside the laptop.

"You need to ask your friend what to do?" Claire asked, straightening herself with difficulty. "They don't trust you to make your own decisions?"

"Shut up."

"Your plan isn't going to work anyway. They know about Gavin."

"Who knows about Gavin?"

"The police," Claire said, mustering all her energy to hide her pain and keep the strain out of her voice. "I went to the station to talk to them. They know he didn't drink. What do you think it's going to look like to the cops when they find me dead of alcohol poisoning in my car, just like him? Two friends, a week apart? You think they won't connect the dots?"

"I told them that!" he said. "I told them they can't play the same trick twice. Not in the same county. The cops aren't that dumb. And they said 'Shut up, Pee Wee. Do your job.' Like they don't want to hear common fucking sense. Like they're..." He ran his fingers through his hair, turned and paced.

"And you work for them?" Claire asked in a tone to pique his outrage. "You're the one who's going to poison me. You're the one who's going to take the rap for their stupid plan, which you know isn't going to work."

"Stupid fucks! Stupid goddamn..." The livid red was rising from his neck to his hairline.

"You want to spend the next few weeks looking over your shoulder? Wondering when the cops will catch up with you? You want to spend the rest of your life in prison?"

He was pacing like the caged leopard at the zoo, like a trapped animal unable to find its way out.

"If you check in for me, it'll buy your boss time to negotiate."

"We don't negotiate."

"Or you can skip the check-in and explain to your friend later how you screwed this up. But—oh, it's all on video. He'll be able to see for himself."

"Shut the fuck up, will you?"

She could see beads of sweat on his forehead now.

"Check me in," she said. "That'll keep Anoop from leaking documents, buy your boss time to make his next move. Puts the ball in his court. Then you can see how smart *he* is. Make it his problem to get himself out of this mess."

"I'm not letting you talk to anyone."

"I don't need to. That's not how we communicate anyway."

"What do you want me to do? Send up a fucking flare?"

"Just let Anoop know I'm good for another day. It's an anonymous check-in. You know, like the spies used to do? Leave a chalk mark on a lamppost. That sort of thing. You don't have to pass any information at all."

"How the fuck does that work?"

"Go to a public website called Zero Hour Survivor."

"And do what?"

"Post a comment."

He eyed her warily, then looked at the overhead camera. She could see the wheels turning, his uncertainty about what to do.

"Explain it," he said, moving toward the laptop. "If it sounds like bullshit, I'll stick my knife in your throat."

"Zero Hour Survivor," she repeated.

She closed her eyes and listened to him type. Her mouth was dry and her hands shook. Don't let that shake come through in your voice, she told herself. Don't!

"Yeah, now what?"

"Find the story called 'Gut Feeling.'"

Deep breath, she told herself. Steady. If I crack here, I lose. And I will *not* lose to *him*.

"And?" he demanded.

"Leave a comment."

"Who's it from?"

"What?"

"It's asking for a name," he shouted. "What name do I put in?" He was shaking.

"Angel."

"Angel? Ha! Some fucking angel you are."

She opened her eyes and watched him type.

"OK, Angel, what's your message? And don't try to feed me some shit like 'I'm stuck in a house in PG County and they're going to kill me.'"

"No."

"'Cause that'll earn you a knife in the gut."

"It's just a simple check-in. Same message I leave every day, so he knows I'm OK."

"What's your message? Spit it out!"

"All quiet on the western front."

"That's it?"

"That's it."

"Well isn't that pretty."

She closed her eyes as he tapped out the message. She pictured the alert popping up on Lincoln's phone. She remembered him showing her how the commenter's internet address appeared, how he could map its location through an IP locator service.

She prayed he was still nearby, that his phone was in range of a signal, that Napoleon wouldn't hit her again, or poison her, or kill her. She prayed for the throbbing pain in her back to stop, and she promised that if she made it out of this alive, she would tell Peter everything.

31

She didn't know how many minutes had passed since the message went out. It seemed like hours, but she knew how fear warped one's sense of time, stretching seconds into agonizing eternities. She had looked for something in the room to count by—a flashing light or recurrent noise—but the green light on the camera shone steadily, and the only sound came from the movements of Napoleon rummaging behind her.

She tried to keep time by counting her breath, but the pain of inhalation distracted her and she couldn't get past three. Her best guess was that somewhere between five and thirty minutes had passed.

Then a door closed behind her. That meant there was another room. She heard a toilet seat bang down, a soft sigh from Napoleon.

She strained to listen for any noise in the night. When she thought she heard the distant knocking of the old Continental, she sucked in a deep, painful breath and held it, hoping to quiet the sound of her breathing. But all she heard was the blood rushing through her ears and the heart pounding in her chest.

She let out her breath, inhaled, stopped abruptly. Was that it? Was that the rumbling beast? The 460 cubic inches Lincoln was so proud of?

No. The only sound now was toilet paper reeling off the roll.

But, she told herself hopefully, Lincoln knows the car is loud. The last stretch of road leading to this house runs downhill. He'd cut the engine and roll in silently. That's what he'd do.

She strained again to listen. The flush of the toilet was like a roar in her ears. Then silence. Then water splashing in the sink.

If you listen hard enough, she promised herself, you'll hear him. You will.

But all she heard was Napoleon patting his hands dry with what must have been a paper towel.

She closed her eyes and dropped her head in despair. She had promised herself she wouldn't cry, no matter what. But what was the point? What did it matter anymore? Whatever unfinished business she had in the world would remain unfinished. Her wrongs would go unrighted, her apologies undelivered. She heard the rush of blood in her ears before the tears came.

Only the rush sounded strange this time. Raspier than usual, like the scrape of rusty brakes.

She jerked her head up.

Was that a click? The driver's door of the Continental? She tried to remember the sound it made when it opened.

She held her breath, waiting for the next noise, the shutting of the door, but there was only silence.

He wouldn't shut it, she thought. The thud would be too loud.

She strained, but heard nothing more.

If he's walking, she told herself, the snow will quiet his steps.

But he has to make *some* noise. Unless he's not really there. Unless I just imagined it all.

She listened through her pounding heart.

There! Someone was twisting the knob of the door, but it wouldn't open. Whoever it was began to knock, lightly at first, then louder and more forceful.

"Use your key," Napoleon shouted from the bathroom.

God, don't let it be Darrell, she thought.

The knock repeated, harder this time.

"Goddamnit!" She heard the bathroom door open behind her, saw him march past angrily, yank open the door impatiently as he shouted, "Use your goddamn—"

A giant fist crushed into his face with a sickening meaty thud, knocking him back onto his ass. Lincoln charged in faster than she ever thought he could move. As the little man tried to stand, Lincoln kicked the side of his knee. Napoleon screamed as his leg buckled. Then Lincoln lifted him with one hand and punched him with the other. Right in the solar plexus. The same place she'd taken it, only with ten times the force. He crumpled to the floor.

"You OK?" Lincoln asked.

She nodded toward the butterfly knife Napoleon had left beside the computer. He cut her free and pulled her up, a little too forcefully in his excitement. A little too much adrenaline. She yelped and fell to the ground.

"You hurt?"

"Get my coat," she groaned. "My shoes, my bag, the laptop, the phone."

32

The old Continental slithered up the snowy wooded drive on treadless tires like a snake on a greased ramp. More than once, Claire thought they would slide backwards into the woods.

"He has a gun," Claire said when she feared they wouldn't make it out.

"Not anymore." Lincoln showed her the pistol. "Besides, he can't walk far enough to get us. I busted his knee, and my fist went just about clear through to his spine. He wants to chase us, he's gonna have to push his liver down out of his throat."

When they reached the road, Lincoln steered the car along the ruts he had made on the way in. There was another set of tracks in the snow, from tires with actual tread. Laid down by Fake Darrell's newer car, they were closer together.

"Where are we?" Claire asked.

"Somewhere between Greenbelt and Fort Meade. Your phone on?"

"Crap. Yeah."

"Turn it off."

"I know."

"I can't pull up a map to navigate," he explained. "Not without broadcasting our location. So we're going to take the long way. Back down to the Beltway, around to two-seventy, up to Frederick. Unless you know of a better place to go."

The cost of keeping her cool through that whole ordeal had caught up with her. "I don't want to see anyone, I don't want to talk to anyone. I just want to disappear."

"Want to go to the cops?"

"Tomorrow."

"Claire—"

"Where are they going to put me? They have to put me somewhere. And how are they going to protect me? They can arrest Napoleon, but Fake Darrell's still out there. And the big drunk. And the two in the alley from last night. And how many more? I'd rather go where I know no one will find me. I'm done with people today. I want to disappear. Please take me away. I'm fucking done."

The pain in her back was getting worse, bad enough that it began to frighten her. But she'd had enough of fear as well. She pushed it away, down into that place where she shoved the other inconvenient emotions.

"What happened in there?" Lincoln asked.

She told him, pausing between breaths to gather her energy against the pain, which instinct and habit forced her to hide.

"So it is a computer drive," Lincoln said.

"Sounds like it." She breathed out the throbbing ache in a long quavering breath.

"Well good work figuring that out. And it sounds like it contains what you think it contains."

She pressed her fingers to her temples. "Sounds like it."

"Ever thought about becoming a detective?"

"Why would I do that?"

"You got a mind for figuring things out."

If she could breathe more deeply, she wouldn't feel so lightheaded.

"Anyone who'd choose to get herself into situations like this is insane."

"Yeah, you got a little of that in you too. Hardheaded woman with all the brains in the world and not a lick of sense. You're breathin' like a woman in labor."

"Just drive."

She felt him eyeing her now and then as the car splashed through the slush of the Beltway. She wanted to steer the topic to something light, to make him stop checking up on her.

She was about to ask if he had spoken to his wife, but before she could get the words out, the car hit a bump and she let out a cry of pain.

"Damnit, Claire, why you gotta hide everything? If you're hurt, tell me."

"It's just a bruise," she said. "I'm not used to getting hit, OK?"

"Yeah, it's just a bruise," he said. "Well I seen you with your grandma, all the crap you take from her, and I know you're tough. If that little bump got a yelp outta you, you're hurt and you need to see a doctor."

"I'll see someone in the morning if it's still bothering me."

"The hell you will. You're just trying to shut me up."

"OK then, take the hint and shut up. I don't feel like talking anyway."

She turned and looked out at the mess of slush rolling by. He'll start talking in two minutes, she thought. He can't hold his tongue any longer than that when there's an open ear nearby.

In two minutes, he was telling her how smart his daughter was, how she had corrected the science teacher twice already this year, how his younger daughter wasn't as bright. She struggled in school and compared herself unfavorably to her sister.

"Now my wife and I, this is where we're on the same page. Trying to get that girl to see her true gifts. 'Cause book smarts ain't everything. There's something to be said for an honest heart. For loyalty and kindness, and the Lord poured those blessings on her in spades."

Yes, thought Claire. There's a lot to be said for loyalty and kindness. What good are your stony defenses if there's no decency or warmth in the heart you work so hard to protect? She bred it into me. Leona drilled her lessons deeper into me than she ever could have hoped. Coldness and distrust right down to the core. It works in your favor when you're dealing with people who really do want to hurt you, but when someone actually loves you, it's a poison. It's fatal. Why would he ever have wanted to marry me?

She twisted the diamond in her ear and reminded herself she'd made a promise. *If I make it out of here alive, I'll tell him everything.* Because he didn't deserve what I did to him. No one deserves that. There *is* something to be said for loyalty and kindness. There is everything in the world to be said for loyalty and kindness.

The drive took so long on the snow-choked roads that even Lincoln ran out of things to say. They passed the last twenty minutes in silence.

Inside the house, Claire took off her coat and turned up the heat. Lincoln sat heavily on the couch, looking tired and worn.

"Come here," he said. His tone was unfamiliar. A command.

"What?"

"You get on over here." He motioned with his hand.

She walked to the couch and he said, "Turn around."

She didn't know why she obeyed.

He lifted her shirt. "I can see it. Whole left side is bruised up fierce. That was some hit that bastard put on you."

"Don't touch it." Claire winced.

"Hold on now..." Lincoln pressed his rough hand gently against her right kidney, then more gingerly on the left. She yelped.

"Tender and swollen and hot to the touch," he said. "That's more than a bruise. The kidney's a bad place to get hit."

Claire pulled her shirt down.

"I'll see a doctor in the morning."

"Or tonight," said Lincoln, "if you can't sleep. And I bet you can't."

"I'll be fine."

"Said the woman who couldn't ask for help. Listen, if you see any blood in your urine, if your pee comes out pink, we're going straight to the hospital. You hear me?"

"I hear you."

33

Lincoln was right. She couldn't sleep.

She lay on the torn mattress in the dry air beside the heater. The skies had cleared, revealing a broad wash of stars and a thin sliver of moon.

As she listened to Lincoln snore on the couch, she thought through what she would say to Peter. She wanted to be clear, not emotional, because she knew that if she let her shame and guilt creep in, she'd lose control and make a mess of things.

At 2:38 a.m., she turned her phone on. Peter silenced his phone at night, which meant she could leave a long message, get it all out without having to confront him.

Listening to the phone ring, she thought, I should have gotten water. It's dry in here. My throat is dry.

The call went to voicemail. He hadn't changed his greeting. The same positive, happy voice she had known seemed to come from some other universe where nothing had changed, where they were still together in the apartment. She wore a ring. They kissed when they parted, kissed when they returned.

When the tone sounded, she took a deep breath. That would be the first thing he heard. Her breathing.

"Peter," she said calmly. "I want to start by saying I'm sorry. I found the ring and I panicked. I don't think I had adjusted yet to moving in with you. To giving up part of my freedom and identity. When I thought about it, I felt like I had given up too much too fast, and somehow I resented you for what was ultimately my decision. We hadn't really talked of marriage— not fully, not all the way through, and suddenly you were talking about children. I couldn't even consider that next step when I hadn't fully processed the last. Every time you started on that topic, my mind went blank. Everything just shut down. I never said a word. I think you interpreted that to mean I was onboard with it all. That we were both on the same page. I don't blame you for thinking that."

Three dull beeps told her the message had cut off. She called back and continued.

"Since I've been in DC, I've buried myself in work. I got Leona into a home and I've been packing up the house that's so full of things I never wanted to see again. I've done all I can to avoid thinking about what I did, and why, and where I'm going without you. When I do think about it, when I'm awake at night like I am now, I feel horrible. I did a horrible thing to you, and I'm sorry. If I could have explained everything that was going through my head at the time, I'd like to think I would have. But I couldn't even explain it to myself. All I felt was panic, and I ran."

Again she was cut off, and again she called back.

"On some level, I was scared I'd never be what you wanted me to be. You talk about children, but I'm not a mothering type. Warmth and nurturing and patience aren't part of who I am. Maybe you think they are, but I can't seem to find them in myself. When you talk of children, you have to remember that family for me means catastrophe. Family is where everything goes wrong. I can live with screwing up my own life, but not someone else's. Not a child's."

Her own thoughts interrupted her in a voice she didn't recognize. *Aren't you being warm now? Aren't you being patient with yourself and your own emotions? Is it not nurturing to make amends to one you've injured?*

She pushed the thoughts aside and continued.

"I guess the main thing I want you to know is that it wasn't your fault. You just stepped on a land mine that you couldn't have known was there. I didn't even know it was there."

The line cut off, and she called again.

"I'm sorry I ran away. I'm sorry I hurt you. I don't expect you to respond, but I do want you to know that you never did anything wrong. You were always good to me. Goodbye, Peter."

This time, she hung up before the beep.

She turned the phone off, dropped it on her stomach, and lay looking at the stars, her right hand twisting the diamond in her ear.

In a few minutes, the pain in her lower back gave way to exhaustion and she drifted off to sleep.

34

When she awoke, it was still dark and her mouth was dry. Where was she?

On the floor in Leona's old house, looking through the window at the stars. Had she already made the call to Peter? Or was that a dream?

She cried in pain when she tried to sit up. She waited, blinking at the ceiling, until the sharp stab subsided into a dull, throbbing ache. Her left lower back was hot to the touch. She rolled onto her right side and propped herself on her elbow. From there she was able to stand and walk to the bathroom. She took her phone with her. She wanted to check the call logs to make sure she had actually called him, that it wasn't a dream.

The cold toilet seat sent a shiver through her. She kept the light off because Lincoln told her he didn't want anyone outside to see where people were moving inside. Paranoid, maybe, but his job was to protect her. She turned the phone on, thinking, Maybe I didn't call if this thing isn't even on.

When she peed, the pain in her lower back increased. She held her breath and winced.

Then she felt a vibration in the floorboards. Was Lincoln up? She didn't hear him snoring. If he was up, why was he being so quiet?

She twisted the diamond with her right hand as she held the phone with her left. The stud was loose. Why? She touched behind her earlobe. The backing was gone. There was nothing holding it in. That made her nervous, but she continued to twist.

The call logs showed she had called Peter four times. The phone's clock said it was now 5:48 a.m.

She heard a noise outside the house. A pop and a hiss.

The vibrations in the floorboards stopped. She held her breath and listened. Another pop, another hiss. The floorboards shook again. Someone was moving in the hall outside the bathroom.

She took a breath, held it and listened. Another footstep, then a soft knock at the door startled her. Her hand jumped, knocked the diamond stud from her ear. She heard it hit the floor beside the toilet.

A man whispered, "Claire."

A pop and a hiss outside.

"Who's there?" Claire whispered.

"Lincoln."

Pop. Hiss.

"Someone's cuttin' the tires," he whispered. "So we can't get away."

Her heart skipped a beat. She reached for the toilet paper. Get out of here, she told herself. Get out of here fast. But...

"You didn't turn that phone on, did you?"

She knelt beside the toilet and felt for the diamond stud. It was gone. She began to panic.

"Claire," Lincoln hissed. "I told you not to turn that goddamn phone on."

"Sorry, I—" She stood, pulled her pants up, knelt again and ran her fingers frantically over the rough wood in search of the diamond Peter had given her.

"You decent in there?"

Footsteps crunched through the snow outside.

"Hold on," she whispered.

175

She felt something hard and sharp in a crack between the floorboards. She tried to dig it out with her nail but couldn't.

She shone the phone's flashlight into the crack. The glinting diamond was wedged in deep.

"Damnit, Claire, turn that light off!"

A shot shattered the glass above her head and splintered the door. Lincoln cursed, flung the door open, grabbed her by the arm.

"Stay low." He pulled her out roughly. She kept her cool, didn't make a sound despite the searing pain in her back.

She stayed low and quiet, just as he wanted. Only she didn't stay low enough to avoid seeing into the toilet.

"Turn that damn light off," he whispered.

She obeyed, tapped it off, and the blood-red water disappeared into the dark.

35

She crawled on all fours as Lincoln, in a crouch, nudged her toward the bedroom. The pain in her kidney throbbed with each heartbeat. She heard a shard of glass fall to the bathroom floor. Then another. Lincoln stepped back, stood, and extended his arm into the bathroom. The shot lit the house, and the scream outside conveyed fear and pain.

The floorboards shook as Lincoln stepped around her. He went into the bedroom, to the window that gave him another angle on the person he had just hit.

The swiping sound of polyester told her someone was moving outside. Running. Two shots rang out from the bedroom, three from outside, and another from within. She pressed herself against the floor, eyes wide in the dark, ears alert for sounds of movement.

The floor shook again as Lincoln passed her, the other way this time, toward the kitchen and the front room.

In the silence that followed, only the shaking floorboards told her he was moving.

A doorknob clicked. Was that the front door? Or the back?

A shot broke the quiet. It came from the front room, or just outside. The shaking floor told her someone was moving again, soundlessly. She held her breath and listened.

Nothing.

A draft of wintry air chilled her feet and ankles, crept to her hands and face. If she crawled forward, she'd get to the bedroom. A dead end, except for the windows, at least one of which had been shot out.

To crawl the other way, she'd have to turn around. That would take her to the source of the draft, to the front room and kitchen where someone might be waiting in the dark with a gun.

The bathroom window was open, a possible exit, but the pane was shattered in jagged shards. Not something you'd want to climb through. And outside, people who might still be alive may be lying in the snow with guns.

The floor shook lightly. Whoever was moving in the front room made no sound. That couldn't be Lincoln, she thought. His heavy steps had more of an impact.

She felt a step, then another, then a sound like paper. What was that?

He's in the kitchen, she thought. One of Lincoln's sandwich wrappers must have blown off the counter. Or he knocked it off. Wait, is he in the kitchen or not?

Outside the bathroom window, a thud, a grunt, and another thud. Someone was getting kicked. The sound was so crisp, so distinct, it could have come from inside, from the bathroom itself. Was someone in there? Or were they really outside?

The figure in the kitchen must have heard it. Why else would he have stopped?

She waited and the floorboards shook. He was coming to investigate. The vibrations in the floor were getting stronger. She could hear him breathing. He was right behind her.

"Get up."

She saw his shadow flash twice against the wall as shots erupted from the open bathroom door beside him. He dropped with a thud and a groan, his gun sending a bullet into the ceiling as it struck the floor. She lunged instinctively to grab it before he could, crying in pain at the sudden movement.

The stab in her back was so sharp, she didn't notice she had grabbed the gun by the wrong end, that the hot barrel was burning her hand. She pushed the pain back by force of will, turned the gun and pointed it at the heap on the floor.

He was cursing, sucking in air through his teeth and letting it out in short, agonized grunts. His breath whistled and gurgled on the way in. The bullet was in his lung.

Now the floor shook hard.

Please let that be Lincoln. Please don't tell me they have a giant too. She raised the gun to shoot the figure storming in. She would have pulled the trigger, kept pulling until there were no more bullets, if the enormous silhouette hadn't had that limp. He came in fast, delivered a thunderous kick to the ribs of the man on the floor, eliciting a muffled scream.

"Where's your gun, buddy? Give it up, 'less you wanna die."

"I have it," Claire said.

"Point it at the floor, and keep your finger off the trigger." He stood on the injured man, pinning him to the ground as he took the gun and helped Claire to her feet.

36

Claire's feet barely reached the pedal. The driver's seat of the Lincoln had been pushed back to accommodate a man six and a half feet tall. She jammed the accelerator to keep the sputtering engine from stalling. Nursing the old beast to life in the bitter cold was like trying to raise the dead. None of this was reassuring. A fifty-year-old oil-burner with four flat tires, and Lincoln—she turned and looked toward the house—God only knew where he was.

He had made a round of the place before hustling her and "all her crap," as he put it, out to the car. Then he'd gone off without saying—

What was that?

An engine roared to life behind her. Her eyes darted to the rearview. A black SUV was blocking the drive. Why hadn't she noticed it when she'd left the house? What *had* she noticed with all that adrenaline rushing through her?

The SUV jerked backwards, swung onto the snowy pavement, kept turning until its rear wheels were in the drainage ditch at the side of the road. The engine went quiet. She saw Lincoln get out, put the key fob in his pocket, his big feet crunching toward her through the snow, left hand pressed to the side of his head.

"There's three of 'em," he said, waving her into the passenger seat. From the unfamiliar phone pressed to his ear, Claire heard a woman's voice. "May I have your name, sir?"

"No, ma'am. But you can get the location from this here phone and send some ambulances." He tossed the phone into the snow and settled into the driver's seat.

"Why do them nine-one-one operators always gotta be so nosy?"

"You called nine-one-one?"

"I don't want them fellas to die." He backed slowly onto the road, then started off toward Frederick. "Well, part of me does," he admitted. "Just not the part that likes to avoid prison."

"Why didn't we take that SUV?"

"Got a tracking system," Lincoln said. "OnStar, or whatever." He pulled a gun from his coat and threw it out the window. "'Sides, a soldier don't leave an injured comrade behind." He patted the dash of the old Continental. "She seems to take the ice and snow better on flats. But it's gonna ruin her rims."

"Where are we going?"

He pointed ahead toward the lights of Frederick in the east.

"Don't you think we should call the police?" Claire asked.

Lincoln pulled a badge from his coat and threw it in her lap. "One of them guys was the police."

Claire inspected the badge. "How do you know this is real?"

"How do I know anything's real?"

"Well there's one cop I can trust. Down in PG County. I'm going to call her."

"Not from here. And not from your phone. If they're tracking us..." Lincoln pulled another gun from his coat and tossed it out the window.

"Where do you keep getting those?"

"I took 'em off them guys back there. Along with their phones. Did you pee?" He looked at her but she didn't answer. "In the bathroom back there? Was there any blood?"

"Just a drop or two," she lied.

"Wasn't no drop or two. I saw it myself. You forgot to flush. You're hurt worse than you're showing and you need help."

"Don't tell me what I need."

"I'm serious. You gotta take care of yourself. And why the hell'd you turn that goddamn phone on? You did, didn't you? Led 'em right to us. I told you not to do that."

"I'm sorry. I had to."

"You didn't have to."

"I made a promise. I made a dying promise, and I had to keep it."

"You didn't have to put your life at risk. Or mine."

This was the first time she'd seen him angry, and she learned that when he was angry, he clammed up. Maybe his wife pissed him off on purpose now and then, she thought, just to get some peace and quiet.

He sped up, and as the car floated left and right like a weaving drunk, he seemed to catch the rhythm of its drifts. He knew just when to turn the wheel, when to accelerate, and when to slow to keep the car on the right side of the road.

"There's gotta be a hospital in this town up here," he said after a record four minutes of silence.

"Maybe. But that ambulance you just called is going to take all three of our friends there."

"Shiiiiit," said Lincoln. "You're right. Where's the next hospital?"

"I don't know. Rockville?"

"This old girl ain't gonna make it to Rockville. But she will do thirty on four flats. Show me a damn Toyota that'll do that."

The engine knocked and sputtered as the blue smoke pouring from the tailpipe began to thicken.

"She's wounded," Lincoln said as the front passenger-side tire began to come apart, slapping at the wheel well. "A few minutes of that'll take out the front quarter panel."

An ambulance passed on its way to the house they had just left.

"You got any cash on you?" Lincoln asked.

Claire winced in pain as she lifted her bag from the floor.

"A hundred and fourteen dollars."

The engine let out a series of knocks like a death rattle, nearly stalling before it caught again.

"In Frederick," Lincoln said, "you get a cab down to Rockville or wherever. Find a hospital and get that kidney looked at."

He turned to look at her as the acrid smell of burning oil filled the car.

"I hate to say this to a lady, but you look like shit."

"I thought I was going to die back there. That doesn't exactly bring out my blush."

"Yeah, well I thought we was both gonna die, and I don't mind saying it scared the living shit out of me. Now I'm worried about them dying," Lincoln said. "I sure as hell don't need no murder rap."

"No one's going to arrest you," Claire said. "When three guys slash your tires and fire bullets through your windows, you have every right to defend yourself."

"What if they really was cops?"

"Then they should have said so. Aim for the middle of town. If we want a cab, that'll be the only place to find one at..." She squinted at the analog clock on the dashboard. "Six oh six in the morning."

The lights of the strip malls were already in view, and Lincoln began to mutter under his breath as he nursed the ailing engine, giving it gas and letting off.

"It's a goddamn crime, assaultin' a defenseless motor vehicle." The car lurched as he punched the gas to prevent another stall. A chunk of the right front tire flew past the window.

"Breaking a mirror on a Volkswagen, that's a misdemeanor. Slashing the tires on a seventy-one Continental, now that's a felony."

"You seriously can't have a single thought without speaking it aloud," Claire said.

"You hear how she's knocking now?" he said, pointing toward the hood. "The timing's off and the valves are going, like an old man's heart. Like an old warrior at the end of the line. Saddest damn sound you'll ever hear."

He turned to Claire with a scowl. "Whichever one of them slashed these tires oughta get reported to the Society for the Prevention of Cruelty to Automobiles. Also, he could use a good kick in the head. You know what happens when you drive on flats? Tears up the rims. Now what am I gonna put on here? Ford wheels? That'd be like bronzing a gold medal."

The engine sputtered and choked as they rolled into town. "Old Bessie here, I think he done wounded her heart."

He shook his head in disgust, and Claire left him to his mourning.

Five minutes later, the old Continental gave up the ghost just one block short of an all-night gas station.

37

The car idling out front had an unlit Uber sign in the windshield. Lincoln rapped on the glass, startling the young driver who was eating a hot dog. The man rolled down the window, looking annoyed. "What?" He wore a black wool cap and had a scruffy beard.

"My friend here needs a ride," said Lincoln. "That's what."

"I'm off duty."

"She needs to go to the hospital."

"Then call an ambulance."

Lincoln pulled the door open and yanked the young man from the car. "If I call an ambulance, it's gonna be for you, pal. Now I'm asking you for a ride to the hospital. How far is that?"

"A... a couple miles," the driver sputtered, looking sullenly at the hot dog on the icy pavement.

"Not that hospital," Lincoln said. "The next one down."

"You mean Rockville?"

"If they got doctors, that's the one I mean."

"That's a long drive."

"Forty bucks oughta cover it." He let go of the man and pulled two twenties from his wallet.

"You have to use the app," the driver said.

"My phone's busted," Lincoln lied.

"I'm off duty anyway."

"Not anymore." Lincoln thrust two twenties into his hand. "And drive slow. She's got a backache."

"Yes, sir," said the driver, straightening his jacket. "Slow it is."

"Take this," Lincoln said to Claire, handing her the stun gun he'd put into her hands on the night they met. "It's charged."

"Where are you going?" Claire asked as he turned to leave.

"You ain't the only one sick," Lincoln said. "Bessie needs a doctor too."

"Are you seriously going to try to fix that car?"

"I told you, a soldier don't leave a fallen comrade. Besides, I gotta clear some stuff outta the trunk, else they might identify me. I don't want nobody going after my family. I'll catch up with you in the hospital."

"Wait," said Claire. "Give me your number."

"You're not putting it in your contacts."

"Just tell it to me. I'll remember."

"You'll remember ten digits, just like that?"

"Numbers are easy. Give it to me."

He told her the number and said don't call from her own phone 'cause they's trackin' her.

"You want my number?" she asked. "Just in case?"

"I already got it," Lincoln said, tapping his temple. "Claire C. Chastain. Area code six-four-six. Had to memorize it as part of the assignment."

She watched him walk back toward the Continental, hands in his pockets, feet crunching through the snow, great clouds of steam billowing around his head in the glaring lights of the station.

38

When they'd gone two blocks and Lincoln was out of view, Claire said, "Take me to College Park."

If her assailants weren't too badly injured, they might go to Frederick. But the hospital in Frederick probably wouldn't have a trauma center. The town was too small to support one. The hospitals in Rockville might. Shooting victims go to trauma centers, she reasoned, and she didn't want to see any more of the assailants who had found her at home, at work, at Rollingwood, and at Leona's old country house.

College Park was a long way away. They'd have no reason to go that far. The university had a hospital and Officer Greer was in Hyattsville, five minutes away. Claire would fill her in on what had happened. If she had to stay in the hospital overnight, Greer could find someone to guard her room.

"College Park?" the driver said. "That's way past Rockville."

"I'll pay you."

"Your friend said—"

"I know what my friend said. We're going to College Park. To the hospital at the university. I'll pay you eighty bucks. On top of the forty my friend gave you."

He glanced in the rearview, not convinced.

"Uber won't be taking any off the top. It all goes into your pocket."

"OK, miss. I don't mean to offend you or anything, but you don't look well. You sure you're OK to travel that far?"

"It's mizz. And I'm sure."

She wasn't really sure. The walk from the Continental to the gas station was only a block, but it left her feeling light-headed and weak. The fact that her health might really be in danger—a fact she now understood on a deep visceral level—scared her. But fear was a useless emotion. It was one of the weapons Leona had used to manipulate her when she was small, and she learned that when she ignored it, it lost its power.

I'm pale because it's winter, she told herself, and because I'm cold. I'm weak and lightheaded because I haven't been eating for weeks.

"Your superpower," Peter once told her, "is making everything look OK when it's really not."

"You'd be surprised how well that serves me in negotiations," she told him.

"But there comes a time when you need to turn it off. Someday, you're going to have to face all the things inside you that are not OK."

"Who are you to say what's inside me?" she snapped. "Who are you to say I have to face anything? You're not perfect either. You could have excelled in business if you'd had an ounce of ambition. You could have found a woman who'd treat you better, the nurturing type you want for your children, if only you had a little more self-respect."

Remembering those words sickened her more than the pain in her kidney, twisting her gut with a wrenching nausea.

Why was I so mean to him? Why was I always angry when I didn't need to be?

Stop thinking about the past, she told herself. Keep your mind on the problems at hand. Someone wants to kill you. You need a doctor. You need protection.

She thought ahead to practical matters. Checking in at the ER. She found her insurance card and license in her wallet so she'd have them ready when she went in. She wondered if they'd keep her overnight. She wanted them to, wanted her life to be someone else's responsibility for a day. She'd call Greer to arrange a guard, tell her about Napoleon and Fake Darrell.

But how long would it take the police to catch them? And how many others worked with them? If the hospital released her in a day, where would she go? How long would she have to keep looking over her shoulder? How long before she could close her eyes at night without fear of someone coming after her?

The only way out of this, she thought, was to find what they were after. Find that hard drive, or whatever it was, and turn it over to the cops, or to Wikileaks, or to someone who would expose it to the world. Once they'd been exposed, they'd know the game was up. There would be no point in going after her anymore because there would be nothing left to cover up.

But how could she find what she didn't have, what had never been given to her in the first place?

I'm passing the torch to you.

Goddamn you, Gavin!

Her thoughts whirled uselessly, exhaustingly, as the car made its way down 270 in the early morning light. When she stopped thinking about her troubles, the pain in her lower back expanded to fill the void, spreading like dark poison into every muscle and bone, a slow death emanating from an invisible inner wound.

It was beginning to scare her deeply.

She began to notice something else now. A pressure building in her bladder. She had drunk nothing since her last visit to the bathroom. She knew what was in there.

As her breathing grew shallower, she told herself, You have to stop. Stop this worrying. Take a breath and get a hold of yourself.

She tried, and a new thought came to her. What if Gavin really had given her the hard drive?

She thought back to their last meeting, thought through every communication they'd had since she'd returned to DC, tried to remember any instance of him giving her anything at all, but she came up with nothing.

By the time they passed Rockville, she was sinking.

The last thought to trouble her mind before she fell asleep was the exchange of phone numbers with Lincoln when they'd parted. Something about it wasn't right. She just couldn't put her finger on it.

39

"Miss?"

Claire's eyes opened to an unfamiliar icy road, her head against the window. The pale sun hung just above the horizon.

"You want the hospital, right?" The driver watched her in the rearview.

"Yes."

"It's in Cheverly, not College Park." He held his phone up to show he'd found it on the map. "We'll be there in three."

"Thank you. And stop calling me Miss. I'm not twelve."

Three minutes, she thought. If I can hold my bladder for three minutes, everything will be fine.

She had forgotten about the pain until she tried to move. The driver startled when she let out a cry.

"You OK?"

"I'm fine."

"You should..." The driver hesitated, scared to provoke her. "You should look in the mirror." He brushed his fingertips across his lips. "Your lips have no color."

"Just drive."

She turned on her phone. Screw whoever was watching her. She'd be at the hospital in a few minutes and she wanted to know how long it would take Greer to get there.

She scrolled through her call history and found the number Greer had called from a few days before. She tapped Call. Two rings and a man answered.

"Hello, I'm looking for Sharice Greer."

"Uh huh. And you are?"

She didn't like the man's tone, the mix of sarcasm and lazy indifference, like she had interrupted him in the middle of his morning read.

"Claire Chastain."

"Greer's out. You want to leave a message? Or you want to talk to someone else?"

"Do you have a number where I can reach her?"

"I said you could leave a message or talk to someone else."

"Or I could just hang up," Claire said. "Asshole."

She opened her shoulder bag and found the card Greer had given her on the night they met. It had two numbers, office and mobile.

She punched in the mobile number as they approached the hospital grounds. A wailing ambulance roared past on its way to the ER and the driver followed.

After six rings, the call went to voicemail. The greeting seemed overly formal. "You've reached Sharice C. Greer. I can't take your call right now..."

The sound of Greer's voice reassured her.

The driver brought the car to a stop sixty yards short of the ER entrance.

"I can't pull up there." He pointed to the crew of four in hospital scrubs that had rushed from the building and swarmed the back of the ambulance.

"Then drop me here."

"You sure you're OK to walk?"

Claire got out without answering, kneed the door shut behind her, grunted at the pain.

"Sharice, this is Claire."

The Uber rolled slowly away.

Sixty yards ahead, the sight of the four in scrubs attacking the man they'd just pulled from the back of the ambulance gave Claire's heart a start. She stopped short.

"Jesus!"

That went into the voicemail.

She watched for a few seconds before realizing the man on the gurney was having convulsions. They were trying to keep him from bouncing out of his restraints.

Claire caught her breath.

"Sharice, I'm at the hospital in..." Wait. Where was she again? She looked around for a sign.

A short man hobbling on crutches across the lot ahead slipped on a patch of ice and went down hard beside a small green car.

"... in Cheverly," Claire said.

She heard the man moan in pain, but she couldn't see him.

"I think I hurt my kidney. Can you come and meet me—"

The beep cut her off.

"Damnit."

Cheverly, she thought. If we had driven south last night instead of turning onto the Beltway we would have ended up here. It's a straight shot down the Baltimore-Washington Parkway from Napoleon's torture hut to this place. Instead we went north and almost got ourselves killed.

She looked at the phone. Should she call Lincoln?

The man who had fallen cursed his heart out amid the clatter of aluminum crutches.

What a mouth, Claire thought. He's got a temper worse than mine.

The glass doors of the ER slid open and swallowed the knot of humanity that had been wrestling behind the ambulance—the EMTs in their dark blue uniforms, nurses and orderlies in light blue scrubs, the thrashing patient on the gurney.

Lincoln's going to look for me in Rockville. I should tell him where I am. But not from this phone.

"Goddamnmotherfuckingstupidasspieceofshitbitchfuckcru tches!" Thump thump thump. The fallen man was smashing his crutches against the side of the car.

Claire picked up her pace. She'd be there in a few seconds, help him off the ground, stuff him into his car, and send him on his way.

I'll call Lincoln from the ER. Tell him I'm in Cheverly. If I don't, he'll worry.

Thump thump smash. The mirror of the little green car took a jab from the end of a crutch.

He must have broken the glass, she thought.

The car looked familiar, but she couldn't place it.

She saw Lincoln standing beneath the lights of the all-night gas station.

The man cursed again. The voice sounded familiar.

She saw Lincoln tap his finger to his temple. "Had to memorize it as part of the assignment."

You've reached Sharice C. Greer.

Why C? Who says their middle initial in...

Lincoln tapping his temple. *Claire C. Chastain. Area code six-four-six.*

Wait a minute!

Wait. A. Minute.

She stopped just behind the green Fiat, dialed Anoop, and put her phone to her ear.

The man on the ground behind the car grunted and cursed as he tried to pull himself up.

Anoop answered on the first ring.

"Did you order a credit card for me? For company expenses?"

"Claire?"

"Answer me."

"It came yesterday. It's sitting on my desk."

She hung up and stepped forward just as the little man got to his feet. For a second, they stood blinking at each other in surprise. His flattened nose was a testament to the power of

Lincoln's fist. The brace that ran from his thigh to his calf immobilized the knee Lincoln had kicked in the night before.

"You!" Claire exclaimed.

Napoleon's creepy smile had just started to show when she pulled the stun gun from her coat pocket.

"What the fuck is—"

She lunged, jabbed the prongs into his throat, and pulled the trigger.

The jolt stiffened him and he went over backward without a word. The back of his skull hit the icy pavement with a jarring crack.

"That's for Li," Claire said. She kicked his crutches under the car. "Don't stop breathing, because I'm not done. The next one will be for me."

40

The rush of adrenaline made her entire body feel like one big pounding heart. All the anger she had felt at being pursued, at having to shower in fear, at the thought of Leona's house being violated, of Li being attacked, of herself being beaten and terrorized—all the rage she'd kept bottled up for years flooded to the surface at once, and poor self-pitying Napoleon was going to be on the receiving end of all of it. If only he knew how deep that well of anger was, how much she had to unload.

He sat with his right hand cupped around the back of his head. The pain showed on his face.

"You broke my fuckin' skull back there."

"Shut up, Pee Wee."

They were in the Fiat. She was driving. She had shoved the passenger seat as far forward as it would go, jamming his immobilized leg into the floorboards so he couldn't move.

"Why are women so goddamn mean?"

"Because you're an asshole."

They were six miles up the Baltimore-Washington Parkway, approaching the area where the turn should be.

She was going to end this once and for all. She knew the answer now, knew her way out.

"Where's the house?" Claire demanded.

"What house?"

"You know what house. Where is it?"

"Up your ass and around the corner."

She pressed the stun gun into his ribs and gave him another jolt. That would shut him up for a few minutes. But it also meant she had to slow the car so she wouldn't pass the turn.

"Fake Darrell said he was going to get my car last night. You were going to put me in it, shoot me full of Everclear, and drop me in a lake. Remember?"

She studied his face while she waited for his response. The pain that had shown a minute ago was gone. Now he was bug eyed, like a man who'd held his breath too long.

"It wasn't my idea," he whined.

"I don't care whose idea it was. It was your fist in my stomach, your fist in my back. Is my car at that house?"

"Yeah," he gasped. He seemed to be hurting worse than her.

"What about the other two? Darrell and the drunk?"

"His name's not Darrell."

"Where are they?"

"How the fuck should I know? Can I push this seat back? It's killing my knee."

"No. Did they leave?"

"Did they leave!" he grunted. "Yeah they fuckin' left. You think I'd be out driving with a busted knee if I coulda got a ride? My buddy was pissed. He was disgusted—"

"Who's at the house now?"

"No one. How the hell did your friend find that place? It's not even on a real road."

"You tell me where to turn."

"Why should I?"

She pressed the stun gun against his shoulder and pulled the trigger. His body convulsed like a cardiac patient beneath a defibrillator.

"How's that for a reason?"

She slowed even more, scanned the road, pointed at the turn ahead.

"Here?"

He nodded silently, his mouth puckered like a fish, eyes bugged in awe of the pain.

The winding wooded road had nothing to distinguish it. Snowy trees on either side, it could have been any road, anywhere. At least the plows had been through. They'd cleared the pavement, salted, left it dry.

Napoleon was breathing irregularly now. When he regained control of his limbs, he put his hand to the back of his head and grimaced in pain. She worried that he may really have fractured his skull when he'd fallen back in the lot.

"Which way?" she asked.

He pointed with his left hand. "Right up here."

She side-eyed him as she made the turn. His eyes blinked a lot. His breathing was labored and shallow.

"Left here," he said.

He guided her through the woods to the unpaved road, the final descent toward the tiny house. In daylight, she could see the stream that ran beside the lane. She pictured herself strapped into the seat of her blue BMW beneath the water of an icy pond.

How'd you like it if I did that to you, she thought, shooting Napoleon an angry glare. She slowed the car as it descended, afraid it might run off into the woods. Down to her left she saw the little house and her BMW. No other cars in sight.

She slowed almost to a stop, thought about getting out and letting the Fiat roll down into the stream with Napoleon in it. It wouldn't be as bad as him sending her into the pond. The creek was only a few inches deep. But his car would be nose-down and he'd have to drag himself up the snowy bank on that aching immobilized leg. That would be adequate payback, now wouldn't it?

But the look of pain on his face began to pain her too. She let off the brake and they rolled down to the house.

She pulled up in front and cut the engine. She would get out, throw his keys in the snow, leave him to crawl around in search of them after she drove off.

But she hesitated before opening the door. His head had dropped forward beneath the weight of the hand cupped behind it. He was still breathing quick shallow breaths. And still blinking, though his eyes were more often closed than open.

"Are you all right?" she asked.

He shook his head.

"What's your name?"

"Gus."

"Hold on, Gus."

She took the keys with her when she got out. The keys to the BMW were in the ignition, and the door was unlocked. Nothing inside the car had been disturbed.

She opened the rear passenger door, picked up the two letters on the back seat. She ignored the one from her old company in New York and studied the name on the other.

Claire C. Chastain.

She never used her middle initial, and most people didn't even know what it was. But Gavin knew it. And when Gavin had given Lincoln the assignment, he'd made him commit her name and phone number to memory. *Claire C. Chastain. Area code six-four-six.*

She felt the outline of the credit card. It was not the company card she'd been expecting. Anoop had told her that card was on his desk. This one, she knew, had come from someone else. Someone who knew her middle initial.

She tore the envelope carefully across the top, unfolded the heavy cardstock on which a bank would have printed her name and address. There was no type, only a note in Gavin's hand.

"This is insurance if things go wrong. Extort the fuckers. They're evil!"

She examined the plastic card. Capital One Rewards. Gavin Corley.

He had cut the EMV chip from the left side, razored out some extra space and jammed a micro-SD card in its place. SanDisk, 64 gigabytes. The same as the one she'd replaced in her phone.

She remembered the conversation they'd had at brunch.

If you want to be really secure, you'll pass a message in a way that no one would know it had ever been passed.

She looked again at the tiny chip. Sixty-four gigabytes could hold tens of thousands of documents. It could hold video, images, and voice recordings. More than enough to expose the wrongdoing of people doing wrong. She dropped the chip into the pocket of her coat.

When she turned to look at Napoleon, the pain shot from her kidney into her chest and head. It went down the other way too, down to her toes, lighting everything along the way in a blazing fire of agony. She saw stars and heard chimes and braced herself against the car to keep from fainting. The adrenaline was wearing off and the toll of the last few days was bearing down on her. Again the fear crept in, and again she tried to push it back. But the weeks of not eating now caught up to her as well. She had been running on fumes and now the fumes were all gone. She didn't have the strength to push it all back.

The world was going white. She had to pee, and she couldn't hold it. She felt it running hot down her leg, watched a scarlet rose blossom in the snow around her foot. She was losing control, her worst fear, and the ringing in her ears made a melody she hadn't heard in a long, long time.

What was that melody? She used to hear it every day.

She pulled the phone from her pocket, saw his name on the screen.

Peter's ringtone. That melody I haven't heard for so long. He got my messages. He wants to talk.

The phone fell into the snow. She stared at his name on the screen, knowing how much it would hurt to bend down, knowing that even if she made it without falling, straightening up again would be even harder.

Two deep breaths to gird against the pain. She winced on the way down, cried aloud on the way back up.

Too late. The call had gone to voicemail.

She turned and looked at Napoleon. His head sagged on his chest, body slumped sideways.

I can't leave him here, she thought. Even if I hate him, it's not right to leave a person like that.

I'll drive him, she thought. Back to the hospital with me. I've held it together this long. I can make it another twenty minutes. Control, Claire. Control. You've got this.

She took a step toward the Fiat and knew she wasn't going to make it. The pain in her back, the weakness and dizziness, everything going white again. It was a simple lack of blood. The blood that should have been in her brain had been leaking from her kidney since last night.

The phone slipped from her fingers. She stared at it down in the whiteness, took a deep breath and knelt, knowing she wouldn't be getting up this time. On her knees, she watched fingers that seemed to belong to someone else dial a number she didn't recognize.

"Nine-one-one, what's your emergency?"

The voice waited quietly.

"Nine-one-one. Hello?"

"I need..." The pain in her back stabbed with each heartbeat. She tried to put her hand to her side.

"Ma'am? Hello?"

"I need help."

41

"Are you having your period?"

The grey-haired doctor had a vaguely Middle Eastern accent.

Claire lay on her stomach, head turned to the left. She didn't remember getting into the ambulance, but she remembered being taken out of the back, being wheeled through the sliding glass doors.

"Where's my coat?"

"Miss Chastain, there's blood in your underwear. Are you having your period?"

"It's mizz," she whispered. "And no."

"Any chance it could be early? When was your last period?"

"No, and sixteen days ago. Where is my coat?"

"I'm concerned about that kidney. The amount of inflammation—how long ago did this happen?"

"Last night."

"Why didn't you come in immediately?"

"Don't take that tone with me. I was dealing with some very difficult people."

"This is nothing to joke about."

"Where's my coat?"

"On the chair behind you."

"I left a message for a friend of mine," Claire said. "A cop."

"I'm here," said Greer.

"Look in the pocket of my coat. There's a little chip—"

"Shh. Less talking," said the doctor. "We're going to give you a CT scan. If the kidney looks bad, or if the fluid prevents us from seeing, we're going to the OR."

"You find it?" Claire asked.

Greer came around to Claire's left, where she could see her. "This?" She showed her the tiny black chip.

"That's your evidence," Claire said. "At least, I hope."

A dark-haired nurse with a gentle voice leaned in closely and squeezed her hand. "We're going to move you in just a minute."

She was too tired now to be scared. She closed her eyes. Her fate was out of her own hands. Time to let go.

42

"Claire!"

"Hello, Sharice."

The bed was comfortable. The pain in her back came more from the oozing incision than from the kidney. The worst effects of the anesthetic had worn off and the first stars were beginning to appear in the evening twilight.

"What did the doctor say?"

"Grade four lacerations," Claire said. "They had to cut me open to look at it."

"Is four bad?"

"Grade five, they remove your kidney. Grade four, it's the doctor's call. He sewed me up and told me I need to take it easy for a few weeks."

Greer breathed a sigh of relief. "Well that's good news."

"I hate taking it easy. I wasn't built for that."

"Well maybe it's time for you to learn something new. By the way, that chip. You hit the mother lode."

"Really?"

"I passed it on to digital forensics and they had the DEA on the line within the hour. They'll be in to talk to you tomorrow, when your head's a little clearer."

"I hope those guys get locked up. I'm sick of running from people."

"We have some of them in custody already. The man who said he was Darrell Gatlin? We got him on a tip from the short guy you were with when you called nine-one-one."

"How's he doing?"

"Hasn't gotten any taller. Bad attitude too, but he's going to be helpful. He's already turned against the others. Listen, there was a shootout up in Frederick County last night."

"I know."

"Two guys wound up at the trauma center in Baltimore. The third is still in Frederick. All of their names showed up in the files on the SD card you gave me."

"What was on there?"

"Delivery schedules. A pharmaceutical company was shipping narcotics out the back door, packaged as other pills. All of it was off the books. No lot numbers on the packaging. They had a network of couriers distributing to sixteen states. DEA said they've been on the case for months, just waiting for a break like this. They still don't know the full scope of it."

"Two million pills last year," Claire said.

"How do you know that?"

"I have a spreadsheet on my computer. What else was in those files?"

"Some scattered accounting. How many pills went to each courier, how much cash came back. And chat logs. Like real-time texts. They were all supposed to be encrypted, running through a server they controlled, so no one else could get eyes on them. But whoever set up that server kept a copy of the encryption key. He was eavesdropping on them. That's what digital forensics tells me. He even dropped into some of their chats and tried to extort them. Told them he'd turn over evidence unless they bought him off."

Claire closed her eyes and breathed slowly. "Shit."

"What?"

"You remember my friend? The one who died in the accident?"

"Gavin Corley?"

"It wasn't an accident."

"How was he involved in this?"

"That's a long story. Not sure I have the breath for it now. Napoleon can probably tell you better than I can." Seeing Greer didn't understand, she added, "The short guy I was with when the ambulance arrived."

A nurse entered with a cup of water in one hand, a tiny paper cup in the other. She nodded to Greer, then asked Claire how she was feeling.

"Tired. And my back hurts."

"Something else," Greer said. "That car that was following you. The Lincoln. Cops found it abandoned up in Frederick. Whoever left it cleaned it out and wiped it down. No prints or anything. So we still don't know who your stalker is."

Claire smiled.

Greer cocked her head. "You know something?"

"Oh, have I got a story for you. But all this is wearing me out."

"Take this," said the nurse, handing her the water and the small paper cup.

"What is it?"

"Oxycodone. For the pain."

Claire picked up the light blue tablet, turned it over in her fingers and examined both sides.

"This is what the fuss is all about?"

"All the money, all the stealing, all the killing," Greer said.

Claire put the pill back in the cup and drank the water.

"You don't want it?" asked the nurse.

Claire shook her head.

"One more thing," Greer said. "Your phone kept ringing while you were in surgery. Same guy calling over and over."

"Peter."

"I finally answered it, told him what was going on."

"Yeah?"

"He's on his way down from New York."

Claire took a deep breath.

"Get some rest," Greer said. "We have a guard outside your door."

43

From nine to ten thirty the following morning, she lay in bed answering questions from the DEA, Prince George's County, and Frederick County police. She told them everything she could, except for Lincoln's last name, which she didn't know.

When they tried the phone number he had given her, no one answered. Was she sure she had remembered it correctly?

"Of course I'm sure. He did say it was a burner though. Maybe he ditched it."

At ten thirty-three, Greer popped her head in and mouthed a single word. Peter.

Claire sat up, winced, put her hand to her back and said, "You all have to leave. Now."

The Frederick County Sheriff's deputy said he had more questions.

"Later," Claire said. "Seriously. Get out of here. All of you."

As they gathered their coats, she pushed herself up from the bed and dropped her feet to the floor. When she stood with a groan, the DEA agent asked, "You sure you should be—"

"Go," Claire commanded.

In a moment, they had all cleared out, leaving only a pile of business cards on the table beside the bed.

Claire was at the window smoothing her hair when Peter came in wearing an overcoat and bearing a bouquet of roses. Yellow, not the reds he used to give her. The easy smile he seemed to always wear was gone. Without it he looked like a different person.

Claire put her hands behind her back and leaned against the wall, even though it hurt.

"Thank you," she said. "There's space on the table beside the bed."

He put the flowers down without a word and made no motion to unbutton his coat.

"Thank you for coming all the way down here."

He didn't respond, just stared at her quietly for a few seconds with a cool, curious look, as if reassessing someone he once thought he'd known.

"Are you going to say anything?" Claire asked.

"I'm glad you're OK."

"Are you? Really?"

"Yes."

"Does part of you wish I wasn't?"

Peter shook his head.

He never used to look like that, Claire thought. So serious. I did that to him.

"I'm sorry," she said.

"You already said that. Listen, Claire, I didn't come down here to win you back."

His bluntness stung.

"I came to make sure you're OK."

"I am."

"Really? Because you always say you're OK."

"No, really. I am."

Peter nodded, still looking at her as if trying to discover something he had missed.

"You get your grandmother all settled?"

Claire nodded.

"That must have been a task."

"It was."

"What are you going to do with the house?"

"Sell it."

He nodded again and looked around the room. "Mmm hmm."

Claire wished he'd unbutton his coat, wished he'd show some emotion other than that grim seriousness. She kept her hands behind her back, shoulders rolled inward like a child awaiting punishment.

"You've lost a lot of weight," Peter said.

"I know."

"You planning on gaining it back?"

She nodded.

"Think you'll stay down here?"

She shrugged.

"Tell me if you're coming back to the city. It'll be hard, to be honest. Avoiding you all the time."

She noted that he said the city, not the apartment.

"I don't think I'm going back."

"What are you going to do then?"

"No idea."

"You're not horrible, Claire. As bad as you may feel. You just don't know yourself."

"Oh, I know myself. Better than before. I've had some time to think."

"I'm as much to blame in this as you."

"No you're not."

"I could see you for who you were. I knew how guarded you were. I knew it from day one. I thought with enough time, I could draw you out. After you moved in, you were distant. I think part of me felt I was losing you. So I tried to push it. I tried to force your hand a little too soon. I should have known you'd react badly to that.

"Whether you want to be with someone or not... Ultimately, it's your decision. I can't make it for you, and you can't make it until you're ready. And maybe you're not ready."

"Maybe not," she said. "No, I know I'm not."

"You're the kind of person who can do whatever you put your mind to. The question is whether you'll ever put your mind to opening up and trusting other people."

"I know," she whispered.

"Well... I just wanted to see you one last time. I wanted to make sure you were OK. Because I do care about you."

"Thank you for that, Peter."

"Good luck, Claire."

He turned and left without another word. She stood against the wall, her head bowed.

What would he have done if I had said I wasn't OK, she wondered. Would he still have walked away?

Greer waited a few minutes before entering.

"How'd that go?"

She didn't have to ask. She could see it in Claire's face, in her downcast eyes, the silent shake of the head.

"No words?" Greer said. "No words is always the worst."

44

Claire laid the yellow roses Peter had given her atop the swollen womb of earth that marked the final resting place of her childhood friend.

"I'm sorry, old friend. If I had known what you were going through, I would have tried to help. It was always hard to tell when you were crazy and when you were just being Gavin."

The first thing she needed to do to get her life moving forward again was to finish packing the house. Then she would arrange the repairs and have it repainted. After that, it would be the realtor's problem. The house would pass into the hands of someone new, a young family, she hoped. They would know nothing of its past. It would become a place of glowing promise. A new girl, unscarred, would play in the woods across the street, hunt crayfish in the stream, come home to welcoming parents, befriend a boy...

She had already told Anoop she was taking an indefinite leave. In her heart, she knew she wasn't going back.

I have to tell him, she told herself. No more hiding things. Not from myself or anyone else. Just tell him I'm moving on. He'll ask where I'm going, and I'll tell him I don't know. I just don't know.

The pure numbers work of auditing didn't engage enough of her mind. She needed to work on problems whose complexity spanned multiple dimensions, problems whose solutions mattered to everyday people, not just to banks and shareholders.

She read the numbers on the headstone. Gavin Corley had thirty-two years from start to finish. Thirty-two years is where I stand now. And what will my allotment be? How will I fill the time?

She felt a change coming, a change in her sense of self, as if someone were about to flip the mirror she'd been staring into all these weeks and show her what was on the other side.

A jarring ring interrupted her contemplation. She pulled her phone from her coat pocket, checked the number. No one she knew. She rejected the call. Seconds later, it rang again.

"Hello?" she huffed, making no effort to hide her annoyance at this intrusion.

"Where the hell you been?"

"Lincoln?"

"I looked for you in the hospital in Rockville. And the urgent care. Went all the way down to Bethesda, but you wasn't there."

"Sorry. I went to Cheverly. I tried calling you but it didn't go through."

"Yeah, I chucked the burner. I didn't know where to look past Bethesda, and then the missus called all gushy-feely, wanting me to come home, so I hightailed it back to Arkansas."

"So that's where you're from."

"I didn't say that. By the way, I heard the DEA busted up a drug ring. I figured that was you."

"And you," she said. "Don't forget your part in all this. Have you talked to the police yet?"

"No. Do I gotta?"

"I think so. Can I give them your number?"

"Might as well. My wife's all pissy about me pallin' around the big city with a pretty young thing."

"I'm not a thing."

"Tell *her* that."

"How would she know what I look like anyway?"

"Sometimes old Lincoln can't hold his tongue. Starts answering questions that wasn't even asked. You know what I'm saying? Go ahead and give the cops my number. If they call, she'll see I was doing real work up there."

"What's your last name?" She turned to walk back to her car.

"Lincoln."

"I thought that was your first name."

"It is. My daddy had a deep respect for the sixteenth president and American luxury cars. How's your grandma?"

"Cranky."

"I figured. You back in the office?"

"No. I don't think I'm going back either."

"What the hell you gonna do then? You ain't gonna sit on your ass."

"I don't know."

"I'll tell you what you *should* do. You should become an investigator. Private detective or something. You don't trust nobody, got a mind like a steel trap, you're persistent to the point of foolishness, ain't got no regard for your own safety, and deep down inside, though you'd never admit it, you're a do-gooder."

"No I'm not."

"Better take another look, Claire Chastain. I only spent a few days with you, and I could see it plain as day."

Claire laughed. "How does a private investigator even make a living?"

"Well now, this is where you can put your business knowledge to work. A little back-of-the-envelope calculation on supply and demand. How many people in this world need help finding the assholes who done 'em wrong? How many assholes need to get what's coming to 'em? Those numbers won't even fit on the back of an envelope. You'll never be outta work."

Claire laughed.

"Think about it."

"All right, I'll think about it."

She told him she'd pass his number on to the cops and he should expect them to call before the day was out.

The sun had warmed the inside of the car. She took off her coat, dropped the phone on the passenger seat, started the engine, and turned her mind back to practical matters. The realtor would be at the house when she arrived. They'd do a walk through, flag everything that needed fixing, gather a list of contractors. Claire would make the calls, do the scheduling, figure out the budget, and run the numbers. A comfortable, familiar set of tasks.

Her mind flashed back to the conversation in Greer's patrol car.

Greer: "What kind of work you do?"

Claire: "Due diligence for corporate purchases. They send me in to do a thorough investigation. I dig through records, interview people, uncover all I can, and write up a report."

Greer: "Sounds like detective work."

Stop that, she told herself as she cruised through traffic on Connecticut Avenue. Focus on the work at hand. Painting, landscaping, refinishing the floors, updating the bathroom fixtures.

She'd make the realtor recommend at least two contractors for each job. She'd find the third on her own, get bids from each and then...

How many assholes are there in the world, she wondered. *How many scammers, grifters, stalkers ruining lives? How many women living for weeks, months, years like you had to live these past few days, always looking over their shoulders, never at ease? How hard would it be to track down blackmailers, con men, frauds, and thieves? Harder than adding numbers in a spreadsheet?*

The voice that intruded on her train of thought to ask these questions was unfamiliar. Speculative rather than practical. That annoyed her.

She pushed the questions away as she approached Chevy Chase Circle, commanding herself again to focus on the here and now.

When the floors are redone, they'll need a lighter stain. The house will be easier to sell if it's brighter inside. If the landscapers plant daffodils along the front walk, they'll bloom while the house is on the market. It'll look that much more appealing.

She had begun to picture it, could see the bright flowers turning their hopeful yellow faces toward the sun, when the thoughts intruded again.

How many times has a person like Sharice Greer stepped in to help a person in need? How many people do you respect as much as her? Not just who she is, but what she does?

Focus, she commanded.

As she rounded the circle onto Western Avenue, onto the last leg of the drive, she counted off the items on her to-do list. Cancel Leona's auto insurance. Have the heat pump inspected. New air filters for the house. Oil change for the BMW.

Listen to yourself, Claire.

Those words used to send her hackles up when Peter spoke them. If he said them more than once, there would be a fight.

"Listen to what?" Claire mumbled as she passed the Shrine of the Most Blessed Sacrament.

You have a mind like a steel trap.

"Nope." She was talking out loud, shaking her head. "I know where this is going, and no. Just, no."

A do-gooder. Persistent to the point of foolishness.

"Uh-uh. Got way too much on my plate already."

You've been looking at your life all wrong. Lamenting your toughness, your wariness, your unerring instinct and unyielding will. All the things that made you fail at love are assets in the right context. They can help someone. Maybe not you, but someone.

The voice was talking sense. The mirror was beginning to flip and she didn't like it.

"No. I have the realtor, the house, the paperwork for Leona's Medicare. I don't have time for fantasies and daydreams."

You never have. Where are you going, Claire? What's next for you?

"I don't know."

Then what's to stop you?

"From what?"

From anything.

"My god, I'm going mad. I'm talking to myself—"

Finally!

"Out loud, like a mad woman."

No. This is sanity, Claire. You're listening.

"I'm losing it."

You said it yourself, remember? When you were alone in the hotel with your notepad. You want to help people. You want to make the world a better place.

"This isn't practical. Fantasies are not practical."

Then do something practical, Claire.

"All right, I will," she huffed. "I'll do something practical right now."

She pulled to the side of the road, picked up her phone from the passenger seat. Her fingers shook with anger as she stabbed out the words. She tapped the blue Search arrow.

What do you see, Claire?

For a moment, she blinked in silence at the screen. This was just the first page of results. There were thousands more behind it.

You said it in the car with Sharice. "If I have a skill, then I have a responsibility to put it to good use, to help people. God knows there are enough people in this world who need help." Listen to your own words, Claire.

She scanned the list of links, calculated the time and expense this would require, the amount she had left in savings.

"But this isn't a career," she protested. "There's no health insurance, no retirement plan. This is something *other* people do. Something people do in books, in movies..."

You ran away for a reason, Claire.

"...exposing the truth instead of..."
Instead of what, Claire?
"Instead of hiding it."
She re-read the question she had typed.

How does one become a private investigator?

"Screw this. I'm not doing it."
She tossed the phone onto the seat, jammed the shift into drive, and peeled out from the curb.
"Nobody tells me what to do."
Not even you. But this time, you're going to listen.
"No I'm not."
Surrender, Claire.
"I won't."
But she was already planning it out in her head. A day job in some office downtown, classes in the evening. Criminal Justice at American University, a straight shot up Massachusetts Avenue from Dupont Circle.

The more she indulged the thoughts, the more powerfully her appetite returned. The physical and mental exertion of the past few weeks, the way she'd pushed herself, the depletion of her body's reserves—she felt it all in a ravenous, insatiable desire for food.

It was the first desire she'd felt in months, the first bodily sensation she didn't want to shun or suppress.

She could smell the cheesesteaks Lincoln loved to eat. Where could she find one? How fast could they make them?
Surrender, Claire.

She turned the car around, back toward the restaurants at Friendship Heights. The realtor would have to wait. For the first time in fourteen years, she would intentionally break an appointment. The painters and the landscapers, the car insurance, the bathroom fixtures, the heat pump—who cares when it all got done? She had a debt to pay. To her body, to herself, to her future.

All that mattered now was strengthening herself for the next chapter of her life, for the work that might help some future Li, deliver some other frightened Claire from the anxiety of being targeted, harassed, and stalked.

As she rounded Chevy Chase Circle, heading away from where she was supposed to be, the voice grew softer, less insistent. It no longer had to clamor for her attention. She could hear it clearly through the noise of her thoughts—friendly, wise, and confident.

Surrender, it said.

Her body shook with hunger.

She nodded quietly in assent, the same deferential bow of humility that had so annoyed her in Li, and to herself she whispered softly, "I do."

TO HELL WITH JOHNNY MANIC

Psychological Thriller / Noir

John Manis, aka Johnny Manic, isn't who he says he is. His money can't ease the burden of his dark secret. The high life, he finds, is a lonely life when you have to live it as someone else. If only someone could see him for who he really was.

Marilyn Dupree has a strange intuition, a spark of recognition when they meet. Her life isn't going right either. Johnny is reckless. Marilyn is passionate and volatile, with too much money and the wrong husband. She and Johnny have a chemistry like nitrogen and glycerin.

"The wiser part of me knew I should have left," Johnny recalls. "But knowing what's right and doing what's right are two different things, especially when you're at war with instincts you can't articulate and don't understand. The important thing was that in the grocery store that morning, Johnny Manic and the raven-haired Marilyn Dupree had found each other. The fuse was lit."

Watching them both is the wary detective Lou Eisenfall, who senses he's going to be very busy in the coming weeks.

A dark tale of deception, murder, and psychological suspense, *To Hell with Johnny Manic* is a throwback to the classic crime fiction of Patricia Highsmith, Raymond Chandler, and Jim Thompson.

"A feverishly readable psychological noir."—*Kirkus Reviews*

"Truly riveting... One of the year's best thrillers." — *BestThrillers.com*

To Hell with Johnny Manic on Amazon.com

GATE 76

Thriller

A mysterious woman fleeing an unknown terror boards the wrong plane at San Francisco International and disappears into the heart of the country. Freddy Ferguson, a troubled detective with a violent past, believes she's the last living witness to a crime that has captivated the nation.

Sifting through the wreckage of her past, he begins to understand who she's running from, and why. Now he must track her down before her pursuers can silence her for good.

A modern crime thriller with elements of Raymond Chandler and the classic pulp mysteries of the 1950s, *Gate 76* weaves a deeply personal tale of witness and investigator, loss and redemption.

A consummate thriller with some of the best characterization you'll see all year. —*Kirkus Reviews (starred review)*

One of the year's best thrillers. —*BestThrillers.com*

- Named to Kirkus Reviews' Best Books of 2018
- Named to BestThrillers.com's best thrillers of 2018

Gate 76 on Amazon.com

IMPALA
Thriller

After four years on the straight and narrow, Russell Fitzpatrick has a boring job, the wrong woman, and an itch for something more. All he needs to get his life going again is a nudge in the wrong direction.

When he receives a cryptic email from a legendary and slightly deranged fellow hacker—his old friend Charlie, whom he knows to be dead—he tries to tell himself it's none of his concern. But the guy who stalks him across town at night, the two thugs waiting in the alley, and a ruthless FBI agent let him know his days are numbered if he doesn't turn over the money Charlie stole.

The problem is, Russ doesn't have it. As his enemies close in from all sides, Russ slowly unwinds the mystery of his old friend's paranoid mind and finds that Charlie left behind something worth much more than the money. And no one but him is on to it...

- A Kirkus Recommended Review - September 2016
- An Amazon Best Book of the Month - Sept. 2016 - Mystery/Thriller
- An IndieReader Best of 2016 Selection
- First Place Winner - Genre Fiction - 24th Annual Writer's Digest Awards
- Gold Medal Winner - 2017 Readers' Favorite Awards

Impala on Amazon.com

WARREN LANE
Mystery/Comedy

Susan Moore is about to hire the wrong man to investigate her philandering husband, Will. There's something not quite right about that detective. Warren Lane drinks too much and has a hard time staying out of trouble. He's just the kind of guy Will's mistress can't resist. And everyone is starting to figure out that Will is hiding a lot more than his affair with a reckless young woman. With a bit of mystery, romance, crime, and suspense, Warren Lane has his hands full.

Warren Lane on Amazon.com

WAKE UP, WANDA WILEY
Comedy/Romance/Satire

Hannah Sharpe has been written out of all eighteen of Wanda Wiley's romance novels. A runaway heroine who won't conform to the plots laid out for her, Hannah has been consigned to a realm of fog deep in the recesses of the author's imagination.

Trevor Dunwoody, the protagonist of a macho action-thriller that Wanda has regrettably agreed to ghostwrite, is single-minded and obtuse, understanding only what he can beat up, shoot, or screw. Like Hannah, he's a character Wanda doesn't know what to do with. When he appears one day in Hannah's fog world, she can't convince him he's in the wrong story.

Hannah knows she'll be stuck in the limbo of Wanda's subconscious until the writer can find a suitable story to cast her in. But Wanda, trapped in a disastrous relationship with the philandering narcissist Dirk Jaworski, is sinking into a deep depression. The pot she smokes to self-medicate impairs her ability to write and thickens the fog of Hannah's timeless isolation.

As Hannah explains her predicament to the thick-headed Trevor, she begins to realize that she knows her author better than her author knows herself. If she can only break out of the limbo of Wanda's subconscious and nudge the writer in the right direction, she can free them both.

But how can Hannah penetrate the fog of her creator's mind from within? The answer is right in front of her in the form of the big, dumb, action-ready tool, Trevor Dunwoody.

"Diamond's prose is funny and barbed, particularly the dialogue between Hannah and Trevor... surprisingly compelling." —*Kirkus Reviews*

Wake Up, Wanda Wiley on Amazon.com

ABOUT THE AUTHOR

Andrew Diamond writes mystery, crime, noir, and an occasional comedy. His award-winning books feature cinematic prose, strong characterization, twisting plots, and dark humor. You can follow Andrew on Goodreads, on his blog at https://adiamond.me, or on Facebook at https://www.facebook.com/adiamond.me.